D0935226

Island Stories:
Unravelling Britain

Island Stories: Unravelling Britain

Theatres of Memory, Volume II

RAPHAEL SAMUEL

EDITED BY ALISON LIGHT
with
Sally Alexander *and*
Gareth Stedman Jones

London • New York

First published by Verso 1998

Verso
UK: 6 Meard Street, London W1V 3HR
USA: 180 Varick Street, New York NY 10014–4606

Verso is the imprint of New Left Books

ISBN 1–85984–965–2

British Library Cataloguing in Publication Data
A catalogue record for this book is available from the British Library

Library of Congress Cataloging-in-Publication Data
A catalog record for this book is available from the Library of Congress

Typeset by M Rules
Printed by Biddles Ltd, Guildford and King's Lynn

Contents

PART IV The War of Ghosts

APPENDIX

Illustration Acknowledgements

John Speed's illustration (page 13) was published originally in his 1616 Latin edition of *Theatrum Imperii Magnae Britanniae* (*Theatre of the Empire of Great Britain*), and is reproduced in *The Counties of Britain: A Tudor Atlas by John Speed* (Pavilion Books, 1988).

Matthew Paris's map of Britain (page 47) is from his *Abbreviato Chronicorum Angliae*, reproduced by permission of the British Library (Cott.Claud.D.VI.fol.12v.).

Alfred Waterhouse's 1869 drawing of Manchester Town Hall (page 62) is from the collection of the Ashmolean Museum, Oxford, and is reproduced in *The English Town* by Mark Girouard (Yale University Press, 1990).

The photograph of the Red House staircase (page 66, left) is from the National Monuments Record collection and is reproduced in *Gimson and the Barnsleys* by Mary Greensted (Alan Sutton Publishing Ltd, 1991).

The photograph of the White House stairwell and the oak chest of drawers (page 66, right, and page 67 respectively) are from the Cheltenham City Art Gallery and Museum collection and are reproduced in *Gimson and the Barnsleys.*

The chocolate-marketing illustrations (page 89) are from the Robert Opie Collection, Museum of Advertising and Packaging, Gloucester, and are reproduced in *Rule Britannia: Trading on the British Image* by Robert Opie (Viking, 1985).

Thomas Shotter Boys's 1842 lithograph of the Tower (page 109) is from the collection of the Guildhall, London, and is reproduced in *Tower of London: A History of England from the Norman Conquest* by Christopher Hibbert (Readers Digest Association, 1971).

The Pennine Way walk photograph (page 142) is taken from *The Rucksack* (the Youth Hostels Association magazine), Midsummer 1948 edition.

John Piper's ink-and-wash painting of Tryfan (page 147) is taken from *Piper's Places: John Piper in England & Wales* by Richard Ingrams and John Piper, and is reproduced courtesy of the artist and Chatto & Windus.

The photograph of Albert Finney in *Saturday Night and Sunday Morning* (page 164) is reproduced courtesy of BFI Stills, Posters and Designs.

The SDP/R.H. Tawney cartoon illustration (page 233) is reproduced courtesy of Peter Clarke and the *Guardian.*

All other illustrations are from the author's private collection.

Editors' Preface

Raphael Samuel intended *Theatres of Memory* as a trilogy. In the Preface to the first volume, published in 1994, he discussed his plans for the second and third:

> The second volume – 'Island Stories' – is about the wildly different versions of the national past on offer at any given point in time, depending on whether the optic is that of town or country; centre or periphery; the state or civil society. It begins with a series of pieces on 'The Spirit of Place'; continues with 'The War of Ghosts' (politics and memory in the 1980s); and concludes with a series of arguments on 'History, the Nation and the Schools'. A final chapter addresses the question of post-colonial history.

In a later outline found amongst his papers, he added that he hoped to complete it with 'an extended essay, "The Difficulties of being English", in which the writer tests the argument of the book against his own unstable sense of nationality, and contrasts his mother's experience of being British with his own'.

Our aim as editors and as Raphael's literary executors has been to produce a volume which followed the author's intentions as closely as we could. Raphael prepared a number of possible contents lists for *Island Stories,* and when he died in December 1996 he left several completed pieces and full drafts for the book. There were also essays in every phase of composition, from a few typed pages to handwritten paragraphs and notes (this latter being the case with 'The Difficulties of being English'). We have assembled this volume solely from the finished manuscripts and the all-but-complete drafts; we have not reproduced any of the work which was in handwritten form only. Further collections of Raphael Samuel's essays, published and unpublished, are under consideration. All the manuscripts will eventually make their way, we hope, into a public archive of his work.

Any attempt to recapture Raphael's thought too literally would have been self-defeating. He always conceived of historical work as experimental, fluid, provisional: Raphael's subtitle 'Unravelling Britain' carries this sense of the continuous, evolving work of the historian. The whole point of Raphael's creation, the History Workshop (the term was borrowed from Joan Littlewood's Theatre Workshop), was to emphasize the inchoate, protean and experimental character of historical work. The workshops held from the 1960s at Ruskin College, Oxford, where Raphael was a tutor in history, were huge gatherings of students, autodidact enthusiasts and professional historians. Like the dozen or so volumes which Raphael Samuel edited in the History Workshop series of books, they stressed the forging and reforging of historical knowledge and its boundaries.* Raphael approached the business of sole authorship in the same spirit. It is impossible to imagine 'a definitive' version of *Island Stories* and certainly were he alive, Raphael would be doing his best to subvert such a notion.

Island Stories shares this sense of openness. It was, nevertheless, always meant to be rather more narrowly focused than Volume I, whose subject is the broad and multifarious uses of the past in contemporary culture, ranging from period decor, 'retrochic' and the discovery of old photographs, to the creation of heritage sites and the new museum culture. *Island Stories* has the 'British Isles' more nearly at its centre and bears a close relation to much recent work and political debate on questions of nationality and identity in the aftermath of empire. The second essay, for example, 'Four Nations History', examines the ways in which, since the 1970s, the possibility of 'the break-up of Britain' has been posed, and the disturbing questions about the writing of British history which follow in its wake. 'Unravelling Britain', and Part I's concluding essay, 'Empire Stories', offer different ways in which the reader may consider the instability of what once may have appeared a coherent entity or cohesive artefact, Great Britain. The United Kingdom might be thought of as one important but transient formation in a succession of political nations forged through wars, invasions and conquests of Romans, Saxons, Vikings and Normans and as the temporary and improvised culmination of a long process of subjugation and colonization of the Irish, Scots and Welsh whose national identities have equally been articulated through imperial ambition, religious absolutisms and creation myths.

Island Stories thus challenges the view that the ideas of nation or nationalism belong only to the recent past. His emphasis upon the mutability and precariousness of the idea of nation takes the author at one point back to Herodotus, 'the father of history'; religion as 'the crucible of the national idea' returns him to the ancient Hebrews at another. The

*The history of the History Workshop movement and of its many offshoots by way of meetings and publications can be found in Raphael Samuel (ed.), *History Workshop: A Collectanea 1967–1991* (London 1991).

romance of origins leads him into the intricacies and depths of medieval Scottish mythmaking whilst a fascination with national stereotypes or collective psychologies is as likely to be uncovered in the work of sixteenth-century cosmographers as to prompt reflections on the 1990s' predilection for the term 'Brit'. Readers of Volume I will recognize here Samuel's claim for legend as a 'prelude to the historical', for the complementarity of myth and history, and for the ubiquity of myth as evidence of the tenacious influence of magical modes of thought today. Even the historian most wedded to the empirical, he warns, might find himself entangled in the deep structures of myth.

Island Stories conjures up a sense of history which is much more than a series of events or even experiences; the essays are equally drawn to the narratives which images offer, the pull of the figurative and the non-verbal in national histories, the place of fantasy and desire. In this way, *Island Stories* builds directly on the three volumes of *Patriotism: The Making and Unmaking of British National Identity* (1989) which Raphael Samuel edited. Amongst his contributions to those volumes were chapters exploring some of the figures of national myth, the changing historical notions of Englishness, and the appeal of the idea of a continuous national history.

There are many different kinds of historical writing in this volume: synthesis, overview and argument, political commentary and literary journalism, travelogue, autobiography ('Country Visiting: A Memoir' insists, characteristically, upon personal experience as a creature of its time). The different terrains, mentalities and periods, the variety of modes of address and habits of mind contained in these chapters exemplify what was argued in *Theatres of Memory* Volume I about the work of the historian. Never satisfied with assertions of official knowledge or the protocols of academic or political orthodoxy, Raphael Samuel looked for the tensions in an argument and deepened them. He undermined temporalities by beginning somewhere else. The purpose was neither to silence nor to discredit, but to proliferate examples, subvert simple causalities, tell more stories, to draw everyone into historical discussion by an unbridled freedom of starting point, matched by a generosity of source material. *Island Stories* typically argues that British constitutional history need not merely be told through the dignified progress of Parliament or the State. It can equally be captured through the forces of custom, children's stories, national exhibitions, or the institutional history of the BBC – though such a history, it is maintained, might be more arresting and revealing were it to find a place for the secretary and the cameraman as well as the Director-General and his policy-makers.

The essays in Part II, 'English Journeys' (one of the alternative titles for 'The Spirit of Place'), widen the search for historical narrative and meaning to include the buildings we make and inhabit, and the places we wander through. In particular they reflect the influence upon Raphael of the recent work of historical geographers. But they also return us to one of the recurring themes of this volume, the presence of the national and the imperial in the local and domestic. In 'The Lost Gardens of Heligan' the business of empire can be found to impinge directly upon the unlikeliest reaches of the kingdom. The origins of these beautifully restored gardens were commercial and imperial, their presence a reminder of the forgotten but fundamental part played by botanical collection and cultivation in the history of exploration and empire from the voyages of HMS Beagle to the vast development of Malayan rubber plantations between the wars.

Raphael Samuel felt impelled – both by inclination and by a communist upbringing – to communicate with as large an audience as possible. By the same token he was keen not to underestimate the general historical intelligence of the public. No other historian on the Left made such efforts to intervene, in the press and on radio and television, in the policy debates about the teaching of history in the schools. A selection of his articles in the national press, in response to the decision of Mrs Thatcher's Conservative government to restore history to the 'core' curriculum of school subjects, make up Part III of this volume. (Further discussion drawing on the History Workshops which Raphael helped to organise under the rubric of 'History, the Nation and the Schools' can be found in issues 29 and 30 of *History Workshop Journal.*) These pieces span six years and address directly the question of writing and teaching a national or 'British' history. They suggest how much the writer believed that the direction taken by school history would do more to shape the public sense of history than any number of learned disputes amongst professionals. School history is a constant point of reference in many of the essays for this volume. The ideal historian for Raphael Samuel was always a historian in the making: perhaps this is why the child is so often at the centre of his historical imagination.

It would be wrong of us as editors to try to impose too much of a unity upon these essays, a unity which perhaps they do not have and which might, in any case, stray too far from what Raphael himself might have wanted to argue about the volume. There were two substantial decisions which we took as editors, however, which have given *Island Stories* a particular cast. The first was to create a newly entitled Part I, 'Nations, States, Empires', kicking off with three essays which were still in draft and unrevised (only 'Four Nations History' was finished); their interest to the reader, and their suggestive power, seemed to us to outweigh any anxieties we had about their preliminary state. Secondly, we have added to the final section, 'The War of Ghosts', which focusses on politics and memory in British politics in the 1980s, 'Ancestor Worship', an examination of Tony Benn's uses of tradition; and the two pieces on R.H. Tawney and the emergence of the Social Democratic Party. These had already been sent to the publishers but whether they were finally meant for this volume was unclear. Their inclusion, together with 'The Discovery of Puritanism', strengthens, in our view, the book's exposition of the ways in which certain political and ideological forces which had held together the always-uneasy unity of 'the four nations' of the British Isles have become either exhausted or radically transformed. The reworking of Puritanism in the hands of Mrs Thatcher and her admirers in the 1980s, the attack on welfarism, the rise of a new middle class which rejects older notions of professionalism and service, are amongst those recent trends in British cultural life which the author teases out as threads in an unravelling Britain.

For however much Raphael Samuel stressed the provisionality and ephemerality of meaning in history, the irreducibly contingent elements in causality, the necessarily partial angle of the historian's gaze; for all his ecumenicism of approach, apparent serendipity in choice of object of investigation; his welcoming of a multiplicity of voices or his eschewing of the more formalised presentation of argument; he nevertheless always put forward large and provocative historical interpretations. In 'Empire Stories', for instance, the apparently whimsical reference to the 'coming of age of the banana' in Britain is part of an argument for the reperiodization of the history of empire where its apogee, as a cultural and, arguably, as an economic and political phenomenon, is located not in the period 1870–1914 but between the wars. This argument also places the emphasis upon ways in which empire entered national consciousness and everyday life quite different from those so insistently foregrounded in 'orientalist', 'racist' or 'rentier-imperialist' readings of the imperial phenomenon. The essay – a first draft – challenges the moralism and reductionism with which the legacy of empire is so often treated.

As Raphael's close friends and co-workers, we found reading his manuscripts a peculiarly painful pleasure. We were hearing his voice again but without the opportunity for that whole process of exhilarating discussion, often conducted over several days of telephone calls, in which Raphael – and we ourselves – so delighted. Our meetings as editors frequently took the form of having with each other the arguments we might have had with him. We have resisted the urge to ventriloquise. We have not seen fit to add endings or to 'tidy up' drafts beyond the editorial necessities of punctuation, spelling and syntax. We have relegated one essay, 'Reading the Runes', to an appendix. It is an unrevised opening to a much longer section on the built environment, but complete enough to add a dimension to the arguments in Part II. Alison Light's biographical note which follows this preface gives a fuller picture of how Raphael worked and of the evolution and status of the text.

Unravelling is of course intended as a pun; it refers to the mental activity of the historian, of this historian in particular, as well as the state of the nation and its histories. These essays represent an exceptional effort to deploy all the resources of historical knowledge to capture the meaning of the present. As Raphael Samuel sometimes remarked, we may not be able to change history, but we can try to understand it.

It is a matter of great regret that we cannot thank, as Raphael would have done, all those who contributed to the essays printed here, offering their thoughts and sharing their work with him over the years. Only a handful of individuals are acknowledged in the footnotes to the essays. We would like to acknowledge those editors who originally published pieces in the press reprinted here: Richard Gott of the *Guardian*, Paul Barker at *New Society*, Steve Platt of the *New Statesman and Society*, Philippa Ingrams at the *Times Educational Supplement*, Ferdinand Mount of the *Times Literary Supplement*, Mary-Kay Wilmers at the *London Review of Books*, and those who published essays in earlier collections, Christopher Smout, Jane Garnett and Colin Matthew. We are also grateful to Tanya Evans for her initial help in finding references and to Steve Cox for his meticulous corrections to the text. All the major essays in this volume were written for Verso, migrating across London between Spitalfields and Soho, in various states of draft. Like Raphael we have come to rely utterly upon the goodwill and encouragement of his publishers. Jane Hindle was unfailingly patient and astute in seeing through a problematic and much-delayed manuscript. Robin Blackburn has acted as a fourth editor, taking his duties way beyond those strictly demanded of a publisher, travelling to Raphael's home on call, sorting through boxes of papers and scripts, and thoroughly relishing discussion of the volume in all its aspects. We have benefited enormously from his help.

Alison Light
Sally Alexander
Gareth Stedman Jones

A Biographical Note on the Text

The incompleteness of some of the essays we publish here is as much a measure of Raphael Samuel's constant, even obsessive, revising and recreating of every project he was involved in, as it is a result of the illness with which he lived for nearly two years before his death. When Volume I of *Theatres of Memory* went to press in 1994, Raphael had already drafted outlines of Volumes II, III and IV, for which he had plenty of material. Volume I was supposed, when it began life, to be a relatively straightforward business of collecting and largely reprinting a group of interconnected essays on the uses of the past in contemporary life (it originally contained a number of the pieces of political commentary which we have printed in this volume). In the event it was a book almost entirely written from scratch, responding especially to the debates about 'heritage' and the heritage industry, though some pieces were published in the press along the way: Raphael liked to give a piece a number of airings, taking on the comments of as many as he could, and incorporating them. On the flyleaf of my copy of Volume I, Raphael wrote ruefully: 'a book we've suffered from all our married life' (seven years at that point); but we both knew that it had never been one book, rather a whole shadowy series of possible books, large parts of which had been written only to be 'kept in reserve'. What might appear, and often felt to him, like writerly paralysis seemed to me to stem from an overflow rather than a paucity of ideas: it was as hard to get him to relinquish material as it was to stop him reworking it. Raphael frequently expressed the lame hope that Volume II would emerge rather less circuitously than Volume I, but the pattern of a new book being written, by sleight of hand as it were, on the back of another – his outlines came to resemble palimpsests on which more and more outlines were superimposed – seemed to be repeating itself, if a little more swiftly than before. Raphael always had several irons in the fire. He could only work with a sense of urgency and a precariously-balanced piling up of deadlines and commitments (a knife-edge existence which also could torment him).

Writing was a species of activism rather than withdrawal: everything must feel, and read, as if it were hot off the press, even if it had been, as it usually had, brewed up for months, even years. He was always *in medias res.*

There was a perfectly respectable book ready to go to press early in 1995, for which a contract was about to be signed, already called *Island Stories* and loosely touching on some of the topics of the present volume. But Raphael then launched himself on a newly ambitious series of essays which would concentrate and interlink rather more the intellectual and political themes of 'Unravelling Britain'. In fact all of Parts I and II of the volume before the reader, with the exception of 'Country Visiting', which is a shortened version of a much older piece begun in 1989, was drafted between the spring of 1995 and August 1996. These were also the months in which he received treatment for the cancer which had been diagnosed in April 1995. Many of the essays for this volume were left unfinished because he was busily caught up in, and excited by, other things equally pressing: an oral history of Green Street, for example, purportedly the first 'ethnic high street' in East London (one of the projects he got off the ground in his new post at the University of East London, setting up a centre for research into London's history); other journalism and broadcasting (we have not included here, for example, a talk given in October 1996 to celebrate fifty years of the Third Programme); soliciting articles for the 'History At Large' section of *History Workshop Journal*; as well as talks and meetings at home and abroad – to mention only what immediately springs to mind. Writing didn't always come first: Raphael's Communist unconscious, as we used to call it, still mistrusted the identity of 'writer', with its overtones of solipsism and self-importance; it held no glamour for him. Every piece had to be as collaborative and sociable as the strict and lonely discipline of writing could allow, generating phonecall after phonecall, relying on the endless quizzing of friends, colleagues, librarians, museum curators, businessmen, or the hapless relative who rang about something else. Every view was noted down, attributed in the notes, and taken seriously. The choice of the word 'theatre' in the main title of these volumes, as a metaphor for the activity of memory, was apt not least because it evoked the collective, shared practices in which Raphael was deeply versed, and the artform he admired most.

As editors of this volume we could cheer ourselves up by imagining that Raphael might have welcomed and been relieved by our imposing an order on a book that was still evolving (he would certainly have called on his friends and his publishers to negotiate the final contents list with him). On the other hand, we also know he would have worked furiously on what finally went in. We nevertheless have decided to publish some pieces, namely those in Part I, in their raw, unpolished condition, often at the stage where they energetically overstate arguments, because the reader can judge how much they expand the intellectual scope and vision of 'Unravelling Britain'. We hope that the collection of essays as a whole represents Raphael at his best and most accessible, and captures something of the centrifugal energy of his intellectual curiosity, the depth and breadth of his historical knowledge.

'Fissiparous' was one of Raphael's favourite words. His own work was in a continual state of fission. Any topic on which he was gathering material was always in danger of splitting off into smaller parts, each of which demanded intensive study and consideration (and might eventually spin off into orbit as an article in its own right). It might interest the reader to know that there were a number of supplements to the essays we print here, all in various stages of development; for Part I, a collection of notes on 'The British Diaspora' intended as a companion-piece to 'Empire Stories', which sprang from Raphael's encounter with Australia and Australian historiography at the Australian Historical Association conference he attended in September 1994; 'National Galleries', together with 'Apocrypha', envisaged as an extension of the arguments about visual history and national myths, especially the notion of fictitious pedigrees glanced at in 'Epical History'; 'Christian Epic', enlarging on the idea that with the decline of revealed religion on the one hand, and the appearance of a multi-faith society on the other, one version of national history likely to be marginalized or forgotten would be that of Christian narrative. What is published here in Part II under the title 'English Journeys' (a heading suggested by Raphael in the preface to Volume I) overlapped with a section he was working up called 'The Built Environment', whose general argument concerned the ways in which history is lodged, but also reinvented, in our buildings and the ways we occupy them: 'The Tower of London' illustrates this theme. We have printed as an appendix 'Reading the Runes', which belongs to this body of work, although it is undeveloped as an argument. Only the week before he died, Raphael was consolidating material and making new notes to include a piece on 'Red Bricks' (municipal and socialist housing and architecture), and finally one on 'House' (he had been, like many, fascinated by the artist Rachel Whiteread's public sculpture, displayed in London's East End late in 1993, though typically his notes range from the dwellings of the ancient Assyrians to the home as a conservative fantasy of safety). 'Island Stories' was originally the title for a long meditative essay on the teaching of national history in schools. The debates about the proposed National Curriculum and history's role within it, together with the workshops held at Ruskin College, Oxford, on 'History, the Nation and the Schools' (in June 1989 and May 1990) were a seedbed for much of his later thinking for this volume.

I have added footnotes to all the major pieces left in draft for Parts I and II: 'Epical History', 'Unravelling Britain', 'Empire Stories', 'The Tower of London' and 'Country Visiting'; and to the literary journalism,

'The Lost Gardens of Heligan' and 'The Voice of Britain'. The debates on the national curriculum, the political journalism in Parts III and IV, and the Appendix have been left unfootnoted, though it is likely that Raphael would have added his own notes. All the information for all of the footnotes has been taken from Raphael's files and filecards. That said, these notes obviously represent my own selection, and therefore my interpretation, dependent partly on taste, on the limits of my knowledge, and finally, practically, on what could be easily found and deciphered. There are a number of lacunae but only, I hope, a handful of unattributed quotations which it seemed worthwhile to leave in at the risk of irritating the reader. Mostly, by the standards of many historians (and I am not one), the selection has been minimal, with the intention of giving a glimpse of the intellectual hinterland to the thought and also a couple of pointers to anyone who wants to pursue a particular path. Now and again I have indulged my own pleasure in footnote-writing and extrapolated beyond the mere reference. I have also signalled in the notes where the script carries a warning about its preliminary state or a fraught message to the publishers.

Historians are notorious for piling up footnotes, sometimes in the attempt to save more of their preciously-mined material from oblivion. They are also, perhaps, especially and rightly susceptible to feeling the weight of past work. To a socialist historian like Raphael, footnotes were also a matter of principle as well as common courtesy, acknowledging one's debts as well as making other people's work available, recognizing that thinking and writing are part of a collaborative, shared culture; like authority, thought is always borrowed, on permanent loan, as it were. I have only been able to acknowledge somewhat randomly in the notes, and where it was most obviously signalled, the contribution of friends, colleagues, librarians, students, and innumerable others whom Raphael consulted over the last two years. That is a great shame. Nor could anyone reproduce the ways in which Raphael's footnotes, at best, were both a teaching device and could act as an alternative text, allowing the opportunity for cameo portraits, minor digressions down one of history's lesser-known byways, pointed summaries or miniature genealogies of an argument or concept. There are, for example, about a dozen crowded files on 'Saxonism', charting the different uses to which the idea of the Anglo-Saxon has been put across the centuries by historians and politicians and in the popular imagination (for a couple of lines in 'Unravelling Britain'); for the merest mention in 'The Voice of Britain' of one example of BBC children's programming – *Toytown* – half a file of notes. Yet where the material is at its richest, I have often found myself most stumped, unable either to select or condense. I have consoled myself by believing that the files were perhaps metamorphosing, advancing towards becoming separate essay topics in their own right. And I reread what Raphael wrote about footnotes in Volume I of *Theatres of*

Memory, where he was musing on the historian's method as involving its own levels of artifice:

> Historians today don't knowingly forge documents. But by the nature of our trade we are continually having to fabricate contexts. . . Footnotes serve as fetishes and are given as authorities for generalizations which a thousand different instances would not prove. (pp. 433–4)

Raphael's files, which I have worked through in order to footnote, speak volumes about the kind of historian he was and the kind or kinds of history he valued. His method of notekeeping, to which he recruited many of his students and fellow-workers, derived from that of the Fabian social investigators Sidney and Beatrice Webb, a method Beatrice describes in appendix C to *My Apprenticeship* (1926). Perfected for the 'scientific historian' in the 1890s and 1900s, it depends upon the employment of quantities of loose sheets of paper rather than 'a conglomerate notebook', each page with only one note or source of information on it, perhaps no more than a line or two, on one side only. The note – be it a transcribed quotation or précis, a cutting, a xeroxed extract or a handwritten thought – is given a heading and grouped, and its source briefly attributed. The beauty of this method, as the Webbs saw it, is that the detached sheets can be shuffled and reshuffled indefinitely, new notes added, headings retitled, and, they believed, in rearranging and reordering new sequences, surprising intellectual discoveries could be made which might overturn one's original presuppositions and biases.

Beatrice Webb unbends a little to give a picture of herself and Sidney playing a 'game with reality', reshuffling their mass of papers and 'backing' rival hypotheses in their studies of trade unions or factory work – 'a most stimulating recreation!', she writes almost skittishly. To a modern (or postmodern) eye this idea of the reinterpretability (the unravelling) of the evidence might seem to sit ill with the Webbs' faith in history as a science dealing in facts. It was this reversible process of notemaking – a method which could be deconstructive as well as constructive, improvisatory as well as accumulative – which I think appealed to Raphael and which he made uniquely his own. Their method relies on a vast amount of 'fact gathering'; it is deeply retentive; but it also allows, indeed encourages, a constant disassembling of ideas. Together with a formidable capacity to collect evidence and devour book after book, Raphael was quite fearless in his capacity to dismantle his own arguments, start again, and even jettison former views rather than treat the case as settled once and for all. (Typically, another of the half-written pieces that had to be omitted from this volume is a reply to the critics of Volume I, 'The Heritage Debate Revisited'.)

Files, just like ideas, could keep on turning into something else: arguments could be abandoned and, in one of his favourite usages, 'revivified'.

Raphael usually adduced a minimum of ten or twenty instances, on separate sheets, for each heading or thought which might eventually become a paragraph, say, on the cult of walking in the 1930s. These in turn could splinter into several subheadings – 'Communism and Walking', 'Walking and Trespass', 'Fresh Air Fads', etc. – and result in a solid phalanx of black A3 'lever-arch' ringbinders, all labelled 'Walking between the wars'. (For many years the 'Clarity' lever-arch file was manufactured and supplied by a longstanding firm, Jockelson, White and Co. of 292/4 Bishopsgate, London EC2, just around the corner from us.) Everything could be 'decanted' and refiled under new headings. Files would later be 'filleted' and then 'cannibalized' as he called it, for ensuing projects. (The culinary metaphors – he also talked of 'gutting books' – were a sign of Raphael's immense appetite for the work, I think; and his need to be fed by it.)

The Webbs' method is profligate with paper. Though they soberly advised identically sized sheets, Raphael's files are crammed with reused paper of all shapes, textures and colours: a motley of notes stuck on the backs of scrap (from college memos to drafts of friends' articles, all themselves interesting, if distracting, reading); cut-ups from xeroxes and press-cuttings agencies, shreds of paper napkins from restaurants where a conversation was hurriedly written down and later dissected. His method involved hours of 'sticking up', using scissors and paste (a large, very unstable Gloy gluepot and brush before the days of PrittStick), turning a great deal of what the Webbs called 'brainworking' into messy physical labour, quite relieving and childlike in its pleasures. In tandem with the cliffs of ringbinders in every available space in our house (except for the kitchen and the bedroom), excitable, ever-mounting piles of file-cards, with their full bibliographical references, were packed uneasily into old Oxo tins, teetering on dusty windowsills or lurking beneath chairs. Since everything could, in theory, be reused, nothing could be thrown away.

Raphael's files are, to use one of his phrases, an '*omnium gatherum*' or, as he described a commemorative volume for twenty-five years of *History Workshop*, a 'collectanea', an assembly of materials in which the attempt to understand a phenomenon or a historical argument might yoke together seemingly disparate evidence, the extract from a scholarly article cheek by jowl with a clip from *Homes and Gardens*, the leaflet which came through the door yesterday jostling with the label off a jar of homemade jam – but all to be synthesized under an infinitely reclassifiable thought: 'the country look in the 90s' or 'the aesthetics of nature' or 'the contemporary idea of the domestic' and so on. The files themselves, like the dozen or so on 'retrochic' for Volume I of *Theatres of Memory*, come to constitute a historical treasury, containing much that is the stuff of history as well as an attempted analysis of it. The Webbs' method was intended to make it possible for someone else to take over one's notes and use them, and the footnotes show, whatever else, that even given Raphael's inventive handwriting, this is indeed the case. The editors of this volume, who are also Raphael's literary executors, hope in the coming year to find a new home for his papers, pamphlets and books, in an archive or archives, so that more people can use them and make of them what they will.

The art of notemaking as espoused by the Webbs only really made sense as part of a *life's* work, something organic and total, always generating and regenerating; the work was simply *never* over. Raphael was predisposed in so many ways, from his Jewish childhood (his maternal grandfather ran a Hebrew bookshop; his mentor, Chimen Abramsky, is a man of great learning) to his Communist upbringing by his mother, Minna Keal, herself an activist and organizer, to find this a sympathetic philosophy. He was a dedicated worker, with an almost nineteenth-century faith in the value of the work, testing his own capacities to the limits, often going without food or sleep, living on 'little nips' of spirits, and lashings of nightmarishly strong coffee, to 'get up a head of steam' on what he was writing. He could spend the day 'in a pit', rewriting the same sentence a hundred times, because, like so many others, he cherished the hope that if he could only find the right word or turn of phrase, the whole argument would be instantly illuminated and the reader wooed into agreement. Raphael was never really 'off-duty' (the notion of his ever 'retiring' was quite shocking and repellent to him); the life and the work were meant to be seamless; their pleasures enhancing each other so much that the distinction between them ought to disappear.

I don't think I ever heard Raphael say that a piece was finished; he was temperamentally, politically, and as a historian, opposed to endings (he couldn't easily follow plots, either, and the average amount of suspense demanded by reading a thriller or watching a television series seemed to baffle and alarm him). One probably apocryphal story which tickled him enormously was of the Oxford don (he said) who firmly believed that the only truly gentlemanly thing to do was to publish posthumously. Although Raphael often spoke of how kind the University had been to him both as an undergraduate and later as a historian, it was Ruskin College's marginal and oppositional place in Oxford and in higher education that he savoured, and where he belonged for over thirty years. Still, he has certainly behaved like his imaginary don and left material enough for several more volumes. Verso hopes to publish at least two of them: one on the philosophy and practice of history; the other on the dreamers and planners of socialist and Marxist history and thought.

*

Producing this volume since Raphael died has been for me, as I know for the other editors in their different ways, a work of mourning as well as a labour of love, a way of remaining close to the sources of Raphael's extraordinary vitality when we were most feeling its loss. As his widow I count myself lucky to have had this chance to be his amanuensis, a role which we both would have resisted strenuously when he was alive.

Alison Light
Spitalfields, September 1997

Bookplate designed by Bernard Canavan for the Raphael Samuel Archive

Part I

Nations, States and Empires

Epical History: The Idea of Nation*

I

The idea of nation, as one learns about it in an English school, is, or ought to be, a source of confusion. Studying early modern England, or what used to be called 'Tudors and Stuarts', children are told that in Britain the nation-state began with the Battle of Bosworth (1485) and the establishment of the 'New Monarchy' of Henry VII. Shakespeare's Chronicle plays obey a similar conceit, and to this day, in the Oxford History School, 1485 is the *terminus ad quem* of feudal society. Ecclesiastical historians, anyway Protestant ones, have long been used to giving us the Reformation as the morning-star of modernity and the Act of Uniformity (1536) as the Magna Carta of national independence – a proposition which the remarkable historian G.R. Elton devoted a lifetime of ferocious polemic and research to amplify in a more secular sense. Recently, though, Anglo-American literary historians, writing under the influence of the 'New Historicism', have taken to giving us an alternative chronology, making the 1590s into a landmark decade – the years when, in the aftermath of the defeat of the Spanish Armada, Shakespeare wrote his Chronicle plays, notably the great patriotic drama, *Henry V*; when the antiquaries rediscovered Boadicea (the leader of the resistance to the Roman occupation, she disappeared from the historical record for more than a thousand years); and when, in the field of language, English triumphed, a 'rude' tongue and vulgar literature successfully challenging the hegemony of Latin.[1] Another alternative chronology which has recently come to the fore, partly under the influence of Linda Colley's *Britons* (1992),[2] but also it may be, if unconsciously, because of a new

* This essay is a version of a lecture entitled 'Modernity and Archaism' given in January 1996 to a seminar on nationalism at the Centre Marc Bloch in Berlin, organized by Peter Schöttler. It is an early draft and was not revised or footnoted.

sense of the precariousness of the Union between England and Scotland, is one which dates the rise of British nationalism to the 1740s, the 'moment' when, in the aftermath of the Battle of Culloden, the United Kingdom emerged as a going concern, the decade which gave us such swaggering national anthems as 'Rule Britannia', and the rise of a Protestant nationalism which gave Britain a world-historical mission.

In 'general' history, school students are presented not with one 'springtime of nations'[3] but with half a dozen. As in England, there is the sixteenth-century challenge to the authority of the Papacy, and the supposed rise of the nation-state, both Reformation and, in the case of Spain, Counter-Reformation in character. Then there is the French Revolution and the *levée en masse* and the republic. The discovery of nation here appears as a discovery of the people, an irruption on to the political stage of a hitherto rightless citizenry. Romantic nationalism offers a quite different optic, Mazzinian rather than Jacobin. The focus here is on the struggle of subject peoples for self-determination – the revolt of the South American Spanish colonies (a movement which, as the textbooks are at pains to stress, the British foreign secretary, Canning, made a point of aiding and abetting); the Greek War of Independence (in which Lord Byron lost his life); and the Polish insurrection of 1831.[4] Then, for those who use the older textbooks, there is the Treaty of Versailles, the break-up of the Habsburg and Ottoman Empires, and the idea of a new world-order based on nation-states. Finally, under the influence of multiculturalism and Third Worldism, one of the major influences on the liberalization of the school curriculum, there is the new attention to the post-colonial societies, and the determination to invest them with *pre-colonial* histories.

Under the influence of Michel Foucault – a greater figure in contemporary Anglo-American historiography and geography than he would perhaps be in his native France – an entirely different problematic comes into view, one in which nations, with a trail of tutelary institutions following in their wake, are forever being fabricated, or 'invented', i.e. foisted on the unsuspecting public. The crystallization of nation becomes a disciplinary affair; it is associated with the rise of modern methods of surveillance and what Foucault called 'the great confinement'; the 'discovery' of the asylum; the invention of bureaucratic records; and the rise of such captive institutions as the workhouse, the factory and the school.[5] In England, the Elementary Education Act of 1870 becomes a landmark date, inaugurating a compulsory and national schooling, just as in France, in the same period, it is the *instituteurs* of the Third Republic who are the missionaries of the national idea. More generally, it is argued that the last quarter of the nineteenth century saw the emergence of 'Englishness', a quite self-conscious doctrine and practice which on the one hand summoned up the ghosts of the past to shore up threatened values, and on the other prepared a master race for its imperial vocation.[6]

One point on which the theorists and the historians of nationalism converge is the essential modernity of the phenomenon. Marxists have classically associated it with the rise of the bourgeoisie (though *The Communist Manifesto* seems to opt for absolutist monarchy), economists with the creation of national and transnational markets. For liberals it is a child of the democratic idea, an expression of the modern movement for self-determination. In Benedict Anderson's *Imagined Communities* (1983) – in the Anglophone world, much the most influential current work in the field – nationalism was in the first place a product of what he calls 'print capitalism', and the rise of a popular, 'vernacular-based', political knowledge (it occupies the symbolic space, one is tempted to suggest, that the Reformation did in the textbooks of yesteryear). Eric Hobsbawm, in *Nations and Nationalism* (1990), though scathing about contemporary manifestations of the phenomenon, sees nation-making as an essential component of nineteenth-century progress. 'It belongs exclusively to a particular, and historically recent period . . . it relates to a certain kind of modern territorial state – the "nation-state", and it is pointless to discuss nation and nationality except so far as both relate to it.'[7] Tom Nairn, a partisan of ethnic nationalism, is anxious to show that it is the wave of the future, a response to the break-up of Empire and to the emergence of pan-European solidarities.[8]

The idea of 'nation', in one or other of its many different versions, is as old as the oldest written histories. In Herodotus, the term is freely applied both to the pastoral nomads of Thrace and to the city-states of Asia Minor and Attica.[9] In classical Latin, where '*gens*' was preferred to '*natio*', the appellation would be applied sometimes to a people, such as those whom Julius Caesar so systematically belittles in his *Commentaries*,[10] sometimes to a community (a usage familiar in the Middle Ages from the civil wars which periodically broke out among the rival student 'nations' at Oxford, Paris and Bologna), sometimes, as in the case of Rome itself, to an Empire on the make.[11] In any of these characters, nations appear as collective actors on the historical scene, now subjugating, or defending themselves, against old enemies, now forming alliances with their nearest rivals.

The nations which appear in the ancient histories, though midget in size compared with those which came into existence in early modern Europe, are very far from negligible. They have developed notions of citizenship and are subject to the overriding authority of the law. They conduct a foreign policy, annex neighbouring territory, and subsume tribal identities in a larger whole.[12] In pursuit of national defence, they maintain elaborately fortified frontier posts. In time of war they act with a degree of unity and self-sacrifice which a modern government might well envy, and indeed Pericles's oration at the tomb of the Unknown Soldier – a great inspiration, in the later nineteenth century, to the classically educated Empire builder – is, as an admiring Oxford editor put it in 1943, one of the supreme expressions of the national idea.[13] Attic comedy, such as the plays of Aristophanes, reminds us of the nether side of these developments, poking fun at 'the never-ending lawsuits and fiddling bureaucrats'.[14] The Romans followed suit, and Plautus's *miles gloriosus*, the bombastic, cowardly soldier, armed to the teeth with loot, is a favourite butt of the satirists. Tacitus, in his *Histories*, when dealing with the wire-pullers who used backstairs influence to acquire lucrative official posts, is hardly less tart.[15]

So far from being tribes, the embryo nations of the ancient world were multi-ethnic in character, as France was to be in the time of the Valois, and Prussia under the augmentations of Frederick the Great. The Venetians, according to Livy, were 'a mixed population of Trojans and Eneti';[16] Rome, though it had an original nucleus of Latins, grew up as a magnet for the diasporic. Its armies were reinforced by drafts of mercenaries from the imperial frontier. Its slave population was recruited from all parts. The city-states of ancient Greece, though reserving citizenship for the native-born, were no less polyglot, and indeed exiles such as Thucydides, the historian of the Peloponnesian war, are among the most characteristic figures of Greek literature.[17] Egypt, a carrefour of Asia, Africa and Europe, was, it seems, even more cosmopolitan. In Herodotus's famous ethnography, where the term is applied to 'all the people who . . . drank the Nile's waters', the inhabitants (as Martin Bernal has powerfully argued) were both negro and white, Ionian and Ethiopian.[18] The Phoenicians and the Syrians had ensconced themselves in the Mediterranean littoral (later they were to make Alexandria one of the great cosmopolitan capitals of the world); Libyans colonized the marsh country in the interior.

A concept of Greek and of Greekness seems to have existed, as a generic term, for at least 2,000 years before the formation, in the 1820s, of the first Greek state. Unknown in the pages of Homer, it is freely invoked by Herodotus, for whom the struggle between Greeks and Persians is the epic event of world history. Thucydides, in his great history, is at pains to explain the change: 'Before the Trojan War there was no indication of any common action in Greece, nor indeed of the name being given to the country as a whole. . . . It went by the name of the different tribes'. War knit peoples and states together, uniting for the pursuit of what he calls 'great and national ends'.[19] The war against Troy was the first of a series of federations against the 'barbarians' (i.e. foreigners) at the gates, and it was only with the onset of decadence that the Greeks – among them his beloved Athenians – began to fight among themselves.[20]

Another precocious source for the study of the national idea is, or ought to be, the Old Testament. Here one is confronted not only with dynasties and kingdoms, ethnic nationalisms and imperial ambitions, but also the whole paraphernalia of the modern state – tax-gathering;[21]

conscription; territorial armies; legal codes. Indeed, with the exception of the word 'state' the whole vocabulary of the nation is in place. More exotically there are the sumptuous palaces and elaborate courts, such as the one where King Solomon received the Queen of Sheba. When Nebuchadnezzar, 'king of kings', wanted to stage a national festival, he gathered together (the Book of Daniel tells us) 'the princes, the governors and captains, the judges, the treasurers, the counsellors, the sheriffs, and all the rulers of the provinces'.[22] The Jewish state, multi-ethnic in character – the tribes of Israel constituted as the Nation of the Hebrews – was proto-national in all the vicissitudes of its development, now swelling into an embryo Empire, now contracting into a satellite and a protectorate. Its capital city Jerusalem, the place where the Temple was built, as well as being the home of administrative kingship, was also the religious centre of a united people. In the rising of the Hasmoneans and the establishment of what Jewish historians call 'the Second Hebrew Commonwealth' it presents us with a fully-fledged struggle for political independence (not the least of the legacies on which twentieth-century Zionism was to build); while in the Sadducees, the wealthy elite who in the last century of the Jewish state were contending with the Pharisees for hegemony, it gives us the very prototype of a nationalist party.[23]

The example of the Hebrew nation – detached, when the Temple was destroyed, from a territorial base, and dispersed to the far corners of the Persian Empire, as they were to be later by the Romans – may serve as a reminder of the way in which religion has been the crucible of the national idea. It might be matched by the recent emergence, as independent countries, of Serbia and Croatia on the strength of historic, if newly reinvented, divisions between Orthodox Christianity and Roman Catholicism. The idea of the 'Holy War', waged, it seems, by the Israelites, until the time of David's United Kingdom,[24] and famous, or notorious, in the present day in the Islamic *jihad,* is one which very often doubles with the idea of national defence, or, as in the case of the Palestinian intifada, the assertion of national being. 'The war against the Irish was driven by divine imperatives', writes John Morrill; Cromwell 'saw himself delivering "a righteous judgement of God"'. He had come, he told the Irish Catholic clergy, 'to extirpate popery'.[25] Blood sacrifice is no less ubiquitous in the struggles of subject peoples, just as religious persecution so often provides the occasion for the call to arms. The idea of the 'elect' nation, which William Haller attributes to the influence of Calvinist theology, and attaches to the Protestant-radicals of the 1560s ('God', said an Elizabethan bishop, was 'English'), also seems to be a universal trope.[26] It is anticipated in the Old Testament idea of the 'chosen people' and the Sadducees' belief that God was a national God, 'the God of Israel only'. It is, or at least it was in the nineteenth century, a favourite conceit in 'God's Own Country' – 'purer, cleaner than the Europe left behind' – and ever since Woodrow Wilson's 'Fourteen Points' it has been a leading feature of US foreign policy. In Britain twentieth-century peace movements (as James Hinton convincingly suggests in *Protests and Visions*)[27] have been no less beholden to the age-old Puritan vision of the nation which gives a 'moral lead'.

The romanticization of war might also be considered as a cultural universal, one which, as the nightmare conflicts which have engulfed former Yugoslavia remind us, enters into the very marrow of the national idea. The disasters of the Gallipoli campaign, by common consent, marked Australia's coming-of-age;[28] are we to say less of the battle of Thermopylae, where according to the ancient historians the idea of a Greek federation was born? By what right do we claim the Maginot line – a theatre of the absurd – for the history of modern nationalism, while leaving the fortifications of Anatolia – an inconceivably more effective instrument of national defence – to the archaeologists?[29] War, waged by those whom Herodotus calls 'nations', is *the* great subject of the ancient histories, and as many commentators have pointed out it is by far the most constant activity reported in the Bible. ' . . . There are few years in the thousand-year period covered by Old Testament history in which there was not a campaign being waged by one of the nations or peoples of the Near Eastern world against another'.[30]

Typologies of national character, fastening sometimes on physical peculiarities, sometimes on behavioural quirks, also go back to the earliest times, and in the written culture of Europe they have a high intellectual lineage. Herodotus, the father of history, as also, according to his critics, the great mother of invention, offers us a whole gallery of them, branching out in the case of the Egyptians and the Thracians to full-scale ethnography. Thus the Scythians suffer from a mysterious infliction called 'the female disease', while the Massagetae, who have many resemblances to the Scythians, are distinguished by the fact that they do not boil the flesh or consume the corpses of their dead. In a less macabre vein, the Persians consider themselves 'in every way superior to everyone else', crediting their near neighbours with being second best; the Lacedaemonians are 'constantly on the move'.[31] A born ethnographer, if a possibly gullible investigator, Herodotus tempers his more fantastical suppositions with the small detail of everyday life, drawing here on travellers' tales, there on personal impressions and quite often (it seems possible) on occult lore. At the heart of his writing – with Homer, surely a kind of prototype for the Mediterranean world of Fernand Braudel – the focus is on habit and custom, fashion and dress, navigation and settlement.[32]

Hippocrates, an altogether more systematizing intelligence, attempted to relate such traits to ecology, explaining them by reference to climate, habitat and soil, and investing the collective subject with psychological attributes – e.g. foresight, ambition and strength or absence of will. It was in this guise that taxonomies of ethnic or national personality are reproduced in Pliny's *Natural History* and later (perhaps only half-understood?

a joke to while away the hours in the scriptorium?) in the medieval encyclopedias, where catalogues of the 'vices and deformities of Nation'[33] – sometimes cribbed from classical literature, but also drawing, it may be, on more grass-roots xenophobias – are offset by encomia on the virtuous. Thumbnail sketches of this kind also figure, from the time of Marco Polo, in travellers' accounts, and they were to have pride of place in the work of the sixteenth-century cosmographers.

The origin of such stereotypes is quite mysterious. Like proverbs and riddles, to which they have some affinities, or the capsule accounts of manners and customs which appear in the *Blasons Populaires*, such characterizations could easily become formulaic. But once established they seem to have been difficult to dislodge, and were endlessly reproduced, a great standby for the popular printers of the seventeenth century as they had been for the scribes and illustrators of the Middle Ages. These legendary commonplaces enjoyed a vigorous after-life, indeed as Hodgen, who has monitored their diffusion, remarks, some are still in active service today. They seem to have survived the New Learning of the sixteenth century, and even to have been taken up by it. The belief that there was a 'proper spirit to every region', and a 'naturall disposiccion' to every people, was the conventional wisdom of the age. Jean Bodin, one of the architects of the New Learning in the field of constitutional law, freely indulged in such apothegms, assigning gluttony to the English, drunkenness to the Italians and falsehood to the Irish.[34] A more elaborate taxonomy finds a place in Mercator's *Mappa Mundi* (1585), one of the foundation works of the new geography, and according to some critical geographers a very charter for three centuries of European expansion:

> The *Francons* are simple, blockish & furious; the *Bavarians* sumptuous, gluttons, and brazen-faced; the *Sweeds* light, bablers and boasters; the *Thuringeans* distrustfull, slovens, and quarrelsome; the *Saxons* dissemblers, double-hearted and opinionative; the *Belgians* good horsemen, tender, docible, and delicate; the *Italians* proud, revengeful and ingenious [this one stuck]; the *Spaniard* disdainful, cautious and greedie; the *Gaules* proper, intemperate, rash-headed; the *Cimbrians* high-minded, seditious and terrible; the *Saramates* gluttons, proud, and theeves; the *Bohemians* cruell, lovers of novelties, filtchers; the *Illyricks* variable, malicious, and ryotous; the *Pannonians* rude, superstitious; the *Grecians* miserable.[35]

Heylyn, the Dutch cosmographer, was equally happy to reproduce proverbial lore, presenting it in the form of a recital of national vices and virtues. Like Shakespeare in his point-scoring interludes, Heylyn leavens his message with verbal play and dialectical wit:

> If we believe the proverbiall speech. . . . The Spaniards are said to seeme wise and are fools; the French to seeme fooles and are wise; the Italians to seeme & be wise; the Portugalls are affirmed neither to be wise, nor so much as to

> seeme so; and not much different from this the Spanish have a proverbe, which telleth us that the Portugalls are Pocus y locus, few and foolish.[36]

Stereotypes of national character, often wildly at variance with each other, or combining all-but antithetical qualities – e.g. 'prudence' and 'courage' – seem to have flourished in England quite independent of such taxonomies. Some took their cue from the flora and fauna (e.g. 'hearts of oak'); some from the climate (in the nineteenth century it was thought to be bracing, in the seventeenth and early eighteenth centuries, distempered), and some expressed fantasies of omnipotence. In one of the earliest and most enduring of generalizations, which dates back to, and is liberally amplified in, Sir John Fortescue's *Governance of England* (1467), the English were represented as a nation of meat-eaters, even, according to some, 'gluttons', a people who lived plentifully while on the other side of the Channel there was a nation who starved. (Arthur Young's *Travels Through France* (1789) – written in the year when the Revolution broke out, and sometimes quoted as prophetic – is a late and influential essay in this vein, and indeed to this day *ancien régime* France is thought of as a place where a million pairs of hungry eyes stared in at the rich man's feast.) In a very different typification, brilliantly represented in Burton's *Anatomy of Melancholy* (1621), and still influential in the eighteenth century, when Dr Johnson built a much-loved character out of it, the English suffered from 'morbid melancholy', a hereditary malady which some attributed to the climate, and some to a national deficiency in milk. Suicide was thought of in the eighteenth century as 'the English disease' – a notion that inspired the title of a medical treatise published in 1733. The writer, Dr Cheyne, attributed England's suicide rate – allegedly the highest in Europe – to the 'moisture' of the air, the 'Variableness' of the weather, the 'Rankness' of the soil, the 'Richness and Heaviness' of the food, and, not least, 'the *Inactivity* and *sedentary* occupations of the better sort (among whom this Evil mostly rages).[37]

The English weather, vilified since the advent of the sun-bathing cult in the 1920s at least until global warming, was often treated in earlier times as one of England's glories. Changeable, where that of others was monotonous, it kept the people on their toes. Mild and temperate, it encouraged 'moderate' government where others less favourably placed ran to tyrannical extremes. The 'wholesomeness' of the English climate was a well-worn theme of the philosophers and economists of the eighteenth century, following in the steps of Montesquieu and relating the genius of the country to its geography. The climate fitted the people for action. It encouraged the martial virtues, promoting 'courage' where those in warmer climes (as a Scottish Enlightenment writer put it) were 'indolent and effeminate'.[38] It was also, Joseph Campbell wrote in his *Political Survey of Britain* (1774) – anticipating what was to be a rich vein in imperial conceit – a bounty for travel and exploration:

> The Variations in our Climate, which some have represented as such terrible Inconveniences, are, if more closely considered, very singular Advantages. Our Seasons, though it must be confessed they do not very nearly resemble those on the Continent, yet give such Vivacity and Vigour to the Natives, and so habituates them to those Changes that are incident to a Life of Travel, that no people . . . perform long Voyages or Journeys with greater Ease, or are less affected by the Hardships to which, in such expeditions, they are almost necessarily exposed.[39]

II

The hall of kings at Holyrood Palace, Edinburgh, can provide the *exemplum* for the argument of this essay, showing how, in modern Britain as in ancient Greece, the legendary can serve as a prelude to the historical, and the imaginary double up with the real. Here, in the picture gallery, visitors find themselves confronted with the spectacle of no fewer than 111 Scottish kings. The pictures are arranged in chronological sequence, starting with Fergus I, the mythopoeic figure who founded the kingdom – a peripatetic warrior who allegedly landed in Scotland in 330 BC – and climaxing in a wall devoted to the later Stuarts. Commissioned by Charles II, though only completed in the reign of his successor, and painted by the Dutch artist, Jacob de Wet, the portraits purport to cover some two millennia of Scottish history, giving fleshly embodiment to those royal genealogies and origin myths in which the idea of Scottish nationality seems first to have taken shape.[40] Adumbrated in the shadow of the Wars of Independence 1286–1328, as a weapon against the English, and as a counter-mythology to the Brutus legend which the king of England advanced when laying claim to all-British suzerainty; given a mass of circumstantial detail by the fourteenth-century scholar, John of Fordun; elaborated in the fifteenth-century *Scotichronicon*; and given popular form by the sixteenth-century Renaissance writer, Hector Boece, this pseudo-history held the ring for some four centuries, dropping one or two of the earlier extravagances but taking on new ones. Not until the learned researches of the eighteenth-century antiquarian Thomas Innes did it come under serious attack.[41] In the pictures themselves there is no pretence at historical accuracy; all of the monarchs, before the Stuarts, are dressed alike, in chronologically indeterminate neo-classical garb, and wearing the short beards favoured by seventeenth-century courtiers; and in fact the first forty of the kings (and the first seven centuries of the history) are fictions. Yet the pictures were solemnly offered, and apparently accepted, as a kind of monarchical Valhalla, an *Iconographia Scotica* designed to show the high antiquity of the nation, and the unbroken line of its royal dynasty.

Galleries of kings and queens (Roy Strong tells us) were a 'fundamental ingredient' of almost any late Elizabethan or Jacobean collection of pictures.[42] They were also a great favourite with the publishers of books and prints. John Speed, in his 1611 *The Theatre of the Empire of Great Britain* – a fundamental work for a century and more of cartography – uses them to illustrate the tribal kingdoms of the Anglo-Saxon heptarchy. To each kingdom he allots a founding father, starting with Hengist, the possibly mythic founder of Kent, and ending with the South Saxon king of 662, Ethelwolfe (each is equipped by the illustrator with sceptre and sword). Galleries like this also had a part to play in state theatricals. In the Lord Mayor's Show, one of the great spectacles of Elizabethan and Jacobean London, and an occasion when policy matters were very much to the fore, historical figures, such as reigning or deposed monarchs, were freely mixed with allegorical and mythological ones, such as Robin Hood, who accompanied by a number of his men 'all clad in greene, with their Bowes, Arrowes and Bugles, and a new slaine Deere carried among them',[43] was one of the novelties introduced by Anthony Munday, the chief choreographer, in the Lord Mayor's Show of 1615. John Webster mounted a chariot of kings – eight in all – when, in 1624, he was pageant master for the procession. He had Edward III give the lead, saying: 'Let all good men this sentence oft repeate/By unity the smallest things grow great'. To which all the other kings replied in a chorus: 'By unity the smallest things grow great'.[44] As in all Lord Mayor's shows, however, it was the effigy of Gog – 'the guardian spirit of London',[45] 'the first recorded patriot in British history'[46] – who headed the procession. Gog was the Cornish giant who, according to the Albion legend, challenged the Trojans when they landed at Totnes, Devon, and after a titanic struggle was dashed to pieces on the rocks.[47]

In foundation myths, visual artifices of the kind practised by court painters are more than matched by verbal apocrypha. In the case of Scotland, the deceptions are so frequent and so strategic that one is tempted to suggest that all the leading items in the national pantheon, with the honourable exception of the Declaration of Arbroath (1320), can be traced back, ultimately, to fakes. Medieval Edinburgh, for instance, one of the finest townscapes in Europe, was, contrary to appearances, quite largely a creation of the nineteenth century, a kind of visual realization of the 'Auld Reekie' of Sir Walter Scott. As Bob Morris writes: 'The Castle and the esplanade were remoulded as a great monument and stage upon which Scotland displayed its new identity as a nation within a nation'.[48] The romanticization of the Scottish Highlands, and with it the Gaelic revival and the rehabilitation of Scottish Jacobitism – the platform on which the National Association for the Vindication of Scottish Rights, the first Scottish Home Rule association, was formed in 1853 – stem directly from the forgeries of Ossian, that wonderful exercise in the Gothic imagination which for some fifty years held all Europe in its thrall (Napoleon was allegedly carrying a copy of Ossian at the Battle of Austerlitz).[49] A still more striking example would be the martyrdom of

Detail of engraved title-page of John Speed's *Theatre of the Empire of Great Britain* (1616)

William Wallace, an event recently screened in the Hollywood-financed epic, *Braveheart.* Almost the only source we have for it is the celebrated poem of Henry the Minstrel, 'Blind Harry', the work which made William Wallace a household name. Written some 150 years after the event, the poem is hardly the eye-witness account it purports to be. It now appears that the author was not Blind Harry at all, but one who took his name as an *alias* to recommend the verse to the public.[50]

It is a fact familiar to all those, like field anthropologists or ethnologists, who have studied the storyteller's arts that myth and history are not mutually incompatible, but coexist as complementary and sometimes intersecting modes of representing the past. Myth, so far from being timeless, is subject to a constant process of change which, as a writer on the Amazon Indians puts it, 'allows it to keep pace with reality'.[51] (If Glastonbury is anything to go by – the 'New Age' and pop music Mecca in England, where mass celebrations of the earth mysteries are an annual event – it will also try to incorporate the results of recent research.) Myths accrete their own history, introducing fresh episodes and adding new characters, as, say, in the sixteenth century, when it became part of rural processioning, the Robin Hood saga added Maid Marian to the *dramatis personae.*[52] Ballads, such as the magnificent collection of *Serbocroatian Heroic Songs* analysed by Milman Parry, would have topical verses added to them, just as the Mummer's Play, telling the story of St George and the Dragon, and apparently lost in the mists of time, would add contemporary characters.[53]

Conversely, historians, however wedded to empirical enquiry, will take on, without knowing it, the deep structures of mythic thought – perhaps by the scholarly ingenuity which they lavish on establishing lines of continuity (in a monograph, and even in a learned article, as in a fairy tale, stories should have a beginning, a middle and an end); or by the symbolic importance they attach to the grand permanences of national life (was this one of the subliminal appeals of the *'longue durée' Annales?*);[54] or because of an unargued-for but pervasive teleology. Nineteenth-century practitioners of what is called in Britain the Whig interpretation of history, secularizing the Protestant doctrine of God's Providence and replacing it with one of national destiny, could simply not accommodate the fact of Roman Britain, disqualified by reason of race and religion, as well as the absence of a written constitution, from having any part in the Island story: the English only became English when they converted to Christianity. An earlier example of the tenacity of mythic thought would be the magnificent narratives of Thucydides. A historian's historian, he scorned hearsay and the conjectural, and would put down nothing which he could not verify. The supernatural (according to Sir Richard Livingstone) plays no part in his pages.[55] Yet, after its own fashion, *The History of the Peloponnesian War* belongs to the same mental world as the *Iliad* and the *Odyssey*. Embassies are sent to annul curses and challenge the judgement of the gods; valiant spirits are driven into exile; naval expeditions are ravaged by plague; garrisons are besieged. The only history which Thucydides has an eye for is the military and the heroic. He is determined to see every engagement as an epic. He consults, or at any rate cites, the oracles, treating their prophecies with wary respect. He puts words into the mouth of his characters, making them say – in high-flown terms – 'what I thought the occasion demanded'. As F.M. Cornford brilliantly argued in *Mythistoricus* his set-piece speeches, one of the great ornaments of his work and a *locus classicus* for Hellenists, are closely modelled on the Euripidean drama of his day.[56]

Prophecy, it seems, was a normal, if occasional, component of the town chronicles of fourteenth- and fifteenth-century London, the first lay histories of their kind. Such histories would often begin with the four ages of man, creating a cosmic and eschatological framework for their narrative, before passing on to the fine detail of trading relations and genealogical descent. Thus in Andrew Horn's *Annales Londoniensis*, the reign of Edward II is introduced with prophecies from Geoffrey of Monmouth and the Book of Daniel: the ram of the Castle of Love, who will darken the whole island with his cloudy breath, and whom Merlin compared to Alexander of Macedon, 'will strenuously take and seize Scotland, Norway, Denmark, France, and all the lands which Arthur, most victorious of knights, acquired by the sword'.[57]

Supernatural events – wonders and marvels – were a stock-in-trade of the monastic chroniclers, even though, for the most part, they were concerned to give a dryasdust record of political and ecclesiastical affairs. Bede, with his comets and his sparrow, enlivening his narrative with intimations of the numinous, had set a high example.[58] William of Newburgh, one of his twelfth-century successors, a proclaimed sceptic and a bitter critic of the fabulous history of Geoffrey of Monmouth, nevertheless thought it worth while to give fairly elaborate descriptions of demons and their activities; to include in his *Historia* a few common portents; and to have an angry God inflict famine and plague on England and Gaul in 1196, to punish their kings for waging war.

In folk historiography, passed down by word of mouth, petrified giants, such as those who figure so prominently in the Albion legend, are perhaps the equivalent of the wonders and marvels of the monastic chroniclers. Usually they are assigned to the British past, and it cannot be an accident that they are most numerous in the ultimate lair of the ancient Britons: Wales and the South-West.[59] In Wales stories of the giants are very thickly scattered and dozens of the beings are specifically named. Cadair Idris, the mountain with a giant chair, frequently resorted to by the Druids, according to local lore, is a well-known example. Stonehenge, the best-known prehistoric monument in Britain, was originally attributed, by Geoffrey of Monmouth, to giants; he believed that, on Merlin's orders, they had transported the stones from the Giant's Ring on Mount

Killaraus, Ireland.[60] (An alternative tradition gives Stonehenge a Welsh name and claims that, like the standing stones of Glastonbury Tor, they were originally transported from mid-Wales.)[61] Another whole class of memory places are those dignified by the presence – quite often the burial – of some legendary person of old. In the villages of the White Horse, Wiltshire, exotica abound. To follow the magnificent ethnography compiled, in the 1910s, by the working-class folklorist, Alfred Williams, every stone can tell a story. It is as though the inhabitants felt bound to make up a history whenever they noticed some peculiarity in the local environment – here it is the site of some old Arthurian battle, there of monastic enterprises.[62]

From the point of view of the national idea, foundation myths, or as they are sometimes called by the anthropologists creation myths, which collapse whole epochs into symbolic moments, are the most enduring and the most influential legacy of magical modes of thought. Historians, warned by Marc Bloch to beware of the 'idolatry of origins',[63] and perhaps uneasily aware that, according to the tenets of postmodernism, the idea that things are determined by their origins is an epistemological mistake, are likely to look askance at these. Yet, whether we acknowledge it or not, they provide us with many of our markers. The Gathelus and Scota myth in Scotland, which had a Greek Prince elope with the Pharaoh of Egypt's daughter to found a nation of Scots, was in its own time, like the Wars of Independence, a sign of Scotland's coming-of-age.[64]

The liberal-radical historians of later nineteenth-century England, such as J.R. Green, conceptualizing history as a forward march in which freedom broadened out from precedent to precedent, began their histories, brilliantly but arbitrarily, with the peasant commonwealths and folk-moots of Anglo-Saxon times.[65] Earlier, in the 1600s, Coke and the common lawyers, seeking a historical ground from which to resist the encroachments of royal prerogative, fastened on the 'ancient constitution' which had allegedly existed in the time of Edward the Confessor, before the Norman Conquest. Each of these was a Saxonist idea, republican in its tendencies. The Brutus legend – the foundation myth for the idea of Britishness – was quite different, borrowing prestige from vanished supremacies (the claim to Trojan origin was also, it seems, quite widely canvassed in early Renaissance France).

Arrival myths, or migration myths, are a subclass of symbolic events which are equally worth a special attention. They provide us with some of history's best-known moments – e.g. the arrival of the Pilgrim Fathers in New England; while in the present day, if the Caribbean immigration to postwar Britain is anything to go by, they play an important part in the making of diasporic ideologies. As with other classes of legend, arrival myths are more interesting for the meanings they subsequently take on than for those which they carried at the time. Just as, in the legend of Hengist and Horsa, the duo who supposedly established an Anglo-Saxon presence in England,[66] lifelike details were added *retrospectively*, so in the case of *Empire Windrush*, the boat whose arrival in Britain in 1949 supposedly inaugurated the epoch of New Commonwealth immigration, the processes of projection, amplification and displacement seem inconceivably more important than the original event.

The essay, which then adumbrates a paragraph on fictitious pedigrees as a variant of foundation myths, is left unfinished at this point.

Notes

1 Raphael Samuel, 'Exciting to be English': Introduction to *Patriotism: The Making and Unmaking of British National Identity*, vol. I, London 1989, discusses some of the different 'moments' in which the idea of a national consciousness apparently crystallized; on new historicism, H. Aram Veeser (ed.), *The New Historicism*, London 1989; Kiernan Ryan (ed.), *New Historicism and Cultural Materialism: A Reader*, London 1996; on language and nation, Richard Helgerson, for example, in *Forms of Nationhood: The Elizabethan Writing of England*, Chicago 1992. For the disappearance of Boadicea, Donald R. Dudley and Graham Webster, *The Rebellion of Boudicca*, London 1962, pp. 113–30.

2 Linda Colley, *Britons: Forging the Nation 1707–1837*, London 1992.

3 This phrase is owed to Christopher Smout.

4 For typologies and definitions of nationalism, Eric Hobsbawm, *Nations and Nationalism since 1780, Programme, Myth, Reality*, Cambridge 1990; Ernest Gellner, *Nations and Nationalism*, Oxford 1983; Anthony D. Smith, *Theories of Nationalism*, 2nd ed., London 1983; Eugene Kamenka (ed.), *Nationalism, the Nature and Evolution of an Idea*, London 1976; Elie Kedourie, *Nationalism*, London 1960; Liah Greenfeld, *Nationalism: Five Roads to Modernity*, Cambridge, Mass. 1993.

5 Raphael Samuel, 'Reading the Signs', part I, *History Workshop Journal*, 32, Autumn 1991; part II, no. 33, Spring 1992, examines Foucault's influence on historians and historiography in more detail.

6 Robert Colls and Philip Dodd (ed.), *Englishness: Politics and Culture 1880–1920*, London 1986, would be one example.

7 Hobsbawm, *Nations and Nationalism*, pp. 9–10.

8 Tom Nairn, *The Break-Up of Britain*, London 1981.

9 Herodotus, *The Histories*, translated Aubrey de Selincourt, Harmondsworth 1954. Herodotus wrote his narrative of the conflict between Greeks and the Persian empire in the middle of the fifth century BC. He called his narrative an 'inquiry' – the Greek word is '*historie*' – and 'thus brought the word "history" in its modern sense into the vocabulary of Europe and the West': John Gould, *Herodotus*, London 1989.

10 The author owes this point to Rosalind Thomas.

11 In Rome the name *natio* was first given to groups of foreigners coming from the same geographical region (the initial concept was derogatory) whose status was below that of the Roman citizens. In this sense – of a group of foreigners united by their origin – there were four nations, for example, in the medieval University of Paris: Greenfeld, *Nationalism*, p. 4; Guido Zernatto, 'Nation: The History of a Word', *Review of Politics*, 6, 1944, pp. 351–66.

12 H.H. Scullard, 'Carthage and Rome', *Cambridge Ancient History*, vol. VII, 'The Rise of Rome to 220 B.C.', Cambridge 1989, pp. 364ff.

13 Sir Richard Livingstone, editor and translator of Thucydides, *The History of the Peloponnesian War*, Oxford 1973 ed., p. xv. Livingstone, perhaps consciously drawing parallels with the British situation in the 1940s, sees Pericles's funeral speech in book II as exemplary in showing how he and his age 'with no definite hopes in a future world, face the bereavements of a great war' (p. 109). Livingstone was the originator of summer

schools at Oxford in 1937–38 for colonial administrators; thanks to David Webb for this information.

14 Peter Green, commenting on Aristophanes's comedy, *The Birds* (414), *Alexander to Actium: the Historical Evolution of the Hellenistic Age*, Berkeley 1990, p. 56.

15 Tacitus, *The Histories*, translated Kenneth Wellesley, Harmondsworth 1964, p. 22. His account probably dates from AD 98, when he appears to have been planning the work.

16 Livy, *The Early History of Rome*, translated Aubrey de Selincourt, Harmondsworth 1974, p. 35.

17 Green, *Alexander to Actium*, p. 155. Thucydides exiled himself for about twenty years after the failure in 424 BC of his command of an Athenian fleet against the Spartans (which he recounts in book IV of his history). Herodotus, who calls himself in the opening words of his work a 'Halicarnassian', was 'to all intents and purposes . . . stateless', and spent most of his life in political exile: Gould, *Herodotus*, p. 14.

18 Martin Bernal, *Black Athena: The Afroasiatic Roots of Classical Civilisation*, vol. I, London 1987.

19 Thucydides, *Peloponnesian War*, p. 34.

20 Livingstone, introduction to Thucydides, *Peloponnesian War*, p. xxv.

21 *Harper's Encyclopedia of Bible Life* observes that tax collectors were held in low esteem not only because the Jews detested the taxes which, like that on land, were payable directly to Rome, but also because other taxes, like those levied on movable property, were 'sold out' to private individuals – tax collectors or 'publicans' – who could make hefty profits from the proceedings (p. 269).

22 Daniel 3:3.

23 O. Eissfeldt, 'The Hebrew Kingdom', *Cambridge Ancient History*, Cambridge 1975, vol II, pt. 2, pp. 537–87; Isidore Epstein, *Judaism*, Harmondsworth 1964. See also *Encyclopedia Judaica* and *Encyclopedia of Jewish History*, Oxford 1986; these points were discussed with Chimen Abramsky.

24 'The Lord is a man of war' (Exodus 15:3); 'But if thou shalt indeed obey his voice, and do all that I speak; then I will be an enemy unto thine enemies, and an adversary unto thine adversaries' (Exodus 23:22). On the Israelites and 'Holy Wars', *Harper's Encyclopedia of Bible Life*, p. 270.

25 John Morrill, 'Three Kingdoms and One Commonwealth: the Enigma of Mid-Seventeenth Century Britain and Ireland', in A. Grant and K.J. Stringer (ed.), *Uniting the Kingdom? The Making of British History*, London 1995, p. 186.

26 William Haller, *Foxe's Book of Martyrs and the Elect Nation*, London 1963. The bishop was Aylmer in 1559.

27 James Hinton, *Protests and Visions: Peace Politics in Twentieth Century Britain*, London 1989.

28 Alistair Thomson, *ANZAC Memories: Living with the Legend*, Melbourne/Oxford 1994, p. 26.

29 On Anatolia, J.G. Macqueen, *The Hittites and their Contemporaries in Asia Minor*, London 1975.

30 *Harper's Encyclopedia of Bible Life*, p. 264; John Rich and Graham Shipley (ed.), *War and Society in the Greek World*, London 1993.

31 Herodotus, *The Histories*, trans. de Selincourt, pp. 57; 101; 69; 33.

32 'Herodotus and the Invention of History', *Arethusa*, vol. 20, nos 1 and 2, Spring and Fall 1987, includes a 'Selective Introduction to Herodotean Studies'; Fernand Braudel, *The Mediterranean and the Mediterranean World in the Age of Philip II*, translated Sian Reynolds, London 1972.

33 Margaret Trabue Hodgen, *Early Anthropology in the Sixteenth and Seventeenth Centuries*, Philadelphia 1964, p. 179.

34 Jean Bodin, *Methodus, ad facilem historiarum cognitionem*, 1566.

35 Hodgen, *Early Anthropology*, p. 181.

36 Peter Heylyn, *Microcosmus, or a little description of the great world. A treatise, historicall, geographical, politicall, theologicall*, Oxford 1621; cited, Hodgen, *Early Anthropology*.

37 Dr G. Cheyne, *The English Malady*, London 1733.

38 Lord Kames, *Sketches of the History of Man*, Edinburgh 1774.

39 Joseph Campbell, *Political Survey of Britain*, London 1774, p. 51.

40 Roger A. Mason, '"Scotching the Brut": Politics, History and National Myth in Sixteenth-Century Britain', in Mason (ed.), *Scotland and England 1286–1815*, Edinburgh

1987; on the development of national origin myths and their association with royal genealogies in Europe, Susan Reynolds, 'Medieval *Origines Gentium* and the Community of the Realm', *History*, lxviii, 1984, pp. 375–90. Robyn White kindly forwarded this article and offered helpful information to the author.

41 In brief, Geoffrey of Monmouth's twelfth-century *Historia Regum Britanniae* records the arrival of Brutus, grandson of the Trojan hero Aeneas, his vanquishing of the giants (like Gog) who are in possession of the land and his building of Trinovantum or London. At his death, he divided the whole island between his three sons; thus the legend was mobilized (by the Norman, Plantagenet, and, later, the Tudor monarchies) to claim that the Kings of England, as Brutus's heirs, had clear title to the crown of Scotland. For an introduction to Geoffrey of Monmouth and British historiography, see T.D Kendrick, *British Antiquity*, London 1950. For the alternative Scottish foundation myths, their literary elaboration and political usages, E.J. Cowan, 'Myth and Identity in Early Medieval Scotland', *Scottish Historical Review*, no. 68, 1989, pp. 120–49; R. James Goldstein, *The Matter of Scotland: Historical Narrative in Medieval Scotland*, London 1993; Roger A. Mason, 'The Scottish Reformation and the Origins of Anglo-British Imperialism', in Roger A. Mason, *Scots and Britons: Scottish Political Thought and the Union of 1603*, Cambridge 1994; Colin Kidd, *Subverting Scotland's Past: Scottish Whig Historians and the Creation of an Anglo-British identity, 1689–c. 1830*, Cambridge 1993, especially the Prologue, 'National Identity in Late Medieval and Early Modern Scotland'.

42 Roy Strong, *The English Icon: Elizabethan and Jacobean Portraiture*, London 1969, pp. 47–8.

43 David M. Bergeron, *English Civic Pageantry 1558–1642*, London 1971, p. 154.

44 ibid., pp. 207–9; the Lord Mayor's Show of 1585, Bergeron tells us, was the first to make a well-known dramatist, George Peele, responsible for the entertainment; thereafter other writers, such as Munday, Dekker, Middleton, Webster and Heywood, became involved.

45 Charles Dickens so dubs him in chapter XI of *Nicholas Nickleby*. For the Gog and Magog procession, F.W. Fairhold, *Gog and Magog, the Giants in Guildhall*, London 1859.

46 Anthony Roberts, *Sowers of Thunder: Giants in Myth and History*, London 1978, p. 42.

47 ibid. The story of Gog derives from Geoffrey of Monmouth's account. For Gog's chequered history, Jennifer Westwood, *Albion, A Guide to Legendary Britain*, London 1981.

48 W. Hamish and R.J. Morris (ed.), *People and Society in Scotland 1830–1914*, vol. 2, Edinburgh 1990, p. 77. On the romanticization of Scotland and Scottish history: Marinell Ash, *The Strange Death of Scottish History*, Edinburgh 1980; Peter Womack, *Improvement and Romance: Constructing the Myth of the Highlands*, Houndmills 1989; Colin Kidd, 'The Canon of Patriotic Landmarks in Scottish History', *Scotlands*, 1, 1994, pp. 1–17.

49 Peter Burke, *Popular Culture in Early Modern Europe*, London 1978, p. 10. For discussion of James Macpherson's collation and creation of 'ancient Celtic' poetry which he attributed to Ossian, son of Fingal, a Gaelic bard (reputedly third-century): Fiona Stafford, *The Sublime Savage: A Study of James Macpherson and the Poems of Ossian*, Edinburgh 1988; Ian Haywood, *The Making of History: A Study of the Literary Forgeries of James Macpherson and Thomas Chatterton*, London 1986; Kidd, *Subverting Scotland's Past*; Robert Crawford, *Devolving English Literature*, Oxford 1992.

50 Goldstein, *The Matter of Scotland*, pp. 217–19; Marinell Ash, 'William Wallace and Robert the Bruce: The Life and Death of a National Myth', in Raphael Samuel and Paul Thompson (ed.), *The Myths We Live By*, London 1990, pp. 83–94.

51 Stephen Hugh-Jones, 'Waribi and the White Men: History and Myth in Northwest Amazonia', *History and Ethnicity*, ed. Elizabeth Tonkin, Maryon Macdonald and Malcolm Chapman, London 1989, p. 54. In the same volume Edmund Leach concludes: 'Myth is not just badly remembered history. But we have no grounds for supposing that mythology is unchanging or that it incorporates no history at all' ('Tribal Ethnography: Past, Present, Future', p. 45). See also Samuel and Thompson, Introduction to *The Myths We Live By*.

52 Stephen Knight, *Robin Hood: A Complete Study of the English Outlaw*, Oxford 1994; Maurice Keen, *The Outlaws of Medieval England*, London 1977; J.C. Holt, *Robin Hood*, London 1982.

53 Milman Parry, *Serbocroatian Heroic Songs*, edited and translated by Albert Bates Lord, Cambridge and Belgrade 1954.

54 The term '*longue durée*' was retrospectively attributed to the method of the first

Annalists by Fernand Braudel, alluding to the notion that historical temporalities should reach as far back or forward in time as the historical phenomena or events demand, embracing, for example, geological time or the workings of the unconscious. For an introduction to the work of *Annales*, Peter Burke, *A New Kind of History*, London 1973; E. Le Roy Ladurie, *Le Territoire de l'historien*, Paris 1973; T. Stoianovic, *French Historical Method*, Cornell 1976; Jacques Le Goff, *La nouvelle histoire*, Paris 1978; Samuel, 'Reading the Signs', discusses the recent work of *Annales*.

55 Livingstone, Introduction to Thucydides, *Peloponnesian War*, p. xv.

56 F.M. Cornford, *Thucydides, Mythistoricus*, London 1965; Charles Fornara, *The Nature of History in Ancient Greece and Rome*, Berkeley 1983; Eric A. Havelock, *The Literate Revolution in Greece and Its Cultural Consequences*, Princeton 1982.

57 Jeremy Catto, 'Andrew Horn: Law and History in Fourteenth Century England', in Davis and Wallace-Hadrill (ed.), *Medieval History*, p. 375 (reference unlocated).

58 Peter Hunter Blair, *The World of Bede*, Cambridge 1970, p. 5.

59 Roberts, *Sowers of Thunder*, pp. 135ff.

60 Westwood, *Albion*, p. 64.

61 ibid., p. 19. Also Rhys Jones, 'Sylwadau Cynfrodor Ar Gor Y Cewri, or a British Aboriginal's Land Claim to Stonehenge', in Christopher Chippindale and others (ed.), *Who Owns Stonehenge?*, London 1990, p. 62.

62 Alfred Williams, *A Wiltshire Village*, London 1912; *Villages of the White Horse*, London 1913; Leonard Clark, *Alfred Williams: His Life and Work*, Newton Abbot 1969; Ronald Hutton, *The Pagan Religions of the Ancient British Isles: Their Nature and Legacy*, Oxford 1991.

63 Marc Bloch, *The Historian's Craft*, translated Peter Putnam, Manchester 1954, chapter 1:4, 'The Idol of Origins'.

64 Cowan, 'Myth and Identity in Early Medieval Scotland', p. 121.

65 J.R. Green, *A Short History of the English People* in four volumes, London 1877–80, begins with the landing of Hengist in 449. For a starting-point in a large literature on Saxonism, Christopher Hill, 'The Norman Yoke', *Democracy and the Labour Movement: Essays in Honour of Dona Torr*, John Saville (ed.), London 1954; reprinted, *Puritanism and Revolution*, London 1958; J.G.A. Pocock, *The Ancient Constitution and the Feudal Law: a Study of English Historical Thought in the Seventeenth Century*, 2nd ed., Cambridge 1957; 'The Rise of Anglo-Saxonism', in H. MacDougall, *Racial Myth in English History*, Montreal 1982; Joseph M. Levine, *Humanism and History: Origins of Modern English Historiography*, Ithaca 1987.

66 In one of his accounts of the Anglo-Saxon invasion, the ninth-century Welsh monk and compiler of British history, Nennius, gives Hengist and Horsa as exiles seeking refuge with the British king: Antonia Gransden, *Historical Writing in England, c. 1307 to the Early Sixteenth Century*, vol. 1, London 1982, p. 10.

Four Nations History*

History notoriously takes wing at dusk, that twilight hour when shadows lengthen, silence thickens and when (according to believers in the numinous) thought flies heavenward and ghostly presences make themselves felt. Something like this – a vertiginous sense of impending loss – may help to account for the current small vogue for the idea of Britishness, occurring as it does at a moment when the very existence of the nation-state is in question (Philip Dodd's 'Demos' pamphlet *The Battle over Britain,* which celebrates Britishness as an *ethnic* identity, is an interesting case in point). It might also explain the discovery, or rediscovery, of 'British' history, and the emergence, during the last twenty years, of a more pluralist conception of the national past, replacing an Anglocentric by a 'four nations' or 'British' perspective, 'breaking down the barriers between England, Ireland, Scotland and Wales', as Rees Davies puts it, 'and . . . seizing the opportunity to enrich our understanding by considering the connection, comparison and contrasts between them'.[1]

As a project, and as a perspective, this idea of a 'British' history crystallized at a time when the nationality question was becoming a storm-centre of domestic politics, and when the legitimacy of the British state was increasingly called into question. The civil war in Ulster was opening a new phase in the history of Irish separatism, with no-go areas and vigilante patrols, on either side of the sectarian divide, taking the place of civil order. In the shadow of the Sunningdale agreement and the Ulster Workers Strike of 1974, the 'loyalists' – intransigent Protestants marooned in a secular world – were as alienated from the government at Westminster, as hostile to British rule, and as murderous in their modes of intimidation, as their Republican and Catholic enemies.[2] In Scotland a more secular separatism flourished, fuelled apparently by the energy

* This article formed the editorial for *History Workshop Journal,* no. 40, Autumn 1995. The issue carried a selection of the contributions to a 'Scottish Dimensions' History Workshop, held at Ruskin College, Oxford, 24–26 March 1995.

crisis and the boom in North Sea oil, and strong enough, by the late 1970s, to put devolution (and what Tom Nairn in 1977 prophetically called 'The Break-up of Britain') on the agenda of Westminster politics. In Wales, ethnic disintegration – the depopulation of the hill farms and the mining valleys – set limits to the nationalist revival, but in the schools, and on radio and TV, as in nomenclature and road signs, the language movement carried all before it, winning parity of esteem for Welsh.

Still more pertinent, in making the idea of Britain problematical, would be the apparent redundancy of the post-imperial state. Here the collapse of British power has been followed by a disappearance of those taken-for-granted certainties – above all, the belief in God-given leadership qualities – which, in the heyday of imperialism, had made Great Britain one of the wonders of the world. The map of Africa, redrawn in the 1960s, was no longer painted British red; in deference to newly emancipated and formerly subject peoples, it was even purged of British names. Disenchantment with the planning idea also put the authority of the state into question. The economy, after decades of attempted modernization, in which government policy hovered between the virtues of rationalization and state-led growth, seemed to disintegrate; entry into the European Common Market, so far from revitalizing it, precipitated a period of free fall; by 1981, at the pit of the recession, the very idea of British industry was on its way to becoming a historical souvenir. By the same token, parliament found itself eclipsed; in an age of multinational companies and supranational authorities, sovereignty was an anachronism.

The break-up of Britain in the present, and the uncertainties attaching to its future, necessarily make us more aware of its contingent character in the past. The unity of the British Isles, so far from being the norm, can appear rather as an exceptional condition, with a lifespan of less than two hundred years, from the Battle of Culloden, say, in 1746, to the Irish Treaty of 1921. We are reminded that Shetland was for many centuries Norwegian, and before that the Romans' *Ultima Thule*; that Scotland, before the Act of Union of 1707, was an independent kingdom; that Ireland is geographically more remote from England than France. Likewise Britishness, instead of being a secure, genetic identity, can be seen as something culturally and historically conditioned, always in the making, never made. The Gramscian question asked by Gwyn Williams, in his provocative essay of 1982, 'When Was Wales?',[3] is one which historians of Britain, adopting a four nations perspective, have felt impelled to address. Unlike Williams, however, who argued that the search for some founding moment was the pursuit of a Nirvana, they prefer to give definite answers, some opting for the thirteenth century, when English overlordship was asserted in Ireland and Wales; others for 1547–48, the 'moment' when, under the influence of a state-led Protestantism, the idea of Great Britain began to be vigorously canvassed, and when the ideological foundations for the union of England and Scotland were laid;[4]

yet others for the 1740s, the patriotic hour which saw the rise of radical Gallophobia and the start of a new cycle of French wars.[5]

An optic like this leaves none of our landmarks untouched. Anglo-Saxon England, which in the pages of Stubbs and Stenton, as in 'Whig' history generally, was a precocious unity – the starting-point of 'our island story' and the foundation of representative government – is now seen as more of a hybrid, politically unstable, racially indeterminate, linguistically pluralist. Place-names, that great enthusiasm of the late nineteenth-century Saxonists, turn out to be polyglot, reflecting the heterogeneous nature of the population, and the makeshift character of settlement. The cosmopolitan character of the Church – a Christianity which owed more to wandering Irish monks and Mediterranean missionaries than to Canterbury-based archbishops – is much insisted on. Where Stenton was only too eager to rid the country of British relics, and to prove that the Anglo-Saxons in England 'adhered to their own native traditions',[6] his successors, on the contrary, have seized eagerly on the evidence of survivals, whether in the form of British, 'half-British' and 'British-sounding' names,[7] sub-Roman metal-work or Celtic field-systems. More and more places are revealed to have a Romano-British past, among them Wharram Percy, the best-known of England's 3,000 deserted villages.[8] Not only the Celtic West (in Cornwall British speech was still dominant in John Florio's time)[9] but also the ancient British kingdom of Bernicia, straddling Hadrian's Wall to the north-east, and Cumbria, its counterpart in the north-west, are singled out for attention. Archaeology, supremely indifferent to political frontiers, and taking the geographical area of the British Isles as its natural province, has done a great deal to challenge the hegemony of the Anglo-Saxon. Cross-cultural in its sympathies and fascinated by the appearance of the alien and the exotic, it has called on the 'rich harvest'[10] of Irish work to redress the balance of the written record and has been delighted to extract Roman and Celtic objects from Anglo-Saxon graves.[11]

The borders of Anglo-Saxon England were fluctuating and shadowy, open to seaborne invasion from without and internecine warfare from within. Offa's Dyke, it is now argued, 'the largest archaeological monument in Britain, and the most impressive structure of its kind in Europe', was less a frontier than a crossing-point, allowing raid and counter-raid on either side of the border, and encouraging a symbiotic relationship between English and Welsh warlords, complementary and antagonistic at the same time.[12] It in no way inhibited English settlers from pushing forward into the Welsh marches, or planting little colonies in the valleys of south-east and north-east Wales. The Anglo-Scottish border was even more uncertain. On the coastal plain to the east there was, on the one hand, a constant warlike pressure from the Scots to carry their overlordship to the Tyne,[13] and on the other Anglian colonization and settlement which extended as far as the Firth of Forth ('Arthur's Seat', one of the seven hills of Edinburgh, is one of their memorials).[14] In the south-west there was the ancient British kingdom of Strathclyde, which stretched from the Clyde to Cumbria and continued in some sort of existence down to the thirteenth century. It seems to have been heavily infiltrated by rival peoples: the Ruthwell Cross, 'the supreme Anglo-Saxon example of realistic figure-work in the classical tradition',[15] comes from southern Dumfriesshire, in the heart of this 'British' territory. Politically, Scotland bore the appearance of a united kingdom; *ethnically*, however, with its northern Irish in the kingdom of Dal Riada, its Picts in the central highlands, its Angles and Saxons in the Lothians and its Galloway Britons in the south-west, it seems to have been inhabited by virtually everybody except the Scots.[16]

'The irrelevance of national boundaries'[17] was famously demonstrated by the Scandinavian raiders of the ninth, tenth and eleventh centuries. They went island-hopping in Atlantic Scotland, brought Magnus Barefoot, King of Norway, to fight sea-battles off the Anglesey coast, and made Dublin and Waterford satellites in a vast seaborne empire whose epicentre was the Baltic and whose tendrils extended from the Bosporus to the Yorkshire Ouse. The strongly marked Viking settlement in Galloway was, writes Nicolaisen, 'the northernmost appendix of the Scandinavian settlement in the north of England'.[18] Coastal Wales 'formed part of a Hiberno-Norse world which stretched from Limerick and Dublin to Chester and York'. The kingdom of Man was the hub of an orbit of power which took in the Hebrides, Caithness, Orkney and Shetland.[19] The Vikings formed alliances wherever they settled, and the place-names attributed to their influence are full of hybrids, inversions and compounds. Chester was one of the inland towns on which the Vikings left their mark. Briefly captured by them in 893, and subject for nearly a century to their raids, refortified by the English in 907 and serving as the administrative capital of what is today north-east Wales, it was, writes Wendy Davies, 'a multicultural city with a multicultural hinterland'. 'Some residents of the area . . . must have been Scandinavian, some English, and some Welsh. The Englishness of the government was no bar . . . to the city's rapidly developing commercial connections with the Scandinavian communities of Dublin and the Irish sea zone . . . '[20]

One way of approaching the 'four nations' interpretation of British history would be to see its appearance as an expression of the retreat from Empire, a local manifestation of what literary theorists have recently taken to calling 'post-colonial discourse'. It was first rehearsed, as a perspective, in 1975, the year in which Britain voted, in referendum, for entry into the Common Market – the mother country turning her back on the Commonwealth and exorcising the ghosts of imperial preference. British history makes 'Englishness' problematical and invites us to see it as one amongst a number of competing ethnicities. It is alive to the importance of dual allegiances and multiple identities: even when it offers us a unified subject matter – as, say, state formation or the forging of national identity – it does so by stressing not similitude but difference. It conceptualizes British history not in terms of church and state, crown and aristocracy, king and commons; nor yet, in the manner of the 'new wave' history of the 1960s, class and class, but rather in the spatial dualisms of core and periphery, metropole and provinces. 'Internal Colonialism' was the title of Michael Hechter's 'four nations' study of 1975, the first major book in the field. It is a paradigm to which his more scholarly successors have constantly returned. The colonial metaphor – 'feudal colonialism' as one recent writer calls it[21] – is very much to the fore in the work of the early medievalists who picture the Celts as potential subalterns and see a newly nationalist England, from the reign of John onwards, building an inland empire. The Treaty of Windsor (1174) is according to some the start of the English colonization of Ireland; the peopling of Pembroke with Flemings (the twelfth-century origin of the 'Little England' there today) prefigures the later plantation of Ulster; Edward I's theft of the Stone of Scone (the one which the Scots stole back again in 1953) is the Elgin marbles of its day. Hugh Kearney, pointing to the 'Normanization' of the monastic orders, argues that colonialism was not confined to the secular world.[22] Gwyn Williams sees the fourteenth-century Welsh as 'a subject people', dispossessed and disinherited by a fully-fledged colonial regime: in the spirit of this he treats the rising of Owain Glyn Dwr as a war of national liberation.[23] Jenny Wormald, in a scintillating account of Anglo-Scottish hostility in the reign of James I, finds the colonial metaphor no less serviceable for the world of courtly intrigue:

> How redolent is the virulent anti-Scottish literature of the early seventeenth century, with its recurrent theme of backwardness, lack of civility, parasitism, of attitudes of British colonists of the nineteenth and early twentieth centuries to the natives of the colonies which enjoyed British rule. How many Indians living under the British Raj would instantly have recognised that theme? The twist to the story in the early seventeenth century, is that the English had lost their desire to colonise Scotland directly; they had no desire whatsoever to go there. What they wanted was to train the 'native' ruler who had, against the odds, become their king, in their values, to turn him into an acceptable king of England. They were therefore trapped in an impossible position. For how does one colonise one's king?[24]

The four nations or 'archipelago' perspective on the national past owes a great deal to the British diaspora. The first explicit agenda, and still by far the most brilliant advocacy of it, was set out in a memorial lecture at the University of Canterbury, New Zealand. J.G.A. Pocock's 'British History: A Plea for a New Subject', subsequently published in the *New Zealand Journal of History*, and then taken up by the *Journal of Modern History*, is a profound meditation which has dominated subsequent thought. The work of a Cambridge-trained New Zealander, teaching then in New Zealand, but later re-locating to Johns Hopkins University in the United States, it combines a discussion of historical method with a rather melancholy series of reflections on the dawning possibilities of what he calls 'archipelago' history and the conditions of existence which have brought it into being. He refers sombrely to the civil war in Ulster, then entering its fifth year, and defines Ulster itself as the 'dark and bloody rump' which has been bequeathed to England by Eire.[25] He is keenly alert to other signs of impending break-up and refers in his opening page to the 'new breed of Orkney and Shetland nationalists who consider themselves a Norse fragment unsatisfactorily subject to alien Scots culture'.[26] He remarks on the apparent eagerness of contemporary Britons to turn their backs on the Commonwealth, and look to Europe instead. And he counts himself among the historically orphaned. 'The British cultural star cluster is at present in a highly dispersed condition, various parts of it feeling the attraction of adjacent galaxies; the central giant has cooled, shrunk, and moved away, and the inhabitants of its crust seem more than ever disposed to deny that the rest of us ever existed'.[27] At one point in the article Pocock worries about whether the term 'Britain' will survive, and it is a measure of his cultural pessimism that he proposes to substitute a value-neutral but ahistorical term in its stead. Behind these fears of historical displacement it does not seem fanciful to suggest a repressed nostalgia for the 'Anglo-Atlantic culture'[28] of the first British empire and the Old Colonial System (he makes a plea for including the New England colonies in eighteenth-century 'British' history, and argues that attention to the Canadian history of the British diaspora offers precious insights into the processes of nation-building in mainland Britain). It may be indicative of this that the name he proposed for the new historical subject – 'the Atlantic archipelago' – is one which would have sat easily in the geopolitics of eighteenth-century mercantilism. (It could also be thought of as having a subtly, and no doubt unconscious, anti-European bias.)

Despite the undertow of melancholy, which surfaces whenever the present heaves into view, Pocock's is generally a modernist text, one which proposes a non-teleological view of the past, and an anti-nationalist view of the future – a history that is 'pluralist' and 'multicultural'. His notion of 'British' is ecumenical, embracing both the Orange and the Green, for instance, in the case of what he calls the British *outremer* in Canada; indeed in a rather strained argument he tries to claim the Irish revolution of 1919–22 as Britain's own. Pocock also anticipates today's fashion for the 'mongrel' – a leitmotiv in contemporary celebrations of Britishness – arguing for an 'intercultural . . . history, concerned with conflict and crossbreeding'. He seizes with zest on those instances of it which come his way. A notable passage evokes the diversity of 'intermediate' and 'counter-reactive' societies in medieval and early modern Britain:

> There are normanized Irish and hibernicized Normans; there are bilingual Anglo-Welsh, as well as monoglot Welsh and English; there are Lowland Scots assimilated to the clan world of the Highlands as well as clans which expand at the expense of others by methods of litigation rather than war; there are Celts who enter a Norse world and Norsemen assimilated to the Celtic pattern. Culture conflicts, the language barriers, the phenomena of the marches, the distinction between highland and lowland zones; these all join to make 'British history' – the expansion of government at the expense of kinship – a history of the constant creation, accompanied by the much less constant absorption, of new subcultures and even subnations.[29]

Hugh Kearney's *The British Isles, A History of Four Nations* (1989) falls still more clearly in the field of post-colonial discourse, though it is not perhaps a term which the author might care to acknowledge. It is the work of one who is even more diasporic than Pocock, a Liverpool-born Irishman, trained as a historian at Cambridge, and then successively a teacher at University College, Dublin (the Catholic alternative to Trinity), the University of Sussex, Edinburgh University (where he was Richard Pares Professor of History from 1970 to 1975) and the University of Pittsburgh. He divides his year now between Suffolk in deepest England and the United States. Kearney has the advantage of belonging to what, in an English context, is a minority, and perhaps this helps to give his book a radical edge. Like Pocock he is anxious to untether British history from its English moorings, and to read the record backwards, in an anti-teleological sense. He is at pains to disaggregate the British Isles and the peoples who, at any given time, inhabit it. His subject is not a nation or a people but, rather, a territory, and the geographical and cultural contrasts within it. Kearney appears to be asking for a larger framework, and his book has the merit of spanning millennia and attempting to relate ancient history (or 'prehistory') and the so-called 'Dark Ages' to modern times. But what really excites him as a historian is not the grand sweep but a molecular sense of difference, the fault-lines of an internally divided series of cultures. Reading him, we are continually being offered worlds within worlds. Thus he gives us in the nineteenth century, quite plausibly, three Scotlands – the Highlands (including the Hebrides but not, for good reason, the Orkneys and Shetland, a subculture of their own) and the Lowlands, divided between an industrial Clydeside and an Edinburgh-based east. Wales is likewise divided into two cultures, which are then subdivided according to religion and class.[30]

At the other end of the methodological or epistemological spectrum, using a 'British' perspective in a unifying sense rather than a disaggregating one, there is Linda Colley's fine book *Britons, Forging the Nation, 1707–1837*, by a long way the most widely read contribution to current debates. Here the author escapes from the confines of a merely English history in an attempt to rehabilitate the notion of greater Britain and to account for the ways in which it became a going concern. She dusts down an almost archaic term, 'Britons', one which in mid-Victorian times was eclipsed by Saxonist notions of 'English', but which in the 1740s was carrying all before it. She shows how it became the site of patriotic allegiance, acceptable and even appealing to those, like the 'North British' in Scotland, or the English in England, who nevertheless clung to their more particular local, regional or subnational identities. Cunningly using caricature and squibs (*Britons* is magnificently illustrated) the author contrives to make the ugly beautiful, and to turn even the most outrageous expressions of xenophobia into emblems of the comic and the robust. She is no less indulgent to the excesses of the Protestant imagination: hatred for Roman Catholics, in her account of it, becomes the crucible in which a wider national consciousness is formed; war with France – for a hundred years the national enemy – is the arena in which it exercises itself. Bombast, intolerance and chauvinism, rendered in 1740s hyperbole or Hogarth graphics, become positively endearing, and it is a measure of her achievement that the words of 'God Save the King', solemnly reproduced, contrive to be moving.[31]

Britons is emphatically *not* a four nations book, a concept which Linda Colley is on record as opposing. She has little to say about 'that most distressful country', Ireland. Her originality is to seize on the Anglo-Scottish dialectic and use it to refurbish a unionist history. Starting from the Scottophobia of the Hanoverian English, she argues that the aftermath of Culloden saw the growth of a new polity in which services to the state were handsomely rewarded, and the ambitious were promoted from the ranks. Empire became, for Scotsmen on the make, 'a profession in itself, an opportunity for power, responsibility and excitement on a scale they would never have enjoyed back home'.[32] Army preferment (Colley tells us that in the middle of the eighteenth century, one in four regimental officers were Scots)[33] worked in a similar direction. The Establishment, too, opened its door to Scots. She regards it as a 'triumphant reversal' that by 1780 more than half of Scottish MPs were government placemen,[34] and she is hardly less enthusiastic about the 'spectacular land deals' of Scotland's most celebrated heiress, Elizabeth, Countess of Sutherland, whom readers of *Capital* will know as an architect of the Highland clearances.[35]

Britannic history invites us to relocate our subject matter. It would be interesting to see what happened to the 'standard-of-living-in the-industrial-revolution' debate – that old Sixth Form favourite – or to complacent notions of the early Victorian era as an 'age of improvement', if the Irish famine of 1845–49, and the astonishing diaspora which followed it, were brought in on the 'pessimist' side of the equation. Across the Irish Channel, the Gaelic Revival of the 1890s, locked in the pantheon of nationalist pieties, would look very different if the English dimension of Irish history were reasserted, as it is in Roy Foster's *Modern Ireland*;[36] the Revival might be seen, in one aspect, as a late product of the

Protestant ascendancy – Trinity College scholarship in particular – and in another, via the Cuala Press, W.B. Yeats and 'Gaelic' calligraphy, of the English Arts and Crafts movement.[37]

Revisionist historians of the seventeenth century, 'studying three, and in some ways more than three interacting histories',[38] have seized on the British dimension to put paid to the idea of an 'English' or 'bourgeois' revolution, and the religious sociology which accompanied it. In place of the Putney Debates and the New Model Army, the arrest of the Five Members and the Ship Money Case, we have the war of the three kingdoms. The supposedly revolutionary England was the last rather than the first in the field. As Conrad Russell puts it, not without a smirk of satisfaction, in *The Fall of the British Monarchies*, England was 'the most docile' of Charles I's three kingdoms 'and the only one in which the king's supporters became a sufficiently large party to turn resistance into large-scale civil war'.[39] Ulster, the seat of the Catholic rising of 1641, becomes 'the crucible of the British problem',[40] and more potent than either London or East Anglia in precipitating the outbreak of civil war, while the 'Bishops' War' in Scotland, and the struggle between Charles I and the Convenanters, is the *primum mobile* of crisis.

Challenging grand narrative and those chronologies which for centuries have provided a grid for the study of the national past; arguing for the coexistence of at least four different histories, and looking for the points of intersection between them, Britannic or 'archipelago' history invites us to jettison our conventional notions of period (what does 'early modern' mean to the Blasket Islands, or 'Tudors and Stuarts' in the Trossachs?). It also positively requires us to experiment with new time-frames. Something calling itself a 'British history' could hardly exclude the Romans and the Celts, as Bishop Stubbs did in his three-decker *Constitutional History of England*, the foundation work for the School of Modern History at Oxford. Nor could it, like J.R. Green in his liberal-radical variant, start with the peasant commonwealths, or forest clearings of Anglo-Saxon times, the imaginatively brilliant but utterly arbitrary opening chapter of his 1874 *Short History of the English People.*

The Norman Conquest, interpreted in a 'four nations' perspective, requires a new chronology. 1066, 'the one universally known date in English history',[41] has no resonance at all in Ireland, where the Battle of Hastings passed unremarked by the chroniclers and where, so far as marauders were concerned, Viking raids from the north – the last of them was recorded in 1138 – produced more perturbation than the Normans. All of the early Anglo-Norman forays into Ireland were indirect, taken on the initiative of military or feudal adventurers, and often by invitation: not until the reign of King John and the expedition of 1210, it has been argued, did monarchy take a hand.[42] Despite the claim to the 'lordship of Ireland' the authority of the English monarch, down to Tudor times, barely extended beyond the Dublin Pale, 'a garrisoned foreign province . . . whose foreignness was proclaimed in law and asserted by violence'.[43] In Wales, Anglo-Norman penetration was both earlier and more intense, but it was 'piecemeal, long-drawn-out, and uncompleted' and it seems possible that peasant and burgess settlers, colonizing the lowlands – 'a second tidal wave of Anglo-Saxon or English colonization' – may have counted for more than Norman warlords. Down to the reign of Edward I border warfare was a two-way affair, with raids and counter-raids which were as much an outcrop of internecine strife within the tribal kingdoms of Wales as of invasion or infiltration from without.[44] The Norman advance into Scotland was another thing again, working in part, it seems, through aristocratic alliance, in part through Anglo-Saxon migration and settlement; while so far as politics was concerned, its effect seems to have been to strengthen an already powerful kingship. Not the least of the Norman legacies, on this view, was the Scottish success in the wars of independence.[45]

Medievalists working in this vein, taking their evidence from the clerisy – the annalists and poets – and mapping the fluctuating fortunes of England's internal empire, have been concerned to backdate ideas of nationhood and highlight precocious expressions of it. Thus we learn that the 'imagined community' of the Welsh, existing quite independently of the tribal kingdoms, was celebrated by the bardic historians and scholar-clerics centuries before the advent of that 'print culture' which according to Benedict Anderson is the precondition for the existence of a national consciousness.[46] It seems to have received a tremendous fillip, and painful redefinition, as a result of what Rees Davies calls the Norman *blitzkrieg*. Elsewhere he writes that 'in spite of . . . political fragmentation' the sense of a Welsh national identity grew rapidly in the thirteenth century:

> It was expressed in a pride in the language and laws of Wales, as symbols of its unity, an emphasis on its historic frontiers and the common and exalted descent of its peoples, the self-conscious cultivation of the concept of 'Wales' (*Wallia*) as a political and historical unit, and the cultivation of the prospect of unitary native rule.[47]

In a kindred spirit, medievalists speak of the emergence, during the twelfth century, of an English ethnic nationalism, defined quite often by relations of opposition to 'barbarian Scots', 'wild Irish', and the 'rude and untamed Welsh'. And they interpret the thirteenth-century growth of law and administration as a sign of English nationalism's coming of age. Edward I's expansionist policies, his planting of castles and his Welsh and Scottish wars are seen as the attempted assertion, within the British Isles, of an English hegemony – John Gillingham indeed writes of a medieval English imperialism manifested by the attack on the Celtic peoples. Here, as elsewhere, one of the merits of 'four nations' history is that it highlights an English nationalism which would otherwise pass without remark.[48]

There is an unspoken teleology behind a great deal of 'four nations' history. J.G.A. Pocock, writing in 1975, described the pattern of 'British history' as 'one of steadily increasing dominance of England as a political and cultural entity'.[49] Elsewhere in the same article he defined British history as the record of 'the expansion of government at the expense of kinship'. The making of the unitary state is a leitmotiv of medievalists' work in the field: they are apt to see parallel processes at work in both the English and the Scottish kingdoms. Linda Colley's *Britons* is a success story, and it may be that that is one of the secrets of its appeal, anyway to an English and diasporic readership. Despite a modernist attention to cultural difference, she offers us a unionist version of British history, and an imperial view of national character. National expansion is the unifying thread of her narrative, the triumph of loyalism its *terminus ad quem.* Moments of convergence and coalescence are highlighted, as for instance the upsurge of patriotic sentiment during the French revolutionary and Napoleonic wars, while she passes lightly over matters where explosive contradictions are more apparent.

If, as seems likely at the time of writing, the break-up of Britain proceeds apace; if the separatism of Ulster, and its alienation from mainland Britain, is confirmed; and if, after the next general election, a Scottish government is established at Edinburgh, followed in due course, as many radicals will hope, by the proclamation of a Scottish Republic, it may be that a very different 'four nations' history of Britain will become the order of the day, one which focuses on the tenacity of our island ethnicities, and allows more conceptual space for schisms and secessions. The 'imagined community' of the British could no longer be conceived of as a Protestant one, if the four nations history wanted to address the confessional differences between Scotland East and West, Falls Road, Shankill and the Ardoyne, or Trinidad and Jamaica. The division between Church and Chapel would also need some space. (Religion may have united Protestant nationalists behind government in the 1740s and the 1750s when England engaged in war with France, but twenty years later, in the American War of Independence, it persuaded many Nonconformists to side with their co-religionists on the other side of the Atlantic.)[50] Against Linda Colley's 'Protestant' construction of Britishness, one would need to set the 'Catholic' construction of Irishness, both in the days of the Penal Laws and in the early years of the Irish Free State. The roots of Ulster separatism might be traced back to the Catholic rebellion of 1641, the folk-memory, both among the newly arrived Scots settlers and among the native Irish whom they displaced, of atrocity, and the siege mentality which it bred.[51] By the same token, according to the persuasive if distinctly Ultramontane reading of Patrick O'Farrell, the roots of modern Irish nationalism are to be sought in Elizabeth I's attempted 'pacification' of Ireland. It raised up against the English, he argues, a holy war, or 'religious crusade', in which the English were cast in the role of heretics and murderers, and the Irish in that of martyrs – a drama re-enacted in every subsequent Irish crisis, and one which found its apotheosis in the 'blood sacrifice' of Easter 1916.[52]

The history of Scotland would surely be told in an anti-unionist sense, as it was by the medieval and mythical *Scotichronicon* (the Caledonian answer to Geoffrey of Monmouth), or by the post-Reformation historian George Buchanan. The attempted union of the crowns under James I would be seen as a failure, desired by neither side; while even the Act of Union of 1707, according to one position vehemently taken up at the 'Scottish Dimensions' History Workshop, might appear retrospectively as a comedy of errors. The whole bias of recent historical scholarship, now joined by imaginative film-making, has been to rehabilitate the Jacobite cause, and it seems likely that a newly independent Scotland will look with a kindly eye on its nineteenth-century memorialists, rehabilitating the work and the reputation of such late Jacobites as W.E. Aytoun, the biographer of the Scottish cavaliers, and James Grant, the military-romantic founder of the Association for the Vindication of Scottish Rights. Sir Walter Scott's successful defence of the Scottish banknote may appear as interesting a historical act as his masterminding of George IV's state visit to Edinburgh.[53]

Looking for the roots of Scottish separatism, such a history might start from the independence of the legal system, or focus on the Kirk as Scotland's *de facto* parliament. Or it might follow the rise of those parallel and intermediate associations, such as Freemasonry, which gave such density and solidarity to Scottish urban life.[54] Attention might be drawn, as it was in the Royal Society of Edinburgh's publication on *Victorian Values*, to the resilience of the parish in nineteenth-century Scotland, the failure to implement the New Poor Law, and the precocious mid-Victorian growth of collectivist and protectionist boards of administration.[55] The creation of a Scottish Office in 1885, hailed at the time as a landmark, would take on an altogether new allure, establishing as it did an embryo of that system of dual power – 'local autonomy within a wider multinational state' – which meant that Scotland's affairs were conducted as those of a separate country even when it was nominally ruled by Westminster.[56]

State formation could fairly be described as the unifying problematic of 'four nations' history. It has been taken up theoretically as the grand project of the *Journal of Historical Sociology*, a publication in which numbers of leading medieval and early modern historians have made their thought explicit. Here writers drawing sometimes on Gramscian notions of hegemony, sometimes on Weberian modernization theory, picture state formation as a 'great arch', a continuous process of development reaching back to the Norman Conquest, and coming forward to the tutelary complexes and disciplinary machineries of the modern state.[57] Even when practised by neo-Marxists, this is top-down, even, after a fashion, drum-and-trumpet history. In the work of the medievalists, lordship, suzerainty and feudal obligation are the framework of the narrative, 'dominant ideology' the unquestioned point of address. Wars matter. Conquest, though subject to revisionist interpretation, provides the narrative with its landmarks, 'if only because military events appear to provide a firm story line and fixed chronological reference points'.[58] The 'three kingdoms' approach to what used to be called the English Civil War is also very much a top-down affair, court-centred or following the tendrils of royal power: both Charles I's failures in Scotland and Ireland, and the outbreak of armed conflict in England, are put down to the phenomenon – and the impossibilities – of 'multiple kingship'. J.G.A. Pocock, though republican in his sympathies, as befits one who draws his inspiration from the eighteenth-century commonwealthmen, is hardly less patrician: dynamism is with the magistrate and the Prince harmonizing the competing claims of liberty and obligation, property and the law, and with those aristocratic (or 'classical') republicans who championed the idea of patriotic duty. The people, whether in the form of 'nationalities', 'peasantries' or the men who took the King's Shilling, are a more or less inert backdrop.[59] Linda Colley has more imaginative space for the popular, especially in her graphics, but it is the 'dynasts and careerists',[60] as she calls them, who are the heroes of her narrative (among them, by virtue of his Scottishness, is Earl Haig, the butcher of Passchendaele),[61] and 'the making of a more authentically British ruling class' which is her measure of ultimate achievement.

In the spirit of the above, some argue that high politics is 'architectonic', and that in any attempt to make a new narrative of British history it should be given pride of place. The selection of papers published as 'Scottish Dimensions' in *History Workshop Journal* begs to differ. Literature is often much more sensitive to the undercurrents of national life, even of state formation, than high politics; in Wales and Ireland (the medievalists remind us) it was the very foundation of the national idea. It can be no less finely tuned to the competing strains in national character.[62] 'Microhistories' too can provide us with the vital clues which grand narrative is too lordly to notice. Even if high politics is the point of address, an oblique or ethnographic approach might be more rewarding than a narrow focus on the mechanics of power. Easter 1916, on any view a crucial turning-point in Anglo-Irish relations, has been illuminatingly contextualized by reference not only to the Catholic revival of the 1880s and 1890s, but also more specifically to the new-found strength, among Catholics, of the missionary idea, and not least to the zeal of Catholic Temperance – the moral crusade in which Padraig Pearse served his agitational apprenticeship.[63]

Religion, if it was studied as a cause rather than as an effect, would give a quite different take on four nations history than the narrative of politics and government. Starting at the level of the parish, like historians of the devotional revolution in Reformation England, or at that of domestic piety in the 'little commonwealth' of the home, it allows for and indeed positively requires a more local, more subjective and more molecular understanding of ideology and consciousness than one which takes its cue from lordship and domination or state power. Liam McIlvanney's work on 'Robert Burns and the Calvinist Radical Tradition' reminds us of some of the ways in which Presbyterianism has been fundamental to the construction of Scottishness, as in the doctrine of resistance propounded by its earliest theologians and enshrined in the deeds of the Covenanters; or the 'system of near-universal education' – and opportunity for the 'lad o' pairts' – which it established by its parochial schooling; or by the appearance in higher education of that 'democratic intellect' which (George Davie has eloquently argued) was the distinctive achievement of Scotland's ancient universities.[64] The Catholic construction of Irishness is an entirely different affair, one in which the Church, while standing for universal values and a cosmopolitan religious community, was also the custodian, even the incarnation, of the race memory of historic wrong, and in which the national cause – like the Christian one – was mixed with the blood of the martyrs. (Bobby Sands, the IRA prisoner who starved himself to death in 1980, possibly did more for the Republican cause in Ulster than twenty years of armed struggle; the same was famously true, as Yeats's poem records, of the summary executions which followed the Easter Rising.)

Demography, 'the numerical study of . . . society', has quite as legitimate a claim to being regarded as 'architectonic' as monarchical ambition, administrative growth or imperial fantasy – i.e. high politics. The fact that, as recently as 1945, London was routinely described as the greatest city in the world – a position it apparently held for two centuries and more – may tell us more about the success of the idea of Britain, and the mesmeric hold it exercised over its subjects, than any number of references to invented traditions of imagined communities. Again, to stay at the level of statistical aggregates, it matters a great deal, from the point of view of reaffirming the importance of the Irish dimension of British history, that before the catastrophe of the Famine, one in three of the population of these islands was Irish, and that in the century of Georgian Dublin and Grattan's Parliament, as indeed for the seventeenth century, the movement of population was into Ireland rather than away from it. Tracking migration flows, studying place-names and field-systems and reading the evidence of material remains, historic demography can map those glacial population shifts which determined the linguistic configuration of the country, as for instance the Saxon colonization of South Wales, both before and after the Norman Conquest, which abstracted the coastal plain from Wales's Welsh-speaking heartland; or the comparable movements of the eleventh and twelfth centuries which made Lowland Scotland Anglophone.[65]

One of the merits of the 'four nations' perspective is that, if only to explain the term 'Great Britain', and the empire with which it was, for some four centuries, coeval, it forces us to consider the imperial dimension of British history. Anyone who has read Sir Charles Dilke's *Greater Britain* (1869),[66] or who has followed the story of missionary enterprise, will know that the British Empire was at least as much a Scottish affair as an English one, and indeed the Scottish diaspora of the nineteenth century was one of the nurseries in which Scottish nationalism was reared. The great period of Scottish missionary work came after 1843, 'when the Disruption brought about a revival of religious zeal throughout the country'. The appearance of 'little Scotlands' in the white colonies, Canada, New Zealand and Australia in particular, belongs to the same period, though to judge by the number of 'Scottish' mountains, rivers and waters (Western Australia is full of them) Scottish explorers may have been there first.[67] At Dunedin, New Zealand, 'the New Edinburgh of the Southern Sea',[68] the religious revival and the colonial settlement came together, the colony taking its start from a party of Free Churchers and its street nomenclature from Edinburgh. 'The place-names of the Southern half of the South Island are evidence enough of the race of men who first colonized it', wrote Gibb in *Scottish Empire*. 'Here, for example, are Bruce, Little Paisley, Ettrick, Campbelltown, Oban, Clutha, Wallace, Roxburgh, Stirling, Fortrose and many others; the Scottish mountain names with Ben have been imitated in such as Ben Nevis, Ben Lomond, Ben More and even Ben Ohau; and the streets of Invercargill are named mostly after Scottish rivers.'[69]

The Celtic diaspora, as it took shape in the later nineteenth century, was definitely part of the imperial heritage, indeed St Andrew's Day was more fervently observed in Bombay and Calcutta, Otago and Queensland than it was in Edinburgh or Glasgow. It is indicative of the importance of these Empire connections, and of the imaginative hold they exercised, that the first Celtic nationalisms, emerging as they did in the high noon of Britian's colonial expansion, had an unashamedly imperial dimension. Indeed it is possible to see the growth of Empire and the ethnic revival of the 1870s and 1880s as two sides of the same coin; each, after its own fashion, worshipped at the feet of race consciousness, that scientistic version of natural selection theory which in the later nineteenth century intoxicated thinkers of all stripes. The idea of a Welsh Colony 'which would become a new and purer Wales outside the bounds of Britain'[70] appears at each decisive moment in the formation of a Welsh nationalism; the fervent welcome to the country's 'exiles', a feature of the Eisteddfodau, helped to keep the flame burning, though it was in Patagonia and the United States, rather than in the Greater Wales of the British Empire, that it was realized.

In Ireland the first Home Rule party, a kind of dissident wing of the Protestant Ascendancy, was ardently imperialist; its Parnellite successor was more hostile to England but looked forward to an emancipated Ireland taking a full and equal part in the British Empire. For this reason it was quite sympathetic to ideas of imperial federation. Sir Charles Gavan Duffy, one of the great advocates of the language movement of the 1890s, and an erstwhile Young Irelander, had been governor of New South Wales, and his later advocacy of self-government was modelled on the Australian example. 'Human nature has the same spiritual warp and woof in the Old World as in the New, and what made Irish Catholics contented and loyal on the banks of the Paramatta and the Yarra Yarra would make them contented and loyal on the banks of the Liffey.'[71] Imperialism burnt with a hard, gem-like flame in Erskine Childers, one of Irish nationalism's Edwardian recruits. In a parallel development, the Edwardian years saw the emergence of a Gaelic and Catholic version of the imperial idea, in which the Irish were cast in the role of spiritual redeemers of the world. In Scotland, where both Tory romantics such as Napier,[72] and Liberal Imperialists such as Lord Rosebery, had some influence on the emergence of a proto-nationalist sentiment, the imperial ambitions were quite open, and they were renewed when the Scottish National Party came into being: 'Scotland within the Empire' (later modified to 'Scotland within the Commonwealth') was a major plank in the party's platform[73] (it won some early support from Lord Beaverbrook), and it is only in the last fifteen years that it has been exchanged for 'A Scotland Free Within Europe'.

A 'four nations' history of Britain widens the scope of scholarly inquiry. It puts in question some of our more cocksure generalizations (the notion that Britain is a country without a peasantry could hardly have won credence if Ireland had been brought into the equation, or *A Scots Quair* used as a text). 'Four nations' history offers a more natural framework for comparative work than those forced analogies and far-fetched contrasts which young researchers are too often forced to adopt, as a way of giving theoretical dignity to their work. A 'four nations' history encourages us to think more geographically, to see London as a world metropolis and Cardiff as a coal one; to map the British diaspora; and to log the two-way traffic in peoples and ideas across the Atlantic, to recover the North Sea and Baltic connection.

Yet a 'four nations' history produces as many problems as it resolves. Being polycentric it has no natural heartland or consecutive narrative. Like any field of study it has its silences and its exclusions. It has so far been more or less gender-blind, though it seems unlikely that the patriarchal assumptions which underpin so much modern nationalism will continue to go unchallenged.[74] It leaves unresolved fundamental questions as to what history should be about. The state? Civil society? Organized religion? Field-systems? Child-rearing? Is politics 'architectonic', as some influential voices contend, or would the built environment serve better as a unifying thread?

Can a 'four nations' history prosper if the United Kingdom continues to unravel? One might argue, to the contrary, that history, ideally, should be, in Walter Benjamin's phrase, 'brushed against the grain'; that historians, as memory-keepers, have a particular vocation to preserve the record and advance the understanding of disappearing worlds; that history is not a mere creature of politics, and that it is at its best when it works counter-cyclically, putting a value on what is threatened with oblivion. On this view, the matter of Britain is a rewarding one for historians to address precisely because it no longer inhabits the realm of the taken-for-granted. To recover the lost English component of Irish history (or the lost Irish dimension of British history) is hardly at the time of writing a popular cause: but it is intolerable that on school maps in England, the twenty-six counties should appear as a blank; and it would be absurd if, in deference to a newly constituted parliament at Edinburgh, the map of North Britain should follow suit.

Notes

1 R.R. Davies, 'In Praise of British History', in Davies (ed.), *The British Isles, 1100–1500: Comparisons, Contrasts and Connections*, Edinburgh 1988, p. 23.

2 Steve Bruce, *The Edge of the Union, the Ulster Loyalist Political Vision*, Oxford 1994, p. 30.

3 Gwyn Williams, 'When Was Wales?', in *The Welsh in Their History*, London 1982, pp. 200–1 for a rhetorically brilliant statement of the conundrum; the same author's *When Was Wales?; a History of the Welsh*, London 1985, does not pose the question so sharply.

4 Roger A. Mason, '"Scotching the Brut": Politics, History and National Myth in Sixteenth-Century Britain', in Mason (ed.), *Scotland and England, 1286–1815*, Edinburgh 1987.

5 An underrated text here is Gerald Newman, *The Rise of English Nationalism, A Cultural History, 1740–1830*, London 1987. More insular and much less comprehensive than Linda Colley's *Britons*, it is nevertheless more alert to eighteenth-century Saxonism, and the radical and 'gothick' elements in 1740s nationalism.

6 F.M. Stenton, *Anglo-Saxon England*, Oxford 1973 ed., p. 315.

7 Susan Reynolds, 'What Do We Mean by "Anglo-Saxon" and "Anglo-Saxons"?', *Journal of British Studies*, vol. 24, no. 4, October 1985, p. 303.

8 James Campbell, 'The End of Roman Britain' and 'The Lost Centuries: 400–600', in James Campbell, Eric John, Patrick Wormald (eds), *The Anglo-Saxons*, Oxford 1982.

9 See his remarks on the impossibility of understanding the Cornish in his translation of Montaigne's *Essays*. Everyman ed., vol. 2, ch. xii.

10 Charles Thomas, *The Early Christian Archaeology of North Britain*, Oxford 1971, p. 8.

11 Charles Thomas, *Celtic Britain*, London 1986; Roger H. White, *Roman and Celtic Objects from Anglo-Saxon Graves: a Catalogue and Interpretation of Their Use*, Oxford 1988.

12 P. Wormald, 'Offa's Dyke', in Campbell and others (ed.), *The Anglo-Saxons*, pp. 120–1; Wendy Davies, *Patterns of Power in Early Wales*, Oxford 1990, pp. 64–72.

13 W.M. Aird, 'St Cuthbert, the Scots and the Normans', *Anglo-Norman Studies*, XVII, 1993, p. 1.

14 A.A.M. Duncan, *Scotland, the Making of the Kingdom*, Edinburgh 1975, p. 76.

15 P. Wormald, 'The Age of Bede and Aethelbald', in Campbell and others (ed.), *The Anglo-Saxons*, p. 91.

16 G.W.S. Barrow, *The Anglo-Norman Era in Scottish History*, Oxford 1980, pp. 5–7; Colin Kidd, 'The Canon of Patriotic Landmarks in Scottish History', *Scotlands*, 1, 1994, pp. 6–7.

17 Barbara E. Crawford, Introduction to John R. Baldwin and Ian D. Whyte (ed.), *The Scandinavians in Cumbria*, Edinburgh 1985, p. 1.

18 W.F.H. Nicolaisen, 'The Viking Settlement of Scotland: the Evidence of Place Names', in R.T. Farrell (ed.), *The Vikings*, Chichester 1982, p. 115.

19 Robin Frame, *The Political Development of the British Isles, 1100–1400*, Oxford 1990, p. 12.

20 Wendy Davies, *Patterns of Power*, pp. 71–3.

21 Robert Bartlett, *Gerald of Wales*, Oxford 1982, p. 2.

22 Hugh Kearney, *The British Isles, A History of Four Nations*, Cambridge 1989, pp. 67–8.

23 Williams, *When Was Wales?*, pp. 87–8, 92–3.

24 Jenny Wormald, 'The Creation of Britain: Multiple Kingdoms or Core and Colonies?', *Transactions of the Royal Historical Society*, 6th ser., no. 2, 1992, p. 188.

25 J.G.A. Pocock, 'British History: A Plea for a New Subject', *Journal of Modern History*, 47, December 1975, p. 601.

26 ibid., p. 601.

27 ibid., p. 621.

28 ibid., p. 606.

29 ibid., p. 609.

30 Kearney, *British Isles, passim.*

31 Linda Colley, *Britons, Forging the Nation, 1707–1837*, London 1992.

32 ibid., p. 129.

33 ibid., p. 126.

34 ibid., pp. 125–6.

35 ibid., p. 159; Karl Marx, *Capital*, London 1949 ed., pp. 753–4.

36 Roy Foster, *Modern Ireland, 1600–1972*, Harmondsworth 1988.

37 Liam Miller, *The Dun Emer Press*, Dublin 1975; Gifford Lewis, *The Yeats Sisters and the Cuala Press*, Dublin 1995. I am grateful to Warwick Gould for these references.

38 Pocock, 'British History', p. 605. Arthur H. Williamson, 'Scotland and the British Revolutions', *Scottish Historical Review*, LXXIII 1, April 1994, pp. 117–27, for a helpful overview. In a large literature, David Stevenson, 'The Century of the Three Kingdoms', in Jenny Wormald (ed.), *Scotland Revisited*, London 1991, pp. 107–18; Mark Charles Fissel, *The Bishops' Wars; Charles I's Campaigns against Scotland, 1638–1640*, Cambridge 1994; J.S. Morrill (ed.), *The Scottish National Covenant in Its British Context*, Edinburgh 1990; Conrad Russell, 'The British Problem and the English Civil War', *History*, vol. 72, 1987, pp. 395–415; 'The British Background to the Irish Rebellion of 1641', in *Historical Research*, LXI, 1988, pp. 166–82; 'The Problem of Multiple Kingdoms, *c.* 1580–1630', in his *The Causes of the English Civil War*, Oxford 1990, pp. 26–57.

39 Conrad Russell, *The Fall of the British Monarchies, 1637–1642*, Oxford 1992, p. 27; Russell, *Unrevolutionary England, 1603–1642*, London 1990, for a collection of essays on this theme.

40 Russell, *Fall*, p. 532.

41 John Davies, *A History of Wales*, London 1993, p. 102.

42 F.X. Martin, 'John, Lord of Ireland, 1185–1216', in Art Cosgrove (ed.), *A New History of Ireland*, Oxford 1993, pp. 127–55.

43 Patrick O'Farrell, *Ireland's English Question: Anglo-Irish Relations 1534–1970*, London 1971, pp. 16–17; Robin Frame, 'England and Ireland, 1171–1399', in Michael Jones and Malcolm Vale (ed.), *England and Her Neighbours, 1066–1453*, London 1989, pp. 139–55; Robin Frame, *Colonial Ireland*, Dublin 1981.

44 R.R. Davies, *Domination and Conquest: the Experience of Ireland, Scotland and Wales, 1100–1300*, Cambridge 1990, p. 64; 'The English State and the "Celtic" Peoples, 1100–1400', *Journal of Historical Sociology*, VI, no. 1, March 1993, p. 11.

45 Barrow, *Anglo-Norman Era*; Judith Green, 'Anglo-Scottish Relations, 1066–1174', in Jones and Vale (ed.), *England and Her Neighbours*, pp. 53–72; Robin Frame, *The Political Development of the British Isles, 1100–1400*, Oxford 1990.

46 R.R. Davies, *The Age of Conquest, 1063–1415*, Oxford 1991, pp. 15–20; 'Law and National Identity in Thirteenth-Century Wales', in R.R. Davies and others (ed.), *Welsh Society and Nationhood*, Cardiff 1984, pp. 51–69; Benedict Anderson, *Imagined Communities*, London 1983.

47 R.R. Davies, *Age of Conquest*, p. 215.

48 John Gillingham, 'The Beginnings of English Imperialism', *Journal of Historical Sociology*, vol. V, no. 4, December 1992, pp. 392–409; Richard Mortimer, *Angevin England, 1154–1258*, Oxford 1994, pp. 137–48, 233–4, 235–43. For an interesting discussion of early medieval ideas of nationhood, Susan Reynolds, *Kingdoms and Communities in Western Europe, 900–1100*, Oxford 1986.

49 Pocock, 'British History', pp. 609, 610.

50 James E. Bradley, *Religion, Revolution and English Radicalism: Nonconformity in Eighteenth-Century Politics and Society*, Cambridge 1990.

51 Foster, *Modern Ireland*, pp. 77–8; Brian Mac Cuarta (ed.), *Ulster 1641, Aspects of the Rising*, Belfast 1994. For the late eighteenth-century reinvention of these divisions, and the birth of the Orange Order, Hereward Senior, *Orangeism in Ireland and Britain, 1795–1836*, London 1966; Foster, *Modern Ireland*, p. 147, for the 1790 invention of the annual celebration of the deliverance of Londonderry; Senior, *Orangeism: the Canadian Phase*, Toronto, 1972; and Pocock, 'British History', p. 618, for the remarkable reproduction of these schisms in Ulster's North American colonies of settlement.

52 O'Farrell, *Ireland's English Question*, pp. 28–31, 52–3, 223–9, 266–7, 290–1. As well as offering a thought-provoking interpretation of post-sixteenth-century Irish history, this book gives one a rare glimpse into the mind of post-1921 Irish Catholic sectarianism; to follow this author W.B. Yeats was disqualified from being fully Irish because he was not a Catholic; Pearse rather than Connolly was the martyr of Easter 1916 because his death was an uncomplicated act of religious sacrifice.

53 J.G. Lockhart, *Memoirs of Sir Walter Scott*, London 1900 ed., 5 vols.

54 R.J. Morris and Graeme Morton, 'Where Was Nineteenth-Century Scotland?', *Scottish Historical Review*, LXXIII, no. 1, April 1994, pp. 96–7.

55 Stewart J. Brown, 'Thomas Chalmers and the Communal Ideal in Victorian Scotland', in T.C. Smout (ed.), *Victorian Values*, Oxford 1992, pp. 61–80.

56 Lindsay Paterson, *The Autonomy of Modern Scotland*, Edinburgh 1994. H.J. Hanham, *Scottish Nationalism*, London 1969, is still a very rewarding starting-point for some of these developments.

57 G.E. Aylmer, 'The Peculiarities of the English State', *Journal of Historical Sociology*, 3, 1990; P. Corrigan and D. Sayer, *The Great Arch: English State Formation as Cultural Revolution*, Oxford 1985.

58 R.R. Davies, *Domination and Conquest*, p. 11. Professor Davies is not here *advocating* drum-and-trumpet history, merely acknowledging its teacherly appeal.

59 J.G.A. Pocock, 'The Limits and Divisions of British History', *Studies in Public Policy*, no. 31, 1979, pp. 9–11.

60 Colley, *Britons*, p. 370.

61 ibid., pp. 163–4. Colley quotes a wartime essay on 'The Oppressed English': 'To-day a Scot is leading the British army in France . . . another is commanding the British grand fleet at sea . . . while a third directs the Imperial General Staff at home'.

62 See, for example, Tom Keymer, 'Smollett's Scotland', in *History Workshop Journal*, no. 40, Autumn 1995, pp. 118–32, and recent work in the new journal, *Scotlands*, in which some of the contributors to the 'Scottish Dimensions' Workshop have a hand.

63 O'Farrell, *Ireland's English Question*, pp. 227–9.

64 Liam McIlvanney, 'Robert Burns and the Calvinist Radical Tradition', *History Workshop Journal*, no. 40, Autumn 1995. George Davie, *The Democratic Intellect*, Edinburgh 1982 ed.

65 'The Pattern of Settlement', in Barrow, *Anglo-Norman Era*, pp. 30ff.

66 'Half the most prominent among the statesmen of the Canadian Confederation, of Victoria and of Queensland, are born Scots, and all the great merchants of India are of the same nation': Sir Charles Dilke, *Greater Britain, A Record of Travel in English-Speaking Countries During 1866 and 1867*, London 1869, pp. 373–4.

67 Malcolm D. Prentis, *The Scottish in Australia*, Melbourne 1987; Eric Richards and others, *That Land of Exiles: Scots in Australia*, Edinburgh 1988.

68 Donald Mackenzie Wallace, *The Web of Empire: A Diary of the Imperial Tour of . . . The Duke and Duchess of Cornwall and York in 1901*, London 1902, pp. 284–5.

69 Andrew Dewar Gibb, *Scottish Empire*, London 1937, p. 301.

70 Philip Jenkins, *A History of Modern Wales, 1536–1990*, London 1992, p. 319.

71 J.E. Parnaby, 'Charles Gavan Duffy in Australia', in Oliver McDonagh and others (ed.), *Irish Culture and Irish Nationalism, 1750–1950*, Canberra 1983, p. 64.

72 Hanham tells us that the Marquess of Bute, the Lothair of Disraeli's novel, was 'a convert to the idea of creating a national legislature for Scotland, even before the Home Rule question became popular': *Scottish Nationalism*, p. 83.

73 Jack Brand, *The National Movement in Scotland*, London 1978, pp. 216–22; Hanham, *Scottish Nationalism*, pp. 152, 157, 163–4. The 1928 platform of the Scottish Party was 'Self-Government for Scotland on a basis which will enable Scotland as a partner in the British Empire with the same status as England to develop its National Life to the fullest advantage'.

74 Helen Corr, 'Dominies and Domination in Nineteenth-Century Scotland', *History Workshop Journal*, no. 40, Autumn 1995, launches this challenge. Angela McRobbie's piece on 'Catholic Glasgow' in the same issue suggests how fragile the idea of Scotland itself might prove when put to the test of subjectivity.

Unravelling Britain*

I

Britain is a term which has a very uncertain future. The Scots, who in the sixteenth century were quite largely responsible for promoting the concept of 'Great Britain', and who were later instrumental in translating it into the lexicon of monarchical and state polity, are now only too anxious to escape it: according to a recent opinion poll, a mere 3 per cent chose to describe themselves as 'British' (among the English the percentage was close to 50 per cent). 'Loyalist Ulster', after two and a half decades of civil war, is as alienated from England, and as hostile to the government at Westminster, as their Republican enemies. In England itself, a multi-faith and multiracial society, inconceivably more cosmopolitan than Ireland, Scotland or Wales, minority identities seem more potent than majoritarian ones.

As a source of symbolic capital, Britain's credit seems to be exhausted. Fifty years ago this country was still a great power – one of the Big Three. It was a beacon of hope to occupied Europe, standing up to the Nazis where others had capitulated or collaborated. The BBC, starched accents and all, was 'the voice of Britain'. Westminster was thought of as an example to the world, 'the mother of parliaments', enshrining the 'rule of law'; the House of Commons, 'in some ways the most typically English of our institutions,'[1] was the cradle in which the idea of democracy had been nursed. Whitehall, home of the great offices of state and nerve-centre of the Civil Service, was run by the best brains in the country, 'Rolls-Royce minds', whose industry was legendary: 'It would be impossible to imagine a body of men who performed the duties laid on them . . . more conscientiously'.[2] London, 'the capital of England, and of the British Empire', was 'the greatest city in the world'.[3] As the principal

* This essay was drafted in September 1995; topical references have been left unchanged; footnotes added.

target of enemy attack, it had a special place in the nation's esteem. Cockney heroism and good humour – the stoical indifference of the air-raid shelter crowd, cocking a snook at 'Jerry', the 'business as usual' of the cabbies, clippies and bobbies – were symbols of national courage, the miraculous survival of St Paul's a talisman of the nation's will.

Today, the House of Commons is widely thought of as a bear-garden; in the eyes of constitutional reformers, an influential and growing band, it is a very emblem of backwardness. When the new Scottish parliament assembles at Edinburgh, as it seems certain to do after the next general election, it will look to Strasbourg rather than Westminster for its models, and will want to make its procedures and its ceremonial as un-English as it is possible to be. London, 'the rudest capital in Europe',[4] is, if anything, in even greater disrepute. Superseded, as a banking centre, first by Zürich and latterly by the Pacific rim, it is now dwarfed as a megalopolis by such Third World monsters as Mexico City and São Paolo. London is also without honour in Britain, deprived of those industries, such as aircraft manufacture and vehicle building, which gave it an interwar eminence, bypassed as an international exhibition or conference centre. The Labour and Conservative parties compete with one another in demonstrating their independence of 'the London effect'; the Royal Shakespeare Company – one of our two great national theatre companies – is now following suit. The World Service of the BBC, like that other ambassador of national culture, the British Council, has been cut down to size; while Radio Scotland, following the example of Radio Wales, has made itself into a front-runner for national independence, voicing a very public disdain for its nominal controllers in London, and asking that Scottish news should have priority over British.

If the United Kingdom continues to unravel, the word 'Britain' may become as obsolete as 'Soviet' is in post-1989 Russia. The recent celebrations of the anniversary of VE Day, on 8 May 1995, are perhaps a portent of the shape of things to come. In Ulster they were taken up by Protestants for a rather desperate display of loyalty to the flag; in Republican areas they were ignored. Scotland, despite urgent appeals to regimental loyalties, gave them the cold shoulder: the only public turn-out was at Perth, where a crowd of some 5,000 watched a march-past of the 51st Highlanders. In London hundreds of thousands of people assembled for a huge day out, with picnics all over Hyde Park, impromptu dancing, march-pasts, fly-pasts and a spectacular fireworks display. Edinburgh, which on VE Day 1945 had danced the night away, with huge crowds on the streets, just the same (to judge by the photographs) as London, gave the celebrations a miss, and indeed the Lothian Regional Council refused to recognize 8 May as a public holiday.[5] At the beacon-lighting ceremony on Calton Hill, attended by the Lord Provost of Edinburgh, there was not a bagpipe to be heard, only a small military

Publicity for the Scottish National Party, 1995

band, a squad of soldiers standing to attention, and a chill circle of bystanders, raising a ragged cheer. There were more VE Day events in Hampshire than in the whole of Scotland, more Scots Guards in Hyde Park than there were on Calton Hill.

By contrast, the Hollywood-style European Gala Première of *Rob Roy*, staged at the Odeon cinema, Princes Street, Edinburgh, on 14 May – a film in which the villains, where not actually English, like Archie, the aristocratic libertine, are their fifth columnists and stooges among the Scots – was treated as a great national event. United Artists spent £1m on the launch, flying in 300 foreign guests, putting out a fleet of Cadillacs and orchestrating a media spectacular.[6] Michael Caton-Jones, the born-again Scotsman who directed the film, graced the occasion, dressed in a kilt, and the international celebrity crowd danced to the music of the Gay Gordons. The razzmatazz has been repeated for *Brave Heart*, the newly released, Irish-made epic about the life and death of William Wallace – Scotland's greatest martyr – and the Scottish National Party have improved on the occasion by using it to launch a mass recruitment drive.

No less striking than the collapse of British power, and this country's relegation to a second- or even third-class industrial nation, is the unravelling of any unitary idea of national character. 'Nations change profoundly in the very respects in which their characters might be thought most indelible', wrote Lecky, in his magisterial history of Ireland in the eighteenth century.[7] He was taking issue with the fashionable opposition between the Teuton and the Celt, but his argument has a more general purchase. Ireland, the 'turbulent sister isle'[8] of post-1918 British politics, and the disaster area of the post-Famine exodus, with its 'congested' district boards, coffin ships and declining population, was in the eighteenth century an expanding society, with a capital city, Dublin, which was at once a showcase of Georgian architecture, a seat of advanced manufactures, and a centre of learning. The Ireland of Bede's *Ecclesiastical History of the English People* (734) was a kind of Christian Shangri-La, a botanic and spiritual Other, a place where the weather was perpetually mild, nature benevolent, and the people in a state of grace.

In the case of Wales, the symbolic reversals, in perceptions of the national character, are no less complete and they take place within a much more limited time-span. For the Anglican ministers of the 1840s – the time of the notorious Royal Commission on the State of Education in Wales – Wales was one of the dark corners of the kingdom. Indeed a writer in 1856 described the Welsh as being 'the most immoral people in Europe, except perhaps the Swedes'.[9] Possibly he had in mind those illegitimacy rates which figure so prominently in the criminal statistics of Victorian Britain, or the practice of 'bundling' which the more voyeuristic of the folklorists delighted to bring to the light of day. Yet within three years Wales was to be the epicentre of a whole new cycle of religious revivals which in the space of twenty years made Chapel culture hegemonic. As Gwyn Williams remarks, 'The first official recognition of a distinctly Welsh people by the modern British state was the Welsh Sunday Closing Act of 1881 . . . a recognition that a Welsh identity at that moment expressed itself in Welsh Nonconformity, which had become almost as much a national church to the Welsh as Catholicism has become to the Irish'.[10]

Around the time of the Great Exhibition of 1851, the English were thought to be, first and foremost, hyper-industrious. The image of the 'busy hives around us' is one which recurs in book titles and the documentary writing of the day. A passage from the *Mechanics Magazine* for 27 April 1860 may serve as representative for what was then a major national conceit:

> There is no doubt whatever that the people of England work harder, mentally and physically, than the people of any other country on the face of the earth. Whether we take the town or country population, the same plodding industry is apparent, and the respites enjoyed by either in the shape of holidays are few and far between . . . We have no desire in stating the fact that Englishmen work harder than their neighbours to make them discontented with their lot; far from it. It is due to their untiring industry and to the natural advantages of the country of which we are so justly proud, that England holds the foremost rank among the nations of the earth.

The term 'Britain' or 'British' with its many variants, corruptions and derivatives – as, say, 'Britons' or 'Brits' – is an unstable one. It takes on qualitatively different meanings depending upon whether the point of definition is territorial or topographical, as in British Isles; political, as in British foreign policy (interestingly, and curiously, 'Anglo' seems to be preferred when there is a treaty to be signed, or negotiations to be conducted, with another country); or ethnic, as in that mythopoeic category which is such a favourite trope in rhetorical address, 'the British people'. Originally the term was tribal rather than imperial in its connotations – a name given to the islands where the Pretannoi, as the ancient Greeks called them, lived[11] – and it is possible that at the present time it is on its way to becoming tribal or ethnic once again.

Linguistically, the word 'Britain' has undergone many mutations in the course of a long career, now adding (or subtracting) consonants, now changing vowels, now blossoming out in grandiose acronyms (as in the 'MAG. BRIT.' which James I, in one of his Roman fantasies, added to the king's head on the coinage),[12] now playing on, or reviving, ancient conceits. One source of semantic confusion in the Middle Ages was the similarity of 'Brittaines' and 'Bretons' – both of them words deriving from the Old French. Geoffrey of Monmouth, the twelfth-century romancer, wild in so much else, is careful to distinguish the insular British from the continental Bretons. Wace, however, one of those who glossed Geoffrey of Monmouth's narrative, uses 'Breton' in a generic sense to cover Bretons, Cornish and Britons.[13] Another source of linguistic confusion was Brut, the alleged founder of the British royal line, and according to the received version of British history, this country's first ruler. Hence perhaps the references given in *OED* to 'Bruttisce spaeche' (1205) and (in Ranolf Higden, 1387) 'Bruttische ocean'.

The geography and the politics of Britain are often out of synch, as they are in Ulster today, where the two nations of Ireland confront one another not only at border towns like Crosmaglen, but in adjoining streets. Frontiers are typically porous, as they were in the time of the heptarchy, where population flows imposed their own grid. To the classical geographers, as to Ptolemy in his AD 168 map, Britannia (sometimes rendered as Albion) was a portmanteau term for the archipelago of offshore islands at the northernmost edge of Europe's trade routes.[14] Politically it was more limited. The Romans used it as a generic term for the provinces which they divided (around AD 197) into Britannia Superior and Britannia Inferior, later into Britannia Prima and Britannia Secunda.[15] Roman Britain occasionally included parts of Scotland, but it never extended to the lands beyond the northern Firths.[16] Ireland was never under Roman rule, though Agricola cast his beady eyes on it (according to his son-in-law Tacitus, he believed that it would be a valuable acquisition and could be taken by a single legion).[17] For Bede, Ireland was a completely separate country. His conception of Britain, writes Hunter Blair, was a geographical one, of two large islands, *Britannia* and *Hibernia*, not of four distinct countries, England, Wales, Scotland, Ireland.[18]

In Caesar's time, northern Scotland was believed by some to be an island, and a similar idea seems to have been prevalent in thirteenth-century England. Matthew Paris's map – one of the many brilliant illustrations to his *Chronica Majora* – connects up the Clyde and the Forth, and calls the northern part of Scotland *Scocia Ultra Marina.*[19] More generally these early maps, so far from picturing the British Isles as a unity, seem to go out of their way to highlight its divisions, elongating peninsulas, widening rivers and turning estuaries into miniature seas.

The idea that the concept of Britain was an invention of the Welsh may not be literally true – the sixteenth-century Scots, both the unionists of the 1540s and the historian John Major, have some claim to it. But it is the case that for a thousand years and more 'Welsh' and 'British' were treated as interchangeable terms. In the dark ages, when the native British retreated to the West Country in the face of the Anglo-Saxon invasions, Wales became the heartland of Britain, and indeed the native Romanized Britons were called by the English settlers *wealas* (Welsh).[20] It is perhaps indicative of this that Geoffrey of Monmouth's *Historia Regum Britanniae* should have been nursed in the Welsh wonder tales, the original source of the wizard Merlin, and that one of the earliest compilations of British history – Nennius's *Historia Brittonum*[21] – should have been the work of a ninth-century Welsh monk. Philologically, the association of what was still being called, in the writings of the late seventeenth-century antiquarians, the 'Britische' tongue with the Welsh one, was an extraordinarily persistent one; in the 1790s the poems of the early Welsh bards were being published as those of the 'antient British'.[22]

Perhaps because of the Roman legacy, perhaps because its boundaries were so ambiguous, the word Britain seemed to attract imperial ambitions. In Wales itself, Wendy Davies tells us, the annalists of the tenth and eleventh centuries, looking for grandiose titles to give their rulers, spoke of Hywel Dda as 'head and glory of all the Britons'; of Llywelyn ap Seisyll as 'head and shield and defender of the Britons'; and of the great Gruffudd ap Llywelyn as 'head and shield and defender of the Britons'.[23] In a kindred vein, the Anglo-Saxon kings, when they had any political ambitions, were apt to designate themselves in royal titles as kings – or even emperors – of all the British, even though their writ did not run further than the limits of their own tribal kingdoms. Geoffrey of Monmouth, who introduced the Arthurian legend that prevailed as the received version of the national past down to the 1590s, gave a vast metaphorical extension to the word 'Britain', and credited it, under King Arthur, with having made an empire in Europe and conquered Rome.[24] 'Great' was originally added to distinguish Britain from Lesser Britain, the pre-conquest kingdom of Brittany. But in the 1540s, when 'Great Britain' was canvassed in both England and Scotland as a unifying title for the two kingdoms, it acquired a definitely imperial connotation. 'British Empire' is an Elizabethan neologism popularized – some years before this country's first overseas plantations and colonies of settlement – by the

Matthew Paris's map of Britain from his *Abbreviato Chronicorum Angliae*

mysterious and hugely influential occultist, Dr John Dee (like Geoffrey of Monmouth, that other great imperial fantasist, Dee was a Welshman).[25]

In its Elizabethan and post-Elizabethan development, when the Roman goddess Britannia was annexed as its tutelary deity, Britishness was dis-severed from notions of ethnicity and attached instead to those of rule and superiority.[26] From the accession of James I to the throne in 1603, 'Great Britain' entered general use as the imperial title for the union of England and Scotland, a relationship formalized in the Act of Union of 1707; while with the plantation of overseas colonies and settlements it embarked on a second career as the flagship of imperial polity. In the eighteenth century 'Briton' emerged as a key term in the patriotic lexicon, while in letters the notion of 'British literature' enjoyed a brief vogue among the anthologists. With the publication, from 1768, of that monument of the Scottish Enlightenment, the *Encyclopedia Britannica*, Britishness began to serve as a synonym for, or promise of, all-embracing coverage.[27]

English, in its twentieth-century usage, is an altogether more introverted term than 'British' and largely associated with images of landscape, beauty and home rather than those of national greatness. It appears an ethnic term rather than a political one even when an unspoken politics accounts for its popularity. Because it is also the designation of a language ('the name English for the language is . . . older than the name "England" for the country') it carries a heavy freight of cultural meanings. Ethically it has often been associated with ideal virtues such as, say, sturdy independence, plain dealing, honest worth. It is also, because of the stress on common origin and descent, closely bound up with the idea of racial stock – its virtues, supposedly, are hereditary. Literature has normally been English; the Empire – it is argued – was always British.

In the patriotic hour of May–June 1940, possibly on account of the splendid isolation in which, by force of necessity, this country found itself, possibly because of the ethnocentric panic which swept the country in the wake of Dunkirk (in face of the imminent threat of invasion, aliens of all kinds, even Jews, were interned), 'English' was the favoured idiom in which the idea of nation was couched, and it was images of the English landscape – most famously the White Cliffs of Dover – which served on the home front as morale-boosters.[28] It was in the name of England that, in May 1940, enraged Conservative backbenchers brought the Chamberlain government to its knees; the 'island race' of Churchill's apostrophes was English rather than British; and when he turned to international outreach, it was in the first place to those he termed the 'English-speaking peoples of the world'. As a literary conceit, the idea of England, and its elevation into the mother of all the decencies, is even more pronounced. Orwell's expressively named patriotic essays of 1940–41 – 'The Lion and the Unicorn' and 'England Your England' in particular – are one legacy of this moment. Another, which nicely registers the vernacular of the time, is the preface of the reissue of Fowler's *Dictionary of Modern English Usage*:

> . . . it must be remembered that no Englishman, or perhaps no Scotsman even, calls himself a Briton without a sneaking sense of the ludicrous, or hears himself referred to as a BRITISHER without squirming. How should an Englishman utter the word *Great Britain* with the glow of emotion that for him goes with *England*? His sovereign may be Her *Britannic* Majesty to outsiders, but to him is Queen of *England*; he talks the *English* language; he has been taught *English* history as one continuous tale from Alfred to his own day; he has heard of the word of an *Englishman* and aspires to be an *English* gentleman; and he knows that *England* expects every man to do his duty. . . . In the word *England*, not in *Britain* all these things are implicit. It is unreasonable to ask forty millions of people to refrain from the use of the only names that are in tune with patriotic emotion, or to make them stop and think whether they mean their country in a narrower or wider sense each time they name it.

Today, by contrast, English is widely and publicly despised, not least by the teachers nominally charged with initiating students into its mysteries or children into its disciplines. Self-enclosed and inward-looking, it is thought to be inherently hostile or indifferent to the new ethnic minorities, while those 'decencies' by which Orwell in 1941 set such store are a turn-off for the young.[29] The teaching of English literature is associated with the missionary position in sexuality, parochialism in high politics and tea-shop gentility in the world of letters. There is now a whole literature dedicated to digging its grave and a generation of cultural studies lecturers who have constituted it as the main enemy.[30]

On the other hand 'British' is a term which is currently enjoying a small vogue, partly, it may be, because it is less loaded than English with cultural baggage, and therefore less exposed to the heritage-baiters, but also because, in current post-colonial usage as in the older imperial one, it is multi-ethnic and therefore more able to acknowledge the emergence of a multi-faith, multi-cultural society. As a political and administrative designation rather than an ethnic one, it can allow parity of esteem, between Black British and White, Muslim and Christian, natives and incomers. It may be too, that after two decades in which the nationality question has been a storm-centre of British politics, and when Celtic separatism is threatening to dismember the United Kingdom, it is a term which seems to reaffirm the historic and geographical unity of the British archipelago.

Particularly striking is the metamorphosis of the term 'Brit' from a shorthand expression of contempt into something which, at least in the vernacular of expats – or those film stars who find themselves on the international circuit – can be spoken of with wry affection. Originally, it seems, an Americanism, it was adopted by the Irish Republican movement when, in the 1970s, the IRA resumed its armed struggle. Today it is a routine journalistic usage. In the newspaper press, struggling to retain an Anglo-Scottish readership, and tacking to the winds of change north of the border, it is now house style to refer to 'Britons,' 'British' or 'Brits' regardless of whether they are English, Irish or Scottish. 'The Brits' is now the most prestigious award in rock music, and it has even spawned an offspring called the 'Brats' (Britain's no 1 pop group at time of writing, 'Blur', have contrived to win both).[31] In an older idiom, 'Brit' seems to serve as a touchstone of stoic virtue, rather as the English stiff upper lip used to be invoked in the days when this country prided itself on understatement. (The newspapers tell us that the headmaster of Charterhouse, involved in an extramarital liaison, 'took it on the chin like a true Brit' when asked by the governors to resign.)[32]

Philip Dodd, in *The Battle Over Britain*, audaciously attempts to appropriate the term British for postmodernist ends. Resolutely ignoring the imperial legacy – or the tribal and primitivist one – he argues that the British have always been a 'mongrel' people. Identity is not something inherited but something made and freely chosen. It is compatible with the coexistence, in any individual, of multiple and competing selves; with the phenomenon of bilingualism and second identities; and not least with the racially polyglot character of our inner cities. Britishness is not a pre-given quality or condition but a potential which can have a host of different meanings. The Ulster settlement, so far from signalling the break-up of Britain, as many Conservatives fear, might rather serve as the imaginative basis for a new unity, a 'political recognition of the legitimacy of difference and of multiple affiliations. What it is to be British ought always to be plural, not singular . . . heterogenous rather than pure; incomplete rather than monumentally finished'.[33]

II

The idea of a homogeneous people, or of a united kingdom, is not one which a historically informed view of the subject could sustain. Linguistically, ethnically, racially – if by that term one means lines of common descent – each of the peoples of the British Isles is a mongrel. The division between the Gaelic Highlands and the Sassenachs of the English-speaking Lowlands was, from the eleventh century onwards, a leitmotiv of Scottish history.[34] That between Scotland East and West, each with its distinctive political profile, religious complexion, ethnic mix and rival capital, seems hardly less momentous. (The recent scandal at Monklands, where the Labour Council was convicted of lavishing favours on the Irish-Scottish half of the constituency, shows how these oppositions can be replicated within the boundaries of a single constituency.) The Orkneys and Shetland, ceded to Scotland as part of the wedding dowry of

Princess Mathilda, were Norwegian-Danish down to 1468–69, and, as the Viking street nomenclature and 'Up-Helly-Aa' ceremonial may suggest, retain a vivid separatism (Bergen, Shetland maps seem to show, is closer, or at any rate easier to reach, than Aberdeen or Peterhead).[35] The Outer Hebrides, 'now the last stronghold of Scottish Gaelic', were for much of the Middle Ages primarily or exclusively Norse in speech, and they are collectively known in Gaelic as *Innseghall*, 'the foreigners' islands'.[36]

Wales, with its half-English border country – Flint in the north, Monmouthshire in the south – its English or half-English enclaves, and its terrible communications (it is easier to travel to Birmingham or London than to go from north to south) is – or was in the heyday of the mining industry – even more polyglot than Scotland.[37] The division between the Welsh-speaking north and west and the Anglophone counties of the south-east is a familiar one. These divisions were reproduced in Pembrokeshire, 'for almost a thousand years . . . undecided about whether to call itself English or Welsh'.[38] Here geology combined with economics and linguistics to produce two wildly contrasted ecologies. South Pembrokeshire, with its English field-systems and Anglo-Saxon place-names, the 'Little England' of the guidebooks, was conquered by the Normans in 1093 and settled by Anglo-Saxon and Flemish immigrants in the reign of Henry I. Here a fully-fledged manorial system developed, and its residues can be seen in the Norman castles and the tall battlemented church towers. Culturally, the conquest was complete. As an Elizabethan *Description* put it:

> The names of the people are mere English, each family following the English fashion in surnames. Their buildings are English-like, in townreds and villages and not in several and lone houses. Their diet is as the English people use, as the common food beef, mutton, pig, lamb, veal and kid, which usually the poorest husbandman doth daily feed on. The names of the county places are altogether English as Wiston, Picton, Haroldston, Robeston . . . so that a stranger . . . would imagine that he had travelled through Wales and come into England again.[39]

In the north, a landscape of moorland and scattered settlements, farms are small and the fields bounded by rough stone walls. 'Churches, farms and chapels look Welsh, and they usually have Welsh names'.[40] Here is Dewisland, 'the only part of Wales . . . never . . . conquered by either the English or the Normans':

> Its inhabitants are the oldest free folk in Britain. The Normans, pious if nothing else, respected the property of the Church, so that Dewisland was spared the battles and sieges that accompanied the annexation of other parts of Pembrokeshire. No stone fortress was built on its soil; no alien garrison stood ward and watch over its inhabitants. The fact that it was the land of Dewi, the patron saint, proved sufficient to preserve it from the grasping hands of the ambitious invaders.[41]

The industrial revolution, more uneven in its impact on Wales, perhaps, than in any other part of Britain, added a whole new layer of internal divisions. Little islands of industry, such as the ironworking villages of Brecon, were planted in peasant countrysides. The coal-mining complex around Wrexham, an isthmus of the industrial revolution in North Wales, was linked by the canal system to Ellesmere Port, and looked east to Cheshire rather than west to Snowdonia. In Nonconformist Wales, as it took shape in the latter part of the nineteenth century, chapel culture and a shared Liberalism concealed the vast gulf which separated rural Wales from the industrial counties of Carmarthen, Glamorgan and Monmouth. In the coal-mining country itself, pit villages existed cheek-by-jowl with hill farms and sheep runs. There was also a deeper divide between the anthracite minters of the Vale of Neath and Ammanford, Welsh-speaking, recruited from a nearby hinterland, and priding themselves on their respectability, and the altogether more uncouth villages of the Rhondda, with their fiery, dangerous pits, where labour had been recruited from as far afield as Devon, Gloucestershire and Hereford. (A.J. Cook, the tragic leader of the miners in the general strike of 1926, hailed from Wookey, Somerset, arriving to work in Porth, Rhondda, at the age of sixteen.)[42] Morally, too, it seems possible, two cultures prevailed, the one God-fearing, chapel-going and Sabbatarian, the other, complained about in nineteenth-century commissions of inquiry, quantified in bastardy rates and (as fantasized in Dylan Thomas's *Under Milk Wood*), Dionysiac.

In Ireland, as the recent 'troubles' remind us, social and political struggle has often taken the form of civil war. According to some recent research, the agrarian outrages of the nineteenth century had far more to do with neighbourhood feuds than with struggle against absentee English landlords, while in 1921–22 the struggle between Treaty and anti-Treaty factions far surpassed in bitterness and bloodiness the fight with the Black-and-Tans.[43] In Ulster, as the 'two nations' school of historians has been at pains to point out, Presbyterian religion, Scottish settlement and tenant right separated Northern Ireland from the other three provinces at an early date, while the industrial revolution of the nineteenth century linked its economic fortunes to England and Scotland at the very time when the disindustrialization of the South and West of Ireland was turning it into a backward economy. No less pertinent, so far as literature and politics are concerned, would be the chasm which opened up in the nineteenth century between the metropolitan culture of Dublin and the Gaeltacht. In 1848, the division between the *littérateurs* and lawyers of Young Ireland and the starving peasantry of Skibbereen and Co. Mayo could hardly have been more complete; it is one which, after his own fashion, James Joyce returns to in his magnificent story, 'The Dead'; and it was one which J.M. Synge and the Abbey Theatre tried to bridge when bringing the everyday speech of Connemara on to the Dublin stage.

Even within England, precociously unified as a state, but internally divided as a culture, lines of discrimination, both horizontal and vertical have been at all times the stuff of which politics is made. Local chauvinism, represented in the back streets of Victorian England by the scuttling gangs, and in the countryside by the folk radicalism of the 'skimmity ride' – readers of Thomas Hardy's *The Mayor of Casterbridge* will recall the one to which Lucetta and Henchard were subjected by the denizens of Mixen Lane – was a force to be reckoned with in the past, as it is today on those East London housing estates where newcomers are subject to racial harassment. In early modern England the municipalities used it to protect their privileges and immunities against interference by royal government or the encroachments of the Church, and it was no less serviceable to the guilds in enforcing monopoly rights. (So late as the 1850s, the Corporation of London, attempting to confine business transactions within the golden mile to freemen of the City, imposed heavy fines on merchants found guilty of trading with foreigners.) Local chauvinism was also a first resort of the authorities in times of plague, when strangers were treated as lepers, and barred at the city gates. A similar principle animated the Old Poor Law – the 43rd of Elizabeth, which governed the administration of relief throughout the seventeenth and eighteenth centuries. As the constables' accounts show, women 'bigge with child' were forever being bundled out of the parish, while paupers were shipped hither and thither to prevent them making a settlement.

The idea of 'two nations' is also one which recurs. In the nineteenth century it was conceptualized sometimes in terms of North and South, sometimes of town and country, sometimes of haves and have-nots. All of these issues came together in the 1840s when what Carlyle called 'the Condition-of-England' question was the subject of a tremendous national debate. 'We may on abstract grounds prefer a country to a manufacturing state', Sir James Graham, the Home Secretary, wrote in 1845, confiding his doubts about the Corn Laws to the Prime Minister. 'But our lot is cast . . .' A later focus of anxiety was the 'residuum', whom the social Darwinists wanted to exterminate[44] and young Mr Beveridge to put in labour camps. For the social investigators of the 1880s – and the social salvationists who followed in their wake – the poor, and in particular the 'casual' labourers of outcast London, were not only a different class but also another race, a lower depths, the inhabitants of a nether world. The eugenicists characterized them as an inferior stock, unfitted for survival. 'Not a man more than 5 feet two inches', one of Booth's investigators noted, watching a funeral crowd in the Bethnal Green Road. As recent research has shown, such observations corresponded to sober statistical fact: the mean height of an inmate at an industrial school, the late Victorian reformatory, was some seven inches less than that of a public schoolboy.[45]

Bilingualism in the present might alert us to the coexistence of rival speech communities in the past. Thus in *Tess*, where Hardy is at pains to chronicle the modernizing forces at work, Mrs Durbeyfield speaks the dialect; her daughter, who has passed the Sixth Standard in the National School under a London-trained mistress, speaks two languages: the dialect at home, 'more or less'; 'ordinary' English abroad, or when speaking to persons of quality.[46] By the same token we might be encouraged to attend to the importance, for greater or lesser periods of time, of minority tongues, as, say, the Erse of the Irish immigrants of the 1850s (at Kensal Green, graveside services would be conducted in it)[47] or the Welsh which the Anti-Corn Law League in the 1840s found it important enough to enlist native-speaking agents to address.[48] Linguistically, this country, however narrowly its boundaries are defined, is made up at any given moment of a myriad of vernaculars, each with its own esoteric vocabulary, and the passage between them is notoriously difficult to negotiate. In Wales, the division between the Anglophone counties of the south-East and the Welsh-speaking ones of the north and west is the rock on which the language movement – and with it the hopes of Plaid Cymru – have foundered. In England the two-camp division between what Bernstein calls the 'restricted' and the 'elaborated' code, or, to use less loaded terms, the demotic and the polite, has been hardly less momentous.[49] Dialect, or speaking 'broad' as it was called in early nineteenth-century Cheshire (as opposed to 'talking fine'), was a matter not only of accent but of an entire vocabulary which kept the stranger at bay. When, for instance, in 1861, a Select Committee of the House of Commons summoned a group of Northumberland miners to appear before them, to give evidence on working conditions, the services of an interpreter had to be engaged.[50] 'Thieves' Latin', the language of the underworld, was notoriously hermetic; so was its near cousin, the 'cant' of the professional tramp. The whole point of rhyming slang, Mayhew's street folk told him, was that it baffled the authorities. The vernacular of the racecourse fraternities which provided Nimrod and Surtees with their humours, and *Bell's Life in London* with its copy, is impossible to follow without a glossary of what Grose called 'the Vulgar Tongue'.[51] At the other end of the social spectrum, the language of the law, and that of the instruments of landownership, has always been heavily Latinate, while officialese, notwithstanding recurrent attempts to reform it, is famously a way of maintaining a distance between the rulers and the ruled.

Dual labour markets are another phenomenon which a more molecular view of the past, and one which built its ideas of national identity not out of similarity but of difference, would have to address. They have been extensively documented in the present day in relation to New Commonwealth enterprises and New Commonwealth immigrants, as for instance those of the East End fashion trade, where family businesses rule the roost, and both labour and capital are recruited on the basis of kinship. Feminist historians too have made a large contribution to the understanding of these dualities, by inquiring into the operation, in the workplace, of the domestically-derived dogma of separate spheres.[52] Nineteenth-century industry was honeycombed with local job monopolies, 'closed shops' (to adopt the terminology of another epoch) in which labour recruitment was by family succession; labour aristocracies who lorded it over their juvenile assistants and combined the hereditary principle with an exclusive sense of place. The Purbeck marblers – one of the great sources of nineteenth-century paving stones – are an interesting example, a company of workers who demanded descent from a quarryman grandfather in both the maternal and paternal lines.[53]

The symbolic opposition between North and South, which could be traced back fancifully to the Synod of Whitby, and the establishment of York and Canterbury as rival sees, is also something which a more molecular view of the national past would want to highlight. In medieval Oxford, where hostilities between northerners and southerners were, it seems, as frequent, and as bloody, as those between town and gown, it was a normal contingency of university life. And it also figured on a larger stage. With its Marcher lordships, such as those of the Percys, and its palatine jurisdictions, such as those of the Prince-Bishops of Durham, the North was a springboard of civil war, and it was of course under the rival standards of Yorkists and Lancastrians that those of the fifteenth century were fought out. 'Hatred between northerners and southerners was intense', a recent account tells us. 'London in 1461 closed its gates to the queen's northern army for fear of spoil "for the people in the north rob and steal and be appointed to pillage"'; a few years later, according to a southern chronicler, Richard III's distribution of land to northerners – 'to the disgrace of all the people in the south' – bulked high among his sins.[54] North and South was also one of the axes on which the earlier phases of the Reformation were fought out, the old religion finding its most courageous defenders in the Pilgrimage of Grace, while on the other side of the divide, the 'Tudor Revolution in Government', in Geoffrey Elton's phrase, was nowhere more in evidence than in the emergency jurisdiction of Henry VIII's Council of the North.

When the opposition between North and South resurfaced in the nineteenth century, it was not as a party label but rather as a point of metaphorical divide in which one was pictured as the seat of manufacture, and the other of landed wealth. For the young Charles Dickens, the North was a kingdom of toil. It was approached by the lunar landscape of the Black Country (there is a nightmare description of it in *The Old Curiosity Shop*); it harboured such monuments to inhumanity as Wackford Squeers of Dotheboys Hall (a kind of Yorkshire Sweeney Todd) and Gradgrind the number-crunching child-crusher of *Hard Times*; and it found some kind of apotheosis in the 'melancholy madness' of the steam-powered machinery and the tall factory chimneys of Coketown. For Matthew Arnold, fastidiously pouring scorn on the vanities of a commercial society, the

North was represented by gloom, smoke and cold; it was a place where people had hideous names – Higginbottom, Stiggins and Wragg are those he singles out for ridicule – where infanticide was practised, as a last resort, by the desperate; and where the spirit of literature was sacrificed at the altar of dogma.[55] These hostilities were reciprocated, and in the dialect literature of northern England, a flourishing genre in mid-Victorian times, Yorkshire 'grit' and Lancashire 'gradeliness' were contrasted to southern effeteness. London, in particular, was pictured as the home of flunkeydom, a place where the dandy and the fop disported themselves, where gentlemen made a living 'doing nowt', and where vicious poverty, of a kind unknown in the industrious North, was allowed to fester unchecked. Joseph Wright, the compiler of the dialect dictionary, and a leading light in the Dialect Society of the 1870s, found his most enthusiastic helpers were from the North and West; elevated, improbably, to an Oxford professorship (he was a Bradford lad who had left school at thirteen), he reverted (his biographer tells us) to some of his boyhood pronunciation; and he included in his dictionary the term *Throssen up*, meaning 'stuffy' or 'stuck up', a word used by his mother to describe ladies from the South.[56]

A still more momentous division, from the point of view of cross-cutting loyalties and fault-lines, would be that between Protestant and Catholic. From this point of view the *failure* of the Reformation in Ireland was quite as important as its success in England. In nineteenth-century Ireland, as Emmet Larkin's studies suggest, the success of the Catholic hierarchy in creating a state within a state, refusing mixed schooling, maintaining an independent university and pursuing, in defiance of Rome as well as London, a proto-nationalist politics prefigured even if it did not explicity prepare the way for the coming of the Irish republic.[57]

Linda Colley, in her book *Britons*, presents militant Protestantism as a great unifying force in national life, the secret of Great Britain's success. Under another optic – one which looked at the fissiparous elements in national life – it might seem to be a more ambiguous inheritance, supporting minority identities and encouraging religious sectarianism, what Matthew Arnold was to call 'the dissidence of dissent'.[58] In the seventeenth century it was one of the great issues at stake in the Civil War of the 1640s. In the eighteenth century, it persuaded many Dissenters, at the time of the American War of Independence, to side with Britain's enemies. (For the same reason, in the 1790s, a quite striking number of Dissenters sided with the French in the early stages of the Revolutionary wars.) In the nineteenth century militant Protestantism was one of the great supports of the Chapel when it defended itself against, or launched guerrilla attacks upon, the overweening arrogance of the Anglican Church. At Ashton-on-the-Hill, Lancashire, as Haslam Mills writes, in an affecting memoir of his 1880s chapel childhood, it served as an all-embracing identity. 'Aunt Margaret, challenged by a sentry, would have said not "English", certainly not "British" but "Methodist".'[59]

Militant Protestantism was also a great crucible of religious tension. In Ulster, where the Orange Order was formed, as a secret society, in the 1780s, spreading rapidly among the small farmers, and serving as a kind of Protestant counterweight to the Ribbonmen and the Peep O'Day boys, it undermined a burgeoning republican movement and persuaded Presbyterians to give primacy to confessional war. Having established itself in Ulster, Orangeism was then exported to England, following the path of Irish migration, and by the 1830s, when its secrecies were the subject of alarmed parliamentary inquiry, it was firmly established in Lancashire and the West of Scotland.[60] Ethnic strife between the English and the Irish poor – sensationally reported in the newspaper press and leaving a trail of documentation in the police records – was an endemic feature of urban life in the third quarter of the nineteenth century. Every town had its 'Little Ireland', often clustering round a St Patrick's or a St Joseph's church, and sometimes with a 'Harp of Erin' public house (and a Walsh or a Murphy funeral parlour) in the near vicinity. As Karl Marx wrote in 1870, at a time when the Irish question was beginning to emerge as the storm-centre of British politics:

> Every industrial and commercial centre in England now possesses a working class *divided* into two *hostile* camps, English proletarians and Irish proletarians. The ordinary English worker hates the Irish worker as a competitor who lowers his standard of life . . . He cherishes religious, social and national prejudices against the Irish worker . . . The Irishman pays him back with interest in his own money.[61]

In the 1860s this civil war produced a remarkable upturn in the electoral fortunes of the Conservative Party, and in the general election of 1868 – the one which followed the passage of the Second Reform Bill, and the first in which there was a working-class electorate – they played the Protestant card for all it was worth, using 'No Popery!' as their rallying cry, making the Irish Church (and Mr Gladstone's proposed disestablishment of it) the question of the day, and accusing the Liberal candidates of being crypto-Papists. In the mill towns of Lancashire it won them a majority support. 'Lancs has gone mad', wrote Mr Gladstone's agent, attempting to account for his defeat in the south-west Lancashire constituency. 'The contest . . . has been one of race, Saxon against Celt.'[62]

In another register, that of sensibility and the culture of the feelings, and from the elevated position of the professorship of poetry in the University of Oxford, Matthew Arnold, setting out to subvert the conventional wisdom of his age and to puncture the conceits of bourgeois England, lit on the Celtic as representative of everything that England was not. His lectures on Celtic literature, published in *The Cornhill*

Magazine in 1866, were a plea for the re-enchantment of the world, counterposing the mysteries of the past to the vulgar materialism of the present. He begins with a remarkable recognition of the disunity of the British Isles.

> . . . While France can truly boast of her 'magnificent unity', a unity of spirit no less than of name between all the people who compose her, in England the Englishman proper is in union of spirit with no one except other Englishmen proper like himself. His Welsh and Irish fellow-citizens are hardly more amalgamated with him now than they were when Wales and Ireland were first conquered.[63]

Then, reaching back to pre-medieval antiquity, he celebrates the bards and storytellers of the sixth century (the sources of the Arthurian legend), and offers them as a kind of indigenous equivalent to Homer. Calling on race theory – then the latest thing – he argued that there were blood differences between the Saxon and the Celt, and that they stood for antithetical principles in national life. The one were doers and achievers, the other a race of impractical dreamers. One went in for 'homely realism', the other for 'fairy-like loveliness'; one was mercurial, the other pedestrian and prosaic; one was wedded to the hegemony of fact; the other was fancy-free. In an argument which prefigured some of the favourite images of New Ageism, Arnold pictured the Celtic temperament as gay, sensual and anarchic. The Celts were Nature's own children. They had beauty, charm and spirituality, but they had no head for business or politics. Nervous, excitable, 'straining after . . . emotion', their genius was essentially a feminine one and was 'peculiarly disposed to feel the spell of the feminine idiosyncrasy'.[64]

Arnold's Celtic epistles are of a piece with his other writings in which the idea of national character looms large. Elsewhere, in his literary criticism as well as in his reports on education, he was apt to speak in derogatory terms of the 'British spirit' or the 'English intellect' and to contrast it unfavourably to the French: the English had energy but were spasmodics; the French had an instinct for order and a passion for education; they knew how to give a high and noble tone to national life. Arnold's epistles were also in line with the advanced thought of his day, in particular those versions of comparative philology in which race characteristics were spoken of as though they were generic. Arnold got much of his interest in the Celts from a reading of Renan's *Poésie des races celtiques* – the work of a leading French rationalist – and his thought also bears the impress of those theories of 'race instinct' and national 'genius' which were an intellectual commonplace of the time.[65] (Max Müller, a guru of the 1850s who had established himself as a professor of linguistics in the University of Oxford, was a possible influence here.) Thus England's greatness, as he conceived it, when putting on the patriotic hat, came from its unique mixture of 'bloods',

Teutonic, Norman and Celtic, the Normans being distinguished by their clarity, the Teutons by their plodding industry, and the Celts by their flair for style.

Celtic was a word to conjure with in mid-Victorian Britain. In archaeology it was used as a portmanteau term to describe almost anything pre-Roman. In the post-Darwinian science of biogenetics it stood for mankind in an aboriginal state.[66] Comparative philology tracked it to the remotest corners of Europe, while antiquarians and curators began to piece together the elements of it as a visual style. The discovery of Cornwall, on the part of writers, artists and musicians, and its celebration as a land of romance, a movement which got under way in the 1870s, also gave the idea of the Celtic a boost: ancient Avalon, as it were – the land of Tristan and Isolde – on England's doorstep. With the formation of the Newlyn school of painters, it also began to attract cultural dissidents.[67] Among them, an enthusiast for the revival of the Cornish language as well as an early practitioner of modernism in music was Peter Warlock. Leaving England for Ireland at the height of the Great War, attacking patriotism, and taking up one of Arnold's favourite themes, he wrote to a friend to argue that a dead language had distinct advantages over a living one. 'What more effective protest against imperialism (in art as in other matters) could you or I make than by adopting, as pure ritual, a speech, a nationality, that no longer exists?'[68]

The Celtic analogy was also to the fore, it seems, though in a negative rather than a positive sense, in colonial theory, where, after the Great Famine, Ireland was invoked as a dread example of what happened when a people failed to put itself into a progressive state. The Anglo-Saxons – enterprising, self-reliant and self-controlled – were a master race, born leaders, the only people, so Dilke believed, energetic enough to impose themselves on all comers.[69] The Celts – fickle, quick to fight and wanting in self-command – were Nature's losers, a 'cheap race', according to Dilke, who undercut the labour of the industrious settler. As *The Telegraph* put it in an article of 1862:

> We say that a little pride is pardonable to an Englishman as he turns his globe, and notes, as they pass under his hand, all these rich and fertile countries coloured 'with one brush' . . . The truth is that a prosperous hive will throw off swarms, especially if the bees feed on northern flowers. There is that old distinction between the Teuton and the Celt . . . Your Celt cannot colonise. He can seize an Algeria or a Cochin China – no one better; or, impelled by hunger, he can leave Limerick and Cork in droves to seek food in the far West; but he is not a founder of nations.

The Economist, in an article acclaiming the triumph of the efficient virtues, played with a similar set of antinomies, but preferred to put the accent on reliability:

> Thank God we are Saxons! Flanked by the savage Celt on the one side and the flighty Gaul on the other – the one a slave to his passions, the other a victim to the theories of the hour – we feel deeply grateful from our inmost hearts that we belong to a race, which if it cannot boast the flowing fancy of one of its neighbours, nor the brilliant *esprit* of the other has an ample compensation in [a] social, slow, reflective, phlegmatic temperament.[70]

The nineteenth century is often thought of as a time when Britain became a much more integrated society, and local particularisms, or liberties, were swept away. The thousands of 'select' vestries (the Webbs counted more than 11,000 of them) who had administered the old Poor Law were replaced by centrally controlled Boards of Guardians. Geographical mobility undermined the closed community. Improved transport opened up the dark corners of the kingdom, making beauty spots or scenic wonders of erstwhile wilderness, and holiday resorts of barren coasts. The schoolmaster was abroad, bringing formal education and standard English to the remotest hamlets. With the Famine exodus there was a dramatic decline in the number of Irish speakers. The Welsh language, famously attacked by the commission of inquiry into the Rebecca riots, was also on the decline, though relatively to the increase in numbers rather than in absolute terms. Through the Reform Act of 1867 the working class was brought 'within the pale of the Constitution', while with the abolition of religious Tests (1872) the children of Dissenters were allowed to enter the ancient universities.

In another way of looking at it, however, the centrifugal forces seem to be more influential than the centripetal ones in giving nineteenth-century society its distinctive shape. The advances in printing technology, for example, and the reduction in the taxes on knowledge gave a quite extraordinary prosperity to the local and provincial press. The commodification of agricultural labour gave an enhanced status to country towns. The advent of iron shipbuilding brought new concentrations of industry on the banks of the Clyde and the Tyne. Economically mid-Victorian Britain, by comparison with the present day, looks remarkably polycentric. The great manufacturers, like Sir Titus Salt at Saltaire, the millionaire who made a fortune out of alpaca, comported themselves as merchant princes, acting as master builders, patronizing the arts, and having themselves buried as though they were Egyptian sun-gods. The great towns, doubling very often in the character of regional capitals, were corporate universes. They enjoyed far more independence *vis-à-vis* the state, and far more power over the lives of the citizens, than either their predecessors or their successors (most nineteenth-century legislation was enabling, so that whether or not a town had a Free Library, or a hospital or a health service was a matter of ratepayer vote). They conducted their affairs as though they were city states, maintaining embassies abroad, staging quasi-monarchical theatricals (crowds of thousands would attend stone-laying ceremonies), and building (often in Renaissance style) the municipal equivalent of palaces. Manchester, the cotton metropolis, was one of the commercial capitals of Europe, and conducted its own foreign policy, backing the Free Trade treaty with France in 1860, and siding with the North against the South in the American Civil War (Ashton-under-Lyne and Stalybridge took the other side).[71] Its Exchange, opened in 1809 and greatly extended in 1838, 'the parliament house of the lords of cotton', was reputedly the largest in Europe, with more floor space and more dealers – some 6,000 of them when the building was further enlarged in the 1870s – than the Stock Exchange in London.[72] (By the same token Manchester Town Hall, which cost a million pounds to build, started in 1868 and completed in 1877, was larger than the House of Commons.) Cardiff, the coal metropolis, was the world headquarters of the sea-coal trade; in the 1890s and 1900s it was also locked into the Basque country, supplying that country with investment for its native industry while taking off its surplus labour for the pits at Merthyr Vale. Its castle was a millionaire's folly, built – in the very heart of the town – with the profits of the coal trade; its civic centre stands comparison with Lutyen's Delhi as a showcase of Edwardian Baroque.[73]

It is a curious fact that the third quarter of the nineteenth century saw the nationalities of Britain drawing further apart, both from each other and from Westminster, or at any rate launching out on paths which can retrospectively be seen to point in the direction of a clearer identity and greater independence. The Irish Home Rule Party was established in 1873 and was soon winning a formidable number of seats, not only in the 26 counties but also in what is today Protestant – and British – Ulster. In Wales, where 'Land of My Fathers', composed for the Eisteddfod of 1856, was already beginning to make its way as an alternative national anthem, there was a tremendous growth in the industrial economy, and a new ambition on the part of the middle class. The clean sweep of the liberals in the 1868 general election served as a rejection of English (and Anglican) hegemony, relegating 'to the position of a minority religion the Church which had so long enjoyed an undisputed social and political as well as religious dominance'.[74] It was followed, in the 1870s, by the foundation of a National University of Wales, a National Library, and a National Museum.[75] Scotland, in the same period, saw the birth of a national party – the short-lived National Association for the Vindication of Scottish Rights[76] – and more pertinently, the establishment of the embryo of home rule, first through a series of *ad hoc*, quasi-autonomous Scottish boards – for poor law, lunacy, agriculture and fisheries[77] – then, in 1885, after a high-level public campaign waged by the advocates and the burghs, through the establishment of a Scottish Office, 'one of the landmarks in the growth of Scottish national self-consciousness',[78] and the origin of today's system of dual power, in which Westminster plays second fiddle when Scottish questions are at stake. (In 1885 the Office

Manchester Town Hall, from a drawing by Alfred Waterhouse, 1869

was transferred from London to Edinburgh; and it became the conduit for collectivist interventions of all kind, from the protection of crofters' tenancies to the establishment of public works.) Reference might be made finally to Ulster, which in the wake of the great Revival of 1859 began to flex its muscles as the champion of militant Protestantism (the Murphy riots of 1867–68, which produced such turmoil in Lancashire, Birmingham and the Black Country, were an outcrop of Ulster Protestantism's new-found electoral militancy), striking out on a path of its own.

As well as the rise of an ethnic politics, the third quarter of the nineteenth century also saw the appearance of a whole series of language movements which had the effect of giving an altogether new symbolic importance to the idea of a folk. In Scotland these movements went hand in hand with the Crofters' agitation and the campaign for land reform; in Ireland they prefigured a deliberate attempt to 'de-Anglicize' the national culture; in Wales they were a kind of antiphon to industrialization. These movements were to a remarkable extent in the hands of exiles. The eisteddfodau had been relaunched, in the 1810s, by the London Welsh, and a similar pattern emerged with the Highland Associations and the Gaelic Societies, all of which seem to have begun life in Scotland's larger towns. J.S. Blackie, the key figure in the Crofters' War of the 1880s, and the great missionary of the Gaelic, was not a Highlander at all, but an Aberdonian, and professor of Greek at Edinburgh University. He had become interested in 'gaeldom' during a series of walking holidays, was capitvated by the people and language of the Highlands, took up the cause of the crofters in the press and gradually became immersed in a kind of Celtic twilight of his own creation. 'He wrote poems about the Highlands, built a house at Oban called Altnacraig, compared the Highlanders with the ancient Greeks, toured the Highlands raising small contributions towards the endowment of a Celtic chair at Edinburgh, and became by far the best known of all the champions of the Highlanders'.[79]

The Gaelic revival in Ireland was a literary and artistic movement before it became a culture and a politics. Thus in the case of Irish calligraphy – of the kind used in the Proclamation of the Republic in Easter 1916 – it seems to have been the publications of the Irish Archaeological Society, begun at Dublin in 1841, which created a taste and established a style. The type-face was based on the Book of Kells, the earliest Irish manuscript; the designer, George Petrie, was an artist as well as an antiquary.[80] It was likewise the *Irish Minstrelsy*, an anthology of Gaelic lyrics published in 1831, and the bardic poetry translated by Samuel Ferguson, 'embodying the legends and sagas of Ireland's pre-Christian, heroic age', which provided both the model for nationalist history and, at least in the case of Padraig Pearse, the inspiration for the Easter Rising itself. (Yeats, though it was not his intention, had made some contribution to this in his play *Cathleen ni Houlihan*, first performed in 1902, which drew on a famous bardic figure to create a secular myth of the nation in arms.)[81] Again, it was the 'contagious grandeur' of the newly rediscovered narratives of the ancient order which led Standish O'Grady to publish, in 1878, volume I of his *Bardic History of Ireland*, entitling it *The Heroic Period* – a warrior vision which, along with others, he was later to embody in a politics.[82]

One of the less noticed features of the Gaelic Revival was its affinities with the Arts and Crafts movement. Yeats spent much of his boyhood and adolescence in Bedford Park, the 'aesthetic' West London suburb where so many of the ideals of English vernacular were first given a public view. It was while living there that Yeats's sisters, Elizabeth and Lily, learnt needlework from May Morris, the original inspiration for the embroidery workshop and Dun Emer Press which they established in Dublin in the early 1900s. In 1902, together with her other sister, Susan, Elizabeth helped to found an Arts and Crafts 'settlement' at Dundrum.[83] Archibald Knox, one of the great pioneers of the idea of 'Celtic design', served his architectural apprenticeship with Baillie Scott, the Arts and Crafts furniture maker who did so much to influence the shape of Hampstead Garden Suburb and Welwyn Garden City.[84] It says something of the kindred feeling of the two movements – each looking back to a vernacular purity – that when Walter Crane, the English socialist artist, wanted to reassert the radical calling of the Arts and Crafts movement, he did so by exhibiting an Irish Nationalist banner of his own design; and it would be instructive to compare the iconography of Crane's May Day banners and posters, with their maypoles, wheatsheafs and indeterminately bucolic peasants, with the shamrocks, harps and round houses which the Gaelic Revival established as of the essence of Celtic art.[85]

Could one speak of an *English* ethnic revival, a movement, in linguistics, in literature and in art, which celebrated the English not as a race of achievers or of conquerors – the place which the word had in the lexicon of later Victorian imperialism – but as a *folk*? The most obvious parallel would be in letters, where, partly through the instrumentality of the local and provincial press, dialect literature, which made a great play with regional types, flourished. In a more scholarly vein there was the founding of the County Dialect societies, a nationwide movement of the 1870s and 1880s, and the printing of the County glossaries – local lexicons in which the Saxon tongue appeared as a kind of Ur-language of England[86] – 'carried in unbroken tradition down to the present' (one of the great enthusiasts for it was James Murray, the creator of the *Oxford English Dictionary*). Independently, but parallel, the 1870s and 1880s saw the crystallization of an idea of what was called, in the publications devoted to it, 'Social England', a history of everyday things, or 'natural' history, a history with the politics left out, but with material culture, in the form of recipes, charms and cures, household chores, affectionately described. Period costume and occupational dress were carefully illustrated – the Elizabethan ruff being a particular favourite – period rooms, showing changes in the domestic interior, lovingly reconstructed. The Englishwoman was given as much imaginative attention as the men. (It is quite wrong to think that women only enter 'our island story' with the advent of 1970s feminism.)[87]

The literary movement had its counterpart in the rediscovery of forgotten calendar customs and the reinvention of local tradition. The Anglican Church, working in the country parishes, gave some sort of lead here, filling out the Christian Year with such restored or reinvented festivities as May games and Harvest Homes, and in mid-Victorian times it was quite often country parsons – Sabine Baring-Gould, the immensely prolific popularizer of West Country lore, and collector of traditional song, is a brilliant example – who began the work of documenting local custom.[88] Later it was the turn of more secular spirits, such as the musicologists who embraced the cause of folk-song, or the protagonists of advanced educational ideas, introducing country dancing into the school curriculum.[89] Cecil Sharp, the 'discoverer' of English Morris, was a Fabian and a progressive, who believed that he was calling on the heritage of the old world to redress the balance of the new.[90] For Mary Neal and her 'Esperance' followers in London's elementary schools, Morris dancing, by putting the children in contact with Nature, would counteract the malodorous influence of the slum.[91]

The discovery of Tudor music, a movement which seems to have got under way in the 1890s, and which by 1920 was sufficiently advanced to support a systematic inventory, detailing holdings in cathedrals, churches and schools, was some kind of counterpart to this in the field of high art, setting in train a musicological search for the taproot of national being, encouraging the idea of a national opera, and promoting the Elizabethan madrigal as the quintessential national song. ('Greensleeves', Vaughan Williams's pastiche of it, composed in 1929, became a kind of unofficial national anthem.)[92]

The Arts and Crafts equivalent of this, practised at such places as the Ancoats settlement or in such community-building experiments as that of C.R. Ashbee and the Whitechapel artisans who established themselves at Chipping Camden in the Cotswolds, was the revival of cottage manufacturers and the protection of regional skills. On the example of Morris and Co., domestic needlework and embroidery were marketed as art products, and sold through the medium of such taste-leaders as Liberty's and Heal's in London. There were strenuous and partly successful efforts to protect the country lacemakers, while hand-thrown pottery was promoted as a kind of artless art. The accent was on the regional and the rustic – the Cotswolds, 'discovered' by William Morris, were at the heart of the Arts and Crafts imagination – but in the hands of modernizing spirits such as Lethaby, in the second generation of the Arts and Crafts

Empire Stories: The Imperial and the Domestic*

I

Mrs Gaskell's *Cranford* (1851) is as provincial a novel as it would be possible to imagine. It is set in a small country town in northern England – to all intents and purposes Knutsford, Cheshire, where the author spent the formative years of her youth. The local society she describes is, on the face of it, 'narrow', 'exclusive' and 'indifferent to the world outside its boundaries', and the narrative entirely domestic.[1] The drama, if it can be called that, centres on the embarrassments and timidities of Miss Matty, an ageing spinster whose little shop is a failure. Yet India is quite an insistent pressure on the story. It provides Miss Matty with her muslin gown, and the more fashionable with their shawls (the cashmere shawl was, it seems, as much an object of desire in early Victorian Cheshire as the twin-set and pearls were to the would-be lady of the 1920s, while the turban was a kind of ultimate in exotica). India also figures as a source of mystery and magic. It is the place where Miss Matty's long-lost brother, Peter, Hindooized into the Aga Jenkyns, makes, if not a fortune, at least a sufficient competence to rescue her from penury, and enable her to live out her remaining years in 'genteel' comfort. And it turns Sergeant Smith, a humble soldier of the 31st Regiment, stationed in India, into the exotically names 'Signor Brunoni' whose exhibition of conjuring, learnt from an Indian juggler, takes the Cranford Assembly Rooms by storm. In recounting the odyssey as told by his wife, Mrs Gaskell takes us to India itself:

> Sam was a sergeant in the 31st; and when the regiment was ordered to India, I drew a lot to go, and I was more thankful than I can tell; for it seemed as if it

* This essay had at least two immediate prompts: one, a round-table discussion on race and racism held by the Commission for Racial Equality in 1994; another, the debates about the place of empire in proposals for school history by the National Curriculum History Working Group. It was left unrevised as a 'preliminary draft' (footnotes 8–14 were appended by the author) at a very early stage.

would only be a slow death to me to part from my husband. But, indeed, ma'am, if I had known all, I don't know whether I would not rather have died there and then, than gone through what I have done since. To be sure, I've been able to comfort Sam, and to be with him; but, ma'am, I've lost six children,' said she, looking up at me with those strange eyes, that I've never noticed but in mothers of dead children – with a kind of wild look in them, as if seeking for what they never more might find. 'Yes! Six children died off, like little buds nipped untimely, in that cruel India. I thought as each died, I never could – I never could – love a child again; and when the next came, it had not only its own love, but the deeper love that came from the thoughts of its little dead brothers and sisters. And when Phœbe was coming, I said to my husband, "Sam, when the child is born, and I am strong, I shall leave you; it will cut my heart cruel; but if this baby dies too, I shall go mad; the madness is in me now; but if you let me go down to Calcutta, carrying my baby step by step, it will maybe work itself off; and I will save, and I will hoard, and I will beg, – and I will die, to get a passage home to England, where our baby may live!" God bless him! he said I might go; and he saved up his pay, and I saved every pice I could get for washing or any way; and when Phœbe came, and I grew strong again, I set off. It was very lonely; through the thick forests, dark again with their heavy trees – along by the river's side – (but I had been brought up near the Avon in Warwickshire, so that flowing noise sounded like home) – from station to station, from Indian village to village, I went along, carrying my child. I had seen one of the officers' ladies, with a little picture, ma'am – done by a Catholic foreigner, ma'am – of the Virgin and the little Saviour, ma'am. She had him on her arm, and her form was softly curled round him, and their cheeks touched. Well, when I went to bid good-by to this lady, for whom I had washed, she cried sadly; for she, too, had lost her children, but she had another to save, like me; and I was bold enough to ask her, would she give me that print? And she cried the more, and said *her* children were with that little blessed Jesus; and gave it me, and told me she had heard it had been painted on the bottom of a cask, which made it have that round shape. And when my body was very weary, and my heart was sick – (for there were times when I misdoubted if I could ever reach my home, and there were times when I thought of my husband, and one time when I thought my baby was dying) – I took out that picture and looked at it, till I could have thought the mother spoke to me, and comforted me. And the natives were very kind. We could not understand one another; but they saw my baby on my breast, and they came out to me, and brought me rice and milk, and sometimes flowers – I have got some of the flowers dried. Then, the next morning, I was so tired! and they wanted me to stay with them – I could tell that – and tried to frighten me from going into the deep woods, which, indeed, looked very strange and dark: but it seemed to me as if Death was following me to take my baby away from me; and as if I must go on, and on – and I thought how God had cared for mothers ever since the world was made, and would care for me; so I bade them good-by, and set off afresh. And once when my baby was ill, and both she and I needed rest, He led me to a place where I found a kind Englishman lived, right in the midst of the natives.'[2]

I have quoted this passage at length, partly because it can serve as an exemplum for the theme of this paper (the interplay of the imperial and the domestic), but also because it may serve to remind us that what Edward Said has influentially called 'Orientalism' was by no means necessarily a pathological affair.[3] It would need a Gaskell scholar to track down the possible sources of this story, and to speculate on how far it corresponded to the deep structures of her thought. But the entire absence of that 'racism' which is allegedly endemic in the English imagination, and which is supposed to be peculiarly virulent in relationship to what used to be called coloured people, is striking; so too is the trust in the goodness and charity of the Indian people and the belief that they shared a common humanity with their alien rulers. It is very much of a piece with that Christian Universalism which – as the scholars of Victorian race theories have shown – was being powerfully canvassed at this time by the Nonconformist and Chapel supporters of the Anti-Slavery cause in the United States, as also for some of the pioneering missionary work in Africa.

Then – a matter which really needs a historian of the occult to elucidate – there is the association of India with mystery and magic. One might inquire here into the nineteenth-century circuses and menageries, perhaps find when snake charmers, or the Indian Rope Trick, first made an English appearance (to judge by Mrs Gaskell, quite early in the century).

Interesting too, coming from the wife of a Christian minister, is the tentative respect shown for Indian religion, a note which was to be amplified and extended in missionary commentary, if only to explain the obstacles faced by India's would-be evangelists. Here for example, appended to a history of the British rule in India, published in 1880, and written by a Wesleyan minister, the Rev. J. Shaw Banks, is the fascinated account of one of its adversaries:

> As the methods and results of missionary labour largely depend upon the general character and circumstances of the people, a few remarks on this subject may not here be out of place.*
>
> With respect to the vernacular languages of India, it is to be observed that most of them are altogether independent of Sanscrit in their origin and structure. Sanscrit is strictly the language of the Brahmins, was introduced and has been exclusively cultivated by them. Whether it was ever spoken in India is unknown. The Brahmins are fond of representing Sanscrit as the parent, not only of all Indian languages, but of all the languages of the world, and support their position by words resembling each other in sound, but connected in no other way. In point of fact, the Indian vernaculars are purely indigenous. As might be expected, those spoken in the north, where the Brahmins, entering by the north-west, first settled, have the largest infusion of Sanscrit; but even in

* One of the best compends on the subject of Hindu life in general is *The Land of the Vēda*, by the Rev. P. Percival (London, G. Bell, 1854), now unfortunately out of print, but sometimes to be met with. On Hindu philosophy and literature, Williams's *Indian Wisdom* is full and trustworthy.

these the substance and structure differ fundamentally from Sanscrit, and in the south the Sanscrit element is much less. Here the influence of Sanscrit is far less than that of Latin on English. There are even translations of the great Sanscrit epics in the purest vernacular. In the villages a Sanscritized vernacular would be unintelligible. Dr. Caldwell in his *Comparative Dravidian Grammar* shows that the vernaculars belong, not to the Aryan, but to the Turanian family. . . .

Sanscrit literature is remarkable for its extent, richness and antiquity. It covers the entire field of mental activity. The most ancient portion consists of the four sacred Vēdas, which are generally placed somewhere between 2,000 and 1,000 BC. These books are objects of extraordinary veneration to the Hindus. But it would be a mistake to suppose that they exert any practical influence, save in the most remote way, on Hindu life. Beyond their names little is known of them in India. It must be remembered that an intelligent acquaintance even with what may be called modern classical Sanscrit is by no means a common acquirement among Brahmins; and the Sanscrit of the Vēdas differs far more from classical Sanscrit than the English of Chaucer does from that of Addison and Pope. Again, the teaching of the Vēdas represents a phase of opinion and faith which India left behind many long ages ago. The Vēdic religion is nature-worship. It knows nothing whatever of the multifarious deities and incarnations of modern Hinduism. The Vēdāntists, who profess a desire to return to the simplicity of the Vēdic faith, represent the latter as a system of philosophical theism; but to do this is simply to read their own ideas into the Vēdic writings. Philosophical theism, or rather pantheism, is the doctrine of the Vēdāntist philosophy, which is a much later development of Vēdic teaching. In India at present 'the Vēda' is little more than a name to conjure by.

In reality, the authoritative religious books which sway the religious life of the masses are neither the Vēdas nor the Purānas – mythological works far more recent, – but the great epic poems, the Mahā Bhārata and Rāmāyana, as these are read in whole or part, known through translations, or rendered into popular song, story and drama. These wonderful creations of poetical genius – perfect forests of legend and myth, in which Eastern imagination has run riot – have for ages shaped popular religious faith in India. The Rāmāyana especially, the story of Vishnu's incarnation in the form of the hero Rāma, has taken a deep hold on the popular imagination, has been reproduced in numberless forms, and may be regarded as the gospel of the Hindus. The higher religious thought of the nation finds perfect expression in the Bhagavad-geeta, an extract from the Mahā Bhārata, which teaches the purest pantheism in the smoothest verse. Of the mere literary works, this is not the place to speak. It may be mentioned, however, that the drama of Shakuntala is beautiful, even in a foreign dress, and in its original form is perfect in grace and delicacy.

The philosophical systems of India remind us of the speculations of ancient Greece, only that they are elaborated and commented on with far greater fulness and precision.[4]

Another 1851 text, in this case the excited accounts of the Indian exhibits at the Great Exhibition, may serve to show how India was freely associated with the marvellous:

We pass from the main avenue into the Indian collection, and examine thoughtfully the products of the Empire in the East. What do they tell us? Those jewels, that rich display of mineral and vegetable produce, those shawls and carpets in which the harmony of colours is so admirably represented; filagree work in silver and gold, brocaded stuffs, curiously executed carvings, rude models of machinery, musical instruments, arms, elephant trappings, naval architecture – how suggestive they all are, and what stories they tell. Here are gathered together the trophies of ancient civilization and arts, marvellously carried down to our own time. Here may be studied the industrial habits of nations preserved through centuries without change or progress, yet still wonderful and magnificent in the eyes of modern labour. Look at those alabaster chairs, how regal they appear, how fitly they represent a country where many dynasties conquered and flourished and were overcome before the British sway was established over its dusky populations. Nearly everything in that collection which is the work of man's hand indicates a vast expenditure of time for its production and a great display of taste. Yet it is nearly all ornamental rather than useful in its character. Whenever the really useful arts appear rudeness of material and design are visible. A warlike weapon will be finished off in the most elaborate style, yet a pair of scissors be manufactured in a manner worthy of the South Sea Islanders. The East India company begin their rule of India as if it were a new country. The evidences of barbaric pomp, the State umbrellas, the cloth of gold, and robes decorated with pearls and diamonds, concern not them. These belong to the natives, to the traditions of the past, and to industries which have been bequeathed from age to age as an heirloom. Our part of the collection is the raw produce – the mineral, vegetable, and animal treasures undiscovered and unused till our commerce and the wants of our manufactures sought them out. Resting upon them, we strive to build on substantial and permanent foundations the structure of empire and government in India; at least, that is the lesson which the Exhibition seems to teach, and the question which each visitor asks himself as he surveys that most interesting collection is, 'Shall we succeed in our attempt?'

Here the visitor may survey the wondrous products of countries whose names are romances – Cachmere, Delhi, Benares, Mirzapore, Gyah – consisting of lovely shawls, muslins worked in silk and gold, carpets in whose downy surfaces the footfall noiselessly sinks, exquisite mats, and metal manufactures, besides a variety of fragrant woods, perfumes, gums, cereals, earths, and dried fruits. The eye catches gilded parasols and glistening canopies, and flowing tissues of cloth of gold. Let us visit the East India Company's gorgeous tent. An admiring crowd blocks up the threshold. Watching our time, we, too, catch a glimpse of that marvellous interior. It is a bit out of the Arabian Nights. The tapestried walls are one blaze of glistening metal, wrought, nevertheless, in the loom. On the ground, heaped up masses of velvet and brocade carpets, piled into thrones for Oriental potentates: screens and chairs of state, marvels of cunning carved work; models and devices, all smacking of the Orient; elephants and camels, moulded from the brightest ivory; fans and wavy brushes, to cool swart and jewelled features of Khan or Rajah. In such a tent might the Peri Banou have spread her carpet – in such a tent might fabled genii have done homage to Solomon – in such a tent might the Caliph Haroun Alraschid have listened to the heedless merchant who flung the date-stones – in such a

A drawing, entitled 'State Umbrellas', used to illustrate this extract when originally published in *The Illustrated Exhibitor*, October 1851

tent might have passed the loves of Noureddin and the fair Persian. To come down to authentic times – the fabrics and the ornaments are wondrous pieces of barbaric splendour, but their true significance is to be found without, in the occupants of the ledge which surrounds the Oriental Pavilion; there stand a legion of MODELS OF INDIAN ARTIFICERS and handicraftsmen and women. Can these be the people who have woven these magnificent fabrics, who have carved these wondrous ornaments in scented wood, in ivory, and in gold? A lean, starved-out regiment of squalid beggars, half naked, or with scanty folds of coarsest cotton flung around their wasted limbs, labouring with rudest, roughest implements – the weaver sitting in holes in the earth before the handful of rickety sticks which constitute the loom; the cook toiling with his pot of ghee and his dish of rice; the snake-charmer piping to the hooded cobra; the musician dolefully thrumming his tumtum; the potter squatted beside his wheel; the husbandman standing upon the bullock-drawn harrow, so as to force the wooden teeth into the ground; the women, always by twos, grinding the corn in the rude, rough hand-mill. How the well-remembered verse comes across the mind as we gaze, 'There shall be two women grinding at the mill – one shall be taken and the other left.'

And still the wonder is, how such people and such tools produce such results as we have seen. Look into the glittering pavilion; you will fancy yourself in fairyland. Look outside – examine the model population ranged all round that gorgeous marquee, and you will dream of a horde of squalid, starved barbarians. Nevertheless, let us examine closer into their labour. See these ranges of cunning potters' work, the cups and goblets shaped with

> native grace and artless symmetry. Look at that inlaid work of elaborately combined metals – hookahs, and jars, and sacred ornaments. Mark all those brazen lamps and candelabra, borrowed from temples and native shrines, and observe the innumerable fabrics of cloths and gauzes, gaudily spotted, and crossed, and striped – some of them coarse and strong as sail-cloth, others light as gossamer – the productions these – with the jewellery and the cloth of gold – of a compound of strangely-constituted nations. Again another range of specimens of pottery stretches out before; observe the exquisite shape of the vases and the jars, the beauty of the curves, the symmetry of the proportion. For thousands of years has the manufacture been probably stationary – for thousands of years has the child imitated the shapes his father taught him. When Alexander conquered India, these vases were probably made as they are made now. May it not be true that all art, as all lore, came from the East – that the old Etruscan caught his inspiration from thoughts conceived by the Ganges or the Indus?[5]

To an Indian historian, remembering the ruin of the handicraft textile trades from the competition of Manchester goods – the time when, as the Governor of Bengal wrote, 'the bones of the cotton weavers are bleaching the plains of India' – such passages as the above may seem obscene. To the English social historian, intent on recreating the lived experience of the past, they are more likely to seem irrelevant – an alien intrusion on a territory which has been staked out for the 'ordinary' and the 'everyday'. The 'new wave' social history of the 1960s, in particular, with its strongly marked preference for the close-up rather than the aerial view, and its preoccupation with such domestic matters as household formation and labour process, or rituals of rebellion and resistance, had not imaginative space for overseas conquest and trade, let alone for such marvels as the Koh-i-Noor diamond or the lure of what the Victorians delighted to call 'the unchanging East'. In their account the Great Exhibition stands as an emblem of progress and improvement, a showcase of mechanical invention in which Britain laid claim to being 'the Workshop of the World'.

Another possible reason for the neglect of such passages is that in British history, as it is taught in the schools, or learned at university, the imperial dimension is apt to crop up episodically – in the form of the eighteenth-century slave trade (subject to a renewed attention under the influence of anti-racism), at the time of the American Revolution (the only point at which it enters the prescribed subjects of the National Curriculum History Working Party), or in the *fin-de-siècle* epoch of the Scramble for Africa and the Boer War.

The 1840s was a decade when the imperial idea was notoriously at a low ebb. Free traders, intent on dismantling the relics of the mercantile system, had no time for it, believing that it was a fetter on, rather than encouragement to, trade. The political economists of the 1830s and 1840s, though ready to consider colonies as a means of siphoning off surplus population, and resettling redundant labour, shied off any other breach with the principles of laissez-faire. For the more radical, the colonies were 'a grand system of outdoor relief for the English upper classes'. In the wake of the Canadian unrest, and the disasters of the Afghan Wars, it was hardly more appealing to the conservative. For Disraeli, in a later incarnation the apostle of imperialism, but in the 1840s a proponent of 'Country party' ideology, colonies were 'a mill-stone round our neck'.[6]

In retrospect, it is possible to see the 1840s as one of the decades in which the foundations of the Second British Empire were laid. In the Indian subcontinent itself, what Marx called the 'ethnographical, political and military frontiers'[7] of the British rule were secured by the compulsory annexation of the Punjab and Sind. Aden, the rock which was to have a pivotal place in British naval strategy down to the 1960s, and which was administered, after the formal establishment of a British Protectorate, as part of the Presidency of Bombay, was occupied in 1839.[8] David Livingstone began his missionary work in Africa in 1841.

Episodes like this could no doubt be singled out in any decade of modern British history, from the plantation of the Virginia colony down to the Suez adventure and the Falklands War. The example of Aden – or the Sikh and Afghan wars of 1838 to 1849 – might be matched by those punitive expeditions – or 'small Victorian wars' – which, as Gallagher and Robinson argued in *Africa and the Victorians*, were as much concerned with imperial defence, and protecting the trade route to India, as with the acquiring of new territories. The history of Britain is for some four centuries a history of Empire. From the founding of the East India Company in 1600, it was quite central to this country's overseas trade – never more so than in the 1930s, the epoch of protective tariffs and imperial preference, when the colonies and dominions accounted for some 70 per cent of the country's imports, and 99 per cent of its capital exports.

It was the war in the Carnatic from 1746 to 1763 which, quite as much as the Duke of Marlborough's campaigns in the Low Countries, established Britain as a great military power, just as it was the conquest of Jamaica which laid the basis of England's pre-eminence in the Atlantic economy.

For a rather brief period, which might be dated from, say, Sir John Seeley's *Expansion of England* (1883) down to, but not beyond, the Great War, Empire appeared in the school textbooks as a kind of ultimate fulfilment of the country's historic mission, and earlier phases of national history were reinterpreted in the light of it. England was, quite simply, the greatest nation in the world ('many countries are larger than England, none is more important'),[9] and the Empire something which had constantly expanded since the reign of Queen Elizabeth, 'and . . . is still growing, almost from year to year'.[10] Egypt, for the compilers of *The Pictorial History of the British Empire* (1889), was the latest acquisition. 'Though . . . not properly a colony of Great Britain, yet in view of the control so long exercised by her . . . and the present administration of Egypt by England, the lands of the Nile may be appropriately included in a review of the colonial labours of Great Britain'.[11] The Canadian Pacific Railway, when completed – 'this grand Imperial highway'[12] – would be the Suez Canal of North America; while Suez itself was becoming as much home territory as the English Channel.

Such gung-ho attitudes did not survive the trauma of the Great War. In the Baldwin era, in history as in politics, a more introverted note prevails. Elizabeth I began to be studied in relation to her troublesome parliaments rather than as the Gloriana of the poets and seafarers; 'independent country gentlemen' replace Empire-builders as Tory folk heroes, while that much underrated anti-imperialistic tract *1066 And All That* punctured the more bombastic claims of drum-and-trumpet history. In the schools (according to a 1927 Board of Education report) this is the time when Green's *Short History of the English People* makes its influence truly felt, while series such as the 'Piers Plowman' histories deliberately turned attention from the history of the state to that of everyday things. The historians of the period – Eileen Power and Sir Lewis Namier provide interestingly contrasted examples – enter into an altogether more affectionate relationship with their subjects, celebrating them no longer for their heroism but rather for their ordinariness.

In history, as in the rhetoric of Baldwin and MacDonald, England appears as a land of villages. The more aspiring (Evelyn Waugh's Mr Samgrass in *Brideshead Revisited* is a well-chosen figure) began to haunt the muniment rooms of the country houses; the more democratic (one might speculate) took part in such symptomatic historical initiatives of the period as the Place-Names Society (founded by Frank Stenton and Professor Mawer in 1923). In economic history (another new academic initiative of this period) the Arcadian note, if less premeditated than in the rhetoric of Baldwin and MacDonald, is unmistakable. Eleanora Carus-Wilson discovered the remote origins of capitalism in the fulling-mills of the thirteenth-century estate; Eileen Power picturesquely associated it with the Woolsack and Perpendicular churches; Clapham and Ashton set the industrial revolution not in dark Satanic mills but in the rural setting of the Pennines. The patriotic note does not disappear – it is indeed in certain respects even more pronounced than in the pre-1914 years – but it finds an entirely fresh terrain, that of old-fashioned character. Whereas before 1914 the English had been apt to praise themselves for abundant energy and will, it now turned out that they were really, at heart, a race of lovable eccentrics, not a military people at all, nor yet intrepid explorers. According to one representation (that of Orwell) they were a gentle, flower-growing people, averse to power-worship and enamoured of private life. According to another (Sir Ernest Barker), they displayed a positive preference for 'muddling through'. A mild people, like the schoolmaster-heroes of *The Lady Vanishes* and

Goodbye Mr Chips. They dressed quietly and kept calm while the rest of the world went mad.[13]

It is a disturbing paradox to anyone who is a partisan of 'history from below', like the present writer, that national history is less nationalistic – or at any rate less ethnocentric – than local history, which avoids the embarrassments and difficulties posed by multiculturalism or race by limiting its attention to those who can plausibly be represented in a unitary fashion, as a folk. A national history must deal in geopolitical realities which transcend national frontiers, addressing itself to such phenomena as wars and conquests, treaties and alliances, trade routes and spheres of influence. It can hardly ignore the imperial dimension of British history, if only because, from the time of the Spanish Armada down to that of the Falklands War, it was central to every British war effort, and bound up with this country's very existence both as a trading nation and a world power.

From the point of view of the imperial dimension of British history, the late Victorian and Edwardian readers, textbooks and primers, with their 'confident' assumption that the British were a master-race, with a God-given mission to set an example to the world, were distinctly superior to today's multicultural and liberal ones, with their fear of doing anything which might offend susceptibilities or arouse uncomfortable passions. Particularly debilitating (in the present writer's view) is the set of anxieties relating to 'identity' and the way, both on the right and on the left of politics, and in the centre, that it is supposed to regulate both what children learn at school and the way they learn it. Consider, for instance, the near-disappearance of Empire both in the recent debates on the place of history in the 'core' curriculum, and earlier, in the Schools Council History Projects. For the 'Progressives' of the 1960s, Empire, the British national identity itself, was something to escape from, and the history they promoted was *either* intensely local *or* global 'Third World' history – 'grandmother's washing day', in one incarnation, pre-colonial civilizations (as in 'Building an Arawak hut') in another. When Conservatives, in the 1980s, began agitating for a return to national history, starting with Sir Keith Joseph in 1984, they were hardly less anxious than the Progressives to avoid anything which might be open to the charge of being a return to 'drum-and-trumpet history'. The most that Kenneth Baker could bring himself to say, when, as Education Secretary, he addressed the Conservative Party Conference in 1989, was that the British Empire had been 'a force for good' – hardly the spirit of *The Man Who Would Be King* or Sir Henry Newbolt's *Vitaï Lampada.*

The valiant attempt of the National Curriculum History Working Group to reconcile the passions of 'progressives' and 'traditionalists', and to produce some consensual prescriptions for the new 'core' curriculum, helps to highlight the difficulties of both positions – as also perhaps the weakness of allowing identity politics, and multicultural politics in particular, to shape the contents of a history curriculum. Honourably determined to promote a spirit of tolerance and a recognition of 'ethnic diversity', the History Working Group adopt a 'four-nations' approach to their country's historical past and show themselves anxious at every turn to give due recognition to 'minorities'. Their way of 'combatting racial and other forms of prejudice', a major preoccupation, is on the one hand to emphasize the 'cultural diversity' of Britain itself, on the other to have children study 'non-western civilizations' (e.g. pre-colonial Africa) 'from their own perspectives'. Space is allotted here for the study of the black presence in Britain – as also for other minorities such as Jews – but with the exception of a single option at Key Stage 3 the British Empire disappears from the island story. The tripartite classification to which they continually return is one of 'Britain', 'Europe' and 'The World', as in 'Britain's relationship to other parts of the world'. 'The World' appears, not as a cockpit of national and international rivalries, but rather as a kind of global space in which 'peoples' are forever on the move and new technologies make their impact. Instead of the Elizabethan sea-dogs, Drake's drum or Lord Fisher's 'Dreadnought' the Interim Report offered that altogether more innocuous phenomenon, 'Ships and Shipping', appealing not to the juvenile Horatio Nelson or Sir Walter Raleigh, but to the youngster perhaps who likes messing about in boats. (The Final Report amended this to the hardly less innocuous 'Navigators and Explorers'.) In a similarly benevolent spirit, there were 'good reasons' for studying European history. 'Britain is part of Europe. Its history has helped to shape and been shaped by that of its European neighbours'. Caribbeans it seems, or Asians, are to be studied in the same spirit, not as the subject peoples of the largest empire the world has ever seen, but as friends and neighbours, 'peoples' who have chosen to settle here, like the Romans, the Anglo-Saxons, the Jews and the Huguenots before them.

II

In the version of history on which I was brought up – a Communist variant of anti-war liberalism, and of the propaganda and thought of Pro-Boer Little Englanders – imperialism was the product of a very definite, and rather limited, epoch, a phase of development in which, as we believed, capitalism turned parasitic, exchanging free trade for protection, and individual enterprise for monopoly. Globally, it was a response to the Great Depression in industry and trade – a pan-European 'glut' of the 1870s and 1880s which squeezed profit margins to a minimum and reduced excess capacity in manufacture. It opened up a vast new field for commercial energies, cushioning the effects of diminishing returns on domestic investment, and bringing windfall gains to those who could corner the international market in raw materials. It also represented a sea-change in commercial organization, being associated with the rise of cartels, syndicates and trusts – combines and co-partnerships which, like the great chartered companies of West Africa, owed their fortune to colonial concessions. Imperialism transformed Britain (so Hobson argued in his brilliant 1902 book on the subject) from an industrial into a creditor state. It replaced factory masters with financiers, such as the international speculators (for the most part, Hobson argued, 'German Jews') who ruled the roost in the Transvaal gold-fields. And it peopled Southern England with rentiers: in the 1900s, the coupon clippers and dividend drawers of the rapidly growing coastal resorts; the retired colonial officials and planters who added the bungalow and the verandah to the stock of English domestic architecture; and not least, according to George Orwell, the quite considerable Anglo-Indian colony, beached up in the West London suburb of Ealing, whose homes smelt perpetually of Trichinopoly cigars, and were so full of spears, blow-pipes, brass ornaments and the heads of wild animals, that the visitor could hardly move about in them.[14]

C.A. Bayly, in *Imperial Meridian*, a challenging study of the foundations of the Second British Empire, complains that theories of Empire have been the preserve of students of the later nineteenth century, 'a period when imperial expansion was all over bar the shouting'.[15] This is certainly true of J.A. Hobson, all of whose leading events take place within a very limited time-span. His list of colonial 'acquisitions' begins in 1874, though he admits that 'in a few instances' portions of the territory may have been earmarked for colonization at an earlier date:

> Though, for convenience, the year 1870 has been taken as indicative of the beginning of a conscious policy of Imperialism, it will be evident that the movement did not attain its full impetus until the middle of the eighties. The vast increase in territory, and the method of wholesale partition which assigned to us great tracts of African land, may be dated from about 1884. Within fifteen years some three and three-quarter millions of square miles were added to the British Empire.[16]

The time-frame of Lenin's *Imperialism* (1917) is also quite limited, though he distinguishes between Great Britain, where he thinks the 'enormous expansion of colonial conquest'[17] should be dated to the years 1860–80, and France and Germany, where the 'boom' in colonial acquisitions belongs to the subsequent two decades. Halévy, in his magisterial *History of the English People in the Nineteenth Century* – a multi-volume work published in the 1920s, but deeply influenced by the perceptions which the author had gleaned in an earlier period of residence in this country – adopts an even shorter time-span, and makes imperialism an even more modern growth. In volume five of his *History*, billed as an 'Epilogue', he brackets 'Imperialism' with 'the Rise of Labour' and dates both to the decade 1895–1905. Imperialism, in Halévy's account of it, is a kind of *fin-de-siècle* fever. With its exploitation of the 'warlike passions of the democracy' it does not belong to the nineteenth century at all. He pictures it as the aggressive, jingoist force which reached a crescendo at the time of the South African war, and then subsided in 'weariness and disillusionment'.[18]

In the school textbooks of yesteryear, the history of Empire is also typically broken up into a series of discrete events, starting perhaps with the Virginia plantation or the foundation of the East India Company and ending with the Boer War. Each episode has a comparatively limited time-span, and all of them are placed quite firmly in a pre-1914 world. Clive's wars in India often have a chapter to themselves; so does the Indian Mutiny. The Scramble for Africa stands out, partly it may be because of its dramatic unity, 'almost the whole country parcelled out among Europeans' (as Townsend Warner puts it) in the space of thirty years.[19] Imperialism itself is seen as no more than a brief passage, linked, perhaps, to the life and career of Joseph Chamberlain, or to that of Cecil Rhodes. It is narrowly defined – as a passion which burned brightly in the last two decades of the nineteenth century, but was then snuffed out, 'discredited' (as a recently published primer puts it) by the disappointments of the Boer War.[20]

In the school textbooks, as in the classroom 'Readers' which preceded them, there was a premium on stories that carried a message, in particular those which exhibited nobility of character, resourcefulness in face of adversity, or – a favourite lesson drawn from the Boer War – the virtues of magnanimity when dealing with a defeated enemy. Incidents double in the character of parables, pointing up lessons in manners and morals. Ideals of service and sacrifice are personified in larger-than-life characters. Intrepid explorers push on into the unknown; martyr-missionaries, like Bishop Hannington, brave the wrath of the cannibals; besieged soldiers, surrounded by howling dervishes, display tremendous pluck. In a kindred spirit, movements are encapsulated in historic moments ('Dr Livingstone, I presume', H.M. Stanley's famously formal greeting, in the midst of the African jungle, gets the same reverent attention in Rhoda Power's 'Kingsway' history as such episodes as Alfred and the burnt cakes in earlier phases of 'our island story'). The more morbid child was invited to contemplate the horrors of the Black Hole of Calcutta or the Siege of Cawnpore, a kind of imperial equivalent to such medieval atrocity stories as the murder of the little princes in the tower.

If the measure of Empire were to be not wars and conquests – its claim to attention in the textbooks – but ways of life, then a case could be made for saying that it was a greater presence in the interwar years, 1918–39, the time when it disappears from the history syllabus, and when grand theory gives it a miss, than in any other period. Territorially, the British Empire reached its maximum extent in the 1920s, in the immediate aftermath of the Great War. Much of Germany's former colonial empire was appropriated by its liberators – the South Africans in German South West Africa, the Australians in New Guinea, the New Zealanders in Samoa, the British in Tanganyika. More momentous, because it enabled Britain, almost at a stroke, to become one of the world's leading oil producers, was the remarkable establishment of an imperial presence in the Middle East, the start of a forty-year period in which nominally independent Arab rulers – among them the King of Egypt and the Shah of Persia – became in some sort clients of the British government.

In sub-Saharan African, as also in the rubber-rich Malay peninsula, the 1920s witnessed a systematic intensification of colonization. In West Africa, where Lord Lugard's principle of 'indirect rule' forbade any attempts to create a plantation economy, this took the form of marketing strategies which had the effect of transforming subsistence agriculture into cash-crop farming – the cocoa-fields of the Gold Coast being a celebrated example. In the newly created East African colony of Kenya an ambitious scheme of 'Empire settlement' brought thousands of ex-officers to the White Highlands, while in the Rhodesias the postwar influx of immigrants persuaded the colonial government to grant the white settlers self-rule.[21] In Malaya, the great rubber boom of the 1920s, which quadrupled production in the space of a few years, brought adventurers from all over the world, from the gin-swilling planters of Somerset Maugham's short stories to the traders and speculators of the English Club in Singapore. Empire settlement in the 1920s also embraced Canada and Australia, where government-assisted emigration schemes had the deliberate aim of keeping up the demographic purity of Empire, and enlarging the British race.

Well before the Ottawa agreement of 1932, and the advent of a system of imperial preference, Britain's overseas trade was becoming increasingly autarkic. As early as 1919 an element of imperial preference was included in the budget, a protective measure inaugurating some two decades of neo-mercantilist legislation. In 1913 Britain was sending 22 per cent of her exports to the Empire; by 1938 the percentage had more than doubled, to 47 per cent.[22] The comparable figures for imports were also striking, rising from 27 per cent in the years 1920–24 to a peak of 37.9 per cent in 1938. The reorientation of overseas investment was even more dramatic. Where before the Great War Britain was still helping to finance transnational and intercontinental projects, such as the Baghdad railway, by 1938 the colonies and dominions accounted for some 99 per cent of this country's overseas investment.[23] The establishment of the Sterling Area in 1933 – like the Ottawa agreement, an attempt to turn Britain and her trading partners into a self-sufficient economic unit – made these biases systematic, imposing a virtual embargo on capital exports outside the Sterling Area, and deliberately insulating Britain and her trading partners from the world crash.[24] At a time of shrinking trade, these arrangements gave the Empire countries a guaranteed market; they also cushioned Britain from the worst effects of the depression, and indeed allowed for a modest prosperity (movements in the terms of trade favoured Britain as a producer of manufactured goods as against the Empire's primary producers).

These autarkic tendencies were hardly less apparent in the interwar British foreign policy. Here Britain, in the aftermath of the Versailles peace settlement, turned her back on Europe and, as relations with France deteriorated, looked to the new world – that of the self-governing dominions – to redress the balance of the old. As in the days of the *Pax Britannica* Britain's whole policy was to limit, or ideally renounce entirely, any continental commitment and to concentrate her energies instead on defending a far-flung sea dominion. Defence was in the first place imperial defence. The First World War was reinterpreted in this light, with an extending recognition of the vast sacrifice of life on the part of the colonies and dominions. From the Locarno conference of 1925 to the Munich agreement of 1938, the British government made strenuous efforts to keep in line with Empire opinion, deeply suspicious as it was of any commitment in Europe. And it was to the dominions that the chiefs of staff turned when attempting to co-ordinate a policy for the armed services. When, in December 1937, the new Minister for Co-ordination of Defence, Sir Thomas Inskip, presented to the Cabinet his list of priorities in defence obligations, he allocated to the Army as its primary role 'the defence of Imperial commitments, including defence at home' and only as a last objective 'which can only be provided after the other obligations have been met' did he list co-operation in 'the defence of the territories of any allies we may have in the war'.[25]

The turn to Empire had been spectacularly anticipated, and imaginatively prefigured, at the great British Empire exhibition held at Wembley in 1924. Britain's greatest show since the Great Exhibition of 1851, and one of the biggest international events of the interwar years (it attracted some 17 million visitors), it was entirely devoted to the spectacle of imperial greatness. Inside the exhibition grounds were fifteen miles of railways with names chosen by Rudyard Kipling. The Indian domes displayed the splendours of the East, including silks, carpets, embroideries, marble and silverware. Canada displayed her forest wealth, Jamaica her sugar and bananas. The newly discovered tomb of Tutankhamun was one of the Wembley spectacles, a sensation to rival the 1851 display of the Koh-i-Noor diamond at the Crystal Palace.[26]

If Empire marketing was one of interwar Britain's successes, it was in part because it ministered to some of this country's new and burgeoning lifestyles. In the most elementary sense, it helped to lower prices and lessen the cost of living. It therefore benefited the great bulk of those in steady employment. Then it encouraged the enrichment and diversification of diet. Tropical fruit, in the nineteenth century a luxury of the

'Chocolate as a national food': 1929 magazine advertisement (left) and Carson's Empire Chocolate box, *c.* 1930

very rich, and of the fanatically ambitious hot-house gardener, was now displayed in the middle-class drawing room as a matter of course (the establishment of the London Fruit exchange, in 1928, could be said to mark the coming-of-age of the banana). Chocolate, glamorously wrapped and extensively advertised on the hoardings, displaced boiled sweets as the nation's favourite comfort food. Milk chocolate, an invention of the 1920s, and sold in penny and threepenny bars, was one impetus to sales, while at the luxury end of the market, chocolate-chewing matinee audiences at the theatre profited from the fancifully beribboned chocolate boxes which were another 1920s addition to the stock of national pleasures. (By 1930 chocolate confectionery sales were double those of sugar confectionery.)[27] The rise of cocoa, which in the late nineteenth century was little more than a temperance beverage, but which emerged in the 1920s as a kind of universal night-cap, was even more spectacular, bringing a whole set of soporifics in its train. (The Gold Coast Cocoa campaign, launched at the Wembley exhibition of 1924, was credited by some with having led to a dramatic increase in sales.) Overall, the Wembley Exhibition could be thought of as a way of popularizing and glamorizing what a recent commentator has called 'produce imperialism'[28] – 'the idea that the Empire meant cocoa from the Gold Coast, diamonds from South Africa, tea from Ceylon and a Prince of Wales sculpted life-size in Canadian butter'.[29]

Improbable as it may now seem, Empire was also aligned, in the 1920s, with modernity. In Kenya it was associated with experimental farming and the introduction of new crops; in Nigeria with advances in tropical medicine; in Palestine (a Jewish National Home, according to the Balfour Declaration) with the kibbutz. The new science of anthropology used the colonies as a laboratory, starting with the islands of the Western Pacific and ending up with the Nilotic peoples of Upper Sudan. The documentary film-makers (financed, in some cases, by the Empire Marketing Board) followed suit, using promo films to create a new poetics of labour. Basil Wright's *Song of Ceylon* (1933), ostensibly a documentary about the tea plantations, contrasts ancient ways of crop-growing with modern methods, but its central dialectic, a radical one, though Raymond Durgnat dismisses it as 'imperialist pastorale', opposes the ancient, traditional Buddhist culture of Ceylon with modern commercial developments.[30]

Empire cruises, a coveted luxury, associated imperial travel with holiday romance, offering an Art Deco mix of cocktail bars, dance-floors and exotic ports-of-call. (Elizabeth Wilson's *Mirror Writing* has an affecting memoir of what such a trip could mean to a family who subsequently fell on hard times.)[31] The first British national airline, operating out of the new terminal at Croydon, was British Imperial Airways. Formed in 1924, signposting such far-flung locations as Cairo (2,000 miles), Johannesburg (6,000 miles) and Sydney (11,000 miles), and modelling its cabins on those of the luxury liners, it was an immediate success, not least as a vehicle for air mail (it carried 250,000 letters in its first year of operations, a number which had grown to 11,000,000 by the end of the decade).[32]

'The miracle of wireless' was also an early recruit to the imperial cause. At the opening of the Wembley Exhibition the BBC microphone was suspended a few inches to the right of the King's head, and through it his voice was carried by landline to the Marconi transmitting station at Chelmsford. 'Never before,' said a *Daily Mail* leader, 'has a King's voice been heard by his subjects both in his presence and in their own homes as well – to the tune of perhaps a million homes. Such a miracle can do nothing but cement the bonds of Empire.'[33] A further miracle of communication was the gramophone record of the King's broadcast. HMV, the gramophone company, recorded it by their new 'electrical' method, and that same night, hundreds of pressings of it were rushed by special messenger to Croydon to be flown by aeroplane to every corner of the globe. Broadcasting to Empire was an early Reithian enthusiasm, and the opening in 1925 of the high-powered transmitter at Daventry made it possible for BBC broadcasts to be heard as far away as New Zealand. 'What a thrill we had here to-day when we heard that crisp, clear voice "London Calling", followed by the News and the Cricket Scores!', wrote an enthusiastic Durban listener. A further step towards the opening of an Empire broadcasting service was taken on 4 January 1932, when in the early hours of the morning a first Empire News bulletin was broadcast on short wave from the BBC Experimental Station at Chelmsford. In December of that year the new Empire Service was inaugurated with the first of the King's celebrated Christmas Day addresses.[34]

Film also helped to glamorize Empire, and indeed in the hands of Anglophile Hollywood directors – or expatriate Hungarian ones – the North-West Frontier, that most embattled of imperial outposts, became almost as familiar territory as the cattle ranches of the Wild West. Alexander Korda's 1938 *The Drum* ('a sop to . . . decayed romanticism' according to a hostile critic in *Left Review*)[35] and Henry Hathaway's 1935 *Lives of a Bengal Lancer*, shot on location in California, with Gary Cooper in the hero's part, established an iconography on which a generation of film-makers was to draw. *Clive of India* (1935) was the subject of an extraordinary Hollywood film which turned the conqueror of the Carnatic into a kind of male Cinderella. Like so many Hollywood movies of the 1930s, the narrative was that of the poor boy made good, the story of a counting-house clerk who rose to fame and fortune (Ronald Colman, one of Hollywood's great smoothies, played the male lead; Loretta Young was his female counterpart). *Rhodes of Africa* (1936), a British film made by an Austrian director, which painted its hero warts and all – a visionary and an idealist who nevertheless engaged in dark conspiracy – and *Stanley and Livingstone* (1939), a Hollywood movie which cast Spencer Tracy in a deeply sympathetic portrayal of the American correspondent, stuck more closely to the historical facts. Reference might be made, finally, to the fascinating *Sanders of the River* (1935) – Lugard's principle of Indirect Rule mediated by the heated imagination of Edgar Wallace, with Paul Robeson in the role of the noble savage and Leslie Banks as the idealized district officer.[36]

The modernity of Empire, as it was developed in the interwar years, is nowhere more apparent than in the field of business, where Empire-based corporate giants such as Shell and BP, the oil companies, Unilever, the soap-and-margarine conglomerate, Tate and Lyle the sugar monopolists (a Leviathan founded by merger in 1921) were front-runners in some of capitalism's newest phases of development. Indeed Lenin's notion of imperialism as the 'monopoly' stage of capitalism could possibly find more data to support it in the interwar period than in the earlier one on which he and Hobson drew. It was at the level of marketing rather than production that these corporate giants came into their own, using their quasi-monopoly powers to corner the market and keep down the prices paid to the primary producers. Thus, for instance, Dunlop, with their processing plant in Singapore and their tyre factory at Malacca, held the entire Malay peninsula in their grip, even though their agents were seldom seen in the interior. Unilever, through their subsidiary the United Africa Company, dealt with a mass of petty producers; so did the cocoa millionaires, though Cadbury, emboldened by the success of their industrial estate at Bournville, attempted to build a model rural community near Accra.[37] In the case of Imperial Chemical Industries, for whom (we are told) 'Empire came to matter enormously and increasingly',[38] it was not raw materials but the monopoly hold on consumers which was the lure (international cartel agreements assigned Empire markets to ICI, while reserving European and American ones for their rivals).

The outbreak of the Second World War had the effect of strengthening imperial autarky, indeed in September 1939, to follow the excited editorials in the newspaper press, there was far more anxiety over whether or not South Africa would declare war (Australia, New Zealand and Canada had already done so) than on the fighting capacity of our notional European allies. Economic resources counted for as much as manpower. With the formation, in 1940, of the Sterling Area, colonial trade was brought under the control of new government organizations, and in effect requisitioned (payments were suspended for the duration of the hostilities, and frozen in the form of Sterling 'Balances').

So far from marking the end of Empire, the Second World War was a time when all kinds of grandiose imperial schemes were dreamed up. Some had to do with agronomy (tremendous hopes were entertained for the elimination of the tsetse fly, and similar wonders were expected of the introduction of new crops).[39] 'Development' (often coupled with 'Welfare') emerged as a key word in the imperial lexicon, joining the ancient ambitions of Milner, Amery and the Round Table to those of Fabian-inspired reform. The homology with the more domestically oriented cult of planning, and the comprehensive schemes of postwar reconstruction, is striking. The incoming Labour government of 1945 embraced these schemes, setting up both a Colonial Development Corporation and an Overseas Food Corporation. It adopted the paternalist idiom of 'trusteeship' with enthusiasm, and indeed claimed (in 1947–48) to have given 'new life' to the Empire. The 'enlightened self-interest' of the mother country, and the development of the colonies, were conceived as marching together hand-in-hand.[40]

Economically, and politically, Britain's dire circumstances at the end of the war put a premium on the success of such schemes of colonial development. In desperate times, when dollar earnings appeared to be the very hinge of national survival, it was Malayan rubber, Rhodesian copper and Middle Eastern oil which allowed postwar governments both to keep the economy afloat and to maintain Britain's claim to great-power status. As in the period of the Second World War, the strengthening of the Sterling Area, and the systematic exploitation of the colonial resource as a way of giving it ballast, appeared as a very hinge of great-power status, and it says something of the success of postwar policy, in maintaining sterling's place in world trade, that at the close of the 1940s it accounted for about half of all international transactions.

III

'Anti-racism', widely adopted by many progressive teachers as a watchword for their classroom projects, has had the great merit, like multiculturalism, of putting the black presence in Britain on the agenda of historical teaching and research, and in the process it has subverted or put in question Anglocentric and unitary views of the national past. It has also made some fine discoveries, unearthing episodes which have been 'hidden from history'. *The Wonderful Adventures of Mrs Seacole*[41] – the life of a woman who contrived to emancipate herself from the limitations of race, gender and class – is in any view a capital text, and arguably a better one for studying mid-Victorian Britain than any others on offer – say Samuel Smile's *Self-Help*, Matthew Arnold's *Culture and Anarchy*, or (another school favourite in recent years) Flora Thompson's *Lark Rise to Candleford*. It is also an excellent one for opening inquiries on the two-way traffic between Britain and Empire, and the cross-cultural exchanges that took place across the boundaries of race and class. Anti-racism also has the merit of asking much harder and more uncomfortable questions than those which are content to remain with notions of pluralism and 'diversity'.

On the other hand 'anti-racism' is an un-historical, and even an anti-historical concept, as essentializing and reductive as 'gender' and 'class' and, because of the passions attaching to it, less capable of qualification and refinement in the light of historical phenomena which fail to answer to it. Transported from a country – the United States – where the dominant ideology is individualist and egalitarian, it surely needs modification when applied to one (Britain) which has been more commonly hierarchical and corporate or collectivist. In any event, the term anti-racism has no explanatory force, and in its current usage seems more designed to stigmatize than to open up historically informed inquiry. Focusing, as it does, on attitudes and identities rather than, say, political economy, trading relations or religious belief, and drawn, very often, from communities of fear, it can hardly hope to account for so expansionist and many-sided a phenomenon as overseas colonization and settlement.

So far as British racism is concerned – or to use a more old-fashioned term xenophobia – imperial ambitions – or even black–white relations – are perhaps less germane than those age-old national hatreds and fears. These can be studied in relationship to No-Popery and anti-Catholicism – a national passion in nineteenth-century Britain as well as the cause of endemic civil war between Anglo-Saxon and Celt in towns of Irish settlement – or in relationship to the French, the national enemy for the better part of a thousand years; the Irish; or, in the periods when they have been permitted to live in this country, and sometimes when they were not, the gypsies and the Jews (four people were hanged in 1592 for no greater crime than being 'Egyptians').[42] As Linda Colley shows in

Britons, any study of eighteenth-century Britain needs to pay heed to the power of anti-Scottish sentiment, very much present, as she shows, in the politics of the 1760s, and one of the midwives at the birth of modern radicalism.

Not only the notion of 'racism' but also the simple opposition of colonizers and colonized seems to offer little purchase on those systems of dual power where the imperial power made its annexationist advances, or administered its rule, in alliance with native elites, and where imperial structures of authority coexisted with indigenous ones. They are plainly inadequate when confronted with British India, a whole subcontinent, with its own indigenous principles of hierarchy and communal division. Reading *Subaltern Studies* as I have done in preparing for a CRE Round Table – the work of committed radical scholars, concerned to discover the psychic and social roots of inequality and oppression, and to challenge the legacy of colonialist historiography – I am struck by the near-absence of the British Raj from many of their detailed accounts.[43] The notion of 'communalism' – i.e. of sectarian divisions based on religious passion – may be a matter of dispute, but one is reminded again and again – if only by absence – of the failure of the Christian missionaries in India, the thinness of linguistic colonization, and the vitality of those caste divisions which had behind them the force of religious taboo. The 'Cow Protection' movement, studied in relationship to the disturbances and riots of the 1890s and 1900s in northern India, may or may not have been class struggle in disguise, but those events clearly have more to do with indigenous social divisions than with anything which, even at second or third remove, could be seen as English racism. The Parsee businessmen whose enterprising spirit so delighted nineteenth-century writers, or the Sikh warriors whom the English conquerors recruited as soldiers and policemen, even the high-caste Brahmins who formed the English-speaking intellectual elites, plainly had their own autonomous spheres of existence, exerting pressures in their own right rather than being mere creatures of the British rule.

It would be absurd to return to 'drum-and-trumpet' history for the sake of restoring an imperial dimension to the study of the British national past, and there are, I suggest, severe limits to any project which takes its problematic from the study of identity. There may be quite other ways in which the realities of Empire could be made central to historical teaching in the new national curriculum. One would be through the study of commodities, as in the tripartite linkage between the Lancashire cotton industry, the slave trade and the plantations of the American South – i.e. the Atlantic economy of the eighteenth century on which, as historians have recently been at pains to point out, so many of this country's new-found prosperities rested.[44] The evolution of the British cup of tea, and its earlier twentieth-century elevation into a national beverage, is one fruitful line of inquiry, as Stuart Hall has often argued, taking us from the potent symbols of wartime Britain, under the impact of the Blitz, to the plantation economies of Ceylon and the Sugar isles. The chronology of rice-pudding might be similarly instructive for the domestic repercussions of the colonization of Malaya, as also, in Britain's relative immunity from the 1930s depression, the comparative cheapness of rubber.

Another way, suggested by the family history societies, would be to investigate the British diaspora, engaging in family reconstitution on lateral as well as longitudinal lines. Julia Bush has engaged in a study like this, as a school exercise, following the fortunes and careers of those who went out from a small group of Northamptonshire villages as soldiers and sailors, traders, settlers and missionaries.[45]

Then there is the history of those whom Stuart Hall once called the 'white settlers of the Surrey Hills', to whom J.A. Hobson was already paying close attention. The focus here would be on the capacity of the expatriates to create make-believe aristocracies, on their role in the creation of the Victorian public school and its twentieth-century epigones, and on the place of Empire in the making of family fortunes.

Some of the more utopian strains in English life, as represented, say, by the open-air movement of the late nineteenth century, and the rise of the Boy Scouts and the Girl Guides, might also be shown to have their original location in colonizing fantasies. Baden-Powell learnt his scouting lore when serving with an Indian regiment of the British Army. Akela, the cub leader, was Kipling's mother wolf. The international 'jamborees' of the Scouts and Guides in the 1920s and 1930s were very much all-Empire affairs. In a quite other sphere of English life – 'Progressive' education – one could look at the influence of Eastern religion and of Tagore in particular on twentieth-century ideas of modernism, on Fabians – most famously Annie Besant, in 1917 President of the Indian National Congress – and on 'New Age' utopians of our own day.

Another vast field of inquiry, which might take its starting point from a visit to Kew Gardens, then go on to consider the transposition of the Hindi term 'jungle' from India to the ancient forests of Africa, and wind up by appraising the role of the rhododendron bush in suburban ideas of privacy, would be the influence of 'Empire' on the idea of nature. Here *The Origin of Species* would be seen to have its origin in those scientific journeys of exploration which the Admiralty was mounting from 1818 onwards, and which deserve a place, quite as much as missionary activity, in projecting the paths of colonization and conquest.

The draft ends here with the familiar and optimistic instruction to editors that there will be 'four more pages' to come.

Notes

1 Peter Keating, Introduction to Elizabeth Gaskell, *Cranford*, Harmondsworth 1976, p. 24.

2 ibid., pp. 160–1.

3 Edward Said, *Orientalism*, Harmondsworth 1978.

4 Rev. J. Shaw Banks, *Our Indian Empire: Its Rise and Growth*, London 1870, pp. 257–9.

5 *The Illustrated Exhibitor*, no. 18, 4 October 1851, pp. 318–9.

6 C.C. Eldridge, *England's Mission: The Imperial Idea in the Age of Gladstone and Disraeli 1868–1880*, London 1973, p. 103.

7 Karl Marx, 'The British Rule in India' (1853), in Marx and Engels, *Selected Works*, Moscow 1952, I.

8 'In the year 1837 a ship plying the British colonies was wrecked near the rock, and those on board barbarously maltreated by the natives. Reparation was demanded by the Government and solemnly promised; but before the agreement had been carried out the Sultan died, and his son refused to fulfil his father's promise. Force, therefore, had to be used, and the place was taken by storm.' D. Mackenzie Wallace, *The Web of Empire*, London 1902, p. 55.

9 *Our Own Country*, London, n.d. [1889?], p. 5.

10 Rev. S.C. Dawe, *Queen Victoria and Her People*, London n.d. [1897], p. 229.

11 *The Pictorial History of the British Empire*, London n.d. [1889], p. 294.

12 ibid., p. 382.

13 The above two paragraphs are reproduced from Raphael Samuel, 'Continuous National History', in Samuel (ed.), *Patriotism: The Making and Unmaking of British National Identity*, vol. I, 'History and Politics', pp. 13–15.

14 George Orwell, *Coming Up For Air*, part II, chapter X, London 1939.

15 C.A. Bayley, *Imperial Meridian: The British Empire and the World 1780–1830*, London 1990, p. 73.

16 J.A. Hobson, *Imperialism*, London 1902, pp. 19–20; Bernard Porter, *Critics of Empire: British Radical Attitudes to Colonialism in Africa 1895–1914*, London 1968.

17 V.I. Lenin, *Imperialism, the Highest Stage of Capitalism*, Peking 1973 edition, p. 91.

18 Elie Halévy, *A History of the English People in the Nineteenth Century*, vol. V, London 1926; 1961 edition, p. 434.

19 George Townsend Warner, *A Brief Survey of British History*, London 1899; 1961 edition, p. 237.

20 Norman Lowe, *Mastering Modern British History*, London 1984, p. 252.

21 P.J. Cain and A.G. Hopkins, *British Imperialism: Crisis and Deconstruction 1914–1990*, London 1993, pp. 214–23; Bernard Porter, *The Lion's Share: A Short History of British Imperialism 1850–1985*, London 1984 ed., pp. 207–77; on the 'White Highlands', see also Ingham, *History of East Africa*, and B. Aogot (ed.), *Economic and Social History of East Africa*, Nairobi 1976, which offers an account of Kikuyu squatters in the Rift Valley.

22 For a contemporary account, see for example the rationale given for 'Imperial Preference' in chapter XVIII of E.B. McGuire, *The British Tariff System*, London 1939.

23 Ian Drummond, *British Economic Policy and the Empire 1919–1930*, London 1972, pp. 17–25; Derek H. Aldcroft, *The British Economy between the Wars*, Oxford 1983, pp. 286–94; see also G.D.H. Cole, *British Trade and Industry, Past and Future*, London 1932, pp. 184–97; C.L. Mowat, *Britain between the Wars 1918–1940*, London 1962, p. 437.

24 On the Sterling Area, Cain and Hopkins, *British Imperialism*, pp. 78–85, 90–3.

25 Quoted by Michael Howard, *The Continental Commitment: The Dilemma of British Defence Policy in the Era of the Two World Wars*, London 1972, p. 116.

26 Wembley History Society, *The British Empire Exhibition*, Wembley 1974; Geoffrey Hewlett, *A History of Wembley*, Brent 1979; Noreen Branson, *Britain in the Nineteen Twenties*, London 1975, pp. 66–7; Mowat, *Britain between the Wars*, pp. 177–8.

27 James B. Jeffreys, *Retail Trading in Britain, 1850–1950*, Cambridge 1954, pp. 253–67.

28 John M. Mackenzie (ed.), *Propaganda and Empire: The Manipulation of British Public Opinion 1880–1960*, Manchester 1984, pp. 111–2.

29 Jeffrey Richards, 'Boys Own Empire', in Mackenzie (ed.), *Propaganda and Empire*, p. 147.

30 Raymond Durgnat, cited by Mackenzie (ed.), *Propaganda and Empire*, p. 86.

31 Elizabeth Wilson, *Mirror Writing: An Autobiography*, London 1982.

32 *The British Empire*, vol. IV, BBC Television Time-Life Books, published in parts, London 1973, p. 2032.

33 ibid.

34 Stuart Hibberd, *'This — Is London . . .'*, London 1950, pp. 31–3, 67, 181.

35 Quoted by Roger Manvell, *The British Empire*, vol. IV, pp. 2215–16.

36 Jeffrey Richards, 'Boys Own Empire', in Mackenzie (ed.), *Propaganda and Empire*, pp. 146–52, discusses these films.

37 Charles Wilson, *The History of Unilever: A Study of Economic Growth and Social Change*, 2 vols, London 1954; Sir Ronald Storrs, *Dunlop in War and Peace*, London 1946; Paul Jennings, *Dunlopera: The Works and Workings of the Dunlop Rubber Co.*, London 1961; James McMillan, *The Dunlop Story: The Life, Death and Re-birth of a Multi-National*, London 1989.

38 Drummond, *British Economic Policy*, p. 20.

39 John Iliffe, *A Modern History of Tanganyika*, Cambridge 1979; Gavin Kitchin, *Class and Economic Change in Kenya*, Yale 1980.

40 Stephen Constantine, *The Making of British Colonial Development Policies 1914–1940*, London 1984; Porter, *Lion's Share*, pp. 278–81; Drummond, *British Economic Policy*, pp. 36–47.

41 *The Wonderful Adventures of Mrs Seacole in Many Lands*, first published London 1857; ed. Z. Alexander and A. Dewjee, Bristol 1984.

42 Raphael Samuel, Introduction to *Patriotism*, vol. II, 'Minorities and Outsiders', London 1989, extends this argument, as do the three volumes as a whole.

43 *Subaltern Studies: Writings on South Asian History and Society*, published by Oxford University Press in Delhi (ongoing).

44 Eric Williams, *Capitalism and Slavery*, London 1964; Robin Blackburn, *The Making of New World Slavery: From The Baroque to the Modern, 1492–1800*, London 1997.

45 Julia Bush, 'Moving On – and Looking Back', *History Workshop Journal*, no. 36, Autumn 1993, pp. 183–94, a special issue on Colonial and Post-Colonial History.

Part II

English Journeys

The Menagerie

KING'S ROYAL

Tower of London.

This ancient Edifice, built in the reign of Edward IV. 1465, for the reception of FOREIGN

BEAST, BIRDS, &c.

Presented to the Kings of England, could never, since its foundation, boast of a more magnificent and splendid VARIETY than it does at present.

First Department.--A beautiful majestic full-grown

BENGAL LION

AND HIS CONSORT, IN ONE DEN,

Being the largest that has been brought to England for many years, and presented to the King by General Watson; the only pair of this kind ever seen in this Country.—FOUR beautiful

AFRICAN LIONS in one Den.--Pair of beautiful

YOUNG LIONS

From the Cape of Good Hope.—Pair of beautiful BENGAL

ROYAL TIGERS

Just Landed. the first that has been in the Menagerie for 20 years.—Pair of

Oriental LEOPARDS, remarkable for docility.---Beautiful PANTHER.

THE STRIPED or UNTAMEABLE HYÆNA,

Beautiful AFRICAN

Leopard & her Cubs

Pair of Spotted or LAUGHING HYÆNAS.--Pair of enormous Black WOLVES

From the Polar Regions; the only ones ever seen alive in England.

PAIR OF ORIENTAL PORCUPINES,

Whose power of raising or depressing their quills renders them so formidable to their pursuers.

Three African BLOOD-HOUNDS.—An enormous GRIZLY BEAR from Hudson's Bay,

WHOSE BULK EXCEEDS THAT OF AN OX.

A fine BLACK BEAR from North America.---A remarkably beautiful

OCELOT, OR TIGER CAT.

This animal excites universal admiration.—The CIVET-CAT, the animal that produces Musk.

COATI MONDIES or Ant-eaters, RACOONS,

With an infinite variety of **SIMIA or MONKEY** Tribe, whose antics and gambols afford the highest amusement.

Second Department.

A Beautiful Zebra,

From Ethiopia.

A BEAUTIFUL MALE NYLGHAU,

From the Coromandel Coast.—A PAIR OF

KANGAROOS,

(Male & Female) Bred in Windsor Great Park.

The MOUFFLON, from Caffraria.—4 EMEWS or

SOUTHERN OSTRICHES.

Three extraordinary fine

PELICANS of the WILDERNESS,

Represented to feed their Young with their own Blood.

ARDEA DUBIA,

Or ADJUTANT of BENGAL, commonly called the Gigantic Crane.

Belearic or Royal Crowned Cranes.—Cyrus or Polish Crane.

Hooded VULTURE from China, & a Bearded VULTURE or GRIFFIN.—Majestic

EAGLE of the SUN

And Golden Eagle,

FROM NORTH AMERICA.

Pair of beautiful Horned Owls, from Hudson's Bay; Pair of Storks, from Elsineur; Pair of Spoon-bills, from Holland.

TWO PAIR OF CURACOA BIRDS, FROM TRINIDAD.

Majestic Elk, from the East Indies.

Chinese Gold and Silver Pheasants, Macaws, Cockatoos, Parrots, Paroquets, and a great variety of other Birds of the most splendid plumage.

The Tapier or Hippopotamus of South America.

Boa Constrictors, or Great Serpents of Jaba,

The largest ever exhibited.

The ANACONDA SNAKE, next in magnitude to the above.

The Beasts are regularly FED at 3 in the Afternoon, which will be found the most interesting time. NO EXTRA CHARGE.
N. B. The highest Price given for every kind of Foreign Beasts & Birds.

Admittance, only 1s. to view the whole Menagerie.

WHEELER, Printer, 87, Bermondsey-St.

Poster advertising the attractions of the menagerie at the Tower, from the period when Alfred Cops had charge in the 1820s and 1830s

The Tower of London*

If ever a building was time-warped, owing its renown to its antiquities, and its public appeal to what Tom Nairn, in relation to the British monarchy generally, has called 'the glamour of backwardness',[1] it is the Tower of London. Rising from an impregnable Norman keep, dating back to the time of William the Conqueror or even earlier (many, among them Shakespeare, believed the Tower had been built by Julius Caesar,[2] and the Tower authorities of the eighteenth century seem to have shared the conceit, referring to the White Tower as 'Caesar's Tower'[3] and naming the muniment room where the ancient customs and usages of the place were deposited 'Julius Caesar Chapel'[4]), it is reputedly the oldest royal palace in the world, older by some four hundred years than the Vatican at Rome or the Kremlin which Ivan the Terrible had built at Moscow. Guarding the eastern approaches to the city, it was a rampart built against both foreign invasion and domestic disorder (it was soldiers from the Tower who put down the Spitalfields weavers during the riots of 1771).[5] Commanding a magnificent prospect of the Thames, it occupied a crucial location in the centuries when the river was London's chief highway, not least for the transport and execution of traitors. Attracting more visitors than Westminster Abbey, it is one of the best-known sights of London, on a par, as a landmark and an icon, with the Tour Eiffel and Arc de Triomphe in Paris, or the Empire State Building in New York. The dress of the Yeomen Warders ('Beefeaters'), guardians of the Tower for nine centuries, reinforces the sense of time-warp. Even in the 1750s it was thought of as anachronistic. They wore then, as they do now, large-sleeved scarlet coats, laced with gold braiding, similar to those of the Yeoman of the Guard; Elizabethan ruffs; and flat-crowned caps decorated with bands of ribbon. (Their name, like their uniform, seems to have been given to them in the 1660s.)

* This essay was written in August 1996; notes 1 to 5 were attached as a sample for its first draft.

Appearances, as so often in these matters, are deceptive. The medieval towers, which figure so prominently on the skyline, the turrets and casemented windows, are for the most part buildings (or rebuildings) of the nineteenth century, and bear the mark of the Gothic Revival architect, Anthony Salvin. The Imperial Crown, 'that all the Kings of England have been crowned with since Edward the Confessor, 1042',[6] is a replica, made on the order of Charles II after the Restoration (the original, together with other ancient regalia, had been stored in Westminster Abbey, and was melted down by parliament, as a fund-raiser, during the Great Rebellion).[7] The barracks, arms depots and powder magazines, which for nearly two centuries occupied the lion's share of space in the fortress, have been swept away.

The Tower is no longer a place of confinement for persons of Quality, 'charged with Misdemeanour, or any Capital Crime';[8] nor does it house the Royal Mint, established there in or before the time of Edward I, which moved to a more commodious site, on Tower Hill, in 1812. The royal menagerie, established in the Tower during the reign of Henry III, and by a long way the greatest visitor attraction in the eighteenth century, decamped in 1834, when it formed the nucleus of the London Zoo in Regent's Park.[9] Today the Crown Jewels are displayed in a newly created, purpose-built block, opened in 1995, where visitors are processed in and out by a kind of travelator. Before then, the Jewel House, opened in 1967, was housed in a subterranean vault of the Waterloo block, the occasion of immense crushes and interminable queues. Prior to that the Jewels had been housed in the Wakefield Tower, in the room in which it was believed Henry VI had been murdered. They had been transferred there after the great fire of 1831.[10] In the eighteenth century, when the Jewels were housed in the Martin Tower, and when it cost a shilling a time to see them, conditions were even more cramped than they were to be in the Waterloo block; according to a foreign visitor who saw the Jewels in 1786, they were kept in an old smoky cupboard in a vault, 'and shown by an old woman by the light of two tallow candles'.[11]

One spectacular absentee is the Royal Armouries Museum, reputedly the largest collection of weaponry in the world, which only this year was removed, lock, stock and barrel, from the Tower to a new glass and concrete, atrium-style museum in Leeds. Formed in the reign of Elizabeth I, it was known for many years as 'The Spanish Armoury' and is often thought to have had, as its original core, trophies and relics of the 1588 Armada.[12] But earlier antiquities excited quite as much attention, among them two immense cannon which Henry VIII took with him to strike terror into the enemy before Boulogne. No less sensational were the clubs, allegedly used by Saxon women in the ninth century to massacre the invading Danes – proof, it was believed by so sober an authority as Sir John Fielding, that the Tower of London had had a continuous existence from at least as far back as the reign of Aethelred II.[13] Trophies from England's eighteenth-century wars swelled the collection, as did such memorabilia as the cloak on which General Wolfe died at Quebec. Among the curiosities of the New Armoury, a spacious room opened to the public in 1851, was the pump of the *Mary Rose*, Henry VIII's man-of-war which sunk in the Solent, off Spithead, and had been found by divers when searching for the wreck of the *Royal George* in 1840. It is, wrote a contemporary guidebook, 'perhaps the earliest specimen of English Naval architecture existing . . . as fresh apparently as it was nearly three centuries ago, before being consigned to the bosom of the deep'.[14] The Royal Armoury, in effect, had blossomed out as a kind of Imperial War Museum *avant la lettre*. Nineteenth-century additions included mementoes of Britain's African wars and India campaigns; the revolver of Lord Roberts, the hero of the Boer War; and at the end, as the HMSO *Guide* of 1938 puts it, 'the sword of Lord Kitchener and his famous Appeal to the Nation for recruits'.

An older absentee, of particular interest to historians, are the Public Records, which were housed at the Tower from early Norman times until 1858, when Sir James Pennethorne's purpose-built PRO in Chancery Lane was opened to receive them. The earliest records, Bayley reports, were the *Chartae Antiquae*, being a collection of grants extending from the reign of Edward the Confessor to the beginning of the thirteenth century.[15] Control in the Wakefield Tower, where the records were lodged in the eighteenth century, seems to have been, from the point of view of modern archival practice, alarmingly haphazard. Von Uffenbach, an eighteenth-century visitor, claimed that he was permitted to tear off a document 'of particular antiquity'.[16] Astle, who became Keeper of the records in 1783, reported that the records were lying in 'total disorder'; that they were blackened with dust; and that the tickets of reference were so obliterated 'that many of them were not legible'. But Astle set to work cataloguing and inventorizing the materials, while Samuel Lysons, the learned London antiquary who became Keeper of the records in 1804, built up the nucleus of an office, increasing the staff from one to six. Finally the insistence of the Ordnance Office (overcoming strenuous representations for the giving of more space to the public records) that the stores of ammunition in the basement should be kept there, despite the extreme risks of fire, and the Duke of Wellington's belief that the Wakefield Tower was the 'best, if not the only place of security' for state prisoners, persuaded the government authorities to move the public records elsewhere.[17]

The environs of the Tower have changed even more strikingly. It is no longer pestered about with mean streets and crowded dwellings, as it was when Stow made his *Survay of London*,[18] but, on the contrary, stands in a landscaped space, a grassed area dotted about with souvenir stalls, ice-cream kiosks, hot-dog stands and all the other paraphernalia of a tourist mecca. The dockers no longer rally on Tower Hill, 100,000 strong, as they did during the strike of 1912 when Ben Tillett famously asked them to raise their hats to God and pray that He strike Lord Devonport (Chairman of the Port of London employers) dead; nor is Tower Hill any longer an open-air pulpit and parliament, as it was in the days of stump oratory and open-air preachers, though the Rev. Donald Soper, an old-time Methodist-radical, still holds forth on Friday lunchtimes, as he has been doing for some sixty years. Still more remote is the time when Tower Hill was a place of public execution, the last occasion being 1746–47, in the aftermath of Culloden, when the four Jacobite lords were put to the axe and beheaded.

It should be evident from the foregoing that the Tower, at any given time, is multi-functional. It has by turn, and often simultaneously, been a military fortress, a royal palace, a state prison, a zoo, a jewel house, a museum, an army barracks, an arsenal, the place where all the gold, silver and copper coin was struck (in 1755, according to *London in Miniature*, the Royal Mint comprehended 'near one Third of the Tower, and contains Houses for all the Officers belonging to the Coinage'), and not least 'the Repository of the antient Records of this Nation'.[19] Like the Kremlin wall, it has been a burying place for notables, albeit those who fell foul of the law. It has also been a pantheon, and indeed served for some two centuries as this country's first national portrait gallery, with a 'Line of Kings', representing the monarchs in their own armour – a 'living history' display first assembled in Restoration times, and purged of its wilder inaccuracies in 1925, when it was moved into the New Horse Armoury.[20]

It should also be apparent that for all its appearance of timelessness, the Tower has been peculiarly susceptible to the demands made on it. The moat, for instance, which the Historic Royal Palaces Agency now proposes, in the name of authenticity, to re-flood, was always subject to competing claims, as it is today when rival schools of resurrectionists debate its future. Excavated, between 1275 and 1281, for military purposes, to help to make the fortification impregnable, it seems to have been encroached upon, at an early date, for civilian use. The nearby residents used it as a rubbish-tip, according to an Elizabethan report; tanners washed their skins in the water, 'poisoning the fish'; the Gentleman Porter of the Tower began leasing the margins of the moat to craftsmen and start-up enterprises, anxious to place themselves outside the City walls and to free themselves from guild restrictions on trade. Later, in the 1820s, it was complained that 'idle and dissolute characters' assembled there for gambling 'and other vicious pursuits'.[21] Drained and infilled in 1843, on the sanitarian argument that its stagnant waters were responsible for the poor health of the Tower garrison, the reclaimed land became, formally, a military parade ground, while alongside it there was a 'tolerably wide' strip of pleasure-ground or garden, 'open to the chief inhabitants and residents'.[22] (In later years local children had a free run of it, using it for pitch-and-toss schools, horseplay and games.) During the Second World War it was commandeered as a giant vegetable garden, a showpiece in the government's 'Dig for Victory' campaign.

The Tower has also been subject to a whole series of internal upheavals and shake-ups, sometimes as a result of military reorganization, as in the eighteenth century when it was converted into an arsenal and a barracks; sometimes because of competition between rival offices of state; sometimes because of ministerial or administrative whim. At any given moment, the Tower appears to be on the eve of momentous changes. This has never been more so than in the present, when it is being systematically made more user-friendly. A concurrence of different influences are at work. There is to begin with the vast increase in the number of visitors and the need for crowd control – the reason why the Crown Jewels have been removed from underground vaults to a light and airy travelator. Then there is the regionalist turn in Arts Council and government policy, one of the reasons, surely, why the Royal Armouries Museum – the incomparable collection of military memorabilia, painstakingly accumulated over four centuries – has been decanted to Leeds. More generally there is the influence of the new museology, with its emphasis on free-standing exhibits and interactive display. In the case of the Tower the appearance on an adjacent space of the 'Tower Pageant' – an initiative of archaeologists from the Museum of London, which offers punters an underground ride through two thousand years of London history, and which has been a resounding tourist success – has made these pressures the more immediate.

The Tower, today Britain's leading tourist attraction, has been regarded as one of the sights of London from at least the reign of Elizabeth I, ('Foreigners would first visit the Tower and the Royal Exchange, and would then proceed up Cheapside to St Paul's');[23] and it has had a museum function, or element, albeit as an adjunct to the royal palace rather than as a public exhibition space, from very early times. The royal menagerie and the Crown Jewels, regarded by some as one of the wonders of the world, seems to have been formed, as a collection, in the same period. Military trophies were put on display in the time of Elizabeth I. So long as the Tower functioned as a royal place, admission to these exhibits was restricted to a select few – court and government officials (Pepys liked taking his ladies to the Tower), foreign visitors, state guests.[24] But by the eighteenth century, though the museum function remained a subordinate one, the Tower's 'Curiosities' could be viewed by the public at large. There was a fixed tariff for the privilege. According to the 1771 *Historical Description* of the Tower, the prices were as follows:[25]

Prices of ſeeing the CURIOSITIES.

Lions, each Perſon, - - - -	Six-pence.
Foot-Armory, - - - - -	Three-pence.
Train of Artillery, - - - -	Two-pence.
Horſe-Armory, - - - - - -	Three-pence.
Spaniſh Armory, - - - - -	Two-pence.
Regalia, in Company, each Perſon,	One Shilling.
——— Single,	One Shilling and Six-pence.

N. B. But if a ſingle Perſon is ſhewn the Foot-Armory, Train of Artillery, Horſe-Armory, and *Spaniſh* Armory, he pays for each double the Price above-mentioned.

In the eighteenth century, as befitted a time of almost continuous foreign wars, the Tower was heavily militarized, becoming one of the nation's principal arsenals, and the site of an army barracks. The White Tower, for instance, the oldest building in the Tower, housed an armoury for 10,000 seamen, 'and war-like instruments of many kinds'.[26] The 'Grand Storehouse' of the Royal Artillery, built by the Ordnance and begun in 1688, dominated the entire complex, rivalling the White Tower in size. The Small Armoury contained complete stands of arms, 'bright, clear, and flinted', for 150,000 men 'besides cannon and pikes, swords and c. innumerable, ranged in regular order'.[27] The military aspect was also very much to the fore in the Tower's museum function, where the show-cases and mounted displays in the Grand Storehouse were filled with recent captures, such as the brass cannon taken from the walls of Vigo in 1704, or those captured from the Highlanders at Culloden.

The Ordnance Office was one of the great departments of state, a kind of War Office and Ministry of Munitions, or Supply, rolled into one. Founded in the reign of Henry VIII, during the invasion scares of 1537–47, it established an early foothold in the Tower.[28] From the restoration of the monarchy in 1660, down to 1855, the year when the Duke of Wellington relinquished his Constableship, its influence in the Tower was paramount. New storehouses were built, offices and lodgings for clerks, barracks for soldiers. Older buildings, too, were converted to Ordnance use – the Beauchamp Tower, for instance, a state prison in its time, marked by the melancholy signatures of the executed, was fitted up by the Board of Ordnance as a mess-room for officers, 'the niches being filled with cupboards and shelves, to the concealment, as well as injury, of the inscriptions'.[29] Others were cleared away to meet the Ordnance's ever-increasing demands for space – in the 1670s, for instance, the Old Palace, 'much of it in a dilapidated state', was demolished 'and with it the Coldharbour, the Jewel House and other accretions along the south side of the White Tower'. As with other departments of state, jobbery was rife: 'All the Ordnance staff . . . had rooms suitable to their rank and the new complex included an impressive wainscotted board room'.[30] Later, in 1774, when the thirteenth-century Lanthorn Tower was damaged by fire, a wholesale clearance followed: 'The old building had not in fact been seriously damaged during the fire, but the Board of Ordnance clearly seized on the occasion to provide themselves with new prestigious quarters.'[31]

Sir Christopher Wren, who did so much to shape Augustan taste, thought of Gothic as a barbarism, and he was delighted that the Great fire of 1666 had swept away so many medieval relics. The buildings which he designed for the Tower were brick, not stone. The Ordnance, who at the Restoration began an extensive programme of military installations and appointments in the fortress, showed no embarrassment about infilling, but were concerned solely with maximizing use. Architecturally, the new buildings made no attempt to conceal their novelty, but were built in the latest style. 'Restoration' was undertaken in a similar spirit. As Lord de Ros, Deputy-Lieutenant of the Tower in the 1850s, was to complain:

> Even the eminent Sir Christopher Wren so entirely lost sight of architectural propriety in his restoration and repair of the White Tower, that he faced the windows with stone in the Italian style, and so disfigured this venerable building, that, until the stranger has entered within its massive walls, and observed their huge thickness and other evidence of its antiquity, he might suppose the White Tower to date no farther back than the time of Queen Anne or George I.[32]

In the eighteenth century the Tower, though admitting the public to see its curiosities, fell into decay, at least as a metropolitan presence. It no longer served as a royal palace, nor, save on exceptional occasions (1715, 1746–47, the Gordon riots), as a state prison. Constables sold the Warderships, allowed public houses to be erected, even against the most venerable towers and ancient buildings, 'and filled every corner with tenants, from whom they collected heavy rents, allowing every sort of encroachment and dilapidation to proceed unnoticed'. The Ordnance spread higgledy-piggledy, converting stables into gunners' barracks and the provision of new soldiers' houses, running up fresh warehouses, storehouses, canteens, magazines and workshops 'on every vacant spot', filling basements with explosives.[33] When the public visited the Tower it was to 'see the lions' (or the armoury), not to gaze with awe on an ancient medieval pile.[34] Daniel Defoe, in his *Tour through the Whole Island of Great Britain*, (1724–26), gives not even a line to the Tower, though he has plenty to say about such sights of London as the Royal Exchange and Temple Bar.

Architecturally, the Tower was a mess. Old decayed towers were intermixed with what an 1817 writer described as 'modern brick offices'.[35] The interior of the St Martin Tower, residence of the Keeper of the Jewels, was 'so disfigured with lath and plaster partitions, and linings of wood, and so cut up into small domestic apartments, that little or nothing can be made of its original details . . .'[36] Additions in the first half of the nineteenth century, though medievalist in intention, added to the confusion. The Waterloo barracks, built after the great fire of 1841 – the last major addition to the military capabilities of the Tower – was 'castellated Gothic of the fifteenth Century'.[37] The White Tower, the most ancient part of the complex, 'that celebrated palatial fortress, so intimately mixed up with the whole eventful history of mediaeval England', was lost amidst the surrounding dross: as the writer of an 1854 illustrated *Guide* to London put it:

> Those who approach the spot with any expectation to be reminded of these associations by any of the old objects and links between the past and the present, usual to such sites, will be utterly disappointed. No fortress of equal age has been so transformed; the two lines of walls and towers being weeded of every original feature, even to a loophole, and betraying their presence only by a few bald surfaces of stone peeping out from the casing and surmounting mass of hideous erections . . . From within this belt of ugliness will be seen rising two piles that replace those burnt in 1841, and are intended to be 'in keeping' with the place – a pretence in keeping with a reality. We may here see *castle* work and *castellated* work in juxtaposition. . . . The fine old pretenceless mass of the White Tower overtops the rest. Of this, again, only the general form and those of the windows remain ancient; everything except the plain surfaces having been remodelled.[38]

The rehistoricization of the Tower, and its transformation from a military arsenal and *omnium gatherum* of curiosities into a national shrine, was the work of many different hands, and took some eight or nine decades to accomplish. It parallels in interesting ways the historicist turn in nineteenth-century British culture. Like church 'restoration' it drew on the labours of antiquarians and archaeologists, architects and builders. It was also beholden to the painters and illustrators, who did so much to fix the melodrama of the Tower in the public mind; to the novelist Harrison Ainsworth; and not least to the compilers of handbooks and guides.

First, in point of time, and ultimately in terms of influence, would be those who in 1796 discovered the numerous memorials on the walls of the Beauchamp Tower, and who in the process rediscovered the *prison* aspect of the Tower, and the high drama of the treason trials and executions with which it had been, for centuries, umbilically tied. The discovery of the inscriptions (others were to follow) seems to have been the work of the antiquarians, being communicated by the Rev. J. Brand to the Society of Antiquaries in the early nineteenth century and made public in the thirteenth volume of their proceedings, *Archaeologia*. Bayley published a large selection of the inscriptions, illustrated by engraved representations of the heraldic and other devices, in his authoritative two-volume *History* of 1821 and 1825.[39]

Reproduction of a coloured lithograph of the Tower and the Mint from Great Tower Hill, by Thomas Shotter Boys, 1842, showing the repaired White Tower and the Small Armouries after the fire of 1841

Charles Dickens, acutely aware, when writing *A Tale of Two Cities*, of the analogies between imprisonment in the Tower and the 'frozen deep' or death-in-life of the Bastille, weaves such discoveries into his fiction:

> 'Pray, Doctor Manette', said Mr. Darnay, as they sat under the plane tree – and he said it in the natural pursuit of the topic in hand, which happened to be the old buildings of London – 'have you seen much of the Tower? . . . They told me a curious thing when I was there'.
>
> 'What was that?' Lucie asked.
>
> 'In making some alterations, the workmen came upon an old dungeon, which had been, for many years, built up and forgotten. Every stone of its inner wall was covered by inscriptions which had been carved by the prisoners – dates, names, complaints, and prayers. Upon a corner stone in an angle of the wall, one prisoner, who seemed to have gone to execution, had cut as his last work, three letters. They were done with some very poor instrument, and hurriedly, with an unsteady hand. At first, they were read as D.I.C.; but, on being more carefully examined, the last letter was found to be G. . . . At length it was suggested the letters were not initials, but the complete word DIG. The floor was examined very carefully under the inscription, and, in the earth beneath a stone, or tile, or some fragment of paving, were found the ashes of a paper, mingled with the ashes of a small leathern case or bag. What the unknown prisoner had written will never be read, but he had written something, and hidden it away to keep it from the gaoler.'
>
> 'My father', exclaimed Lucie, 'you are ill!'
>
> He had suddenly started up, with his hand to his head. His manner and his look quite terrified them all.[40]

The inscriptions in the Beauchamp Tower seem to have been the inspiration for Harrison Ainsworth's historical romance, *The Tower of London*, published in monthly parts in 1840. The preface to the novel has an eloquent plea for the rehabilitation of the Beauchamp Tower – it was being used as an officers' mess – and for it to be opened to the general public.[41] The text, focusing as it does on the treason trials and executions of the 1550s, turns the hieroglyphics into a Grand Guignol historical narrative. Ainsworth, a friend of Dickens and an early mentor, had been a Newgate novelist in the 1830s, writing 'Hogarthian' fictions about outlaw-heroes and low-life characters. Like Dickens, he was instinctively on the side of the underdog, and when he turned to writing novels about old London buildings, as he did in 1840, it was to write about the horrors of the past. 'Bring out your dead!', re-enacting the terrors of the Plague, seems to have been a favourite cry of children who fell under the spell of his *Old St Paul's*, while incarceration and execution, for those who adopted his *The Tower of London*, featured in counting games or theatricals.[42]

Ainsworth's Newgate novels enjoyed an immense diffusion through being adopted for the popular stage. *Jack Sheppard* was a great hit when it was put on at the Surrey side theatres. *Rookwood*, as well as inspiring scores of highwaymen 'penny dreadfuls', also provided the scene for one

'The Execution of Jane', a drawing by George Cruikshank used as the frontispiece for William Harrison Ainsworth's *The Tower of London* (London, 1840)

of the great set-pieces of the Victorian circus, 'Turpin's Ride to York and the Death of Black Bess'.[43] (It is the equestrian feat being performed by Sergeant Troy in Hardy's *Far From the Madding Crowd.*) It seems that *The Tower of London* had an even longer after-life. Daphne du Maurier, as a little girl, found it serviceable for bringing her sisters into line. Through Ainsworth's novel, she writes in *Myself When Young*:

> I knew every inch of the ground and precincts before we were first taken there, walked without hesitation to stand by Traitors' Gate, and then pointed out, correctly, the name of every tower commanding the walls. Had I not beheaded Jeanne, time and again, on Tower Green? I knew the identical spot where the block had stood. 'How nobly she walks to her death', I heard one of the maids whisper, when Tower Green had been the garden of the moment. Jeanne, strutting past, certainly made a moving figure, her curls pinned on the top of her head, while I, the axeman, waited, walking-stick in hand – the crook of the hand forming the axe – and, as was the rightful custom, dropped on one knee to ask her pardon before I felled her with a single blow.
>
> Angela always took the women's parts. She was splendid as Bloody Mary, for whom she vowed she had a real affection, but the trouble with Angela . . . was that she soon lost interest, once a game had started. . . . Jeanne showed more enthusiasm and, being nearly four years my junior, proved malleable to my direction, switching from role to role . . . but more often the hapless victim of the executioner's axe. I have no recollection of ever suffering that hideous fate myself, though on occasion I would stretch myself upon the rack, or better still writhe, attacked by rodents, in the notorious Rat Pit.[44]

Ainsworth's remarkable achievement, as the above passage may suggest, and as Geoffrey Parnell convincingly argues,[45] was to seize on an almost accidental feature of the Tower – its occasional use as a place to hold prisoners of rank, a quite minor feature of its daily life when compared with the activities of the Royal Mint, or, in later years, the Ordnance – and turn it into a place erected for the incarceration, torment and eventual execution of the famous. He made it an ancient, mysterious labyrinth where tragic personalities spent their time in basemented rooms (the Tower in fact has none) waiting for the axeman's call. Like the Newgate novel of the 1830s, and Gothic romance generally, its whole narrative is a drama of entrapment. Hence the brilliant but quite arbitrary limitation of the novel to the reign of Bloody Mary.

The inscriptions which moved the young Lord Macaulay were the tablets in the chapel of St Peter Ad Vincula, marking the tombs and burial-places of those who had been beheaded as traitors. He writes, in a famous passage, that there is no sadder spot on earth:

> Death is there associated, not, as in Westminster Abbey and St. Paul's, with genius and virtue, with public veneration and imperishable renown; not, as in our humblest churches and churchyards, with everything that is most endearing in social and domestic charities; but with whatever is darkest in human nature

and in human destiny, with the savage triumph of implacable enemies, with the inconstancy, the ingratitude, the cowardice of friends. . . . Thither have been carried, through successive ages, by the rude hands of gaolers, without one mourner following, the bleeding relics of men who had been captains of armies, the leaders of parties, the oracles of senates, and the ornaments of court. Thither was borne, before the window where Jane Grey was praying, the mangled corpse of Guildford Dudley. . . . There has mouldered away the headless trunk of John Fisher, Bishop of Rochester and Cardinal of Saint Vitalis, a man worthy to have lived in a better age, and to have died in a better cause . . . Here and there, among the thick graves of unquiet and aspiring statesmen, lie more delicate sufferers; Margaret of Salisbury, the last of the proud name of Plantagenet, and those two fair Queens who perished by the jealous rage of Henry.[46]

Narrative artists and illustrators, focusing on the Tower as a place of incarceration and execution, amplified these effects, making memorable images of martyred women and murdered innocence. One of their great subjects was that beau ideal of Victorian femininity, Lady Jane Grey; another, the little princes in the tower, who in Delaroche's enormously influential painting of 1831, as in Sir John Millais's velveteen figures, mysteriously contrive to become twins. George Cruikshank's brilliant illustrations to Ainsworth's novel, focusing as they do on gloomy vaults, secret stairways and despairing prisoners, helped to establish a macabre iconography of the Tower in which black-faced executioners were forever stalking their victims, sharpening the axe, and bringing the narrative to a climax.

Guidebooks and topographies follow suit, highlighting the cruel fate of those who fell victim of the law, drawing attention to cursed and damned spots where blood had been spilled, and making much of the inscriptions – an 1854 *Guide* gives three pages to them. Here is a selection; interestingly, the focus is especially on the Catholics executed under Elizabeth I:

On entering the building the visitor will notice on the ground floor the following curious device,

but of its carver, Walter Paslew, no authentic records exist. The name "Robert Dvdley," at one corner, is that of the celebrated Earl of Leicester, who when a young man was imprisoned here, having been tried at

Guildhall, on a charge of high treason and sentenced to death in 1554, but was liberated afterwards by Queen Mary.

Over the doorway of the small cell at the foot of the stairs, is the following

and underneath the name, are the letters

I. H. C.

Ascending the stairs near the loophole, is seen a mutilated inscription

"Thox Jenkins, 1672."

On the right of the fire-place, is the following beautifully executed device, bearing the name of "John Dudley," Earl of Warwick, eldest son

of the Duke of Northumberland, and brother to Lord Guildford, who died here in 1553. It consists of a shield containing the well known armorial bearings – the bear and ragged staff. The shield is surrounded by flowers, well-designed and cut, and which are probably intended to allude to the names of his four brothers – viz. the roses for the R in Robert; the honeysuckles for the H in Henry; the acorns on the oak sprig for the A in Ambrose: and the plant which resembles a geranium for the G in Guildford. The inscription at the bottom of the device is as follows:–

> You that these beasts do well behold and se,
> May deme with ease wherefore here may they be.
> With borders eke wherein *there may be found*
> 4 brothers names who list to serche the ground.

The words in italics are unfinished on the stone.

Underneath is the following memorial of Robert Bainbridge, who was imprisoned in 1586, for writing a letter offensive to Queen Elizabeth.

On the left of the second recess is an inscription which is thus translated "Grief is overcome by patience." G. Gyfford, August 8th, 1586.

To the right of the above is an inscription, partly cut away, as follows:– I. II. S. 1571. Die, 10 Aprilis. Wise men ought circumspectly to see what they do – to examin before they speake – to prove before they take in hand – to beware whose company they use, and, above all things, to whom they trust. Charles Bailly.

He was an adherent of Mary Queen of Scots, and suffered the tortures of the rack without making any disclosures of importance. In different parts of the room may be noticed, other memorials of this unfortunate prisoner.

On the right of the recess is this inscription:–

Typping stand and bere thy cross,
For thou art catholyke, but no worse,
And for that cavse this by-eer space,
Thou hast conteant wedin great disgrac
Yet what happ will hitt I
Canot tel, but be death
Or be well, content swet good.

Outside this recess is the following:–

1570
IHON STORE
DOCTOR

He was educated in the University of Oxford, and created doctor of laws, 1538. Refusing to take the oath of supremacy he was executed at Tyburn, June, 1571.

From *The Tower of London: A Handbook Guide for Visitors* (1854) pp. 66, 68–9

Some indication of the climate of expectation this set up may be seen in the account of a Frenchman who visited England in the 1850s. He approached the Tower as a 'sinister necropolis':

I was all impatience to visit the Tower of London, of melodramatic fame. The historical monuments of this country, I notice, are popular in proportion to the horrors committed within their walls. Every self-respecting castle has a legend of bloodshed and murder. . . . Have you any recollection of Tyrrell's clothes in *Les Enfants d'Edouard*? Well, the guards of the Tower of London are got up exactly like that! A square hat with feathers, a dagger in the belt, a scarlet hauberk and tunic fastened down the back, with the Tudor arms and Henry VIII's motto embroidered in gold on the breastplate. They carry a Gothic halberd and wear a starched ruff. 'Tame bluebeards!' whispered one of my companions . . . We were ushered in through a sort of gully within the ramparts. The first tower to the left is a round one. It is the belfry. It was used as a prison for Queen Elizabeth, who having ample opportunity for meditating the fate of Anne Boleyn, her mother, and on that of Jane Grey, so lately beheaded by order of Queen Mary, can scarcely have had a very cheery stay. Further along in the wall to one's right can be seen a half-sunken ogee, framing a heavy door – this is 'Traitor's Gate', through which state criminals made their entrance. Opposite is an ominous-looking postern, surmounted by a tower of the most lugubrious appearance pierced by small, iron-barred windows. It is the 'Bloody Tower', where the little princes were murdered by the savage Gloucester. In the thickness of the masonry, under some stone slabs, their skeletons have been found. In the adjoining, cylindrical, Wakefield Tower is shown a large octagonal room where Henry VI was done to death . . .[47]

The medievalizing (or remedievalizing) of the Tower of London, though it had many cross-overs with the Gothic, had a rather different chronology and was subject to rather different influences – the novels of Sir Walter Scott, for instance, rather than those of Bulwer Lytton, Harrison Ainsworth and Charles Dickens. It was closely connected in its early phases with the cult of chivalry. A key figure here is Samuel Rush Meyrick, the solicitor turned antiquarian who was knighted for his services to the Tower in 1832.[48] His *Critical Inquiry into Antient Armour* (1824) placed the study of armour on a new footing of expertise, Mark Girouard tells us.[49] He brought the light of scholarship, and a sense of period, to the Tower's celebrated 'Line of Kings' – the collection of English monarchs, mounted on horseback and clad in armour, which had been perhaps the Tower's major visitor attraction, ever since it was first displayed in 1680. Meyrick purged the display of such absurdities and anachronisms as the 'Musket of William the Conqueror of great length and thickness'.[50] At the same time, in remodelling the Tower armoury, he combined showmanship with scholarship and in the process introduced a narrative to what had previously been a fancy-free collection of oddments. Insistent on period accuracy, he was no less cavalier than his predecessors in labelling the Tower's vast collection of armoured figures: 'banners were hung above each figure with the title – real or fictitious – of the owner of the armour and the walls were embellished with heraldic colours and devices'.[51] More pertinent, perhaps, for the increasingly 'Gothic' perception of the Tower, would be the instruments of execution and torture which Meyrick had prominently displayed in the New Horse Armoury. The *Tower Guide* of 1854 describes them as follows:

VI INSTRUMENTS OF TORTURE

These specimens of the refined cruelty of our ancestors, may be thus described –

I. THE BILBOES; consisting of iron links, to secure a lot of prisoners together by the ankles.

II. THE SCAVENGER'S DAUGHTER – This 'infernal instrument', for confining the whole of the body – head, hands, and feet – and compressing all the limbs together in a space incredibly small, would have been more correctly called 'The Devil's Masterpiece'. A more horrid piece of machinery for extorting confession – inflicting pain of the most agonizing description – could scarcely well have been conceived of the most cruel tyrant of ancient times.

III. THE THUMBIKIN – These thumbscrews, like the Scavenger's Daughter, were used by our humane ancestors for the purpose of extorting confession from prisoners who were accused – innocently or not – of any high crime, or misdemeanour against the State. The refined mode of operation was to compress the thumbs of the victim between two pieces of iron, by means of a screw, and there made secure by a lock.

IV. THE COLLAR OF TORMENT – This is an iron collar, weighing upwards of 14lbs; the inside being studded with pointed knobs of the same metal about half an inch in length. The amount of torture such a cravat would inflict upon the unfortunate wearer may be imagined. This, however, is not of English origin; it having been captured from one of the ships forming the Spanish Armada, in 1588.

The transformation of the Tower from a cabinet of curiosities and military encampment into a historical monument was very largely the work of the second half of the nineteenth century. A concurrence of different influences were at work. In the first place there was the phenomenal increase in visitors: in 1851, the year of the Great Exhibition, when a regular ticket office was installed, they were running at the rate of 10,000 a year; by the end of the century numbers had risen to more than half a million.[52] Behind this there was a growing public interest in historic buildings, and a growing public appetite for historical spectacle. From some time about 1860, 'the old town', an imaginative reconstruction of the medieval walled city, became a feature of international exhibitions, while in the manufacturing districts of Lancashire and Yorkshire, local cults developed around such monastic ruins as Kirkstall Abbey, Leeds – well described in Charles Dellheim's *The Face of the Past: the Preservation of the Medieval Inheritance in Victorian England.*[53]

Then there was the long-term withdrawal of the Ordnance from the Tower, and its replacement, so far as building projects were concerned, by the much more historically-minded Office of Works – the department of state which had overseen the mounting of the Great Exhibition of 1851. The great fire of 1841 apparently dealt a death blow to the Tower as the nation's principal weapons store, while the development of purpose-built barracks at places like Aldershot made it, as a military encampment, redundant. In the third quarter of the nineteenth century the great bulk of military encroachments were swept away, the personnel departed and the garrison was run down. When, in 1904, responsibility for the Armouries was handed over to the Office of Works, a century-and-a-half-long hegemony finally came to an end.[54]

The medievalization (or remedievalization) of the Tower was the work of one of the leading castle architects and Gothic revivalists of the day, Anthony Salvin. Starting with the restoration of the Beauchamp Tower, his first commission, where he had new battlements 'and windows of an appropriately mediaeval style' put in, he waged systematic war on sash windows, brick buildings and later accretions of all kinds, while at the same time vigorously promoting the addition of battlements, turrets, and winding stairways.[55] By the time his labours came to an end the fortress had taken on its modern aspect as a forest of stonework towers.

There are some wider questions which would need to be raised if one wanted to account for the ways in which the Tower of London became the historical monument we know today. One would be the nineteenth-century romanticization of war. The Gothic Revival is usually discussed in relation to ecclesiology, and Pugin's advocacy of a return to the high Christian architecture of the thirteenth century. Yet in the early nineteenth century, as Mark Girouard shows in *The Return to Camelot,* it is much more closely associated with the 'discovery' of ancient armour and

Osbert Lancaster's gentle mockery of the Scottish Baronial style, from *Here, Of All Places* (London 1959)

the building of make-believe castles. Samuel Rush Meyrick's remodelling of the armouries at the Tower of London was followed by his work on the new armoury at Windsor Castle. Salvin's remedievalization of the Tower was of a piece with his earlier remodelling of Balliol College, Oxford; both had been preceded by Wyatville's well-known work at Windsor Castle, a purist restoration which had the effect of making the medieval look spick-and-span. Sir Walter Scott's Abbotsford, a showcase for his remarkable collection of armour, was the enormously influential precursor not only of 'Scottish Baronial' – *the* style of many later nineteenth-century warehouses, factories and grand hotels, as well as of country seats – but also of castellated suburban villas. Mr Wemmick's 'Walworth Castle', gently satirized by Dickens in *Great Expectations,* is a

'THE DAYS SEEMED VERY LONG AND DREARY TO THE TWO LITTLE BOYS'

The princes in the Tower, from Henrietta Marshall's *Our Island Story*, illustrated by A.S. Forrest

well-known example – a suburban retreat where, as at the Tower of London, the drawbridge was raised each night and a ceremonial cannon fired. No less extravagant is William Burges's military-romantic fantasy of Cardiff Castle, the lifelong obsession of the third Marquis of Bute – a little town of towers taking the place of what had previously been a medieval ruin.[56]

One would also need to reflect upon what Carolyn Steedman, in *Strange Dislocations*, calls the nineteenth-century 'sacralization' of childhood, and Peter Coveney, in *Poor Monkey*, the cult of childhood innocence:[57] this might account for the new centrality given to victimhood and especially to the story of the little princes in the tower, which, in children's history books, such as Henrietta Marshall's *Our Island Story*,[58] was given the symbolic place, as an instance of cruelty and injustice, which a later generation of school textbooks was to give to chimney-sweep boys and child labour down the mines. It is worth recalling here that Shakespeare in *Richard III*, when evoking the horrors of the Tower, gives all his attention to the murder of the Duke of Clarence, while allowing the assassination of the little princes to take place offstage. (Ian McKellen's brilliant 1995 screen version of *Richard III* eschewed Victorian sentiment, reminding us that the princes were in one case an adolescent of about thirteen and in the other a much more juvenile boy of nine when they disappeared in 1483.)[59]

The essay is unfinished here, with a note, 'two or three paragraphs to conclude'.

Notes

1 Tom Nairn, *The Enchanted Glass: Britain and Its Monarchy*, London 1988, part 3, pp. 213–322.

2 PRINCE EDWARD I do not like the Tower, of any place.
Did Julius Caesar build that place, my lord?
BUCKINGHAM He did, my gracious lord, begin that place,
Which since succeeding ages have re-edified.
PRINCE EDWARD Is it upon record, or else reported . . . ?
BUCKINGHAM Upon record, my gracious lord.

Richard III, Act III, Scene i

3 G.T. Clark, 'The Military Architecture of the Tower of London', in *Old London*, London 1867, p. 23.

4 Sir John Fielding, *A Brief Description of the Cities of London and Westminster*, London 1776 ed., p. 96.

5 For the Spitalfields weavers' riots, which produced the ultra-protective Spitalfields Act of 1773, M. Dorothy George, *London Life in the Eighteenth Century*, London 1925, p. 118.

6 *An Illustrated Description of the Tower of London*, London 1771, p. 62.

7 Martin Rivington Holmes, *The Crown Jewels at the Tower of London*, Department of Environment, London 1974, p. 15.

8 *London in Miniature, Being a Concise and Comprehensive Description of the Cities of London and Westminster*, London 1755, pp. 8–40.

9 Phillip Drennon Thomas, 'The Tower of London's Royal Menagerie', *History Today*, August 1996, p. 35; see also E.T. Bennett, *The Tower Menagerie, Comprising the Natural History of the Animals Contained in the Establishment*, London 1829.

10 S. Mordaunt Crook and M.H. Port, *The History of the King's Works*, vol. VI, 1782–1851, London 1973, p. 490.

11 Malcolm Henry Ikin Letts, 'Eighteenth Century London', in *As the Foreigner Saw Us*, London 1935, p. 80.

12 *The Tower of London: Its Armouries and Regalia: A Handbook Guide for Visitors*, Clarke and Co., London *c.* 1850. These and other guidebooks to the Tower were consulted, with the help of David Webb, the librarian at the Bishopsgate Institute, London.

13 Fielding, *Brief Description*, p. 97.

14 *The Tower of London: Its Armouries and Regalia*, p. 40.

15 John Bayley, *The History and Antiquities of the Tower of London*, 2 vols, London 1821 and 1825.

16 Letts, *As the Foreigner Saw Us*, p. 70.

17 Crook and Port, *History of the King's Works*, pp. 488–90.

18 John Stow, *A Survay of London: Contayning the Originall, Antiquity, Increase, Moderne Estate, and Description of that Citie, Etc.*, first published 1598; vol. XV, part II (1934 ed.).

19 *London in Miniature*, pp. 19, 12.

20 Geoffrey Abbott, *The Tower of London As It Was*, Nelson 1988; Abbott lived in the Tower for eight years as a Yeoman Warder and his book is based on his extensive collection of postcards of the Tower.

21 Geoffrey Parnell, 'Getting into Deep Water', *London Archaeologist*, VII, no. 15, Winter 1995, pp. 387–90; 'Diggers Probe for Treasures of Tower Moat', *The Independent*, 31 May 1996.

22 HMSO Guide to the Tower, 1938, p. 5; William Lennox, Lord de Ros, *Memorials of the Tower of London*, London 1866, p. 2.

23 Letts, *As the Foreigner Saw Us*, p. 15.

24 Derek Wilson, *The Tower of London*, London 1958, p. 186.

25 *An Historical Description of the Tower of London, and Its Curiosities*, Carnan and Newberry, London 1771, Preface.

26 *The London Guide, Describing the Public and Private Buildings of London, Westminster and Southwark*, London 1782, p. 26.

27 David Hughson, *Walks Through London*, London 1817, vol. I, p. 23.

28 Howard Tomlinson, 'Ordnance Building at the Tower of London', *History Today*, April 1982, p. 43.

29 Lord de Ros, *Memorials*, p. 4.

30 Wilson, *Tower of London*, p. 186.

31 Geoffrey Parnell, *The Tower of London*, London 1993, p. 88.

32 Lord de Ros, *Memorials*, p. 27.

33 ibid., p. 13. When the Duke of Wellington became Constable of the Tower in 1826, he was confronted by a thousand or so miscellaneous inhabitants of the place, and about a hundred yeoman warders 'who hired their quarters out as lodgings or public houses and who made it their business to extort money by way of tips from visiting antiquaries and tourists': Jill Allibone, *Anthony Salvin: Pioneer of Gothic Revival Architecture*, Cambridge 1988, p. 39.

34 One eighteenth-century visitor dismissed the Crown Jewels and the relics with the advice that seeing these 'would take you several days, and would be to your cost', preferring the menagerie, which contained 'ten lions, one panther, two tigers and four leopards', and a 'tiger man': Rosamund Bayne Powell, *Travellers in Eighteenth-Century England*, London 1951, p. 68. According to Lord de Ros the stock had dwindled by 1815 to 'one lion, two lionesses, one panther, one hyena, one tygress, one jackall, one mountain cow and one large bear': *Memorials*, p. 272. John Britton and E.W. Brayley observe that 'the common phrase of "seeing the lions"' had been in use 'almost down to our own times', noting that when Mr Alfred Cops succeeded to the office of keeper in 1822, the Menagerie 'consisted of the grizzly bear, an elephant, and one or two birds': *Memoirs of the Tower of London*, London 1830. Richard D. Altick gives a vivid portrait of the Tower as one of the eighteenth-century 'sights and resorts' of the capital in *The Shows of London*, Cambridge, Mass. 1978. See also Edward Smith, *Foreign Visitors in England and What They Have Thought of Us*, London 1889.

35 Hughson, *Walks*, p. 21.

36 G.T. Clark, *Medieval Military Architecture in England*, London 1884, p. 234.

37 Parnell, *Tower of London*, p. 90.

38 H.G. Bohn, *The Pictorial Handbook of London*, London 1854, pp. 128–9.

39 Bayley, *History and Antiquities of the Tower of London.*

40 Charles Dickens, *A Tale of Two Cities*, Harmondsworth 1970, p. 131. Dickens wrote that he conceived the idea for the novel 'when I was acting, with my children and friends, in Mr Wilkie Collins's drama of The Frozen Deep': Preface to *A Tale of Two Cities*, 1859.

41 'The Beauchamp Tower, . . . the walls of which, like a mystic scroll, are covered with inscriptions – each a tragic story in itself, and furnishing matter for abundant reflection' is, Ainsworth argues, 'the property of the nation, and should be open to national inspection': *The Tower of London*, London 1840, pp. iv–v. For Ainsworth, see his biographer, Stewart Marsh Ellis, *William Harrison Ainsworth and His Friends*, 2 vols, London 1911.

42 *Old St Paul's*, 3 vols, London 1841. 'The history of the Plague is, of course, mainly founded on Defoe's wonderful *Journal of the Plague Year*, but . . . infused with actuality, with human interest.' Ellis, *Ainsworth*, p. 423.

43 Keith Hollingsworth, *The Newgate Novel 1830–1847*, Detroit 1963, pp. 105–6.

44 Daphne du Maurier, *Myself When Young*, London 1977, pp. 29–30.

45 Parnell, *Tower of London*, p. 112.

46 Thomas Babington Macaulay, *The History of England* (1849–61), in two volumes, 1877 ed. pp. 306–7.

47 Francis Wey, *A Frenchman Sees the English in the Fifties*, ed. Valerie Pirie, London 1935, pp. 96–9.

48 According to the *Dictionary of National Biography*, Meyrick, whilst working as an advocate, accumulated his own magnificent collection of armour; he was elected a Fellow of the Society of Antiquaries in 1810, and contributed frequently to the *Archaeologica*; his three-volume *A Critical Inquiry into Antient Armour as It Existed in Europe, but Particularly in England, from the Norman Conquest to the Reign of King Charles II, with a Glossary of Military Terms of the Middle Ages*, with eighty plates, was 'practically the first on the subject'.

49 Mark Girouard, *The Return to Camelot: Chivalry and the English Gentleman*, London 1981, p. 30.

50 C. Ffoulkes, *Arms and the Tower*, London 1939, p. 47.

51 C. Ffoulkes, *Inventory and Survey of the Armouries of the Tower of London*, vol. I, London 1916, p. 28.

52 Parnell, *Tower of London*, p. 112.

53 Charles Dellheim, *The Face of the Past: the Preservation of the Medieval Inheritance in Victorian England*, Cambridge 1982.

54 Wilson, *Tower of London*, p. 227.

55 Allibone, *Salvin*, p. 141.

56 On Scottish Baronial, see the first three of the five volumes of David MacGibbon and Thomas Ross, *The Castellated and Domestic Architecture of Scotland*, Edinburgh 1887–92, the source for much of Charles Rennie Mackintosh's lecture of 1891, 'Scotch Baronial Architecture', published in Pamela Robertson (ed.), *Charles Rennie Mackintosh: The Architectural Papers*, Glasgow 1990, and see the accompanying essay by Frank Arneil Walker on 'Scottish Baronial Architecture'; James Macaulay, *The Gothic Revival 1745–1845*, Glasgow 1975. These references are owed to Gavin Stamp, whose unpublished paper on 'Scotch Baronial', for the History Workshop conference on 'Scottish Dimensions', May 1995, argued that 'the real interest of Baronial . . . is that it is an attempt at creating, or recreating a national style; as such, it is a pioneer in European terms' (p. 3). For Burges, R.P. Pullan, *The Architectural Designs of William Burges*, London 1883; Stefan Muthesius, *The High Victorian Movement in Architecture 1850–1870*, London 1972.

57 Carolyn Steedman, *Strange Dislocations: Childhood and the Idea of Human Interiority 1780–1930*, London 1995; Peter Coveney, *The Image of Childhood. The Individual and Society: A Study of the Theme in English Literature* (originally published as *Poor Monkey*, 1957), Harmondsworth 1967.

58 Henrietta Marshall, *Our Island Story: A History of England for Boys and Girls*, London 1905, gives an entire chapter to 'The Story of the Two Little Princes in the Tower', in

which the smothering of 'the two pretty children' – 'they could not scream, they could not breathe' (p. 284) – is described in some detail.

59 As Ian McKellen notes in his screenplay, it was nearly two hundred years later that bones, apparently of two children, were excavated within the Tower and reburied in Westminster Abbey (*Richard III*, Doubleday 1996, p. 210).

The Lost Gardens of Heligan*

Botanical gardens, a legacy of the seventeenth-century scientific revolution, of physick gardens, and of the early years of pharmaceuticals, as well as (indirectly) of the expansion of Europe, do not figure in classical accounts of the rise of capitalism, though the instrumentalization of the natural world is, or ought to be, one of its capital themes. Nor do they have a place in accounts of the British Empire. The older histories are preoccupied with the administration and annexation of territory: the traffic in species, even though it was a global one, is beyond their ken. The newer histories, sailing under the flag of post-colonial discourse, and intent on pinning the convict's badge of racism on anything that moves, have neither conceptual nor imaginative space for those intrepid plant collectors – 'botanical travellers' as they were called by one of the eighteenth-century founders of Kew Gardens[1] – who risked life and limb exploring the Empire's outer rim.

Plant-hunting is as old as the voyages of discovery (*Drymis winteri*, the therapeutic bark rich in vitamin C, is attributed to Drake's circumnavigation of the globe),[2] but it was in the epoch of mercantilism, roughly from the late seventeenth to the early nineteenth century, that, in Britain as in other European countries, it became systematic, a means of developing colonial trade and maximizing colonial resources. For Sir Joseph Banks, the effective founder of Kew Gardens, this was a lifelong vocation. After serving his botanical apprenticeship leading the scientific party on board Cook's *Endeavour* (and returning from the three-year voyage to the Antipodes with the dried specimens of some 3,600 species), he settled in England, where he masterminded a worldwide transfer of plants, using a vast network of agents, donors and collectors, and developing a chain of satellites in the colonies.[3] The Calcutta Botanic Gardens, founded by the East India Company in 1787, had the more explicitly mercantilist aim of

* This article first appeared in the Christmas issue of *New Statesman and Society*, 15 December 1995.

collecting rare plants 'not for the purposes . . . of curiosity . . . but for . . . the extension of the national commerce and riches'.[4]

In the nineteenth century Britain laid claim to being the plant metropolis of the world. As early as 1825, John Claudius Loudon, the horticultural writer, claimed that this country was growing nearly one-fourth of the estimated flora of the world.[5] Later, the early Victorian revival and extension of Kew was explicitly undertaken to make it 'an efficient institution for the promotion of botanical science throughout the empire'.[6] Its most brilliant coup, from the point of view of economic botany and imperial development, was the transformation of *Hevea brasiliensis* into the raw material of the Malayan rubber industry.[7]

Cornwall had a distinctive place in the transoceanic transfer of plants. Enjoying the warmth of the Gulf Stream, its mild frost-free winters, high rainfall and acid soil made it a hospitable terrain for exotica which, elsewhere in Britain, would have perished. 'The immediate neighbourhood of Penzance is remarkably well suited for the acclimatization of plants,' remarks J.S. Courteney in his 1845 *Guide*. 'A considerable number of New Holland and New Zealand plants, which . . . the late Mr Aiton of Kew Gardens was for many years accustomed to forward to a lady resident here, have appeared quite at home in her grounds . . . Among these, several species of *Eucalyptus pulvigera*.'[8]

As Courteney's comments suggest, the authorities at Kew seem to have used Cornish gardens as outstations. Joseph Hooker, the superintendent at Kew, is reputed to have been a frequent visitor at Menabilly, the 'Manderley' of Daphne Du Maurier's *Rebecca* (Hooker Grove there is named in his honour). Sikkim rhododendrons, raised from seed collected by Hooker during his celebrated expedition of 1847–51, were a feature of some of the leading Cornish gardens, and so successfully did they acclimatize themselves there that when the authorities at Kew, completing their Temperate House, wanted to display mature specimens of Himalayan rhododendrons, it was from Cornwall that they obtained their supply.[9] Cornwall indeed was the heartland of the Himalayan rhododendron. According to Edgar Thurston's *British and Foreign Trees and Shrubs in Cornwall* (1930), the Great Western Railway was overrun with them. 'At St Austell the train ran into what was a rhododendron walk rather than a railway station. Big flowers hedged the line for full a mile, and, at Bodmin Road . . . there were more of them than are to be found at Kew.'[10]

Cornish gardens established themselves as a repository for transoceanic exotica in the early and middle years of the nineteenth century. It was a time when, because of its advanced mining technology, Cornwall was one of the industrial wonders of the world; fortunes were being made out of mining, engineering and shipping, and surpluses were freely invested in landed estate. The Foxes, Quaker shipping agents at Falmouth, founded some half-dozen great gardens in the years from 1820 to 1860, among them Trebah, using ships' captains as a source of plants as well as the London or Truro seedsmen. At Penjerrick, near Falmouth, the main development, 'especially in the way of semi-tropical trees and shrubs', was done by Robert Were Fox (1789–1877), an FRS on the back of his mineralogical discoveries.[11]

Heligan, miraculously restored to life in the past four years, is, like many gardens, a palimpsest, on which wildly contrasting styles have left their mark. At one stage it was an ornamental garden, with a *ferme ornée* in the picturesque manner of the 1790s. The very rococo grotto, built around 1810, was a late eighteenth-century folly. Little more than a decade later, Heligan was acquiring exotica. The most famous shrub, the *Cornus capitata (Benthamisa fragifera)*, was planted there with seeds from its native Nepal, brought back by Anthony Buller, a local MP who had contrived to secure a Bengal judgeship: '. . . when Mr Tremayne made the drive in 1832, he planted this splendid tree on either side'.[12] (Since Buller was a government placeman, it is a puzzle how the tree came to acquire its radical name.)

The restoration of Heligan, undertaken by enthusiasts, led by media refugee Tim Smit, is as different from those of the National Trust as it is possible to imagine. For one thing there is no country seat 'in family occupation' to drool over; the brick-built manor house was sold off some years ago and converted into flats. Then there are no formal walks or vistas. Thickly planted and overgrown, the 70-acre gardens are a kind of labyrinth. Overhanging branches have not been lopped back, to preserve or restore some period-proper vista; visitors have to duck under them. 'Where things have been blown down, they are left.'[13]

This is not to say that Heligan is a wild garden. The restoration has been undertaken with scrupulous regard to the old maps, and it has made use of a vast amount of forensic skill. There is a slight melancholy air about the place; the wishing-well and the grotto, with their mildewed, ivy-covered stones and circumambient mosses, are of a piece with the altogether more spontaneous chaos of 'the Jungle' – the name given to Heligan's magnificent assembly of exotica. Here, fantastic shapes have developed, encouraged by seventy years of neglect, with self-seeding trees and overgrown shrubs running riot. The 'lost' effect is carefully cultivated by the restorers, and is indeed the rationale of their whole project. So many of the gardening staff perished in the Great War, they argue, that the gardens 'went to sleep'. Losing heart, the Tremayne family abandoned any attempt to renew the plantings. The gardens, Tim Smit argues, are a 'sleeping beauty', and not the least of the objects of restoration is to allow that sleep to continue undisturbed.[14]

For all the affectation of wildness, the restoration of the lost gardens of Heligan is underpinned by historical science. Metal detectors identified the Victorian drainage system; for its Georgian predecessor, regulating the picturesque aquatics, the services of a dowser were engaged. When restoration began in 1991, with a band of volunteers hacking their way into the undergrowth, the paths were identified using the 1839 tithe map. Thomas Grey's plan of 1800, work of the landscapist who also redesigned Menabilly, was no less crucial for the garden layout, setting out a basic grid that has subsisted to the present day; earlier features, such as the Northern Summerhouse, are dated by reference to a plan of 1770. An 1890 photograph is serving as the guide for the Sundial Garden's restoration. A more macabre exercise in historical reconstitution follows the fate of those who, on the eve of the Great War, scrawled their names on the plaster of the 'thunder box' – the toilet next to the dark house. Using work books found in the Devon Country Record Office, the Heligan *Guide* tells us: 'As 1915 arrived, one by one the names were prefixed with the word "enlisted", and the next time the names appear is on the war memorial at St Ewe.'

One distinctive feature of the restoration is the salience given to human labour. On many National Trust properties this is invisible – the gardens appear to be the realization of a landscape artist's dreams, or the proprietor's whim. Here, on the contrary, it is the gardeners who are omnipresent, most of them engaged in the vegetable garden, or the engine-house, forcing or retarding the growth of hot-house plants. The vegetable garden, 'the only full working Victorian kitchen garden in the country', is a hive of activity, standing at the centre of the site and worked by a crew of six or more. Before the mass-production of wire, it required two men working seven weeks each year to train the walled fruits. The heating apparatus for the melon house and the pineapple pits was even more labour-intensive, and visitors are directed to the Little Bothy where a boy gardener would pass the night, watching that nothing was amiss.

The internationality of Heligan also marks it out from conventional notions of the English garden. Flora's garden, the green sward that seems originally to have been a ride, was in the 1850s turned into a showcase for Hooker's Himalayan rhododendrons. Nearby are storyboards that link the species with the plant hunters after whom they are name – e.g. the 'Douglas fir' at the end of the ravine (after an extraordinary career in both the Americas and the East, Douglas met his death in a Hawaiian gin-trap). The 'Valley Garden' as it was called in a *Gardener's Chronicle* report of 1897, has been renamed. 'The Jungle' and the giant Brazilian rhubarb (*Gunnera manicata*), growing rankly and in clumps, gives it in places the appearance of a swamp. Reference should be made also to the abundance of Australian tree ferns (*Dicksonia antarctica*), imported in the later nineteenth century by a well-known family of local nurserymen, the Treseders of Truro and Adelaide.

Like any restoration, that of the lost gardens of Heligan has its hidden aesthetics, and the results are sufficiently remarkable to make it worth speculating on what these might be. There are notions of authenticity here that Victorians might have found strange. As the *Guide* points out, the idea of growing 'organic' vegetables would hardly have appealed to

The author in 'the Jungle' at Heligan, November 1995

those in the habit of using arsenic to force on growth. More fundamental, perhaps, is the idea of the 'secret garden'. This is an idea that has an ancient resonance in European literature, where the enclosed garden stands for magical and mysterious space – an arena where feeling has free play, and desire is untrammelled.[15] Heligan's 'Jungle' is an example of this. It might seem to invite the derision of the heritage-baiters and to be vulnerable to deconstructive critics (many of the trees, so far from being tropical, come from the temperate zone forests of Chile and New Zealand). But 'Jungle', it seems, was a name adopted in deference to local lore. For years 'the Jungle' had been a favourite courting-place for couples from the nearby fishing village of Mevagissey; indeed, according to tradition, something like half the population was conceived there. Four years into what has been hailed as the garden restoration of the century, the Lost Gardens of Heligan still seem like a place where *A Midsummer Night's Dream* could happen.

Notes

1 'Plant hunters, or "botanical travellers", as Sir Joseph Banks preferred to call them': Kenneth Lemmon, *The Golden Age of Plant Hunters*, London 1968, p. ix. This piece grew from notes made in discussion with staff and helpers at Heligan in November 1995. Chris Gardner and Toby Musgrave, a garden historian, of Gardner Musgrave Associates, offered a great deal of information concerning the redesign and layout of the gardens. Thanks are also due to Tim Smit, the original force behind the gardens' restoration, and John Nelson, his partner; the latter patiently took the author on a lengthy and extremely informative perambulation of the gardens in freezing cold Cornish weather during a second visit late in December that year. The piece was left unrevised and unfootnoted.

2 The bark is named after Captain James Winter, who commanded one of the ships in Drake's fleet and was apparently advised by Tierra del Fuegan Indians to feed soup made from the bark to the scurvy-ridden, mutinous crew. The ship's log notes its restorative effect. The author is grateful to Colin Howlett, Director of Marketing at Heligan, for supplying anecdotes and materials regarding the plants and plant hunters, and to Major Tony Hibbert of the Trebah Garden Trust for other historical notes on the gardens in Cornwall.

3 For Banks, Ray Desmond, *A Century of Kew Plantsmen*, London 1993; *Kew: The History of the Royal Botanic Gardens*, London 1995.

4 Lucile H. Brockway, *Science and Colonial Expansion: The Role of the British Royal Botanic Gardens*, New York 1979, p. 75; Ray Desmond, *The European Discovery of Indian Flora*, Oxford 1992.

5 Cited by Lemmon, *Plant Hunters*, p. 217.

6 Desmond, *Kew: The History*, p. 147.

7 'In 1876 the British removed wild rubber seeds from Brazil to start plantations in India, Ceylon, Malaya. . . . By 1913, Ceylon's exports of rubber were worth £4.5 million and rubber exports from the Malay peninsula £3.1 million': Brockway, *Science and Colonial Expansion*; p. 141.

8 Cited by Edgar Thurston, *British and Foreign Trees and Shrubs in Cornwall*, Cambridge 1930, pp. 4–5; W.T. Aiton succeeded his father as Royal Gardener at Kew in 1793.

9 Desmond, *Kew: The History*, p. 279.

10 Thurston, *Trees and Shrubs*, p. 198.

11 ibid., p. 60.

12 W. Roberts, *Gardeners' Chronicle*, xx, 1896, p. 747.

13 A comment made by Chris Gardner.

14 Since the publication of this article a full account of the restoration has been published by Tim Smit, *The Lost Gardens of Heligan*, London 1997, to tie in with a Channel Four television series.

15 The Heligan brochure affectionately mentions the inspiration of the Edwardian children's classic by Frances Hodgson Burnett, *The Secret Garden*, London 1911, a tale in which an orphaned and depressed child is restored to love and hope by the discovery and cultivation of a hidden garden.

Country Visiting: A Memoir*

I was brought up on a very different version of the country cult to those which seem prevalent today; one which, though by its own lights purist, was the very reverse of the Arcadian. Not buttercups and daisies but gorse and heather were its flora and fauna, not quiet meadows but rocky heights its *ultima Thule*.[1] For my mother, at once a 'progressive' and a romantic, nature was essentially wild, 'the more primitive the better'.[2] It was not a source of tranquillity but an energizer, a kind of objective correlative to the idea of storm and stress. As in her love of pottery – the only ornament of our otherwise rather bare living-room – or in her taste for literature (*The Wind That Shakes the Barley*, a romantic life of Burns, was one of the very few books on her shelves; Grassic Gibbon's *A Scots Quair* another), so too in the countryside she identified the primitive with the natural, the beautiful and the good.[3] A woman in revolt against the servitudes of domestic life (and, it may be, motherhood), she scorned comfort and revelled in the freedom of unruly open space. A born organizer, in her wartime work at an aircraft factory working to fine limits, she could indulge here a taste for the boundless or, in the words of one of her favourite ballads, 'the lonely sea and the sky.'[4] On our climbing expeditions we were hugely excited when we were caught up in the swirl of mountain mists, or the skirts of a cloud, such as the low-lying ones which circled the apex of Ben Lomond. One of the delights of the New Forest was losing oneself in the darkness of the woods. On Dartmoor, where we spent a week youth-hostelling, the great challenge was to find one's way across a trackless waste.

For working-class ramblers, a sizeable army in the 1930s and 1940s, the country was an escape from the dirt and grime of the city. For my mother it was rather, perhaps, a reverse image of 'The Suburb' – the Hampstead

* This essay is a shortened version of an unfinished piece variously entitled 'The Scenic Gaze' or 'The Country Look', part of a larger exploration of the changing notion of 'aesthetic geography', which is discussed below. It was unfootnoted.

Garden Suburb where we had lived before the war and which she had escaped to work in a factory. In my childhood demonology – learnt, I'm sure, at my mother's knee – 'The Suburb' was synonymous with conventionality and boredom. But it was also, as any visitor will see, a showcase of the picturesque, an ambitious exercise in English vernacular which combines cottage or cottage-style architecture with carefully landscaped 'Walks' and 'Closes' and 'Ways'. It certainly seems to have defined, by negative example, my mother's tastes. She had, and has, a sovereign contempt for the 'pretty pretty'. It was not quiet which she sought in the countryside but tumult – the thunder of the waterfalls, the turmoil of the mountain cataracts, the melancholy echo of the sea. She steered clear of the cosy and charming. She thrilled to the spectacle of the untamed.

Rambling involved too, it may be, a rejection, or partial rejection, of femininity. It required stamina and strength, 'practical' clothing and 'sensible' shoes. It emancipated women from thraldom to the milliner, the dressmaker and the hairdresser. To wear shorts – something like a uniform among hikers – was still quite a daring thing for women to do in the 1940s, while the idea of roughing it in all weathers hardly conformed to traditional notions of the maidenly, the matronly or the maternal. Rambling encouraged women to dress like men, to look like men, and to act like men. It was, in some sort, an emancipation from the sex. My mother's walking kit – shorts, windcheaters and stout shoes, such as those in the accompanying photograph – were in this very much of a piece with the dungarees which she delighted to wear in her Slough factory; her preference for slacks over stockings; her impatience with fashion, flounces and frills. It was also of a piece with an aesthetics which conceptualized nature in terms of rude strength: bold scenery, rugged coastlines, grey granite and crags. Our chosen landscapes, I now realize, were exclusively masculine. We preferred the mountain peaks to the valleys, the rocky cliffs to the golden sands. We had no images at all of fertility, such as those associated with seed-time and harvest; no interest in wildlife; no taste at all for the drowsy or the lush.

Our interest in nature was, it seems, first and foremost symbolic. On our country walks, self-absorbed and unnoticing, or perhaps if we were in a party, singing, we never stopped to admire (or identify) the field and woodland flowers, but strode on purposefully to the uplands, beating our way through the bracken, or scrambling up stony paths. Indeed I was brought up in such complete ignorance of plants that when, a few years ago, I was caught up in the gardening mania, I ruined my first year's efforts by planting indoor shrubs outside. Before the war, when we lived in Hampstead Garden Suburb, my mother had kept a rockery, but I think she must have taken against gardens – even 'Alpine' ones – at the same time as she turned against 'The Suburb'. Certainly, after breaking up the home we never had a garden again. For the same reason, perhaps, and in a similar spirit – a radical impatience with the comfortable and the

Building 'The Hut' at Long Dene School, 1942 (author second from the right); and, left, Minna Keal, the author's mother, kitted out for hiking

kempt – my mother came to look down on parks, and when we returned to London after the war we seldom set foot in one. Regent's Park, with its ornamental flower-beds, was 'artificial'; Hyde Park (except for political demos) was uninteresting and flat. Only Hampstead Heath, a hilly wilderness, was real. My mother also seems to have lost whatever taste she had for flowers, and to this day dislikes having them in the house. As a child,

I am sorry to say, I thought them 'cissy'. I was fascinated by the scarlet bloom on the runner beans (in wartime Britain, the one splash of colour one saw in the back gardens when travelling about by train), and I loved snowdrops and crocuses as early signs of spring. Otherwise I had no eye for flowers at all, and associated them not with the country but with 'The Suburb'. When, at boarding school, I was given a garden plot of my own, I used it exclusively to grow vegetables, my prize crops (which I would carry home as 'presents' at the end of the week) being radishes and potatoes.

My mother, like other emancipated people of her generation, was a fresh-air fanatic, counterposing the claustrophobia and 'stuffiness' of the Victorian with the freedom of light and space. As a baby I was brought up on the principles of Truby King, a New Zealander (the Dr Spock of his day) who believed that windows should be kept wide open; that parental breath was poisonous; and that the ideal place for children to sleep was on the verandah.[5] I was put out in the snow, my mother tells me, when I was only a few days old. At boarding school, where I was sent at the age of six, an evacuee from wartime London, the regimen was hardly less severe: our day began at 6.45 a.m. with a cold bath and a barefoot run round the paddock. Conditions were more relaxed in my later childhood, but it remained a matter of principle, and indeed personal pride, to wear an open neck, short-sleeved shirt (preferably Aertex)[6] in all the seasons of the year, never to feel the cold, and to enjoy going out in all weathers.

Like other 'progressive' schools, Long Dene in Buckinghamshire believed in everyday contact with 'the essential simple life of nature'.[7] Lessons were perfunctory (English and woodwork are the only ones I can remember) and we spent much of the day out of doors, hanging about the stables or the orchard, building rafts and floating them off in the lake, practising high jump in the paddock, or playing football and rounders. The school made a fetish of manual skills, and I think we must have been encouraged to become juvenile builders. We spent our afternoons in 'The Hut', one of a series of little houses which we built for ourselves in woodland clearings on the school estate. As can be seen from the accompanying photograph, it was quite an elaborate affair, running, at one stage, to two storeys, with tarpaulins to keep out the draughts, a window to let in some light, and a stove where we baked potatoes. For the school authorities it was no doubt a Thoreau-like communion with nature,[8] but for a little group of homesick children, huddling together for warmth, it was perhaps rather a way of getting up a fug.

Long Dene subscribed to a variety of nature mysticisms. Our classes took their name from wild life (I was a 'Beaver', my best friend Christopher Webb was a 'Kestrel'). Johnny, the headmaster, practised Yoga, though we never saw him at it; Karis, his wife, instructed us in eurythmics, or 'creative' dance'; Fred the head gardener was a vegetarian and a Conscientious Objector. Mary, the English teacher, was an Irishwoman who believed in ghosts; Constance, the matron in charge of our dormitory, told us that the churchyard in Stoke Poges which abutted the school – the one where Gray wrote his *Elegy* – was haunted. Halloween was the only festival which, as befitted a non-denominational school, Long Dene observed, and it was celebrated (if that is the word) with real and frightening fervour – the most memorable night of the year. As a juvenile Marxist I was naturally against all this, but at night it was only the reassuring sound of ack-ack fire which soothed me to sleep – a distant echo of London, where the anti-aircraft batteries were taking on enemy bombers.

Long Dene practised its own version of 'Back to the Land'.[9] It prided itself on being, at least so far as fruit and vegetables were concerned, self-supporting, and quite a bit of our time was spent helping out in the kitchen garden or being employed on ancillary tasks: shaking the trees for fruit, or working in the apple loft are the ones I remember best. The headmaster was a partisan of 'organic' farming who believed that what he called 'materialism' was ruining British agriculture. His address at the beginning of the school day – 'Johnny's Blah' – would be given over to such matters as the iniquities of chemical fertilizers, and the message was amplified at our Sunday evening film shows, the place where I first saw *The Plow that Broke the Plains* (a documentary about 'Dust Bowl' America) and *Man of Aran*, Flaherty's tribute to a livelihood snatched from the sea.

King Alfred's, the London day school of my later childhood – another 'progressive' school – was, if anything, even more committed to Arts and Crafts than Long Dene. It did not practise nature mysticism, but, as befitted a school which numbered Cecil Sharp among its founders, it taught 'country dancing', and school sing-songs, a high point of the term, were devoted to country songs.[10] Within its own more restricted limits, King Alfred's was no less fetishistic than Long Dene about fresh air. As *The Modern Schools Handbook* (1934) put it:

> The school grounds comprise an area of six acres . . . This enables London children to get the nearest approach to country conditions possible within a few miles of Charing Cross. There are trees to climb; bushes, among which 'huts' may be built; a pool for paddling, and the possibility of watching the processes of the seasons, as well as the opportunity for playing hockey, cricket, footer, netball, tennis and fives, all within the boundaries of the school estate.[11]

School assembly was held each morning in Squirrel Hall, an al fresco auditorium where we seated ourselves on logs while the register was called and buttoned ourselves up, as best we could, against the wind and the rain. School work, according to the 1934 handbook, was 'conducted as much as possible under open-air conditions'.[12] I do not have a memory of this, but as a fanatic footballer I needed no encouragement to stay in the open air, and spent as much of the day as I could on the playing field. We did not, like our predecessors in the 1930s, go 'tracking' and fishing on Hampstead Heath, which adjoined the school to the north. But we did go tobogganing there when the snows set in, as they did so spectacularly during the winter of 1946–47. And the school took us there for cross-country running. It was one of the few things I was good at, and one of the prouder moments of my childhood was when I came eighth in a West Middlesex juvenile championship (if I had come sixth I would have got a medal).

From the age of nine, when I was taken climbing in the Lake District, long and strenuous walks in the country were a central part of my childhood. My mother was forever getting up or joining walking parties, usually for no more than a weekend, but at Christmas and Easter for the holiday break, and once or twice a year for the entire week.[13] 'Woodlands', a Communist holiday camp in the North Downs, where we slept in rough chalets and spent a very good Christmas in 1946, was one frequent venue: 'Netherwood', a Bohemian guest-house run by a rather saturnine spirit-rapper, was another.[14] Then there were the Sunday rambles organized by the Workers Musical Association, of which my mother was membership secretary as well as singing in the choir, and the summer camps organized by the Woodcraft Folk or the Young Communist League, one of which, at New Milton, initiated me into the mysteries of the New Forest. I would also be taken walking by family friends; by my school; and from time to time by adults who adopted me (I spent a good deal of my childhood looking for surrogate parents).

Although I did not follow my mother in all her enthusiasms, I was, if anything, even more Gothic in my tastes. As a child obsessive, I conceived a passion for mountains, craving to be taken to them on holidays, drawing them, peak upon peak, in my classroom doodles, and imagining myself climbing impossible heights. Later I developed a comparable fascination with moors, though it owed more perhaps to reading than to walking experience. Egdon Heath, that 'vast tract' of unenclosed wild, fascinated me when, about the age of fourteen I came upon Hardy's *The Return of the Native*; so did the spectre-ridden fastness of *Wuthering Heights.* British films of the period – I was an avid cinemagoer – no doubt amplified these effects. They were also reinforced by the revolutionary romanticism of Russian Communism in which, along with the rest of my family, I was immersed. A picture of Lenin and his companion Krupskaya, climbing in the Alps, is one that has lodged itself in my memory. Another – taken from the film *My Universities* – is of the young Maxim Gorky, a stormy petrel peering out to the far horizons. Of the choruses we belted out, one – a Polish workers' song of the 1920s – seems particularly pertinent:

> Whirlwinds of danger around us are swirling
> Overwhelming forces of darkness and fear,
> Still in the fight for the freedom of humanity
> Red flag of liberty that yet shall prevail.

This brings sharply and unexpectedly to mind the first film I ever saw, at the impressionable age of six – a show organized by my mother in the village of Aspley Guise, in Bedfordshire, where we were evacuated. The film – a parable of the 1905 revolution made into a Bolshevik folk-tale – was called *Lone White Sail.* It tells of a group of children in a remote Caucasian village who come upon a refugee from the mutiny on the *Potemkin* – a revolutionary sailor on the run. They shelter him from the police and bring him food, rather in the manner of Pip and Magwitch in the opening sequence of David Lean's *Great Expectations.* The film ends with his getaway. The children assemble on the cliff, shouting their farewells into the distance as the boat makes for the open sea, no doubt to the accompaniment of swelling chords on the sound-track; the fugitive sailor, wrapped up in his greatcoat, stands before the mast, while the lone white sail streams against the wind.

I am not sure what I felt about the countryside as a child. At boarding school, surrounded by nature mystics and in daily communion with nature, I was both homesick and – as a self-proclaimed 'materialist' – at odds with the school authorities. I was also cut off from 'the news', one of my obsessions at that time. The staff-room copy of the *Daily Telegraph,* which I cycled down to the lodge to fetch in the early morning, was my only contact with the outside world. Holidays in Belsize Park, London, where I stayed with an uncle and aunt, and Saturday mornings at my mother's factory in Slough gave me an enthusiasm for the urban which has lasted throughout my life. On the other hand Burnham Beeches, one of my mother's favourite Sunday outings, had for me the magic of the Forest of Arden. My mother's climbing expeditions were an even more complete escape from school, as were seaside holidays with my father's family in Wales. Saddleback in the Lake District, where I braved the perils of 'Sharp Edge' was in my mind's eye a Matterhorn; Plynlimon, the third highest mountain in Wales, where we got no further than the foothills, an Everest.

I was, if anything, even more enthusiastic for the youth-hostelling weekends of my later childhood, after we returned, in 1945, to London, and I have the fondest memories of the Communist holiday camps and guest-houses. But I suspect this had to do less with the scenery and the walks than with the company, and above all the fact that here I was surrounded by adults, people who would listen gravely to my 'views' and no doubt flatter me in my conceits. I hated being a child and got on badly at school, on account both of congenital lateness (or what the school termed 'anti-social' behaviour) and of a wildly unpopular politics (I was expelled from the school debating society). Weekends away were the one place where I did not have to defend the party line, a refuge from Cold War anti-Communism. They were also a kind of apprenticeship, providing me with a whole succession of mentors who took me under their wing. Going to the countryside, in short, was a way of being grown-up.

Later I discovered other ways of growing up. I developed an obsession for watching football, attending the home matches of both Arsenal and Spurs. I spent my Saturday mornings (and my pocket money) in the bookshops of Charing Cross Road. My mother found it increasingly difficult to drag me off to the countryside and when, at the age of fifteen, I joined the St Pancras YCL I gave up rambling entirely. Yet my tastes seem to have been set in a time-warp, and whenever I have returned to rambling it has been in effect to the landscapes of my childhood. Five years ago, walking in the Cevennes, it struck me that I had been seeing the same scenery all my life, even though it was in different places and under different names, and it is no doubt of a piece with this that when, two years ago, I got married, we spent our honeymoon in the Shetlands – perhaps the bleakest and certainly the most treeless place I have ever seen. My literary and historical pilgrimages seem to have followed a similar course – Stonehenge with its memories of Hardy's Tess and Angel Clare; the Brontë parsonage of Haworth; the Chartist caves at Llangattock, that bare mountainside where the Newport insurrectionaries of 1839, a ragged battalion of ironworkers and colliers, met at dead of night.

For my mother, working during the war at an aircraft factory, and later 'cooped up' in a London office, walking was a kind of religion, a secular form of uplift in which 'fresh air', 'exercise' and 'scenery' took the place of the Holy Trinity. Holidays were a sacrament, a way of leading the Simple Life. They were not so much a relaxation as a way of strengthening body and soul, indeed they only became meaningful if they involved an element of hardship and sacrifice. My mother was content to let nature remain a mystery and perhaps preferred it that way. The whole point of the countryside, in our particular version of it, was its otherness. We had no desire to settle in the country, no ambition to colonize it. The idea of taking a cottage for the week – standard practice among holidaymakers today – was beyond our imaginative ken. Like many other Youth Hostellers we were content to be transients and strangers, delivering ourselves to the mercy of the elements and trusting in an ultimate benevolence.

Our topography of beauty was substantially different from that to be found in the tourist maps, or the heritage trails of today. The Cotswolds, promoted today as 'the heart of England', did not figure in our itineraries, in fact until I became a student at Oxford in the 1950s I am not sure that I had heard of them. Nor, except where it became Weald or marshes, did 'the garden of England', Kent. Suffolk, 'the Constable country' as it has now become, was, like the rest of East Anglia, a blank. We had no feeling for the 'Englishness' of the countryside: on the contrary the less English it was the better. Our ideal landscapes were on the Celtic fringes and provided us with a measure; if we went to the Downs it was because in the Home Counties it was the nearest thing to the Highlands, just as Fairlight Glen, a cross-country walk from Hastings, was our surrogate for a Cornish cove. Fort William, in my mother's conversation, was a fabled place, the scene of her one good holiday with my father, and it was a great moment in my childhood when we made a pilgrimage there. Later, in middle age, ever restless, she transferred her affections to Connemara and the Blasket Islands.

The countryside only became interesting when it was 'hilly'. It only qualified as scenery when it was bleak. Indeed the lonelier the aspect, the more sombre the setting, the more barren the landscape, the more authentic the view. Glencoe, the high point of our holiday in Scotland, was a treeless mountain pass, strewn with boulders and stones, a melancholy spot which had been the scene of a Highland massacre. 'The Devil's Gorge', a seething whirlpool, was the high point of our week in mid-Wales, a glimpse of the unfathomable abyss. Meteorologically, too, we seem to have had a taste for the severe, and indeed in my jaundiced recollection, the ultimate gauge of authenticity was to arrive back from a walk 'wet through'.[15] We walked Borrowdale in what was euphemistically termed a 'fine drizzle', Loch Katrine in what was unmistakeably driving rain. In Cornwall our tents, pitched on the bare hillside, were blown down in a gale. On Dartmoor we lost our way in a blizzard.

In none of these versions of the rural did man-made landscape play any part. Scenery only began where the cultivated fields came to an end. Buildings of whatever kind – with the possible exception of upland farms – 'spoiled' the view. We never stopped to look at the villages through which we passed, let alone admire them. The country house, which anyway in those days was not open to the public, had only negative associations for people who were Communists or Socialists, and indeed except for Long Dene, where I went to school, I have never been inside one in my life. Churches and cathedrals were barred on account of religion (we were militant atheists), though curiously my mother was quite ready to visit the Sacré Coeur and Notre Dame when in 1951 she took me for a week's holiday to Paris.

It was very much of a piece with this indifference to the built environment that we had no interest in, or eye for, rural antiquities. At Stoke Poges, when my mother came to take me home for the weekend, we would walk arm-in-arm through the churchyard without so much as a glance at the graves of the 'mute, inglorious Miltons' or Village Hampdens buried there.[16] In the Lake District, though Wordsworth was one of my mother's favourite poets, it never occurred to us to visit Cockermouth or indeed to treat Keswick as anything more than the place with the nearest shops. We never, to my remembrance, stopped at a market cross, or attended a country fair. We never stopped to look at ruins, or made a detour to see a burial mound, though presumably they were marked on our Ordinance Survey maps. In fact the very idea of sightseeing was anathema. At the seaside, where I passed my summers, I would spend long and solitary hours on the rocks, waiting for the tide to come in and hoping that a storm would get up. It never seems to have occurred to me to go in hunt of fossils or (even in Cornwall) go exploring smugglers' caves. In short, we had no historical sense of the countryside, no feel for natural history. Our reverence for nature was quite abstract.

Curiously for people who called themselves Communists, we also seem to have shown not the slightest interest in rural life. The Youth Hostels perhaps helped to insulate us. They were usually sited well away from the villages, and the packed lunches they provided obviated the need to stop at wayside cafés or pubs. Even so our indifference seems to me, retrospectively, astonishing. We would not lean over the gate to watch the ploughmen, nor pause in the farmyards when we went to ask for a fill of our water-bottles. Even when we stayed on a farm, in Cardiganshire, it was only for the sake of the walks. A week's wartime work stooking sheaves in the cornfields – an initiative of some comrades in Leicestershire – seems to have inoculated us against any idea that harvesting was picturesque. Perhaps our stay in Aspley Guise, where in 1940–41 we were billeted on a farm labourer's family, had done the same in relationship to villages. In any event I am ashamed to say that though I remember their excellent breakfasts I do not know the names and cannot now picture the faces of the people who were good enough to take us in. In the winter of 1941–42, when Moscow was under siege, my mother had half the village knitting socks for the Red Army, but I cannot think that Aspley Guise was fertile ground for Communist propaganda. It was only when my mother plunged into factory work that she came into her own, falling in love with a fellow engineer, recruiting some fifty workers to the party, and starting a Union branch.

My mother liked to think of herself as unconventional, and indeed she went further than most in kicking over the traces, abandoning the comfort of a home to go to work in a factory, throwing herself heart and soul into both her war work and her agitational activity, abandoning any notion of security or career. Even by the standards of Simple Lifeism her tastes were Spartan. Her taste in landscape seems to have predated her rambling (as an adolescent she was transfixed by the Niagara Falls), and no doubt, as with anyone, it would need to be explained in terms of psychic and imaginative needs. My own formation, at odds, in some sort, with both school and home, was even more peculiar. Yet, piecing together this memoir and attempting to make sense of it, I am struck with how much we were creatures of our time.

Hiking was a mass enthusiasm of the 1930s, as distinctive of its time as, say, ballroom dancing or greyhound racing, and indeed in the early 1930s when the Great Western Railway was running a 'Hiker's Mystery Express' from Paddington, while the Southern Railway countered with a South Downs 'Moonlight Walk' (forty had been expected for the excursion, 1,400 turned up), it took on the character of a national craze.[17] It had a

Hugh Dalton and colleagues on the Pennine Way walk, 1948; from left to right are Hugh Dalton, MP, Arthur Blenkinsop, MP, George Chetwynd, MP, Hostel Warden Mr Bolton partly hidden by six-foot-six Julian Snow; sitting on the hostel steps is Geoffrey de Freitas, MP

cult following among the young. The Youth Hostels Association, founded in 1932, and the Ramblers' Association, leading the agitation for access to the mountains, were its representative public bodies; and it was also promoted by an array of now forgotten organizations such as the Workers' Travel Association. Rambling in the 1930s was a cause, and it was fought for on occasion by direct action – most famously in the 'mass trespass' of Kinder Scout in the Derbyshire Peak.[18] It was very much a part of the unofficial culture of the British Left, among Labour people hardly less than Communists, and it is indeed in the diaries of such figures as Hugh Dalton and Beatrice Webb that one can take some measure of the place which it occupied in the weekly and seasonal round.

The idea that fresh air made better people had been vigorously canvassed by housing reformers for some three generations.[19] It was the leading inspiration of the 'garden' suburb and the 'garden' city, as it was to be of the New Towns built after 1945.[20] In an age haunted by the spectre of tuberculosis it was also the grand specific for public health, the first principle of both hygiene and convalescence. For the progressives in English education – among them the headmistress of my mother's Hackney School – 'out-of-doors' education was an article of faith. It had been pioneered, before the First World War, by Rachel and Margaret

McMillan, in their open-air nursery in Deptford, and it was to be given a brilliant realization, after 1945, in the open-plan architecture of the new primary schools.[21] The 'Green Belt', instituted by the Labour LCC in 1935 and earlier campaigned for by Octavia Hill, had been promoted as the 'lungs' of the city. The municipal playgrounds, swimming pools and lidos which were the pride and joy of Labour councils were supposed to bring fresh air and sunlight to the slums.[22] In a more philanthropic vein much the same inspiration lay behind the Children's Country Holiday Fund which, long before wartime evacuation, was sending tens of thousands of London children to country cottages.[23] The fresh-air cult was given a spiritual or mystical dimension in the Woodcraft Folk and the Kibbo Kift – the flourishing 1920s children's movements of the Left – and a more imperial one in the Boy Scouts and Girl Guides.[24] It was given a further extension by the sunbathing craze of the 1930s (like youth hostelling, an originally German movement); and by the Physical Fitness Movement, which in 1938 received the accolade of a government subsidy; in wartime Britain when physical fitness was the first item of the day on the BBC Home Service, it was given a national stage.[25]

Our idea of natural beauty – or what was called in the 1930s and 1940s 'scenery' – was also very much of our time. The fetishization of the unspoiled might plausibly be related to the agitation, on both Right and Left of the political spectrum, as well as among aesthetes and snobs of all kinds, against what was seen as the menace of 'ribbon' development.[26] If we turned our back on the Home Counties it may have been in part because they were the heartland of those arterial roads, dormitory towns and bungalows demonized by the rural preservationists of the time. 'Scenery', a vogue word, meant something altogether more spectacular than 'landscape' does today. The accent was on large and open vistas – in the words of C.E.M. Joad, one of the most influential propagandists of the open-air movement, 'Nature in the grand'.[27] The optic was that of the outsider, one for whom villages were mere dots on the horizon. The favoured views, whether of the grass-topped hills and rolling downs of southern England, the rugged coastland of the West Country, or the mountainous crags of the North, were panoramic. 'Beauty spots' (another vogue word of the time) were, by definition, uninhabited, and ideally places where there was not a soul to be seen. Likewise our adoration of the rugged could be seen to echo, or reproduce, albeit unconsciously, the 'aesthetic geography' of V.J. Cornish,[28] an influential prewar writer who anatomized the scenic appeal of mountains and coasts. It corresponds, also, to the Youth Hostels Association maps of the period, with their cluster of green triangles wherever the uplands thickened. Romantic primitivism seems to have been particularly strong among the young, mainly working-class ramblers of the North, who treated the Pennines and the Peak District as their Mecca. 'It was just wild country', one of them recalls, making the contrast with the Lancashire mill town of

Parks, open spaces, swimming pools for healthy men and women of to-morrow

Wouldn't you like to live in a new London? A London with fields right round it, with more parks and playgrounds and swimming pools than any other city in the world. A beginning has been made on this great plan. Labour on the L.C.C., led by Mr. Herbert Morrison, has already acquired new "lungs" for London at Shooters Hill, Hainault Forest, Becontree, Brockley and Eltham. On May 25, 1936, at Victoria Park, E., Mr. Morrison opened the first of the great new London Lidos (see picture above). Labour plans more London Lidos, with special provision for the children and open-air swimming for everyone.

PULL TOGETHER FOR A BETTER LONDON

[P.T.O.

London Labour Publications promoting fresh air between the wars

Labour's great ideas—

THE GREEN BELT AND THE 3-YEAR PLAN

We need fresh air! As London stretches further out, it becomes more and more expensive for Londoners to get into the open country. *The London Labour Party's Plan will stop this.* Mr. Herbert Morrison, as leader of the L.C.C., invited all the County Councils around London to apply for grants towards the cost of establishing a *GREEN BELT AROUND LONDON.* The L.C.C. itself is planning to preserve within three years immense open spaces, North, South, East and West. This three-year Labour Plan of health for London includes sports grounds, lidos, bowling greens, gymnasia, paddling ponds, and playgrounds on every side.

The Plan will pay for itself

At present much of London's money goes in building and running hundreds of hospitals, convalescent homes, tubercular clinics, etc. The cost is high because to-day London cannot breathe. Eleven die per 1,000 in London every year compared with 4.9 in Welwyn Garden City. Labour's Plan will reduce the illness burden. The L.C.C. will save money. So the swimming pools, playgrounds and Green Belt will pay for themselves.

Labour is making a better London

[P.T.O.

No. 1/36. Published by London Labour Publications Ltd., 258-262 Westminster Bridge Road, S.E.1, and printed by the Victoria House Printing Co. Ltd., 55 & 57, Drury Lane, London, W.C.2.

his youth: 'The great attraction was that so easily you lost any sense of . . . civilization, you felt you were alone in the world'.[29] For the young ramblers of the North, too, the countryside was seen as an energizer; their intention was not so much to see the landscape as to experience it physically, to walk it, climb it or cycle through it.

Our spirit of place, or scenic 'gaze', could also be related to that of the neo-Romantic school of British Painters, though we were certainly unaware of their work. Our topography was closely in line with their itineraries, and so too, it seems, was our preference for a landscape without figures. John Piper, 'attracted by the ruggedness of Snowdonia rather than the smaller-scale scenery of Pembrokeshire', was ineluctably drawn to the mountain waterfalls; he enjoyed rough weather; and to judge by his field notes, was never more at east than when enveloped in mountain gloom:

> Mist blowing across all day: visibility about 15–20 yards only; curious sensation in presence of giant boulders, giant coffin slabs, pale trunk-shaped rocks, disappearing into grey invisibility even at close range. The affectionate nature of the mountain is not changed by the acute loneliness and closed-in feeling induced by the mist: but the atmosphere of an affectionate cemetery.[30]

The taste for sensationalist landscape is, of course, even more pronounced in British films of the time. The thunderous seas which make up the opening sequence of *Rebecca* (1940) and which provide *I Know Where I'm Going* (1947) with its climax – the first an essay in Cornish romanticism, the second a phantasmagoria of the Scottish isles – are those of my childhood dreams; while the graveyard sequence of *Great Expectations* (1947), with its twisted trees tossing and turning in the wind, and sinister marshland setting, possibly did more than anything else to overcome rationalist scruples, and awaken a taste for the Gothic.

The great absences in our version of the countryside could also be related to the politics and aesthetics of our time. Country houses, very few of which were open to the public in the 1940s, represented a way of life that not only Socialists and Communists but also many Conservatives believed to be doomed, and which was represented in the British films of the period as grotesque. Villages, inconceivably scruffier than they are today, and poorer, hardly invited the attention of the sightseer, and when they did so it was not on account of their film-set glitter, as it is today, but rather because of what John Piper termed at the time 'pleasing decay'.[31] Neither fields nor farming were thought of at that time as picturesque. British agriculture had been for some twenty years a depressed industry; the farm labourer, in his 'tied' cottage (the subject of annual resolutions at Labour Party conferences), was regarded as second cousin to the serf, and the cottages themselves, so far from being regarded as *objets d'art*, were though of as rural slums, with rising damp, leaky roofs, tiny windows, and squalid interiors, 'without water supply, sewerage or lighting'.[32]

John Piper's uncompromising ink-and-wash depiction of Tryfan, North Wales, 1945–46

The absence of a historical sense – and the determination not to take a 'sentimental' view of the countryside – was of a piece with a much more widespread 'progressivism' which looked to the future rather than the past. It is nowhere more apparent than in the campaigning writings of the rural reconstructionists of the interwar years. An interesting example here would be C.S. Orwin, director of the Agricultural Economics Institute at Oxford University, and an advocate in the 1920s and 1930s of land nationalization. His idealized picture of the village future, written during the war, contains no hint of a sentimental attachment to the past:

> Let us try to reconstruct the scene, then, which might greet the eyes of another Rip Van Winkle, who had fallen asleep, say, in 1940, and awakened a generation later, after the nation, freed from its preoccupation with war, had set itself to solve some of the problems, industrial and social, of the countryside.
>
> The landscape, as it first greeted him, would show notable changes. While the appeal of the rural scene, always fresh to the country lover, affected him as strongly as ever, there was now a spaciousness and order about it which was new. The many awkward little fields, the pastures too often full of thistles and sometimes of thorns, the overgrown hedgerows and choked ditches, all were gone. The trim hedges enclosed larger fields, more of them were in crops of various kinds, and where grass appeared, it had the strength and vigour associated more with clover mixtures than with aforetime permanent pastures and meadows. There were no horses to be seen; all the field work in progress was being carried out by the agricultural tractors, which he remembered as just coming into general use. Some of the implements were familiar, enlarged to give full scope to the power of the tractors, but others were quite new to him. Everywhere there was the suggestion of technical changes, all of which seemed to promote a greater activity on the land.
>
> As he approached a homestead, he found himself walking along a good concrete roadway, and he soon discovered that all the approaches to the buildings, and the roads and paths about them, were of the same material. The farm manager and his men, the implements and livestock, all could move about the place free from the muck and mire which were the universal accompaniments of farm work as he remembered it. But there were far greater changes than these. Gone were the dilapidated old barns (all the corn was now cut and threshed in one operation in the harvest field); gone, the dark and dirty cowsheds (the cows were now milked in the fields by travelling milking machines, a system which made for healthier cows and cleaner milk and which saved so much labour that a man and boy could manage between 50 and 100 cows); gone, the ranges of pig hovels, constructed so that nothing larger than a pig could enter them (pigs were now kept in houses designed for healthy living conditions, and for economy of labour in feeding and attention such that one man could feed several hundred pigs); gone, the open sheds and dirty corners in which valuable implements and machines rusted and deteriorated, or served, at best, as poultry perches (there was ample shedding on concrete floors for all the farm equipment). In short, the homestead impressed him, just as the fields had done, with its air of order and efficiency,

and its suggestion of a live and progressive enterprise which was so remote from most of the farming which he remembered.

He wondered at the number of young men he saw about the place, and learned from the manager that this reconstructed homestead was the headquarters of a large farming enterprise, built up from an amalgamation of several smaller farms. Only through the larger unit had it been found possible, he said, to give full scope to highly qualified management, to modern machinery and to skilled workers. By these means English agriculture had been enabled to hold its place in the world food market with its products, and in the home labour market with its opportunities.

The isolated cottages in the fields, remote from neighbours, public services and the amenities of village life, seemed to have disappeared. The homestead itself was placed centrally for convenience of management, but it was sited, also, on a good road. Nearly all the men, it seemed, lived in houses in the villages, and came to their work on motor bicycles. The farming, he found, was carried on much more intensively than in the days he remembered it, and there were large acreages of potatoes and green crops. They caused a considerable demand for seasonal labour, and Rip Van Winkle learned that lorries went daily from the farm at these times to the surrounding villages as transport for such workers.

His conversation with the manager had taken place in an office, with all the paraphernalia of modern business organization. He noticed, too, that the building equipment included what appeared to be a mechanic's workshop for the repair of farm machinery.

It was with a feeling of slight bewilderment that he betook himself, next, to the village of his youth. As he approached, it was obvious that the place had grown, but not beyond recognition. New houses came out to meet him, pleasant houses, larger than those which he had known, each with a good garden and plenty of space about it. Some were on the roadside, while others lay back from it, and there was a coherence and economy about the lay-out, as far removed as it could be from the exploitation of roadside frontages of the old days. As he walked on, the new houses merged almost imperceptibly into the old village without incongruity, new and old being drawn together even more closely by the insertion, here and there, of pairs of new ones on vacant sites in the village itself. Most of the new houses were occupied, it seemed, by workers in a factory which had been moved out of Birmingham and set up on a site about five miles away.

Reaching the green, the old familiar scene came back to him, for here the changes were fewer. The church, with its fine Norman tower, still dominated the scene, but the ugly Victorian vicarage-house was transformed. It had been too large for modern requirements and for the parson's stipend, but now it was larger still, and Rip Van Winkle learnt that it had become the Community Centre – the focus of all the social activity of the village. The great, untidy garden was now laid out with tennis courts and bowling greens for young and old. The new wing added to the house was the Village Hall, with a stage for plays and concerts. The rest of the house served for the Health Clinic, the County Library, clubrooms, adult education classrooms, a canteen and restaurant, dormitories for a Youth Hostel and so on. A smaller, labour-saving vicarage-house, erected on glebe land near the churchyard, now accommodated the vicar.

The school in which Van Winkle had been educated, and the school-house, had gone, and in their place was a new and larger building. Instead of the one classroom in which all standards had been taught, there were now several, and instead of the Gothic windows of his childhood, too small for their purpose and too high to see out of, it was obvious that the admission of light and air was an important part of the design.

Otherwise, the surroundings of the green had changed little, except that the growth of the community had called for further trading facilities. A branch of the local Co-operative Society occupied the site of what had been the wheelwright's shop and yard. There was a new and larger general shop, and a butcher's business where none had been before, but the same little Post Office still served, and it still sold sweets, cigarettes and picture postcards. On the far side of the green there had been the same sort of housing development as that which he had seen on his approach, but there was no suggestion about the place of a divided community, of an old village and a new housing estate. On the contrary, Rip Van Winkle had an impression of a virile, well-knit society, as though there had been a blood transfusion into the old body corporate, which had caused it to expand and to develop, both physically and mentally. There was a vigour and activity about the place which it had never suggested as he remembered it, and he found it good.[33]

The essay was unfinished.

Notes

1 For the chequered history of gorse and heather, alternately vilified as weeds by farmers and improvers, celebrated as picturesque, or romantically championed, see Keith Thomas, *Man and the Natural World: Changing Attitudes in England 1500–1800*, Harmondsworth 1984, to which this essay is indebted.

2 This memoir owes much to Minna Keal, the author's mother, who submitted to several telephone grillings about the past, and to Ray, Peter and David Waterman for their memories of progressive schooling and of Communist walking culture.

3 James Barke, *The Wind that Shakes the Barley: A Novel of the Lives and Loves of Robert Burns*, London 1946; Lewis Grassic Gibbon, *A Scots Quair*, London 1946, a trilogy of novels charting the struggles of his Scots peasant heroine, Chris Guthrie, from the First World War years to the 1930s.

4 'I must go down to the seas again, to the lonely sea and the sky,/ And all I ask is a tall ship, and a star to steer her by . . .' John Masefield, 'Sea Fever', *The Golden Book of Modern English Poetry*, London 1926, p. 230.

5 Dr Frederic Truby King was one of the pioneers of 'mothercraft', scientific, planned motherhood. *Mothercraft* states firmly that 'a Truby King baby' is fed at regular four-hour intervals (with no night feeds), is completely breast-fed for nine months and then weaned, and brought up without 'pampering': 'A baby who cries simply because he wants to be picked up and played with must be left to "cry it out"': 17th impression [n.d. 1940s], p. 172.

6 'Gay cellular-woven shirts had come in by 1933 for the use of both sexes: their mesh of fine holes gave the skin the prescribed healthy ventilation': Robert Graves and Alan Hodge, *The Long Weekend: A Social History of Great Britain 1918–1939*, London 1940, p. 277.

7 For 'simple lifeism', Jan Marsh, *Back to the Land: The Pastoral Impulse in Victorian England from 1880 to 1914*, London 1982, who gives us the three basic elements of what

was at heart an anti-industrial movement: 'the return to the land, the revival of handicrafts and the simplification of daily life' (p. 7); for the connection with progressive ideas in English education between the wars, *The Modern Schools Handbook*, ed. Trevor E. Blewitt, London 1934; R.J.W. Selleck, *English Education and the Progressives 1914–1939*, London 1972; W. Boyd and W.T. Rawson, *The Story of the New Education*, London 1965; also Michael Young's account, *The Elmhirsts of Dartington*, London 1982.

8 Henry David Thoreau's return to nature included building his own timber house – 'the student who wishes for a shelter, can obtain one for a lifetime at an expense not greater than the rent which he now pays annually': *Walden or, Life in the Woods*, Norton Critical Edition, New York 1966, p. 33 (first published 1854).

9 Marsh, *Back to the Land*; Dennis Hardy, *Alternative Communities in Nineteenth Century England*, London 1979; W.H.G. Armytage, *Heavens Below: Utopian Experiments in England, 1560–1960*, London 1961.

10 For Cecil Sharp, see 'Unravelling Britain', notes 90–92; Sharp founded the English Folk-Dance Society in 1911.

11 *The Modern Schools Handbook*, p. 86.

12 ibid. It continues: 'The classes have been housed in wooden army huts. . . . It is noticeable how quickly children respond to the call of the sun in winter, and it is no uncommon sight to see them sitting out when the snow is on the ground . . .'

13 The superiority of walking is taken for granted by most contemporary guidebooks, as for example by E.F. Davies in an Odhams anthology, *The Countryside and How to Enjoy It* (undated but late 1940s), which advises the reader that 'there is no other way of getting into the heart of mountains and moorlands' and 'of all modes of travel, walking is the most natural' (p. 310).

14 For this, and other aspects of a religiously Communist childhood and upbringing, Raphael Samuel, 'The Lost World of British Communism', *New Left Review*, no. 154, November/December 1985.

15 *The Countryside Companion*, London 1939, edited by Tom Stephenson (a campaigner for rambling and general editor of *The Rucksack*, the magazine of the Youth Hostels Association in the late 1940s), in a chapter devoted to 'rugged peaks' and 'crazy pinnacles', for 'scramblers and climbers', waxes especially lyrical at the delights of 'a soaking': 'when you are literally soaked to the skin, you will doubtless be surprised at the nonchalance with which you can face what you had imagined to be unutterable misery, and at the way you can stride contentedly along defying the gale and laughing at the storm. Home from the hills after such a day, a hot bath, or even a vigorous towelling, will soon set you aglow, and make you feel no end of a fellow, undaunted by the worst of weather' (p. 413). Such experiences were very much of a piece with what David Elliston Allen calls 'the energetic restlessness' of ramblers and hikers: 'people with arched backs and wind-beaten faces, who preferred scrambling over rocks or hurtling down screes to the calmer, gentler processes of sketching or studying them': *The Naturalist in Britain, A Social History*, London 1976, pp. 226ff.

16 Thomas Gray's 'An Elegy Written in a Country Church-Yard' (1751) was composed at Stoke Poges in Buckinghamshire.

17 Graves and Hodge, *The Long Weekend*, p. 275, where the authors group hiking with pacifism and nudism as 'libertarian fashions'. Public school animus against the 'crankiness' of such pursuits, dismissing as faddish or alien to socialism the long history of alternative or progressive, communitarian and utopian ideas, was given its most famously splenetic expression in George Orwell's tirade against 'every fruit-juice drinker, nudist, sandal-wearer, sex-maniac, Quaker, "Nature Cure" quack, pacifist, and feminist in England': *The Road to Wigan Pier*, London 1937; reprinted Harmondsworth 1966, p. 152.

18 For an account of the Kinder Scout campaign and other mass rambling movements and federations, Howard Hill, *Freedom to Roam*, Ashbourne 1980; John Lowerson, 'battles for the Countryside', in Frank Gloversmith (ed.), *Class, Culture and Social Change*, Brighton 1980.

19 The Arts and Crafts Movement, for example, as modernists and experimentalists, championed light, space and freedom, and were pioneers of both 'rational dress' and 'simple lifeism': G. Naylor, *The Arts and Crafts Movement, A Study of Its Sources, Ideals and Influence on Design Theory*, London 1990; Fiona MacCarthy, *The Simple Life: C.R. Ashbee in the Cotswolds*, London 1981, notes Ashbee's conviction that 'fresh air made better people, and contact with nature much improved the moral fibre' (p. 83).

20 For the garden suburb and city, M.H. Baillie Scott, *Houses and Gardens*, London 1900; Raymond Unwin and M.H. Ballie Scott, *Town Planning and Modern Architecture at the Hampstead Garden Suburb*, London 1909.

21 Margaret McMillan, *The Life of Rachel McMillan*, London 1927; Albert Mansbridge, *Margaret McMillan, Prophet and Pioneer: Her Life and Work*, London 1932; Carolyn Steedman, *Childhood, Culture and Class: Margaret McMillan 1860–1931*, London 1990.

22 For Octavia Hill, one of the three founders of the National Trust, E.H.C. Moberley Bell, *Octavia Hill*, London 1942; *Life of Octavia Hill as Told in Her Letters*, ed. C. Edmund Maurice, London 1913; for the promotion of open-air lidos, Raymond Postgate, *The Life of George Lansbury*, London 1951.

23 *Practicable Socialism*, by the Rev. and Mrs Samuel Augustus Barnett, London 1913: the experience, they believed, 'makes a foundation of quiet and pleasure on which to build the strenuous days and anxious years of the later life of struggle and effort' (p. 49). Henrietta Barnett, who had come under the influence of Octavia Hill, was the founder of Hampstead Garden Suburb: having read in September 1904 a paper by Raymond Unwin, she immediately decided that the architect was 'the man for my beautiful green and golden scheme': Michael G. Day, 'The Contribution of Sir Raymond Unwin and R. Barry Parker', in Anthony Sutcliffe (ed.), *British Town Planning: The Formative Years*, pp. 181ff (reference unlocated).

24 On interwar nature cults, Derek Edgell, *The Order of Woodcraft Chivalry, 1916–1949 as New Age Alternative to the Boy Scouts*, 2 vols, Lampeter 1992; D. Prynn, 'The Woodcraft Folk and the Labour Movement 1925–1970', *Journal of Contemporary History*, vol. 8 1983, pp. 79–95; John Springhall, 'Green Jerkins and Back-to-Nature', *Youth, Empire and Society: British Youth Movements 1883–1940*, London 1977; and on nature mysticisms, Anna Bramwell, *Ecology in the Twentieth Century: A History*, London 1989, especially chapter 6.

25 Lowerson, 'Battles for the Countryside', p. 274.

26 Clough Williams-Ellis, *England and the Octopus*, London 1928, and *Britain and the Beast*, London 1938.

27 C.E.M. Joad, *The Horrors of the Countryside*, London 1931; *A Charter for Ramblers*, London 1934.

28 Vaughan Cornish, *National Parks and the Heritage of Scenery*, London 1930; *The Scenery of England*, Council for the Preservation of Rural England, 1932; *Scenery and the Sense of Sight*, London 1935; *The Beauties of Scenery: A Geographical Survey*, 1943; Denis Cosgrove gives a brief discussion of Cornish's work in *Social Formation and Symbolic Landscape*, London 1984, pp. 266–7.

29 Tom Stephenson, recorded by Marion Shoard in Cosgrove, *Social Formation*, p. 268.

30 Malcolm Yorke, *The Spirit of Place: Nine Neo-Romantic Artists and Their Times*, London 1988, p. 97; Yorke notes that Piper, like Paul Nash and Graham Sutherland, produced landscapes 'swept clean of all human inhabitants' (p. 16); on the neo-Romantics and landscape, Richard Ingrams and John Piper, *Piper's Places: John Piper in England and Wales*, London 1983; David Mellor (ed.), *A Paradise Lost: The Neo-Romantic Imagination in Britain in 1935–55*, London 1987; David Mellor, Gill Saunders and Patrick Wright, *Recording Britain: A Pictorial Domesday of Prewar Britain*, Newton Abbot 1990; Raphael Samuel, 'Genealogies', *Theatres of Memory*, vol. I.

31 'Pleasing Decay', a chapter of John Piper's *Buildings and Prospects*, London 1949.

32 C.S. Orwin, *Problems of the Countryside*, Cambridge 1945.

33 ibid., pp. 105–9.

North and South*

'This is a story of simple working people – their hardship, their humours, but above all their heroism.' The epigraph which introduced the 1939 screen version of *The Stars Look Down* – the words are possibly those of A.J. Cronin, the novelist, rather than of Carol Reed, the film's director[1] – signalled a remarkable turn-around in attitudes to the miners, as well as prefiguring what was to be the leading idiom of British wartime cinema.[2] The success of the film itself (fear of censorship had held it back for three or four years) encouraged a spate of 'grimly honest' realist dramas.[3] As Graham Greene remarked of one of them, the colliery winding gear, silhouetted against the sky, the pit disaster and the warning siren became as cinematically familiar as the Eiffel Tower or the Houses of Parliament.[4] A.J. Cronin, the best-selling novelist whose fictions arguably did as much as the Beveridge report – and certainly more than the Thirties poets – to secure Labour's landslide victory in the 1945 election, had served one of his medical apprenticeships in the Rhondda valley; amputating the leg of a miner trapped in a rock fall had been his initiation in this work[5] and it seems that the disaster in the Scupper Flats, which is the climax of *The Stars Look Down*, though set in Co. Durham rather than South Wales, was based on a real-life rescue operation in which, as the local doctor, he was called upon to take a part.[6] *The Stars Look Down*, showing the ways in which human greed put the miner's life at risk, helped to turn nationalization from a Fabian dream into something approaching a popular cause.

The heroic narrative, in which the miner appeared both as the symbolic victim of capitalism and as the indomitable survivor, was not peculiar to Britain. *Germinal* was the great literary original, and the prophetic lines which close the book, a black avenging host preparing to stand up for their rights, the seed-corn of the future 'slowly germinating

* This essay first appeared in the *London Review of Books*, 22 June 1995, as a review of *Coming Back Brockens: A Year in a Mining Village* by Mark Hudson. The notes are the author's.

in the furrows', anticipates the epiphany of *The Stars Look Down.* Pabst's *Kameradschaft* (1931), one of the first talkies, a narrative built around a terrifying pit explosion in which the rescue teams, recruited from both sides of the Franco-German border, serve as a kind of allegory of human solidarity, was a filmic progenitor; and Hollywood played a big part in putting British 'social consciousness' drama on the silver screen (*The Citadel,* the first of Cronin's novels to be filmed, was an MGM production of 1938; *How Green Was My Valley* a Darryl F. Zanuck film of 1941).[7] But there was good reason why this narrative should have a special resonance in Britain. The country owed its manufacturing greatness to steam power and machinery, and at the peak of this activity a million men, no fewer than one in ten of the male work-force, were employed in the mines. Then, the coalfields had been the scene of this country's only epic class-confrontation, the General Strike of 1926 – a seven-month Calvary for the miners, a nine-day wonder elsewhere. It was also from the coalfields that the first Hunger Marches had set off. Finally, the frequency and magnitude of pit disasters made the perils of the miner's life headline news, and lent credence to the charge of 'blood on the coal'. As Labour propaganda had it, coal mining was not so much an industry as an atrocity.

In the interwar years, when so many of Britain's new industries seemed to dispense with the need for heavy physical labour, and when so many of the older ones, like cotton textiles, came under the hammer, the miner also came to occupy the symbolic space of the Vulcan at the forge, the weary Titan who figures so largely in nineteenth-century industrial art, undertaking an 'almost superhuman' job, performing Herculean tasks of labour. For George Orwell, in his sulphurous account of underground labour, 'the line of half-naked kneeling men' looked as though they had been hammered out of iron. Famously, he thrilled to the spectacle of their physique, the wide shoulders tapering to splendid supple waists, the 'small pronounced buttocks' and sinewy thighs 'with not an ounce of waste flesh anywhere', the 'huge' shovels being driven under the coal 'with stupendous force and speed'.[8]

The Martyrdom of the Mines was an ancient image, descending from those line drawings of juvenile entombment which illustrated the Children's Employment Commission of 1842. No less archetypal, stemming perhaps from the great Durham lockout of 1844, was the pithead confrontation of masters and men. The discovery of the coalfield ballads, a phenomenon of the 1950s, and the very basis of the Folk Club movement, powerfully renewed these memories, and cast them in epic form (Arthur Scargill's first job, when he joined the Barnsley Young Communist League, was to be made 'Ballads and Blues' secretary).[9] In another sphere, Aneurin Bevan, a glittering representative of the South Wales coalfield, and the most accomplished orator of his day, made the mining industry a vivid presence in the sphere of high politics. 'Unimaginably brave and resilient', ruthlessly exploited, alternately seen as a helot and an 'elemental',[10] the miner, engaged in 'the . . . difficult and dangerous job of coal-getting',[11] was as representative a figure of industrial Britain as the sharecropper of Dust Bowl America, or the peasant of *la France profonde.* Such images, embedded in the national unconscious, and springing to life in times of crisis, were sufficiently potent to win the miners an astonishing breadth of public support during the national strike of 1972. Harold Macmillan, who as MP for Stockton in the 1930s had referred indignantly to the 'Passchendaele' of the South-West Durham coalfield, gave moving expression to his feelings in his last public speech, when intervening on behalf of miners during the strike of 1984–85. They never gave up, he said, recalling those who had fought alongside him in the trenches, and speaking of them as though they were still alive.[12] So late as the autumn of 1992, when Middle England rose in revolt against the annihilation of the industry, the miner's labour was identified so completely with the cause of manufacturing industry that a newly elected Conservative government found itself in deep trouble with its own supporters when it tried to enforce wholesale closure of the pits.

In recent years, these heroic narratives have been overtaken, or overlain, by a new imaginative complex in which militant masculinity is cast as the villain of the piece. The mining communities are here seen as a relic of patriarchy. Politically they are one of the original heartlands of that 'old Labour' from which Mr Blair is attempting to extricate his party. Ecologically they are associated – as in the monstrous, smoke-belching Nowa Huta, in Poland – with the manufacture of toxic poisons. Broken-backed, since the defeat of the 1984–85 strike, marooned in desolate landscapes, the ex-coalfield communities become the breeding grounds of delinquency and drug abuse, attracting notice through murder cases rather than strikes. Beatrix Campbell, in *Wigan Pier Revisited,* a book published on the very eve of the 1984–85 strike, presciently rehearsed some of these themes, arguing that the famed militancy of the miners was premised on the exploitation of women.[13] She has amplified and generalized the argument in subsequent writings. A refusal to mourn the passing of the pits in Ashington, Northumberland, fairly represents her distinctive voice:

> This Northumberland community was once the biggest colliery village in the world . . . It voted Labour, of course, but its traditionalism derived less from the party or the place than from the absolute power of the men . . . Ashington man was the archetypal proletarian, the archetypal patriarch . . . As in the Army and the Stock Exchange, men's companionship did not produce social cohesion; it fostered power and privilege for men within their own class and community . . . No day matched Sunday for desolation. Up with the children, the women kept them quiet while the man had his lie-in, made the dinner while he sank a skinful at the pub, kept the kids quiet while he slept it off, made the tea, put the kids to bed while he ended the day down the club . . .

> Monuments to the martyrdom of men dominated the social landscape. Miners' clubs along the north-east coast were the cathedrals of their communities, the space where men had their pleasure and their politics. Their homes, however, remained some of the worst in Britain.[14]

Mark Hudson's *Coming Back Brockens* – subtitled 'A Year in a Mining Village' – extends this antiheroic narrative, though from the standpoint of a travel writer and a man of letters rather than, as in Beatrix Campbell's case, that of embattled feminism. The book was handsomely reviewed when it first appeared last year, and it has now been given the accolade, and the financial reward, of the AT & T non-fiction prize for 1995 – 'the biggest literary prize in the UK'.[15] People shrink under Hudson's investigative gaze; incidents lose their epic character; idols turn out to have feet of clay. The self-improving ethos, and with it the grand narrative of what Hudson refers to insistently as 'the Raising of the Working Class',[16] has disappeared without a trace (we are twice told that there is not a single bookshop in East Durham, but only the rack of thrillers and romances in the Asda store). Solidarities, if they ever existed, were short-term affairs. Both the Union and the local Council seem to have been managed as fiefs, with epic beer-treating, pint-buying sessions to lubricate the wheels of the electoral process.[17] The Labour Movement itself (with a capital 'L' and a capital 'M' as Arthur Henderson, a County Durham architect of the modern Labour Party, once put it) is no more than a ghostly presence. The Durham Miners' Gala, to which Hudson devotes two set-piece descriptions, has shrunk to a shadow of its former self. Horden colliery closed in 1986, though the Union committee meet every Wednesday in the Miners' Hall to process death benefits and compensation claims.[18] The Big Club, Horden's 'legendary working men's club', turns out to be virtually shut up, save for a doorman levying a toll of tenpence a time to deter non-existent visitors, and a dwindling band of cantankerous septuagenarians. Ingrained with nicotine (throughout this book cigarette smoking serves as a negative signifier), the Club exhibits the kind of desolation 'only found in all-night mini-cab offices'.[19] Early in 1994 it was sold up and gutted prior to redevelopment as a multi-bar complex aimed at the youth of the area.[20] Charlie Kemp, leader of the 'Broad Left', radicalizing faction in the 1970s National Union of Mineworkers, was, when Mark Hudson visited him, busy looking at the *Financial Times* index on Ceefax (he had spent his redundancy money on buying stocks and shares and had invested shrewdly);[21] the village's lone Communist, no longer working in the pit, was studying for a sociology degree, and wrestling (not very happily) with the mysteries of Durkheim.[22]

A particular disappointment is the author's grandfather, Percy, the attempt to recover whose memory was Hudson's ostensible rationale in taking up residence in Horden, and engaging in the research for this book. In his father's talk, Percy was a great trade union man, a passionate socialist, and a great talker, intent on 'putting the world to rights'.[23] He is now remembered in Horden, by those few who still remember him, as a 'quietish sort of fellow'[24] who made a point of never getting involved in controversy; a fixer in the Union and on the Council rather than a campaigner (no one can remember any causes which he took up); a man who was frightened of talking politics at home, because his first wife Jenny objected to them.[25] Percy, we learn, was 'very narrow-minded'.[26] He had kept his son and daughter at grammar school, thus enabling Mark Hudson's father to make his escape from Co. Durham, but he seems to have had no intellectual interests of his own. So far from being a working-class hero (Mark Hudson concludes) he was 'just a bloke in a collarless shirt and a cloth cap who liked his garden'.[27]

In a kindred vein, Hudson plays with the idea of the death of the past – both the recent past and the ancient past – and the impossibility of making meaningful connection with it. His investigation of his own family history proves singularly unrewarding – few people remember his grandfather Percy, even though he was a big figure in the village and only died in 1966[28] – and he ends up feeling angry with his forebears 'not only for having left so little of themselves . . . but because the life they lived had been so easily reduced to nothing more than an old man's memories of snacks'.[29] The village seems to be suffering from a kind of collective amnesia; where folk memory ought to be there is nothing more than titbits. The big riot of 1910, a by-product of the 'People's Budget' election, when Horden Colliery Social Club was burned to the ground, when troops were sent in to restore order and when five men were sentenced to long terms of imprisonment, was already forgotten (Hudson tells us) in the 1930s, when it still lay within the field of living memory.[30] Even the 1984–85 miners' strike, passionately supported in the village, is now it seems on the way to becoming a blank. 'It was all such a short time ago, but how little evidence there was of that zeal and passion in Horden today. Like the enthusiasm and loyalty many of the men had undoubtedly felt towards Arthur Scargill during the course of the strike, the zeal of the women had all but vanished, even as a memory.'[31]

Coming Back Brockens is cast in the form of a quest narrative, a voyage of exploration and discovery which has as its object the delineation of 'What Horden is really about'.[32] Hudson does not go in for lay sermons, in the manner of Orwell in *The Road to Wigan Pier*, nor yet for self-exposure, a leitmotiv of Clancy Sigal's *Weekend in Dinlock*, where the narrator is a very active protagonist in the story.[33] He prefers to position himself as a dispassionate recorder. Hudson has a traveller's eye for detail and a topographer's interest in place-names (he is good on the etymology of the weird and wonderful titles adopted by the individual collieries).[34] Gobbets of technical or historical information are offset or mixed up with stories, so that the reader can more easily digest them. He enjoys mimicking the dialect and goes to great pains to reproduce its lilt and cadence in an invented orthography. Descriptions of the miner's work are rendered in 'pitmatic', the dialect of the pits (the title of the book is taken from the terminology of bord-and-pillar working).[35] Hudson is a keen listener, and the book proceeds through dialogue and quotation rather than set-piece argument and description. He has a good ear for the flotsam and jetsam of colloquial exchange; he is also an eager collector of tittle-tattle, and one of the values of this book is the way it acts as a repository for local gossip, albeit mostly that of the older men.

The curious effect of all this is to make Horden seem more, not less remote. As the book unfolds the writer finds himself progressively more alienated both from the village's past and its present. Trading on consanguinity, and using the family name as a kind of open sesame to interviews, he yet betrays no sense of fellow-feeling with those whom he encounters. As the family's grand narrative disintegrates, the 'tenuous links'[36] as he expressively calls them which connect him to Horden (until undertaking this book, he seems never to have visited it) look increasingly threadbare. In a year's residence he does not seem to have made a single friend, nor to have found any kindred spirits with whom to compare his impressions. What begins as a quest narrative ends up as something like an extended obituary, in which not only the past but also the present registers itself as in some sort dead. The book's dust-jacket, showing the torso (apparently) of a miner – gnarled hands, heavy boots, shapeless trousers – headless and therefore mindless, as in the pornography of the female nude, contrasts singularly with the photograph of the author on the spine – a head and shoulders portrait with high cheekbones, sensitive nostrils and withdrawn, secretive eyes.

It seems to be the nature of his project that Horden should be a quintessence of otherness, as remote from the quotidian life of Southern England as the Gambian women who were the subject of Hudson's previous prize-winning book. Horden appears as a kind of tribal reserve, inhabited by a race of primitives. Caught in a time-warp, the people disport themselves in ignorance of the world outside. They hang on to consumer society by their fingernails, believing that Safeways and Boots, the big stores in Peterlee, are a kind of ultimate in sophistication. Moronic types, simian physiognomies and subhuman faces figure quite largely in his narrative – here a man whose face looks as though, like a red potato,[37] it would burst; there a misshapen woman, dragging bawling bairns besides her. He notes the 'Neanderthal'-like appearance of the denizens of a difficult housing-estate.[38]

Hudson is particularly severe on young people, and after describing them in various unpleasant postures concludes that 'Biffa Bacon', *Viz*'s grotesque northern yob – an invention, it seems of middle-class wits in Newcastle – a lad dressed in shorts and bovver boots – is not a caricature of a certain type of working-class life, but 'a perspicacious piece of social realism'.[39] In a shopping crowd at Peterlee, where there were 'a fair number of people it didn't seem wise to stare at', he notes 'feral' young men slinking their way in twos and threes, pursuing their dark errands.[40] The young girls at Horden youth centre would like to exterminate the elderly.[41] Motorcyclists, 'their expressions darkly and grimly closed off', slump helmetless on the pavement.[42] Outside the Wine Bar, on a Friday night, lads and lasses 'plied their mouths with great slithering chunks of pizza' while at the brick bus-stop 'dozens of couples could be seen groping in the glare of the car headlights'.[43]

Northern diet is a subject of particular disgust, as it was for Edwina Currie during her period of office as junior Health Minister in Mrs Thatcher's government, and as it is for the Statistical Office's *Regional Trends* in their reports on the incidence of the killer diseases. The people, whippet-like in the past, are today obese. In the pages of *Coming Back Brockens* they appear as a race of gluttons, eating food in the streets with their fingers, stuffing themselves with carbohydrates, making a religion of their fry-ups. The 'dense, smoke-filled interior' of Sparks' Bakery, 'the most congenial of Peterlee's three cafes', is hardly more appetizing than the stand-up snacks outside Horden's solitary wine bar. Hudson's voyeuristic account of it runs as follows:

> The girl who'd served me at the counter had an oppressed, benumbed air, as though she were on day release from a labour camp, while behind her, a young woman who was supposed to be defrosting a sack of peas and carrots was describing her previous night's hilarity to an older woman. 'We were on wa backs!' she crooned. 'Oh aye' said the other. 'We were wettun waselves!' 'Charming'. The young woman opposite me who had achieved the kind of glamour to which the girls who work in banks and building societies and travel agents of Peterlee aspire – the glamour of celebrity guests on game shows I've never heard of: tight skirt, elaborately streaked and crinkled perm, overzealous attention of the sun-ray lamp, boatloads of make-up – the sort of girl who in London would be lunching on two lettuce leaves, if at all, was tucking into a plate of chips and gravy. People here ordered chips as a kind of cultural rite. 'I'll just have chips', they said, as though this were a gesture of tremendous originality.[44]

One great absence from this book is love. There are no stirrings of sexual interest – other than repulsion – in anyone he sees, no intimations of beauty, or dignity or grace. His interlocutors are typically represented as wary, often as suspicious. Nobody seems to make the author welcome in their home. Nobody is funny. Nobody is wise. Hudson has not a word to say about religion or faith. He never stops to talk to or watch the children, but treats them as irritants. Dogs occasionally howl at him, but he seems uninterested in household pets or – save as a flyblown scenario, yards, gardens and allotments. Despite giving himself the task of family reconstruction, Hudson does not warm to the work. He has not a touch of the historian's itch to find out more, elation at clawing back the frontiers

Notes

1 Reed disclaimed any political intention in making the film, and said that he could have as easily taken the other side in the argument over coal nationalization: British Film Institute, Carol Reed collection, item 27; Tony Aldgate, 'Ideological Consensus in British Feature Films, 1935–1947', in K.R.M. Short (ed.) *Feature Films as History*, London 1981, p. 105. Cronin, on the other hand, had an outsize social conscience, as can be seen from his autobiography, and a fierce Scottish radicalism, engaging as readily with the Dublin poor, among whom be briefly practised, as with the South Wales miners. A scholarship boy, with, as he writes, 'a passionate desire for wealth and fame' (he had wanted to be a top specialist in Harley Street), he was no less passionately attached to the idea of social justice: A.J. Cronin *Adventures in Two Worlds*, London 1952.

2 Peter Stead, 'The People as Stars', in Philip M. Taylor (ed.), *Britain and the Cinema in the Second World War*, London 1988.

3 Peter Stead, *Film and the Working Class. The Feature Film in British and American Society*, London 1989, pp. 112–19.

4 *The Spectator*, 15 March 1940, quoted in Stead, *Film and the Working Class*, p. 117.

5 Cronin, *Adventures*, pp. 122–4.

6 ibid., pp. 149–57.

7 Stead, *Film and the Working Class*, p. 112; Russell Campbell, 'The Ideology of the Social Consciousness Movie: Three Films by Darryl F. Zannuck', *Review of Film Studies*, vol. 3, no. 1, Winter 1978. For the British background to two of these Hollywood films, Richard Findlater, *Emlyn Williams*, London 1956, pp. 53–5; Derrick Price, '*How Green Was My Valley*: a Romance of Wales', in Jean Radford (ed.), *The Progress of Romance*, London 1986. Interestingly, Emlyn Williams's *The Corn is Green*, a West End play in 1938, a Hollywood film in 1945, transposed the drama – an autobiography of his own scholarship boy career – from North Wales to a South Wales pit village.

8 George Orwell, *The Road to Wigan Pier*, Harmondsworth 1966, p. 21.

9 Arthur Scargill, address at Ewan MacColl 70th birthday celebration, Queen Elizabeth Hall, London, Spring 1985.

10 D.H. Lawrence, *Lady Chatterley's Lover, passim.*

11 Wilfred Pickles, *Ne'er Forget the People*, London 1953, p. 17.

12 *Hansard*, November 1984 (reference unlocated).

13 Beatrix Campbell, *Wigan Pier Revisited, Poverty and Politics in the Eighties*, London 1984, pp. 97–115.

14 Beatrix Campbell, 'Dependable Props of the Ashington Pit', *Independent*, 8 December 1993.

15 *Independent*, 13 May 1995. The newspaper, by way of observing the occasion, devoted its feature pages to an extract from the book. For some other comment, Daniel Johnson, *The Times*, 13 May 1995; Julia Llewellyn Smith, *The Times*, 6 May 1995. For some of the earlier reviews, *Independent*, 21 October 1994; *Times Literary Supplement*, 9 December 1994; *Sunday Times*, 30 October 1994.

16 Mark Hudson, *Coming Back Brockens: A Year in a Mining Village*, London 1984, pp. 8, 129.

17 ibid., p. 244.

18 ibid., p. 135.

19 ibid., pp. 37, 42.

20 ibid., p. 301.

21 ibid., pp. 227 ff.

22 ibid., pp. 223 ff.

23 ibid., p. 10.

24 ibid., p. 88.

25 ibid., pp. 100–3, 116–7.

26 ibid., p. 31.

27 ibid., p. 304.

28 ibid., pp. 17, 79.

29 ibid., p. 78.

30 ibid., pp. 50–1.

31 ibid., p. 218.

32 ibid., p. 155.

33 Clancy Sigal, *Weekend in Dinlock*, New York 1961.
34 Hudson, *Coming Back Brockens*, p. 173.
35 ibid., p. 22.
36 ibid., p. 280.
37 ibid., p. 257; for a similar male grotesque, whose face seemed to swallow up his neck as he grew apoplectic, p. 209.
38 ibid., p. 253.
39 ibid., p. 258.
40 ibid., p. 257.
41 ibid., p. 251.
42 ibid., p. 272.
43 ibid., p. 95.
44 ibid., pp. 256–7.
45 'Row as Story of Village Scoops Top Book Prize', *Independent*, 10 May 1995; 'They Invited Me Hoping for Controversy', *Times*, 6 May 1995.
46 Paul Theroux, *The Kingdom by the Sea; a Journey Round the Coast of Britain*, London 1983, p. 173. At Hartlepool (p. 264) he 'wondered . . . how people could stand to live in such a place'; Jarrow (p. 263) 'had the poisoned and dispirited look of a place that had just lost the war'; Sunderland (p. 264) 'had a sick imprisoned atmosphere; there was simply nothing to do there'. On the Cumberland coast, Maryport, once an important coal and iron port, was 'just sad'; Workington with its steelworks – 'another insolvent industry' – was 'huge' and 'horrible'; Parton and Harrington 'small' and 'bleak' (p. 180).
47 Ian Jack, *Before the Oil Ran Out, Britain 1977–1986*, London 1987
48 Robert Chesshyre, *The Return of a Native Reporter*, London 1987.,
49 Beatrix Campbell, *Goliath, Britain's Dangerous Places*, London 1993. For a critical Tyneside view of this book, David Bryne, 'Dangerous Places? A Response', *North-East Labour History Bulletin*, no. 27, 1993, pp. 75–81; and for a feminist questioning, Barbara Taylor and Rosalind Coward, 'Whipping Boys', *The Guardian*, 3 September 1994.
50 Moving between the primary poverty of the Third World and the plight of the underclass in the metropolitan countries, Jeremy Seabrook, in a series of vivid ethnologies, has been concerned to argue that consumerism, as well as impoverishing the primary producers, ambushes the intelligence, waylays the development of children, stunts growth and reduces people to a state of abject dependence upon bogus goods. '. . . All that prosperity promised, which should have meant release from the ancient experience of exploitative and ill-rewarded work, became instead the source of a new kind of pain. The end of primary poverty and those disciplines that went with it should have put an end to that injury of body and spirit. But for that freedom, the determining power of the market-place has been substituted, a dependency on it so complete, that the social identity of the whole generation has been formed by it. In this way, one of the most significant aspects of human development – the social part – has been subordinated to and determined by the selling of things'; Jeremy Seabrook, *Working-Class Childhood, an Oral History*, London 1982, p. 248; cf. also the same writer's *Landscapes of Poverty*, London 1985, pp. 52–5, 85, 92. In a feeble echo of all this, Hudson, after recording his disgust at the shopping facilities in the new town of Peterlee, gives vent to the tired thought: 'The proud old ways of resistance and communal enterprise had gone leaving only a slavish acquiescence at the lowest level of consumerism'; *Coming Back Brockens*, p. 79. The book's interest in the 'proud old ways' does not extend either to the Co-ops or to the corner shop, to neither of which is there so much as a reference, either in the past or the present.
51 Charles Jennings, *Up North, Travels Beyond the Watford Gap*, London 1995, p. 70.
52 Beatrice Webb, *My Apprenticeship*, London n.d., pp. 133, 137, 139, 147.
53 ibid., p. 134. '. . . A six-miles' walk with him across the country' seems to have been her first source for the social profile of Bacup. 'I have seen two more Aked brothers', she noted in her third letter from Bacup. 'They are all delicate-featured, melancholy men, with beautiful *hands*' (p. 140). In 1887 the Akeds, mother and son, stayed with her in London. 'I love these Lancashire folk', she wrote in her diary. 'I showed them all over London; the one thing they delighted in was the endless galleries of books in the British Museum . . . Olive Schreiner . . . was staying here; she is a wonderfully attractive little woman brimming over with sympathy. Titus Aked lost his heart to her; her charm of manner and conversation bowled over the simple-hearted Lancashire laddie, with his

straight and narrow understanding. He gazed at the wee little woman with reverence and tenderness, and listened intently to every word she said' (p. 147).

54 Carolyn Steedman, *Childhood, Culture and Class in Britain: Margaret McMillan, 1960–1931*, p. 103; cf. also Fenner Brockway, *Socialism Over Sixty Years: the Life of Jowett of Bradford*, London 1946, pp. 60–2; June Hannam, 'In the Comradeship of the Sexes Lies Hope of Progress and Regeneration'; and 'Women in the West Riding ILP, c. 1890–1914', in Jane Rendall (ed.) *Equal or Different, Women's Politics, 1800–1914*, Oxford 1987,

55 Mary Elliston (ed.), *Support for Secession: Lancashire and the American Civil War*, Chicago 1972, is a sustained attempt to question this. The author argues that in Lancashire support for the South was at least as apparent as that for the North, and that it was the rhetoric of John Bright, who used the American Civil War to establish himself as the tribune of English radicalism, which annexed the cotton operatives to the Yankee cause. Gladstone's famous 'conversion' to the cause of electoral reform, which he attributed to the steadfastness of Lancashire during the Cotton Famine, also played a big part; see Peter d'a Jones, 'The History of a Myth', in Elliston, (ed.), *Support for Secession*, pp. 199–218. For a restatement of the older view, and a critique of Mary Elliston's work, Eugenio Biagini, *Liberty, Retrenchment and Reform: Popular Liberalism in the Age of Gladstone*, Cambridge 1992, pp. 69–82, 379–85.

56 Llewellyn Smith, one of the leading investigators in Booth's multi-volume survey of metropolitan poverty, put it this way, when evoking what he thought of as the chaos of East London; 'Why is there so little local life and sentiment in East London? Why is it hardly possible to conceive an excited throng crying "Well played, Bethnal Green", with the same spirit which nerves the men of Bradford to crowd enthusiastically to the football field on a cold and drizzling November afternoon?' H. Llewellyn Smith, 'Influx of Population', in Charles Booth (ed.) *Life and Labour of the People in London*, 1st ser. 3, London 1904 ed., p. 58.

57 J.M. Baernreither, *English Associations of Working Men*, London 1889, pp. 217–19; using the Poor Law Returns of 1815 and the percentage of persons in membership of the societies shown in the figures produced by the Select Committee of the House of Lords in 1831, Gosden finds that Lancashire in the 1820s had the highest proportion of its population in friendly societies, 17 per cent, 'nearly twice as many as the next largest total, 80,684, for the West Riding': P.H.J.H. Gosden, *Self-Help; Voluntary Associations in the Nineteenth Century*, London 1987, p. 13. The Oddfellows always had their main strength in the North, Gosden tells us in an earlier work, but the Foresters, though beginning with Lancashire and Yorkshire as their citadels, later recruited heavily in the agricultural counties of the south-east and the south-west and had a more evenly spread membership; P.H.J.H. Gosden, *The Friendly Societies in England, 1815–1875*, Manchester 1961, pp. 30, 141–7.

58 H. Oliver Horne, *A History of Savings Banks*, Oxford 1949, pp. 186–91. For the role of the West Riding in the building society movement, E.J. Cleary, *The Building Society Movement*, London 1965, pp. 11, 12, 72.

59 Catherine Webb, *Industrial Co-Operation: the Story of a Peaceful Revolution*, Manchester 1904, p. 106. Gosden, *Self-Help*, pp. 186–7, for the geographical distribution of Co-operative societies in the 1870s. The exceptional strength of the Co-ops in the mill towns of Lancashire was explained by Escott as follows: 'Lancashire earnings are not so large and are much more regular than in mining neighbourhoods; consequently expenditure is much more carefully made by textile artisans and their families than by miners, and, as might be expected, the co-operative movement has never attained in Yorkshire anything like the same successful development which has fallen to its lot in Lancashire'; T.H.S. Escott, *England: Its People, Polity and Pursuits*, London 1890, p. 78.

60 *My Apprenticeship*, p. 307. For the history of the Hebden Bridge society, Benjamin Jones, *Co-Operative Production*, Oxford 1894, vol. I, pp. 332–8; vol. II, pp. 772–5.

61 Biagini, *Liberty, Retrenchment and Reform*, pp. 394, refers interestingly to 'the Puritan "mass intellectualism" of the northern counties'. 'Theatres, music-halls, and excursions round Manchester provide ordinary amusements', writes Escott (*England*, p. 80), 'while literary institutes and entertainments are very popular with the mill-hands, who are often great readers and frequently keen politicians'; cf. also James Routledge, *Popular Progress in England*, London 1876, pp. 578–9. For a more recent commentary on the autodidact culture of the North, Martha Vicinus, *The Industrial Muse*, London 1974; Patrick Joyce, *Visions of the People: Industrial England and the Question of Class, 1848–1914*, Cambridge 1991, pp. 215–304.

62 Toshio Kusamitsu, 'Great Exhibitions Before 1851', *History Workshop Journal*, 9, spring, 1980.

63 Quoted in Mabel Tylecote, *The Mechanics' Institutes of Lancashire and Yorkshire Before 1851*, Manchester 1957, p. 258.

64 Thomas Kelly, *History of Public Libraries in Great Britain, 1845–1965*, London 1973.

65 Tawney, on graduation, went to live in Toynbee Hall, Canon Barnett's East End settlement house. 'He pretended to be happy in a workmen's Club at Bethnal Green though I knew he couldn't be', wrote William Beveridge (Anthony Wright, *R.H. Tawney*, Manchester 1987, p. 155n.). It was the WEA classes at Longton, in the Potteries, and at Rochdale which set him on his lifelong pedagogical and ethical career. See Ross Terill, *R.H. Tawney and his Times*, Cambridge, Mass., 1974.

66 Quoted by G. Lowes Dickinson in Gilbert Beith (ed.), *Edward Carpenter, an Appreciation*, London 1931, pp. 39–40; and cf. generally, Edward Carpenter, *My Days and Dreams*, London 1916, pp. 99–189.

67 John Hill, *Sex, Class and Realism, British Cinema, 1956–1963*, London 1986, is a good critical discussion, alive to such contrasting but contiguous movements as the 'Carry on' films, which are not usually admitted to critical discussion.

68 Richard Dyer and others, *Coronation Street*, London 1981; E. Buscombe (ed.), *Granada, the First Twenty-Five Years*, London 1981. As viewers of the first episode will know, the soap began as the narrative of a scholarship boy, closely modelled on Hoggart's *Uses of Literacy*.

69 On *Z Cars*, Stuart Laing, *Representations of Working Class Life, 1957–1964*, London 1986, pp. 169–79.

70 Ben Pimlott, *Harold Wilson*, London 1992, p. 267. The obituarists, in May 1995, were unable to decide whether he was a chip off the old block – the son of an industrial chemist, 'Puritan' in his earnestness and plain-speaking – or a Yorkshire equivalent of Arnold Bennett's *The Card* (cf. 'Lord Wilson of Rievaulx', *Independent*, 25 May 1995).

71 Jack, *Before the Oil Ran Out*, p. ix; cf. also Chesshyre, *Return of a Native Reporter*, pp. 38–9 and *passim*; Richard Critchfield, *Among the British, an Outsider's View*, London 1990, parts II and III.

72 Theroux, *Kingdom by the Sea*, p. 171.

73 Beryl Bainbridge, *English Journey, or the Road to Milton Keynes*, Bath 1986, p. 132. Her picture of industrial Tyneside (p. 157) is also of terminal decay.

74 Jennings, *Up North*, p. 72.

75 Hudson, *Coming Back Brockens*, pp. 11, 13.

76 'Another $1m made, then Back in Time for School', *Independent on Sunday*, 21 May 1995.

77 Bill Lancaster, 'Newcastle – Capital of What?' in Robert Colls and Bill Lancaster (ed.), *Geordies, Roots of Regionalism*, Edinburgh 1992.

The Voice of Britain*

I

Institutional histories are almost by force of necessity self-inflating and self-obsessed. Founders, however small the world they inhabit, take on the symbolic role of titans – in one idiom, architects and master builders; in another, visionaries and seers; in a third, administrative geniuses. Thus Dorothea Beale, the spiritually incandescent headmistress of Cheltenham Ladies College, becomes a modern saint, according to her own favourite analogy, St Hilda *rediviva;* Solomon Edwards, the South Wales entrepreneur who gave Cardiff its first bus service, is remembered as 'a Napoleon of commerce'; Edward Holden, the aggressive chairman of the Midland Bank in its glory days and an impresario of the Edwardian merger movement, was a financial wizard, 'a colossus', 'a kind of superman in the banking world'.[1] By the same token, the opening up of new premises – a leitmotiv in jubilee histories of the Co-ops – is a milestone on a magnificent journey. Departmental reorganizations, such as the 1943 Eden reforms at the Foreign Office, are discussed as though they were epochal events. Likewise, in a trade union history the word 'historic' dignifies quite ordinary administrative consolidations – a change of rule, say, the relocation of Head Office, amalgamation with a brother society. In another register, the appearance of new brooms is treated as tantamount to revolution. Thus, in the volume under review, the Young Turks who in the late 1950s invaded the BBC newsrooms are treated as heralds of a bright new dawn, while *That Was the Week That Was*, the satire programme to which the author devotes some thirty pages, spells the death-knell of deference.

* This essay extends a review of *The History of Broadcasting in the United Kingdom*, vol. 5: *Competition*, by Asa Briggs (Oxford 1996). A shorter version of it, without section I, and unfootnoted, was published as 'London Calling' in the *Times Literary Supplement*, 8 March 1996.

Chronologies and periodization follow suit, taking their markers from corporate acts and their dynasties from the succession of corporate leaders. A change of direction, when one principal is succeeded by another, involves 'the passing of an era'; incumbency in high office – or in the case of a hospital, the position of leading surgeon – is the equivalent of a monarchical reign. Epochal divisions like this have long been *de rigueur* in school histories; indeed the author of one centenary volume, celebrating a North London grammar school, remarks that so perfectly did the headmasters match the different phases of the school's natural history that it was as though Providence itself had had a hand in making the appointments. 'Mr Cumberland, the First Decade', runs one of his chapter headings, delineating 'Combo', the man who put the school on the map. 'Dr Crockett: The New School' is another. 'With him the School may be said to have entered on an era of liberal humanity displacing the discipline and rule of marks of the Davis era, which had itself superseded the paternalism of Mr Cumberland'. For this writer, a change in the school uniform, even the advent of a new cap, is a landmark; so is the composition of the school anthem, even though it is barely distinguishable from a thousand others.[2]

Commemorative volumes have today become a normal part of corporate image-building. Big-spending local authorities have made a speciality of them, commissioning municipal histories on the flimsiest of pretexts and using them for ceremonial presentation when there is some exchange of favours to be solemnized. In the spirit of the jubilee volumes of yesteryear, these books are handsomely printed, nicely bound, and lavishly illustrated. A municipal coat of arms will often serve as the frontispiece and there will be photographs or portraits of local worthies. A great feature will also be made of founding charters, and formal documents of all kinds will be reproduced verbatim.

Institutional histories, for all their formality, will often have a strong, if unspoken, autobiographical element. Commissioned on the occasion of some anniversary – a coming-of-age, a centenary, a jubilee – they are often assigned to old hands – a retired official in the case of a trade union, a superannuated teacher or distinguished alumnus in that of a school. Some double in the character of testaments, distilling the perceptions of a working lifetime, trotting out old stories, giving thumbnail sketches of well-remembered characters, and using personal reminiscence to bring the dry bones of the record to life. Others are more in the nature of an apologia, setting the record straight, and offering a blow-by-blow account of a stewardship. Bernard Sendall's *Independent Television in Britain*, a book which vividly conveys the energy of the BBC's upstart rival, was written by one who was for some twenty years a leading executive of the Independent Television Authority.[3] It provides an excellent foil to the volume under review, covering the same years from an entirely different, indeed, from a BBC point of view, an 'enemy' perspective. Unlike

Asa Briggs's work, it is thoroughly conversant with showbiz and never happier than when re-enacting gala occasions. William Kiddier's *The Old Trade Unions* (1930), by far the best account we have of the eighteenth- and nineteenth-century trade societies, was in some sort valedictory, the swan-song of a once proud but, by the 1920s, dying culture. It was written by one who was a master brushmaker rather than a union man, but he had spent his lifetime in the craft, and wrote, as he said, 'in the pleasant smell of the pitchpan' and 'obsessed with the spirit of the Old Clubhouses'.[4]

One of the delights of these books, anyway for someone who wants to use them as a historical source, is that they are all-inclusive. Thus in a history of St Thomas's Hospital we are given the menu for the governors' farewell dinner, held at 'The Albion', Aldersgate Street, on the occasion of the hospital's move from Southwark to Lambeth.[5] A history of the Bradford Sunday schools takes time off to describe the consternation among the officials when, in 1902, an ice-cream cart positioned itself outside the chapel, and attempted to ambush the scholars. In the Jubilee histories of the Co-ops – shelf-fulls of them were produced in the first thirty years of this century, heavily illustrated with photogravures – everybody gets a mention sooner or later, from the tea-boy to the President. Likewise in the Jubilee histories of the Methodist chapels, there are comprehensive lists not only of the ministers and circuit officials, but also of the Sunday School superintendents, quite often with photographs to match.[6] In the school histories, as at Founder's Day celebrations, every kind of achievement gets its space – goal averages or *proxime accessit* in a Cup, as well as summer theatre and Christmas entertainments.

Professional historians, even if they are commissioned to write an institutional history, will have no truck with any of this. Jealous of their editorial independence, and believing that history must be, above all, objective, they maintain a fastidious distance from the here-and-now. Practising, according to their own lights, a higher learning, they seek their task as that of compiling a critical history rather than a commemorative one, not chronicling events in more or less random succession, but monitoring innovation, delineating change and unravelling patterns of development. As institutional historians they are more interested in policy-making than in personalities. Where the amateur may give us a whole gallery of remembered characters, with idiosyncrasies and nervous tics very much to the fore, the professional is more likely to be concerned with the evolution of decision-making mechanisms. Professional historians are equally on guard against the parochial. Rather than offer a simple narrative of the internal history of an organization, they pride themselves on giving it a wider setting, and never tire of reminding us that no institution can be self-sufficient.

Professional historians bring a new level of intellectual ambition to the writing of institutional history. They want their work to be definitive.

Ideally it should offer a comprehensive and authoritative account of matters which had previously only been seen as fragments. They will also make large claims for the strategic importance of their chosen subject matter, either because of its representative character, or because it can be seen as a catalyst to future growth, or because it throws a new and brilliant light on matters which had been hidden from history in the past. They may also want to dignify their work, and give it a larger meaning by offering it as a case study in some currently fashionable theory. Thus for instance the 1970s and 1980s saw a whole crop of books on 'carceral' or captive institutions – schools, prisons, hospitals, madhouses – which took their inspiration from Foucault's *Birth of the Clinic*, Goffman's *Asylums* or more generally from the counter-cultural and antinomian currents of the time.[7] Where the chronicle history, rather breathlessly, follows *faits divers*, the professional historian offers, ideally, an integrated whole. The multi-volume history of Oxford University, now nearing completion, was meant to register a complete break with the parochial. The medieval volume stressed the European dimensions of university education, while the twentieth century volume took time off to discuss the impact of Oxford – Oxford Leftism in particular – on national politics. In Trevor Aston's conception of the history, it was to mark an alternative way of approaching the history of ideas, concentrating not on great thinkers, but rather on schools of thought. More generally, in the expansive spirit of the 1960s, the aim was to put higher education on the map of historical research.[8]

T.F. Tout, whose six-decker *Chapters in Administrative History* is a monument to the medieval scholarship of yesteryear, believed himself to be writing, in some sort, the biography of the state, picturing a stage-by-stage development in which the personal offices of the royal household, such as the Wardrobe and the Chamber, were gradually brought within the public sphere and transformed into the nucleus of government departments.

A still more ambitious project was the *History of Parliament* on which L.B. Namier spent the last ten years of his life, a mighty labour on which a large team of researchers were employed, and which drew from Namier himself a final burst of scholarly energy. When the project was first launched, in 1929, Namier viewed it as a way of seeing a world in a grain of sand. Pioneering, after his own fashion, the idea of micro-history, he believed that the mightiest of social forces could best be understood by reference to their molecular make-up.[9] The House of Commons, 'that marvellous microcosm of English social and political life, that extraordinary club', offered itself as the key to Hanoverian social structure.[10] Patronage could be traced through it, as in those aristocratic cousinhoods which it was Namier's particular delight to unravel; government influence; the decay or the prosperity of the boroughs. Here too the larger conflicts were played out, as those between court and country, government placemen and Squire Western-like primitives. The people had a look-in too, if only as bystanders at the hustings.

II

For the larger view of institutional history (readers of Asa Briggs's *magnum opus* may conclude) the BBC is an ideal candidate. Straddling some eighty years of national existence; operating, influentially, in both the public and the private sphere; speaking simultaneously to both the very old and the very young (as early as 1923, in its salad days, the BBC was making a particular pitch at children), the Corporation has been quite fundamental to twentieth-century character formation, and it is perhaps some token of the imaginative hold which it exercised on the mind of reformers that Ellen Wilkinson, Minister of Education in the Attlee Labour government, looked forward to a time when the entire nation would be Third Programme listeners.

It is indeed remarkable how many of the defining moments in modern history are associated with broadcasting events. The outbreak of war, in September 1939, is a prime example. In the absence of parliament, which was in recess, it was to the listening public, 'huddled round the . . . wireless set to hear the fateful crackling broadcast',[11] that Chamberlain delivered his declaration of war. The lugubrious effect was amplified by the air-raid warning which followed closely on its heels. Earlier, in the summer of 1939, it was above all the BBC, it seems, which had alerted the country to the danger of war. By merely reporting the menacing turn of events on the Continent it set the alarm bells ringing. In June angry letters began to appear in the press accusing the BBC of being alarmist and spoiling the summer holidays; *Punch* produced a cartoon showing a well-dressed suburbanite hurling a book at his Cassandra-like radio; and there were even claims that a number of suicides had resulted from listening to the BBC news bulletins.[12] Radio was even more decisive in Britain's darkest hour, June 1940, when up to 60 per cent of the population heard those remarkable addresses in which Churchill warned the nation of its peril.[13] Almost as many heard J.B. Priestley's *Postscripts*, the Sunday evening broadcasts which, beginning in the very shadow of Dunkirk, released an astonishing wave of hope. Homespun where Churchill was high-flown, they pictured the evacuation of the British Expeditionary Force as a civilian victory rather than a military defeat – an epic in which the seaside fishing-boats and pleasure steamers had responded magnificently to the national SOS, and sailed into the inferno.

The BBC was born as a national medium, even though it was only in 1930 that it acquired transmitters powerful enough to cover the country in a single programme. It claimed monopoly rights over the airwaves. Whereas in the United States – for half a century and more the dread example of that rampant commercialism which it was the object of public service broadcasting to avoid – cut-throat competition ruled the roost, in Britain the whole effort was to provide a nationwide service. Formed initially, in 1922, as a merger of private companies, the BBC rapidly assumed the character of a public utility, independent of government and parliament and yet a civil power. Incorporated by royal charter in 1927, answerable to governors who were Crown appointees, the BBC was the prototype of an institution of a new kind, the public corporation, a new Leviathan, licensed to act unilaterally. The original local radio stations set up in the days of the private companies were amalgamated into a single network. From 1930, when the 'National' programme was established - 'so-called because it is the most far-reaching British programme'[14] – the listening public was confronted with a single choice, 'available to all and the same for everyone',[15] and it was not until the establishment of the Forces network, in 1940, that they were offered an alternative service.

The ending, in 1955, of the BBC monopoly of air time by no means put an end to such ambitions. Wrongfooted by Independent Television, and losing, for a time, the greater part of the viewing public, the BBC was able to stage a remarkable comeback, and emerged from the cultural revolution of the 1960s with its broadcasting leadership substantially intact. After an initial period of hesitation, it embarked on a series of aggressive innovations, adopting new and more theatrical modes of news presentation, exploiting colour TV (and making Britain a world leader in the use of it), and creating, in *Juke Box Jury* and *Six-Five Special*, a showcase for British Pop. In a similar spirit, sound broadcasting saw off the competition of the radio pirates by adopting their disc jockeys as its own, and giving over two whole airwaves to their patter. Later, in the 1970s, when other public-sector corporations were being forced into cost-cutting exercises, the BBC was able to use the ever-growing income from colour licensing to sustain expansion and growth. Even in the present day, after more than a decade of cost-cutting exercises and almost unremitting government hostility, the BBC can still appear as one of Britain's success stories – indeed almost the only one we have left. As Andrew Marr, the political correspondent of *The Independent*, recently put it, the Corporation was still 'more important in keeping these islands glued together than any political party'.[16] (From this point of view the current tensions between Radio Scotland and Portland Place ought to be as worrying to unionist politicians as it is to senior executives in the BBC.)

Reith, the first director-general of the BBC, was an ardent centralizer, who disliked provincial cities and treated the regions as a kind of dumping-ground for the unwanted.[17] For all his Scots formation, he was thoroughly metropolitan in his political and cultural tastes. The glamour of London, and in particular the West End, was one of the great excitements of the BBC. The Company's first home had been Marconi House,

Aldwych, many years later the nerve-centre of the BBC World Service. Then it moved to No. 2 Savoy Hill, 'a fairly ramshackle building'[18] on the other side of the Strand. It looked across to the back of the Savoy Hotel, and according to one who worked there had previously been 'a slightly *risqué* block of flats'.[19] Circled by eating-houses and pubs (the 'Coal Hole' in the Strand 'was practically the official BBC pub')[20] shadowed by theatreland and Covent Garden (then an all-night market) on one side and the down-and-outs of the Embankment on the other, this was a distinctly raffish part of London. Once it had been a criminal sanctuary, the 'Alsatia' of Scott's *Fortunes of Nigel*, and as befitted an ancient riverine parish, there was a nocturnal population of rats. Here, amidst the 'old world slopes'[21] running down to the Thames, the BBC spent nearly nine years of its life, before moving to purpose-built headquarters in a no less metropolitan, if rather grander, part of London, Portland Place.

Not the least of the appeals of wireless was that it brought a touch of high life to the suburbs. The tennis club blade, preparing for the annual ball, could practise his steps to the strains of top-notch dance bands, broadcast live from a grand hotel. The doctor's wife, preparing for her annual outing, or planning to meet her sister in town, could sample the London shows (according to BBC folklore, it was an outside broadcast from the Victoria Palace which saved the musical *Me and My Girl* from premature closure at the start of its record-breaking run).[22] The musical appreciation circle or the gramophone record club could tune in to Covent Garden, which the BBC began subsidizing in 1923, or the Proms, which, in one of its most remarkable contributions to British music, the BBC took over in 1927. The Savoy bands, the Savoy Orpheans and the Savoy Havana Band, became 'practically synonymous with British broadcasting during the dancing craze of the late twenties', writes Maurice Gorham. '. . . Young people all over the country rolled back the carpet and fox-trotted to the wireless, happy in the knowledge that they were sharing the music with the favoured few in London who could afford to put on evening dress and dance at the Savoy'.[23] The religious public, too, was London-orientated. Dick Sheppard's monthly broadcasts from St Martin-in-the-Fields (a work continued by his successor, when Sheppard resigned in October 1926) made it the best-known church in Britain. 'For years a large proportion of listeners would have parted with almost any item in their programme rather than the broadcasts from the church in Trafalgar Square'.[24]

On Saturday nights, at 6.30, 'then considered to be one of the "peak" hours of the week',[25] the BBC transported the entire nation to some imaginary vantage point in the West End, stopping the roar of London's traffic and the plangent London street-cries to introduce the capital city's visiting celebrities. A shop window for metropolitan show business, *In Town Tonight* was for some twenty years BBC radio's flagship – in the 1940s it was notching up listening figures of 20 million or more: the flower girl murmuring 'Sweet Violets', a familiar voice in Piccadilly, reached out to the remotest listener.[26] London was also a location to conjure with in the news bulletins. The announcers were dressed, West End style, in dinner jackets; they were cued by the time pips of the Royal Observatory, Greenwich, introduced in 1924, and the sonorous chimes of 'Big Ben', Westminster ('the most amazing clock of its type in the world', 'the most familiar sound ever broadcast from Britain').[27] By a well-established convention, retained from the days of 2LO, 'London calling' or 'This is London' were the announcer's opening words; and it is perhaps symptomatic of the metropolitan ambience of the Savoy Hill and Portland Place studios that Stuart Hibberd, the BBC's senior announcer, makes *This Is London* the title of his autobiography.

Like London Transport, under the inspired leadership of Frank Pick, or the eclectic pylons of the National Grid, the BBC was an avatar of inter-war British modernism ('Radio in Every Room' says a still bright neon sign in the King's Cross hotel district of Argyll Square). It is perhaps indicative of this that Broadcasting House with its swing doors and noiseless corridors, its sound-proofed studios and its batteries of blinking lights, should be – like the Wells Coates 'Ekco' radio set – a monument to Thirties functionalism, while its Eric Gill bas-reliefs (those 'questionable statues' referred to by Winston Churchill) could be seen as late offspring of the Tutankhamun craze of the 1920s.[28] The BBC pioneered a new form of mass communication which by the late 1930s reached out to a great majority of the English people (though not yet, interestingly, to those in Wales, Scotland and Ulster). It coincided with, and was possibly a market leader in, the rapid increase in the proportion of houses with mains electricity (only one in seventeen in 1920, some two-thirds by the 1930s)[29] and a remarkable increase in the production of electrical goods. (By 1936, Whiteleys, the up-market Bayswater store, were advertising their Burgoyne radio set in an all-electric hearth.)[30]

After its own fashion, the BBC gave its support to twentieth-century ideas of domestic science, extolling the virtues of the labour-saving electrically-powered home, introducing listeners to the precepts of the Truby King school of mothercraft; seconding the physical culture movement of the 1930s, and putting keep-fit fanatics through their paces. Like the Women's Institutes, a mushroom growth of the 1920s, or later *Woman's Hour* (a programme which began life in 1946), it taught the precepts of good housekeeping and preached the virtues of companionate marriage. It gave gardening lessons to the new suburban householder, ministering to the first of the Do-It-Yourself enthusiasms. Later, during the Second World War, The Radio Doctor, 'exuding good humour and common-sense', introduced a whole series of hitherto forbidden topics. (A particular sensation was his open reference to the state of the bowels, his praise for 'that humble black-coated worker, the prune', and his advocacy of a regular daily visit to what he called, in a bawdy that turned out to be surprisingly acceptable, 'the throne'.)[31] Through the medium of such doubtful gurus as Dr Saleeby, the eugenicist, the BBC brought the idea of preventive medicine into the public arena. In nutrition, a great 1930s enthusiasm, it celebrated the virtues of fresh vegetables, and explained the mysteries of protein and vitamins.

The BBC also helped to introduced a new order in the home. Its advent was closely related to the emergence of the lounge as a family living space and to the modernization of household routines. Where the cinema marked itself off as an arena of the exotic, building Moorish picture palaces and giving them Mediterranean names, radio was emphatically a home service, the province of the armchair listener, the place for a fireside chat. Domestic habits were closely attuned to the wireless day, with the weather forecasts and the news bulletins serving as more or less continual time checks (some accused the BBC of being responsible for the national obsession with punctuality). The cricket fan was the slave of the lunchtime scoreboard, the racecourse punter of the Saturday afternoon commentaries. For the housewife, accustomed to putting on the radio as background noise, a more discrete form of time-budgeting seems to have been the order of the day, with programmes signalling the time for a well-earned break. Palm court orchestras seem to have been a favourite for afternoon tea. Morning music was less dreamy. 'If you heard a burst of classical music from *Housewives Choice* you knew the time must be running up to ten o'clock'.[32] So far as children were concerned, the BBC did whatever it could to second the interwar fetish of early bedtimes (on *Children's Hour* Uncle Mac closed the programme – at 5.45 p.m.! – with 'Good night children, everywhere'); indeed so late as the 1950s, BBC television was still religiously observing the idea of 'toddler's truce' (the hour when no programmes were shown, so that mothers could get their little ones to sleep).[33]

It seems possible that the BBC's greatest 1930s success was one of which it was largely unaware – its contribution to the emancipation of women. Women made up, it seems, 'a remarkable number . . . quite one third' of the Saturday visitors to the 1933 'Radiolympia',[34] making a bee-line for the new user-friendly, mains-operated sets; and at least until the advent of the car radio – a phenomenon of the 1950s – they were a great majority of the daytime listening public.[35] Radio arrived at a time when labour-saving domestic devices, and the advent of the two-storey house, were creating the possibility of domestic leisure, and when, in families which practised birth-control, women were freed from the burden of perpetual child-bearing. Radio, it was claimed, provided women with a daytime 'good companion'.[36] Through the news, listened to compulsively if only for the time-checks, it kept them abreast with current affairs. Morning talks on such subjects as cookery, hygiene and child management – listened to by some 30 per cent of those in one of Rowntree's York surveys – introduced them to advanced ideas in the sphere of body politics.[37] More generally, there was the influence of the BBC's popular lecturers in giving an airing to matters of public controversy. Suspected of being radical by Reith, who sacked two of its principals, the BBC Talks Department, both under Hilda Matheson from 1928 to 1934, and her successor, seems to have set itself up as a kind of home university, acting by turns as a citizens' advice bureau, an extramural class, and a public lecture forum. Women especially (Hilda Matheson argued in her 1935 volume on *Broadcasting*) were the beneficiaries, winning access, if only vicariously, to the public sphere, and profiting from the 'wider outlook', 'greater interests' and 'more up-to-date practical knowledge' which wireless brought.

III

At least until the coming of *Dallas* and *Dynasty*, in the late 1970s, the BBC was the most English of the media, and it is perhaps indicative of this that national pride is a distinctive note in Asa Briggs's concluding volume. '. . . British television, BBC and ITV, remained essentially British, not American or Americanized' he notes with quiet satisfaction on p. 143. Top BBC ratings in 1959 were for British, not American programmes – they included Jimmy Edwards in *Wack-O!*, The Billy Cotton Band Show, quiz programmes like *What's My Line* and, 'above all', sports programmes like *Sportsview*. 'The BBC's offer . . . of a prize consisting of a fortnight's holiday for two people on the island of Sark contrasted sharply with the offers made on American television of huge sums of money or bundles of commercialized gifts'. British sitcom was distinguished from that of the United States by the fact that the scripts were written by named writers 'and not by teams' (p. 210). *Face to Face* borrowed the idea of interviews in depth from Ed Murrow, 'Yet . . . was to be as British in style and content as *Monitor* or *Panorama*' (p. 169). *Juke Box Jury* was based on an American idea (the BBC had to pay a copyright for it), but 'as in the case of other transatlantic transplants', there was no American programme quite like it (p. 206).

In the field of communications, the BBC cast itself in the role of elocutionist to the nation, enlisting the services of Professor Lloyd James, 'the great expert on phonetics',[38] setting up an Advisory Committee on Spoken English, and issuing lists of 'correct pronunciation' for its announcers. In its more utopian moments it seems to have believed that it had so far succeeded in its aim that the whole of Britain was speaking in a single voice. According to one sanguine report, broadcasting had made the British people speech-conscious and at the same time attuned them to the realities of a wider world. 'The prevalent habit of daily listening to the news'; the opportunities ('formerly denied to the poorer sections of the population') for enjoying music and drama; and 'the increased familiarity with a standardized diction and a greater vocabulary', all had the effect of 'equalizing national life' and overcoming 'parochialism of outlook'.[39]

After its own fashion, the BBC could be said to have gone about nationalizing the arts. Book talks, such as those of G.K. Chesterton, gave autodidacts their cultural cues, rather in the manner of *John O'London's Weekly* (after the Haddow Report of 1927 there was an attempt to organize them into reading circles). In the person of Sir Oliver Lodge, who in 1924 was initiating listeners into the mysteries of the atom, it also found its H.G. Wells to popularize the findings of modern science. Not levelling but cultural upgrading, or, as Reith put it in *Broadcasting Over Britain* (1924), 'to bring the best of things into the greatest number of homes', was the watchword. Above all, the BBC made strenuous efforts to promote a hearing for 'good' music, introducing the adventurous to modernism (in 1928 a talk by Percy Scholes under the title 'Is Bartok Mad or Are We?' provoked a storm of controversy), while at the same time maintaining full-time orchestras for performance of the classics. In Sir Walford Davies, an organist and composer, 'a fine musician . . . an able pianist' it found the ideal pedagogue, a broadcaster who established himself immediately as a 'personality', and who wooed his audience through the microphone (his exercises in musical appreciation are still gratefully remembered by older listeners).[40] 'The BBC was our sole musical mentor', writes John Osborne of his boyhood. '. . . For almost a year when I was in bed with rheumatic fever, I listened all day to both the Forces and Home programmes, discovering how to pronounce Dvŏrák and Dohnányi and what the mysterious "Köchel" might be'.[41]

The BBC, under heavy pressure from native composers and performers, as well as responding to a powerful, if diffuse, cultural nationalism, also played its part in the renaissance of English Music. From 1929 it decreed that Thursday evenings at the Proms would be devoted to British music. A year later, *The BBC Year Book* noted the emergence of a 'national' school of composers, who were creating an essentially 'English' kind of music. Later, in 1936, the young Benjamin Britten was cutting his teeth on the writing of incidental music for BBC programmes, while the newly formed British Council, desperate for counters to fascist propaganda, was proposing a 'Foreign Office tour abroad' for the BBC Chorus.[42] The Second World War, it seems, strengthened these tendencies. Not only did it lead to an enormous increase in musical appreciation, 'another good result' (according to Antonia White's front-line report, *The BBC at War*) 'is that we have been rediscovering our own national music. . . . Since the war one quarter of the broadcasting time for serious music has been devoted to British composers old and new. Listeners have heard many works by Byrd, Purcell and Gibbons as well as by Elgar, Vaughan Williams, Peter Warlock and William Walton'. In a kindred vein, there was also a new alertness to British folk-music. 'From Scotland, Ireland, Wales and all parts of England', she wrote, Sir Adrian Boult, the BBC's musical director, had been collecting local and traditional music and presenting it on the wireless. 'These programmes, given by folk-singers, choirs, fiddlers, pipers and accordion players, are among the most interesting of musical broadcasts since the war'.[43]

The BBC, from as early as 1924, when King George V was persuaded to make a broadcast from the British Empire exhibition at Wembley stadium, was a vigorous promoter of state theatricals. It celebrated royal birthdays and closed its programmes for the day by a solemn playing of the national anthem. It acted as choreographer on great national occasions, such as state visits by foreign dignitaries. It served in some sort as pageant master at royal weddings and funerals, on Lord Mayor's Day and at the State opening of Parliament. (In his autobiography, Reith boasts that there were only two organizations which could be trusted to stage-manage such ceremonial 'with supreme courtesy, efficiency and effect – the Royal Household and the BBC'.)[44] On Remembrance Sunday, the BBC transmitted to the peoples of the Empire the Cenotaph service in the morning and the evening Festival of Remembrance, with its performance from massed choirs, at the Royal Albert Hall. With the advent of outside broadcasting, from 1927, the BBC also turned sporting events into great national occasions, and indeed created a ritual year around them, making a great feature not only of the Cup Final and the Test matches, but also of the Wimbledon tennis championships, the Grand National and the Derby, Rugby internationals and the Oxford and Cambridge boat race. (The recent revolt of the House of Lords, where a great majority of peers refused to countenance the contracting of such events to Rupert Murdoch's Sky TV, testifies to the umbilical cord which still ties these events to BBC commentary, and indeed according to cricket fanatics, among them the former Prime Minister, John Major, summers have never been the same since the departure of the veteran commentator, Brian Johnston.)

The BBC also helped to promote the pleasing idea that Britain was a nation of 'do-gooders'. Television charity extravaganza, such as Terry Wogan and Esther Rantzen's *Children in Need*, a star-studded appeal marathon which takes over BBC1's entire evening schedule on the third Friday in November, has its obscure origins in a Christmas Day programme first broadcast in 1927. Likewise *Blue Peter*'s annual appeals – among the best-remembered have been those for Guide Dogs for the Blind, horseriding centres for handicapped children and equipment for Romanian orphanages – could be seen as a late amplification of those 'Radio Circles' which in the earliest days of broadcasting put funds into children's charities.[45]

Paternalism, a feature of the Corporation from its earliest days, and one of the substantial bases of that 'bleeding-heart liberalism' against which Mrs Thatcher and her supporters, in the 1980s, attempted to take an axe, was crossed with an altogether more popular sense of constituency. Charity, so far from being a privilege of the rich, or an expression of *noblesse oblige,* was projected as a work in which all might take a hand, the children who subscribed to one of Uncle Mac's Christmas appeals for invalid and crippled children (in one year it raised as much as £18,000), no less than the wealthy philanthropist. SOS messages, a feature of the news bulletins, served as tear-jerking reminders of the plight of the lonely, the invalid and the elderly. (As Stuart Hibbert knew, not the least of the tasks of the announcers, when wishing listeners 'Good Night', was to bring them words of comfort.)[46] Documentaries, too, or what were sometimes called in the 1930s 'actuality' programmes, could also have that effect. Here, for instance, is D.G. Bridson's account of *Coal,* a Co. Durham documentary which he made, in 1938, with Joan Littlewood:

> . . . Response to the broadcast was more than a matter of critical bouquets: money poured in from all sides, with requests that it should be passed on to the miner in question. He was the lucky one: I wished there had been enough to have helped the ones who had not been mentioned. But one of the letters gave me particular pleasure. Enclosing his own contribution, the writer told me that the broadcast had given him a new pride in his office. It was signed by the Lord Lieutenant of County Durham.[47]

Long before *Cathy Come Home* and the 'new wave' charities of the 1960s, the BBC was serving as one of the great launching pads for charitable campaigns. This was also a frequent tactic in *The Week's Good Cause,* where well-known personalities – quite often actors or actresses – were wheeled on to support their favourite charity. First broadcast in January 1926, and occupying a prime-time niche on Sunday evenings, *The Week's Good Cause* held its own for some thirty years, exciting sympathy for the disabled and drawing attention to the plight of the abandoned. The programme constituted the listeners as a philanthropic public, by turns harrowing them with tales of need and heartening them with parables of achievement. It flattered them in the belief that, if only vicariously, they were taking part in rescue work.

One of the good causes which the BBC embraced in the 1930s was the countryside. When the Council for the Preservation of Rural England, mobilizing opinion against the horrors of bungaloid development, wanted to launch a new crusade, the opening salvo was a strategically placed radio talk, making use of popular broadcasters – J.B. Priestley and C.E.M. Joad – to add lustre to the cause. Earlier, the open-air movement had been receiving the BBC's active support. When the Youth Hostels Association was launched in the 1930s, G.M. Trevelyan, the first president, gave a radio talk on its aims and needs, broadcasting in the first few months of the YHA's existence, and this was followed up (Oliver Coburn's *Youth Hostel Story* tells us) by regular appeals in *The*

Week's Good Cause. BBC country programmes enriched, and perhaps helped to prepare the way for, the hiking craze of the 1930s. (An early broadcasting sensation, in 1924, was the sound of a nightingale recorded live in the Surrey Woods; later, the bird-song programmes of Ludwig Koch enjoyed a huge following.) BBC schools broadcasts helped to popularize the idea of Nature Walks, while in a less didactic, or more theatrical vein, there was the popularity of the long-running Children's Hour feature, 'Out with Romany', a series of country walks conducted by one who had been brought up as a gypsy, which employed a battery of sound effects – not least the 'Wuf, Wuf' of Romany's make-believe dog, Raq – to sustain the illusion that the programme was being recorded, not in the BBC Manchester studios, but in the wild solitudes of the Pennines.[48]

'The Projection of Britain' was one of Reith's major causes. It found one expression in the Empire Service, inaugurated in 1932, another in the King's Christmas Day broadcast, a ritual address which the BBC sought to humanize by an elaborate feature which celebrated the British diaspora, and attempted to give flesh and blood to the idea of a family of nations. A more direct 'projection of England', one which was to win the BBC a global public, were the foreign-language broadcasts inaugurated in 1938, a brainchild, it seems, of Sir Stephen Tallents, but also – in its insistent distinction between news and propaganda – Lord Reith's last legacy to the BBC.[49] During the war, the vast expansion of this Service, first to occupied Europe, then to the world, turned the BBC into a kind of universal ambassador for Britain, a position which, as Briggs shows in some excellent pages on Bush House (pp. 679–717), it somehow contrived to maintain in the postwar world.

In a more anti-heroic vein, Little England rather than Greater Britain, the BBC did a great deal to create that peculiar conceit, so potent as a mobilizing force in the dire circumstances of 1940, according to which this island was peopled by a race of loveable eccentrics, averse to power worship, addicted to gardening and never happier than when laughing at themselves.[50] Where British cinema depicted a nation of warriors, with gallant commanders scouring the far horizons, Young Mr Pitt seeing off the threat of French invasion, and intrepid pilots reaching for the stars, the BBC, wedded by the circumstances of its being to a more domestic view of the British people and discovering or rediscovering its comic muse, created an imaginary England of clodhoppers, starting with Robb Wilton, the slow-witted Yorkshireman who believed that his Home Guard platoon would bring Hitler to a halt, going on to ITMA's small-town Bumbledom, the Office of Twerps, and ending up with the defiantly non-combatant aerodrome of Much-Binding-in-the-Marsh, where the aircraft were used for WAAFs and bicycles to lean on, and the radiators to brew up tea.[51]

IV

The BBC is, or ought to be, a researcher's dream. Obsessed with monitoring its own performance, minuting every stage in its decision-making processes, punctilious in time-tabling its programmes, and accountable for its lightest actions to bureaucratic audit, the Corporation has generated a vast amount of paperwork, keeping a record of everything, it seems, from performance chits to CVs. A series of official inquiries, starting with the Sykes Report, have kept it firmly in the public sphere, while at the same time mapping the limits of its autonomy. The *Radio Times* – 'the Bradshaw of broadcasting' as Peter Eckersley called it[54] – has led a continuous existence since 1923, while the *BBC Year Books*, the reverse of congratulatory in the 1920s, faithfully record *lacunae*. *The Listener*, 'a sort of BBC Hansard' in Lord Reith's conception of it, though a succession of editors tried to turn it into a literary weekly, flourished for some sixty years.[55] More recently, matching the salience of the media in contemporary British life, there has been a quite extraordinary outpouring of printed memoirs, as though every series required its 'inside story', *Blue Peter* (the subject of a notable biography by Biddy Baxter) no less than *Face to Face* or *Dr Who*. To study the footnotes of Briggs's concluding volume is to be reminded of a whole gallery of half-forgotten personalities, chat show hosts and compères, cricket commentators and newsreaders, court reporters (there are at least three biographies of Richard Dimbleby, as well as Audrey Russell's *A Certain Voice*) and foreign correspondents.

The appearance of the present volume, some forty years after starting work on the project, is a remarkable tribute to the author's tenacity, as also to the pleasures and satisfactions of the historian's craft. Dovetailing his *BBC* with a press of other scholarly and pedagogic tasks, Asa Briggs has somehow found time to equip himself with encyclopedic knowledge, not only producing five mighty tomes, but also acting as catalyst to the formation of one of the more remarkable written archives of our time. Taking up his brief as a young and relatively untried historian, at a time when the study of mass communication was still in its infancy, and when there was virtually no secondary literature to draw on, he seems to have started out with a majestic conception of the work, seeing his task as nothing less than that of writing what he called, quite explicitly, 'total' history, 'not personal, nor, for that matter, purely institutional history' (p. 8) but one which addressed a whole epoch of development.

Without the megalomania (or the brilliance) of a Namier, Briggs is nevertheless determined to see his subject in the round. He distinguishes between 'institutional history' and 'house' history (p. 10), believing that only the first is worthy of respect. He wants his material to illuminate episodes in national history and pays almost as much attention as Namier to the conduct of general elections. In the present volume he is keen to relate changes in BBC programme strategies to the competition and rivalry of what he calls sometimes 'the competitor', sometimes 'the opposition' (i.e. commercial TV). In a series of fascinating passages he traces the two-way traffic in personnel and ideas which produced a BBC–ITV 'duopoly', the very reverse of that free-for-all which had been envisaged by the pioneers of commercial television. He likes matching developments within the Corporation to parallel movements in the world outside – e.g. the satire boom of the early 1960s – and is very ready to invoke the *Zeitgeist* when explaining the success of a particular programme. 'The BBC . . . cannot be understood at any point or during any period without careful attention being paid to the politics, society, culture and often the economics of Britain' (p. 28).

Asa Briggs has always been a modernizing spirit, forward-looking and progressive. As a young Oxford don he exchanged the cloistered calm of the city of dreaming spires for the altogether more rumbustious atmosphere of early Victorian Birmingham, the subject of one of his early contributions to historical research. Later, as a notably liberal Vice-Chancellor of Sussex, he did much to place that university in the van of interdisciplinary courses and innovatory methods of study. Volume five of his *BBC* breathes a similar spirit. He is deeply sympathetic to what he conceives of as the 'Greene' revolution of the 1960s (the reforming efforts of the BBC's ultra-liberal Director-General), and gives enormous space to the iconoclasm of *That Was the Week That Was.* He makes a great point of keeping up to date with technical developments, devoting lengthy passages to the achievements of the BBC engineers, not least in the development of colour TV, and monitoring the transfer of skills from sound to vision. Signs of the times excite him, and he is never happier than when identifying 'break-dates' when all things are made anew. He pays a proper tribute to Pirate Radio, the offshore buccaneers who provoked the BBC into starting Radio One, arguing that it should have 'an unassailable place in the history of British broadcasting' (p. 506); he also tells us that the music which had been 'most in my . . . ears' throughout the writing of volume five was 'the noisy sound of "pop"' (p. xx).

As well as being determinedly up to date, Briggs displays more traditionally scholarly virtues. The footnotage is extensive, testifying to the density of the research and the determination of Briggs and his collaborators (a team of three worked on this volume) to follow up every lead. He has a keen eye for the snakes and ladders of departmental politics and is forever telling us whose star is in the ascendant, and whose on the wane. He is no less alert to 'hassles' over schedules and resources, e.g. the effect of 'family viewing time' on TV programming. When a programme interests him, he will take time off to account for its visual success ('The cameras played on the oddest and most incongruous of the dancers as well as the coolest and most adept', he notes of *Six-Five Special*). One particular quality on display – a skill which he first developed in his work on the language of class in early nineteenth-century England – is his interest in key words. Thus we are told that 'chat show' was a new term in Britain in 1956; that 'zombie' was a key word of the period; that 'professional' was a word that became fashionable among broadcasters in the 1950s; that 'liveliness' and 'pace' were the buzz words of the BBC modernizers; that 'Swinging London' was a neologism coined by the editor of *Encounter*; that 'balance' was a favourite word of the redoubtable Grace Wyndham Goldie, earth mother to a whole generation of Young Turks; and that the word 'élitist' had not yet been invented when, in the early 1950s, the Third Programme came under attack.

Curiously for a historian who made his name by highlighting the importance of region and locality, and who in other spheres has shown a very particular interest in material culture and the small detail of everyday life (in the 1950s he was one of the founders of the study of urban history), Briggs's *BBC* is top-down history of a very old-fashioned sort. He will give limitless space to anything which resembles a national political event – some seventy pages, for instance, in the present volume, to the Suez crisis, and almost as many to the role of broadcasting in the general election of 1959. In an even more antiquated mode, volume three, which covers the period of the Second World War, gives the lion's share of its space to the relationship between BBC External Services, the Foreign Office, and the Special Operations Executive of the Ministry of Information (the organization which had charge of black propaganda and disinformation in occupied Europe).

So far as internal developments are concerned the focus is relentlessly on policy-making, on the merger or subdivision of departments. Briggs is fascinated by career structures. Not broadcasting but policy-making is the true subject of this work, and the unifying thread of the five volumes, leaving little or no space for the initiatives which welled up from below, or which flourished on the peripheries. Reverent attention is given to the various outside committees, appointed from time to time by government or parliament, which sat in judgement on the BBC. The dance-band leaders who enjoyed a following of millions do not even get a walk-on part in the drama. So far as the programmes themselves are concerned we are offered little more than lists. What seems to really arouse his intellectual passion is the exegesis of bureaucratic reports. Thus in the present volume, which cannot spare a paragraph for *Blue Peter* and has barely a line on the TV playwright Dennis Potter, there are some ninety pages given up to politics of that now half-forgotten document *Broadcasting in the Seventies*, which represented a kind of *summa* of liberal opinion at the time.

Asa Briggs, for all his democratic beliefs, has a very strong sense of hierarchy. He goes out of his way to claim that such and such a person was 'distinguished', to the point of compulsively telling us (in brackets) when they later acquire a handle to their name. Thus for instance, in a note on

TV opera productions, we are told that a 1966 selection from *Billy Budd*, which won 'considerable acclaim', was conducted by Charles 'later Sir Charles' Mackerras. Elsewhere we are told that 'James (later Lord) Callaghan' appeared side by side on an ITV programme with the cricketer Ted Dexter, cracking harmless jokes; that 'Charles (later Sir Charles) Carter' was made Chairman of the School of the Broadcasting Council in 1964; and that 'David (later Sir David) Frost' was – in one contemporary judgement – 'the most remarkable man to emerge since television began' (p. 355).

Briggs is preternaturally alert to power play, and to the rise and fall of reputations. Career moves represent, in his mind's eye, a kind of summit of achievement; he follows them with bated breath and writes about them in the vernacular of a personnel officer. Thus we are told of one man that he was 'near the end of his BBC career' and of another, Pelletier, that he 'was to be further promoted, but was to lose influence', a distinction which it would take a medieval schoolman or a Machiavelli to unravel. An enormous amount of importance is attached to the senior executives, not only the Director-General but also the Chairman and the Board of Governors; indeed the triangular relationship between them could fairly be described as the narrative heart of the volume under review. Potted biographies, or career profiles, make this, in one aspect, a kind of BBC *Who's Who*. The acronyms of the controllers and planners – broadcasting's chief executives – are solemnly reproduced as though the BBC's Byzantine command structure was equivalent to the pecking order in one of the great departments of state. Thus, on p. 745 of the volume under review, Stephen Bonarjee hides behind the formidable initials Prog. Ed. C.A. (S), which (the reader is told) stands for 'Programme Editor, Current Affairs, Sound'; Huw Weldon, 'on his way up' in 1962–63, is H. Doc. P. Tel – 'Head of Documentary Programmes, Television'; while Paul Fox (later, as he tells us elsewhere, 'Sir' Paul Fox) is H.P.A.P. Tel – 'Head of Public Affairs Programmes, Television'.

Steeped in what appears, from the footnotage, to be an overwhelmingly bureaucratic set of documents, researching and writing in one of the inner sanctums of Broadcasting House – from 1979 until its recent disbandment, the History of Broadcasting Unit had its own office suite – it is not perhaps surprising to find Asa Briggs, in spite of himself, taking on a corporate voice, and adopting, as if by osmosis, corporate conceits. Thus we are told that the organization behind *Panorama* 'was at least as efficient as that of the Foreign Office'; that, in 1975, Lady Plowden 'was . . . to make history' by exchanging the Vice-Chairmanship of the BBC for Chairmanship of the Independent Broadcasting Authority; that the general election of 1974 was as much that of Robin Day, TV's Grand Inquisitor, as it was that of Harold Wilson and James Callaghan, the ostensible victors. Briggs is apt to refer to oppositionist members of staff as 'disgruntled' and to treat critics of all kinds as troublemakers. Kenneth

Adam is rapped over the knuckles for writing 'in BBC time' (!) (i.e. while still employed by the BBC) a series of articles for the *Sunday Times* implicitly critical of his erstwhile mentor, Hugh Greene (the DG described the articles as 'poisonous nonsense' and claimed to have detected twenty-seven errors of fact, a view which Briggs appears tacitly to endorse). Briggs dismisses *Prospero and Ariel*, the testament of one of the leading spirits in 'Features', D.G. Bridson, as a 'highly personal document' (would it have carried greater weight if it had been as bureaucratic as the volume under review?), and he is no less scathing about *Ariel and All His Quality* (1944), the BBC autobiography of R.S. Lambert, the erstwhile editor of *The Listener*. Adopting the language of the schoolmaster, Briggs describes it as 'one of the first "nasty" books about the BBC', and elsewhere, in a nicely chosen putdown, characterizes the author as 'impetuous' and 'quixotic'.

A more unofficial history of the BBC, taking its cue perhaps from Maurice Gorham's excellent memoir, *Sound and Fury*, would have much more to say about 'that figure of legend, the BBC Secretary',[54] not least those who played such an important part in Lord Reith's fantasy life (Miss Shields, his first secretary, sported a monocle and found time to drive a Bugatti at Brands Hatch; Betty Nash, one of her successors, persuaded him to visit her horologist).[55] It would have a place for radio's penny-a-liners, the freelance playwrights and scriptwriters, scraping a living in the republic of letters, who looked to the BBC for a commission, while cursing the hand that fed them; for the foreign correspondents living out of suitcases and perhaps doubling as secret agents; and for the old soaks at Bush House, gathered from the four corners of the world, doing their all-night stints, and comforting themselves with the bottle. It would not only acknowledge, but even build from, a recognition of double standards ('I never knew an office where sex played so large a part', writes Gorham of the BBC's Savoy Hill days, 'where so many people lived with their secretaries, where the hunters and the hunted were so conspicuous as they went about their sport').[56] It might also pay attention to that peculiarly metropolitan phenomenon 'which the BBC of the late twenties shared with the theatre, the ballet, and the book business', but to which Reith – though he had practised his own version of it – was apparently blind; male networking. And it might scour the records for evidence of those simmering hatreds which very occasionally exploded in the public sphere. (The diaries of J.R. Ackerley, the long-serving assistant editor of *The Listener*, might serve as a corrective to top-down pictures of corporate harmony.)[57]

A child's history of the BBC would in some respects be more interesting than a high-level administrative one. If it focused on the ensemble of programmes, it might consider the influence of the BBC on the learning process – the ways in which the Shipping Forecast may shape early ideas about climate and geography, or in which comic turns, such as Frankie Howerd's Roman slave, create historical myths. If it focused on children's programmes, it would need to say a great deal more than Briggs does about the development of the performing arts and about the role of theatricality in popular education. Children's programmes might turn out to be the crucible in which sound effects were perfected and animation brought to the screen, and in which optical illusion became the common currency of visual communication. *Toytown*, the most popular of all *Children's Hour* series, first performed in 1929, might turn out to be the grand original of those imaginary Englands which did so much to sustain national morale in the years of the Second World War,[58] just as the more recent *Grange Hill* might throw a flood of light on changing ideas of national character.

It would be churlish to end on a critical note. Alone among historians, Asa Briggs had the wit to see that the history of broadcasting was a tremendous subject, worthy of encylopedic coverage and the full resources of scholarly inquiry. He has brought a catholic and ecumenical outlook to a subject in which writers are only too apt to indulge their own prejudices. He has given us an open text, one which positively invites the addition of new characters, the use of alternative records, the pursuit of contrary inspirations. Determinedly unfashionable and seemingly untouched by the apparent disintegration of a unitary broadcasting authority, his book is nevertheless a marvellous vindication of the possibility of a truth-telling contemporary history.

Notes

1 Josephine Kamm, *How Different From Us: A Biography of Miss Buss and Miss Beale*, London 1958, pp. 120–2; John F. Andrews, *Keep Moving: The Story of Solomon Andrews and His Family*, Barry S. Williams pub. limited edition, 1976, p. 10; A.R. Holmes and Edwin Green, *Midland, 150 Years of Banking Business*, London 1986, p. 122.

2 T.D. Wickenden, *William Ellis School 1862–1962, The History of a School and Those Who Made It*, London 1962.

3 Bernard Sendall, *Independent Television in Britain*, vol. 2, *Expansion and Change 1958–68*, London 1983; vol. 1, *Origin and Foundation* (1982), covers the years 1946–62.

4 William Kiddier, *The Old Trade Unions*, London 1930, p. 7. Kiddier also wrote two books on brushmaking and its history.

5 Eilidh Margaret McInnes, *St Thomas's Hospital*, London 1963, p. 105.

6 One such commemorative volume, for the *Jubilee of Girtlington Wesleyan Church 1870–1920* (no date or publisher), Bradford, gives vignette photographs of its ministers from 1866 to 1878 (it also mentions the opportunistic ice-cream cart); these histories were consulted, with the help of the librarian, David Webb, at the Bishopsgate Institute in London, where there are many such volumes.

7 For example, D.J. Rothman, *The Discovery of the Asylum: Social Order and Disorder in the New Republic*, Boston 1971; Michael Ignatieff, *A Just Measure of Pain: The Penitentiary in the Industrial Revolution 1750–1850*, London 1978; A.T. Scull, *Museums of Madness*, London 1979; M.A. Crowther, *The Workhouse System 1834–1934, The History of an English Social Institution*, London 1981. Thanks to Pat Thane for discussion of this point.

8 The author is grateful to Ros Faith, Brian Harrison and Ralph Evans for information concerning the history of Oxford University.

9 Linda Colley, *Lewis Namier*, London 1989; Julia Namier, *Lewis Namier: A Biography*, Oxford 1971.

History's Battle for a New Past*

History has had a better deal from the present Conservative administration than it would from any imaginable Labour one. At least, as their passionate attacks on 'the New History' suggests, Conservatives care about the subject. While left-wing ideologues splash about in the shallows of post-modernism, their right-wing counterparts think up Trafalgar Day as a public holiday, celebrate the glories of the country house and dream of a return to 'Our Island Story'. The enthusiasm of the Education Secretary for the subject is unbounded – albeit for a history cruelly caricatured by Sellar and Yeatman in *1066 And All That,* and put to the scholarly axe, some sixty years ago by Sir Lewis Namier.

Kenneth Baker's predecessor, Sir Keith Joseph, treated history with unqualified respect, and it is partly as a result of his efforts that it is now to be mandatory in the core curriculum. The pleasure (or relief) which anyone who cares about the subject may feel at this is tempered by the 'traditional British history' flag under which it is being conducted; by the imposition of 'performance indicators' as benchmarks; and the dictatorial manner in which the new curriculum will be imposed. Whereas earlier classroom innovations have typically had to prove their worth by trial and error, experiment and competition, this one is being legislated by ministerial ukase.

The new dispensation is also being prepared with what, at least to an outsider, looks like unseemly haste. Appointed only last week, the Minister's working party on the new curriculum is to give its interim advice by 30 June and draw up its final report by Christmas 1989. There hardly seems time for that 'wide consultation' with teachers, unions, local authorities, professionals and outsiders, which, in 1987, Mr Baker was promising for the change; still less for those extended pilot studies which attended the Schools Council's 'New History' projects. Remember that 'new history' existed for some twenty years as a minority practice in

* This essay was first published in the *Guardian,* 21 January 1989.

the classroom, before it found a recognized place in the examination syllabus.

The 'new' history has been subject to many criticisms. Like any modular course it appears 'bitty' to those brought up in traditional disciplines. It sacrifices breadth for depth, leaving children – Conservative opponents claim – ignorant of many of the leading events in national history. The immediacies of its 'patch' approach – history in depth, at particular moments in time – are necessarily achieved at the cost of long-term perspectives. It exalts method at the expense of content: reconstruction – it is alleged – becomes an end in itself.

New History's notion of 'empathy' (in truth a liberal rather than a socialist one, though it draws much right-wing fire) has excited particular derision, blurring – it is claimed – the line between fact and fancy, the imaginary and the real. Like other versions of 'history from below' it is charged with concentrating on the minutiae of social life at the expense of larger questions. Like other 'multicultural' studies it is accused of giving undue space to foreigners.

Yet the starting-point of the 'new history' – a 'skills' approach based on the critical reading of documents and original materials – is one which the research historian is likely to find sympathetic. It focuses, in a way history has so often failed to do, on subjectivity – or what the Annales school in France calls *mentalités*; and it has a place for the kind of subject, e.g. seventeenth-century witchcraft, which the finest modern scholarship has opened up to historical inquiry. It leaves space, as any child's history should – especially in a country where Dickens is favourite reading and Hogarth a father of national art – for the comic and the grotesque. In terms of examination, the desire to test children on what they can find out rather than on what they can remember seems admirable.

It seems unlikely that a set of 'agreed topics' – one of the ideas at the heart of a 'core' curriculum – will make school history 'coherent'. Nor does it seem likely that the restoration of longer chronological time-sweeps will itself produce a principle of order. The fetishization of dates, a leitmotiv in criticism of the 'New History', privileges great events and foregrounds the state at the expense of civil society, elevating public over private lives. It puts a premium on that age-old stand-by of the crib-books – the 'turning-point' or 'water-shed'. It devalues, or ignores entirely, those more molecular processes in which domestic life and personal identities are shaped.

The unifying themes proposed by the Minister and his predecessor (in Mr Baker's case, 'how a free and democratic society has developed over the centuries' – in Sir Keith Joseph's 'the value of liberty for the individual under the law') have the advantage of a celebratory and positive approach. But they fly in the face of present-day perceptions and discontents, and ignore the fruits of some six decades of historical reflections and research. They return us to a Whig view of history as a progressive development, and a parliamentary one (untouched it seems by public disenchantment), which sees the Houses of Parliament at Westminster as the summit of national achievement.

As a view of the constitution, that would have been out of date in the time of Dicey, as anyone who has read his *Law and Public Opinion* (1905), with its diagnosis of the enormous increase in the powers of the state, and inexorable trend from individualism to what he called 'collectivism', will know.

A constitutional history which took as its vantage point the rights of the subject rather than the rhetoric of the lawmakers would be an altogether more chequered affair than that of Mr Baker or Sir Keith Joseph. It would need to take account of the fact that the poor – at any rate the 'mendicant' and 'undeserving' poor – were treated for some three centuries as the untouchables of society; that husbands and wives were forcibly separated in the workhouse (a recording of 'My Old Dutch' might be used to bring the point home); and that down to 1918 'paupers' were automatically disqualified from the vote.

In the eighteenth century such a history might concern itself with the building blocks of what Jonathan Clark has rightly called Britain's *ancien régime* – for instance the Press Gang, Settlement Orders, the Penal Laws directed against the Irish, the Test and Corporation Acts which excluded the Dissenters from public life. In the nineteenth-century with the Master and Servant Acts, which made workers the property of their employers. In the twentieth-century with conscription or, say, prosecutions for attempted suicide or imprisonment for homosexuality. 'Equality before the Law' might be considered in relation to the status of women and their treatment as legal 'minors'.

An entirely different narrative, no less peppered with the requisite 'great events', could be written around the growth in the power of central government, the rise of surveillance and the police, and the spread of corporate bureaucracies. Taking a cue from Bagehot and as an exercise in critical thinking, children might be invited to distinguish between the 'dignified' and the 'efficient' parts of the constitution, and to question such venerable fictions as the sovereignty of parliament (the secret treaties which led to the outbreak of the First World War, juxtaposed with *All Quiet on the Western Front* or facsimile reproductions of the trenches cartoons of Bruce Bairnsfather, might make a memorable lesson).

One grand theme which recent research might suggest would be the loss of local rights, a process which the present government, not least in the Education Reform Act itself, seem to have brought to some kind of point. Here the National Health Service of 1948 might be considered not only as a foundation of the Welfare State but also as a determined attack on local and voluntary initiatives; the New Poor Law of 1834 as a major and successful attempt to wrest power away from the vestries. Children – at any rate children in ILEA schools – might be asked to consider the 'liberties' of London. Above all, if it were to attempt to bring past and present into relationship with each other, such a history would need to explain how a country subscribing to the idea of liberty became (as Maitland was already pointing out in 1906) one of the most closely governed in the world.

The collapse of British power – a phenomenon of the last thirty years – gives us a novel vantage point for reworking our understanding of the national past. In the light of it Trafalgar Day, even if the government succeed in making it a national holiday, may be less rewarding as a topic of study than, say, the fall of Singapore, the invention of the spinning mule less thought-provoking than the closure of the Lancashire mills. Instead of (or as well as) considering the development of Britain as 'a world power', as Mr Baker recommends, it might be more profitable to consider this country as part of a larger whole – an offshore island, say, in medieval Europe (which is how it appears in Hereford Cathedral's Mappa Mundi), or in the eighteenth-century (as Gwyn Williams has argued), part of an Atlantic economy.

Subject ourselves to multinational companies and supranational authorities, we might be more ready to consider the ostensibly indigenous in terms of developments whose epicentre lay elsewhere. 'Americanization' might be studied as a major theme in the making of twentieth-century 'English'- working-class culture; the French connection studied in relation to the Restoration aristocracy and court. English foreign policy, in the aftermath of 1688, was subordinated to that of the Dutch – the only reason it seems, why William of Orange bothered to come here. Ninth- and tenth-century Britain was part of a Viking world whose centre was in the Baltic. The centre of the Angevin Empire was Anjou not England. The largest single source of royal income of the Plantagenets was the Bordeaux wine trade. The medieval wool trade had its Staple at Calais. Such interdependencies, arguably, grow more not less important, with the growth of British power.

It is usual, on *both* Right and Left of the political spectrum, to oppose 'multiculturalism' – one of the sins of which the 'new history' is accused – to some more unified national self. But the two are not necessarily mutually exclusive, and it might be rewarding to study the second in the light of the first. The existence of bilingualism in the present might alert us to the plurality of speech communities in the past (when a Parliamentary Commission, in 1861, was interviewing Northumberland miners, the services of an interpreter had to be engaged). Likewise the recognition of ethnic diversity in the present might serve to put in question the notion, so dear to Tory atavism, of some all-English past.

The Irish, to take an obvious case in point, formed a religious and social underclass in nineteenth-century Britain when civil war between the Orange and the Green was an endemic feature of life in the industrial towns and seaports (one of the bases for emergence of that popular, or working-class Toryism whose influence, to put it mildly, is by no means extinct today). Anti-alien sentiment, though only surfacing occasionally in organized political form, might nevertheless appear (if it were historically examined) a systematic feature of national life. It was very much to the fore in England's 'finest hour', 1940, and even more so in the aftermath of victory in 1919, when 'Yellow Peril' fears swept the country. Likewise the division between the 'established' and 'the outsiders' might appear as a normal feature of British social life, with make-believe aristocracies, at every level of society, occupying, according to their own lights, a pinnacle of esteem.

The recrudescence of Celtic separatism might also encourage a more molecular view of the national past – one which took its perspectives from Connaught or the Lothians, Dublin or Edinburgh, as much as from Westminster. Scotland, after all, was a foreign country for much of what is today called 'British history', while Ireland – anyway Leinster – was an integral part of it from the time of the Anglo-Norman conquest down to the Treaty of 1921. The 'English' or 'Puritan' revolution of the 1640s has its 'first beginning' in the Covenanters' revolt in Scotland; and it was the great Irish rising of 1641 which transformed the constitutional crisis into a civil war. A less Anglocentric view of British history might find more space for the eighteenth-century Scottish Enlightenment as the cradle of English liberalism; it would, like Marx, see the Highland clearances as part of the story of Victorian 'improvement', and the Irish famine of 1845 as integral to the history of Free Trade.

There is no reason to suppose that British society in the past was more homogeneous than it is in the present. Oppositions between town and country and between North and South are major themes in our literature. Militant particularism has been for some four centuries an organizing principle of religious life, nor is it less apparent in the history of trades unionism. One possible object of national history would be to identify the minority communities of which, at any point in time, the majority community of the British was composed. Such a view is not necessarily inimical to the idea of a nation. As the Conservative philosopher, Edmund Burke, put it, it is by our attachment to the 'little platoons' that we become members of the great society.

The issues which divide the 'New History' and its critics are by no means novel, and there is no reason to suppose that they can be resolved by a ministerial memo. The rejection, or attempted rejection, of 'drum-and-trumpet' history goes right back to J.R. Green's *Short History of the English People* in 1874; Marjorie Reeves's 'Then and There' series has its precedents in such popular interwar textbooks as the Piers Plowman histories, the *History of Everyday Things*, and Eileen Power's much-loved *Medieval People*. The rival claims of a 'skills' approach and a 'knowledge' approach, as also of British national history against a more 'world' approach, were being vigorously agitated in the Historical Association during the Great War. It was Lord Acton, one of the founders of the academic study of history, who called for the study of 'problems not periods'. His views were echoed by the protagonists of the 'concentric' method in the 1890s, when history was first introduced to the Board Schools.

'Empathy' is not some invention of the 'new history' but a basic procedure in historical inquiry, albeit one which involves a degree of self-delusion. It is brilliantly exemplified in the work of such Tory historians as G.M. Young and Sir Lewis Namier. And at an earlier stage in the present debate, it was forcefully advocated by Sir Keith Joseph. He told a conference of the Historical Association in February 1984: 'We somehow need to convey . . . the fact that, without condoning their actions, we should not condemn intelligent and even noble men who saw no contradiction between humanity towards their fellow men and the institution of slavery, or for whom liberty was a much less significant value than order.' Sentiments so impeccably right-wing seem to have escaped the attention of the Conservative think-tanks; it is only when they take on the accent of 'concerned' liberalism that they are subjected to ridicule and contempt.

There is nothing ignoble or illegitimate in trying to unify the subject matter of a course, or attempting to identify a core of common problems. But it is self-defeating to think that this can be achieved by stifling teacher initiatives, straitjacketing children, or regimenting the schools. At a time when politicians of all stripes are uniting behind the idea of a uniform curriculum, it seems necessary to enter a plea for pluralism.

Historical knowledge is by its nature contingent, and unless the government succeeds in strangling higher research (admittedly, a real possibility) any history course is going to be undermined by fresh discoveries. The sources of historical knowledge, whether the Education Secretary cares to recognize it or not, are promiscuous, and in a society where we are continually bombarded with images of the past – not least in the built environment – an alert history course ought surely to face up to this.

The argument between the 'skills' and the 'knowledge' approach, between synchrony and diachrony, between history in breadth and history in depth, shows no sign of being settled. The rival claims of the state and civil society on the historian's attention have been agitated for more than a hundred years. Is it beyond the wit of Mr Baker (or the Examining Boards) to allow teachers to choose between rival approaches, and even more important, in the future as in the past, to bring their own intuitions and interests to bear on what they teach? Do we really want every child in the country to parrot the same set of answers to the same set of questions? And if so, Why?

No university would countenance the degree of uniformity which is now to be mandatory in the schools, yet the constituencies of interest and need are inconceivably more various in the second than in the first. Is there not as strong a case for history being made more diverse rather than less?

Heroes below the Hooves of History*

I teach British history, I study British history, I love British history, and I am delighted that there is to be more of it in the schools.

Unfortunately, it does not seem to be the same kind of history as Robert Skidelsky outlined recently on this page ('Battle of Britain's Past Times', 22 August), or rather, though I am ready and indeed glad to draw on his kind of history, as he is an authority on high politics in the 1930s, he does not seem ready to acknowledge the legitimacy of mine.

The issue is not one of 'skills' versus 'knowledge', but rather of the competing claims of the public and the private sphere or, if you like, 'history from above' and 'history from below'.

Can I give an instance of this, since it is one which Skidelsky returns to twice in his *Independent* article? I wrote, in a conference item 'History, the Nation and the Schools', a passage which apparently needled him, that while the Battle of Trafalgar might be momentous even in the annals of naval warfare, it was less important, *from the point of view of family history*, than the Married Women's Property Act of 1882.

Let me elaborate. The Battle of Trafalgar was no kind of turning-point in the Napoleonic wars, indeed French historians (admittedly a chauvinist lot) barely mention it. It was immediately followed, in December 1805, by the most crushing of all Napoleon's victories, Austerlitz, and by the collapse of the Third Coalition. It did not even succeed in saving the kingdom of Naples from the French.

Were it not for the heroic circumstances of Nelson's death and perhaps (a subject worth more inquiry) the nineteenth-century romanticization of war, it is possible that we would know no more of it than we do the Battle of Copenhagen or the landing at Tenerife.

The Married Women's Property Act, though it gets no more than a footnote in *Haydn's Dictionary of Dates*, is a landmark in the history of women's rights and arguably in the idea of companionate marriage. It is

* This essay was first published in the *Independent*, 31 August 1989.

also, in teaching practice, an excellent vantage point for looking at a system which kept public life as an all-male preserve while making the husband lord and master in his own home.

So far as the civil law was concerned, women – at any rate married women – were for the greater part of this country's existence rightless, not only in relation to goods and chattels but (as many Victorian family histories testify) in relation to custody of their children. 'In law husband and wife are one person,' declared the great eighteenth-century jurist Sir William Blackstone, 'and that person is the husband.'

If the 'free-born Englishman' is to be the eponymous hero of 'our island story', something needs to be said about how the other half of the nation lived, even though they were, legally and politically speaking, invisible.

History is a house of many mansions and its narratives change over time. It can be about structure and process, or events – how people lived or what they did. In one major line of interpretation the past is a prologue to the present, connected up by 'lines' or 'stages' of development. In another, the past is constructed as a kind of reverse image of the present – the world we have lost.

The rival claims of the state and civil society on the historian's attention have been vigorously canvassed ever since Macaulay wrote chapter three of *The History of England* – a dazzling ethnography of the Condition-of-England question as it presented itself in the 1680s. Likewise, in teaching methods, the rival claims of 'history in depth' over 'history in breadth' have been a flashpoint of recurrent controversy.

Robert Skidelsky argues that history deals with 'large' and 'dramatic' events, those which take place in the public sphere and have a transformative effect on people's lives. 'That explains the concentration on acts of government and great people.' The bigger an event, it seems, the greater its claim on our attention. 'Those who suffered in silence have no history.'

One could argue that almost the reverse was true. So far from being uninterested in failures – 'those who suffer in silence' – history, anyway British history, reserves some of its liveliest sympathies for the dispossessed, be they medieval Lollards, Elizabethan recusants, eighteenth-century Jacobites or nineteenth-century hand-loom weavers. It is fascinated by 'primitive' rebels and impossibilists; by the survival of outmoded structures; by the tenacity of ancient ideas. Rehabilitating the memory of forgotten luminaries (as in Frances Yates's work on the seventeenth-century occultists), rescuing the defeated (such as the Luddites and the Southcottians) from the 'enormous condescension' of posterity, has been for some thirty years a leading inspiration in historical research – giving names and faces to the anonymous, and voices to the inarticulate.

Ever since the Great War, and initially very much as a revulsion against it, British historical work has typically been *anti-heroic* in its bias, toppling the great from their pedestals and questioning the status of Skidelsky's 'great events'.

School history, under the influence of the Quennells and the 'Piers Plowman' histories, turned, at least in junior classes, from the biography of great men to the history of everyday things. Namier, a fierce iconoclast as well as a pioneer anthropologist of power, offered a new theatre of eighteenth-century politics in which the epic struggle of King and Commons was replaced by a kind of comic-opera of wire-pullers.

History certainly needs to be memorable, as Skidelsky rightly argues, if it is to whet children's appetites. But there is no reason why its narratives should be drawn so exclusively from high politics.

The story of the Irish famine of 1845–49 is (to put it mildly) as 'exciting' as the gladiatorial contest of Peel and Disraeli over the repeal of the Corn Laws, though traditionally it is the latter which have monopolized attention in school-teaching and university special subjects. If it is 'period' we are concerned with – or what used to be called 'the spirit of the age' – would not one of the great Victorian manias or moral panics be as instructive as the Home Rule split in the Liberal Party? There is no reason why a history course should not have room for both.

Similarly if, as Skidelsky seems to be suggesting for medieval and early modern times, we are to return to a history of kings and queens, might we not, taking a cue from the 'human interest' stories in the tabloid press, pay more attention to the sexual politics of the court and, in particular, from the hounding of Piers Gaveston to the assassination of the Duke of Buckingham, the murderous hatreds directed at royal 'favourites'?

Who are to be the *dramatis personae* of 'our island story'? Must they be, as Skidelsky argues, 'great people', and if so, what is to be the measure of their greatness? Not, evidently, the sensation which they made at the time, or children would be confronted with an impossibly crowded canvas.

In the early days of university history, when the subject was thought of as a schooling for the public service, statesmen were automatically singled out for attention. No mind in human history was more interesting to study than Napoleon, 'the most entirely known as well as the ablest of historic men' declared Lord Acton, the Regius professor at Cambridge. Today, when history is no longer a training ground for an imperial race, one might hope that individuals would be singled out not for their political weight, but for the way they personified their times.

Heroes and heroines in humble life as, say, Gracie Fields or Tommy Farr or Bruce Bairnsfather, might be as rewarding to study for our twentieth-century history as Lord Kitchener or Lord Curzon. And might not 'characters' such as Dr Johnson, the best-loved figure in English literature, or Squire Western make a more inviting introduction to the eighteenth century than Carteret, the Pelhams or the Pitts?

If one were not, like the historians of high politics, mesmerized by the glamour of power, one might suggest that horses were more interesting to study than politicians and, at least for younger children, more appealing.

There is now, following Michael Thompson's pioneering study of horses in Victorian England, a rich historical literature on them, while Keith Thomas's magnificent *Man and the Natural World 1500 to 1800* could encourage teachers to position the subject in the widest cultural and ideological setting. Sporting prints and landscape art could be used to match 'chalk and talk' with stunning visual effects.

Such a study could bring children very close to 'history as it was'. It would enable them to follow the baggage-train of the army and watch the cavalry charge, to travel with the narrow boats, to drive, metaphorically speaking, the haywain and the horse-gin, to ride into town with the political cavalcade, to travel with Bible on horseback.

The opening page of *Black Beauty* – a warning against mixing with the 'rough colts' in the meadow – would give teachers as good a text as they could wish for the moral economy of the nineteenth century, and the psychic divisions between boys and girls, men and women, the patrician and the plebeian.

The point here is not to draw up a league table of historical topics, and certainly not to question the utility of knowledge, but to argue that the new core curriculum should not turn its back on the major historical insights of our time. We live in an *expanding* historical culture in which vast new fields of inquiry compete for attention, and whole new classes of evidence have been brought into play.

The public appetite for history has never seemed greater. Conservationism, a minority cause of the 1960s, has acquired the character of a national passion, and whatever one's misgivings about the way it is manipulated, its starting-point is a respect for the past, even – to judge by the present craze for anniversaries – an obsession with it.

Within the universities there has been a proliferation of sub-disciplines, each with its own sources and own problematics. Among the public at large, 'do-it-yourself' enthusiasms are enlarging the notion of the historical. Family history societies, a mushroom growth of recent years, fill record offices and local history libraries with researchers. Photography has come into play as a major historical resource. New museums open, it is said, at the rate of one a week, preserving residues of dying cultures even as economic change consigns them to the scrap heap. We are bombarded with historical representations on all sides.

It would be absurd – or in Robert Skidelsky's phrase 'counter-intuitive' – for the new core curriculum to turn its back on this. The History Working Party, whatever its compromises on other matters, shows no signs of doing so. In a splendid statement, widely picked up in the national press, it said: 'The rough feel of woven cloth, the smell of the stable or of primitive sanitation, the taste of food smoked over an open fire, the sounds of horses' hooves on the cobblestone can evoke images as strong as the written or spoken word.'

'History from below' is not enough, since without some larger framework it becomes a cul-de-sac and loses its subversive potential. But a history of carriage folk which ignored the horses' hooves, or a narrative of battles which only had eyes for the general staff, would be as airless as a bunker.

The rejection of drum-and-trumpet history: the title page to the Quennells' popular *A History of Everyday Things in England*, first published in 1918

One in the Eye: *1066 And All That*[*]

Reprinted some fifty times since it was first published in 1930, *1066 And All That* has been passed from hand to hand by generations of sixth-formers as scholarship's equivalent of a dirty book.

If it is true that only the really serious can be flippant, and that comedy is ideology in motley, then it might be given a place in the library shelves alongside Namier's *Structure of Politics at the Accession of George III*, the renowned modern classic, published the previous year.

Certainly the authors, Sellar and Yeatman, though writing in the pages of *Punch* rather than the *English Historical Review*, deserve a niche in historiography's Valhalla, as pioneers in the art of revisionism. They took an axe to the Tory, or 'great man' theory of history just as effectively as Namier, that prince of iconoclasts, had done to the Whig. Indeed, that it is impossible for the Prime Minister to get a serious hearing for the idea of returning history to a regimen of famous names and dates may have less to do with the achievements of 'history from below' than with recall of Sellar and Yeatman's send-ups – Alfred the Great, for instance, 'never fighting except against heavy odds'.

Sellar and Yeatman are no less undermining of liberal verities, anticipating by a year Butterfield's famous essay on *The Whig Interpretation of History*. Their burlesque leaves no imaginative space for the idea of progress, for 'freedom broadening down from precedent to precedent', or for the 'development of liberties under the law'. How can we take seriously the coronation oath of 1399 – a landmark in the development of parliament, the constitutional historians tell us – when we remember that it marked 'the accession of Henry IV–Part I'; or think of Magna Carta as the free-born Englishman's birthright when we remember its provisions as follows:

> 1. That no one was to be put to death save for some reason – (except the Common People).

*This essay was first published in the *Times Educational Supplement*, 18 May 1990.

2. That everyone should be free – (except the Common People). . . .
6. That the Barons should not be tried except by a special jury of other Barons who would understand.

In Marxist terms, *1066 And All That* was very much a product of its times, and in particular of that disenchantment with ideas of national greatness which followed the trauma of the Great War. Like Eileen Power's *Medieval People* it treated the characters of the past as familiars; like the Quennells' *History of Everyday Things* (a four-decker and beautifully illustrated primer for junior classes, which began publication in 1918), it helped to promote an *anti-heroic* view of the national past. The British were no longer conceived as a master-race, gifted with a vocation for world-leadership – the place they had been allotted in the Edwardian schoolroom – but as a nation of loveable (or laughable) eccentrics, pursuing the peaceful arts. Kings and queens were no longer good or evil, as they had been in the days when history was conceived of as a form of moral uplift, but muddleheads; the 'self-sacrificing determination to become top Nation' (signalled in the preface to *1066 And All That* as the leitmotiv of 'Our Island Story') was treated as absurd.

1066 And All That was written at a time of rising anti-militarist sentiment, when *Journey's End*, which had taken London by storm in the previous year, was helping to release a flood of autobiographies, novels and memoirs directed against the tyrannies of the leadership cult, and the mendaciousness of war propaganda. The futility and cruelty of war is a unifying thread in Sellar and Yeatman's narrative and so it does not seem fanciful to ally it to that literature of delayed recoil which in the following years was to make peace-pledging into a mighty national movement. Here, for instance, is the account of Victoria's 'small wars':

1. *War with China.* Fought on moral grounds, because the Chinese government were disposed to impede the importation of Empire Opium into China. . . .
4. *2nd Burmese War.* Cause: there had only been one Burmese war. Burmese cut to pieces. Burma ceded to the Crown. Peace with Burma. . . .
7. *War against Zulus.* Cause: the Zulus. Zulus exterminated. Peace with Zulus.

1066 And All That bears the marks of the civil war between 'aesthetes' and 'hearties' which scythed undergraduates at the ancient universities (both Sellar and Yeatman were students in Evelyn Waugh's Oxford) and produced stirrings of rebellion in the public schools. It could also be seen as a late expression of 'Young Anarchy', the generational revolt against the 'hard-faced men who had done rather well out of the war', and their patriarchal Victorian predecessors.

It is clearly a piece of 'debunking', a literary fashion which swept all before it in the wake of Lytton Strachey's *Eminent Victorians* (1919).

Indeed in one aspect the book could be seen as an illustration of the epigraph of Strachey's book, in the iconoclastic account of General Gordon, the imperial martyr, which did more than anything else to secure *Eminent Victorians* its *succès de scandale*:

> At any rate, it had all ended very happily – in a glorious slaughter of twenty thousand Arabs, a vast addition to the British Empire, and a step in the peerage for Sir Evelyn Baring.

Debunking the past was a kind of national sport in the 1920s, a way perhaps of anaesthetizing the pain for those, like Sellar and Yeatman, who had walked the fields of death, and for others, marking a break with their elders and betters. Bloomsbury helped to make it a major theme of English letters; Namier and Butterfield established it in the world of historical scholarship.

It also had its echoes, or its answering chorus, in the music halls, where the anti-heroic is as characteristic of popular hits as bombast and boasting had been in the imperial heyday. 'I'm 'Enery the Eighth I am' is one of the best-remembered examples:

> I'm 'Enery the eighth, I am,
> 'Enery the eighth, I am I am
> I got married to the widow next door
> She's been married seven times before
> Every one was an 'Enery
> She wouldn't have a Willie nor a Sam
> I'm the eighth old man called 'Enery
> 'Enery the Eighth I am

Likewise 'Sam, Sam, Pick Up Thy Musket', the best-remembered of Stanley Holloway's Lancashire monologues, celebrates the feats of an anti-hero on the fields of Waterloo; while Billy Bennett, 'the Trench Comedian', offered parodies of those imperialist anthems, such as the 'Road to Mandalay', which had made a previous generation thrill with the pride of being British.

Sellar and Yeatman hardly figure among the avatars of the progressive movement in English education, the former being a schoolmaster at Fettes and the latter a journalist. Yet they made their contribution to those antinomian and subversive currents which were liberalizing and modernizing the curriculum in some of the newer public schools and which, under the benevolent gaze of the Board of Education (see the notably enlightened *Handbook of Suggestions for Teachers*, HMSO 1927), were finding a footing in the jungle classes of the elementary schools. Rote-learning is their invisible adversary, and the excruciating examination questions which finish off their chapters follow the spirit, if not the letter of the crammers and cribs:

1. Sketch vaguely, with some reference to the facts: (1) The Southsea Bubble, (2) The Ramillies Wig. . . .
4. 'An Army marches on its stomach' (Napoleon). Illustrate and examine. . . .
11. Write not more than two lines on the Acquisition of our Indian Empire.
NB – Do not on any account attempt to write on both sides of the paper at once.

In a perverse way, *1066 And All That* could be said to be a kind of tribute, albeit an unintended one, to the way in which, in the space of little more than thirty years, history had been established as a teaching subject in the schools; fastening as it did on those memorable incidents and characters which loomed so large in history lessons and drawing too on those more apocryphal figures and stories which were in some way lodged in the national unconscious: the medieval chronicles of Alfred and the burnt cakes, or Cnut and the waves. The fact that its targets were so instantly recognizable might make us look again at those 'outlines', 'readers' and 'primers' which were the staple fare of the board schools in the 1890s, and try to fathom their appeal.

Like Richmal Crompton's *William, 1066 And All That* appealed to the juvenile anarchist and John Reynolds's splendid drawings gave it ready-made graffiti. Its black humour ministered to that morbid taste for horrors which makes the dungeon a favourite spot on school visits, and the cruelties of the past one of the most effective ways of capturing classroom attention. It would not be difficult to show its continuing appeal in the recent versions of history in *Monty Python* or *Blackadder*. If the traditionalists win their way in the current debate on the 'core' curriculum, teachers might do worse than order some reprints for the school library, not only as a way of inoculating children against the more vainglorious ways of telling 'Our Island Story', but also as a way of remembering it.

Top nation

Dawn of British heroism

Very memorable

Britain muffles through

Illustrations of history's ironic certainties by John Reynolds, for *1066 And All That* (London, 1930)

The Return of History*

The restoration of history to the school 'core curriculum', if it takes place, and if it survives the counter-pressures in the Government towards TVEI (Technical and Vocational Educational Initiative), will represent one of the more remarkable pedagogic reversals of our time. The privileged place which the new curriculum gives (in my opinion, quite rightly) to British history is in singular contrast to the implosion which has taken place in English studies, and the abandonment – now endorsed by the National Curriculum Council – of both English literature as a separate classroom subject, and set texts, the 'cultural heritage' which it was the special mission of school English to transmit.

For some thirty years the whole tendency of educational reform has been cross-curricular and multidisciplinary. In the modernizing moment of the Sixties, historians, the younger and more ardent spirits at least, were only too anxious to present their work in terms borrowed from other disciplines and even to present their findings as illustrations of theoretic models and truths. 'Excessive' specialization, according to the conventional wisdom of the time, was 'academic', divisions in knowledge 'artificial', subject-based learning an obstacle to comparative perspective. The winds of change required a frontierless open space, in course design no less than in campus architecture. In the new universities, then the pace-setters for educational innovation, history was absorbed in larger frameworks and organized not in departments but in inter-disciplinary schools – 'Comparative Government' at the University of Essex, 'Cultural and Community Studies' at Sussex. There was a similar pattern at the polytechnics, where from the start single-subject honours degrees were unknown, and where modular courses moved towards a Post-Modernist 'pick and mix'.

Sociology was a dominant influence on the 'new wave' history of the time. In the new cottage industry of urban history, monographs, when

* This essay was first published in the *London Review of Books*, 14 June 1990.

they began to appear, typically focused on stratification and social structure. *Past and Present*, at the apogee of its influence in this decade, treated history as a branch of the behavioural sciences, following the destiny of achievers in Ancient Rome, patterns of leisure in the industrial revolution and rituals of riot. The Cambridge Group for the History of Population and Social Structure, which began its official life in 1964, devoted its whole initial effort to establishing the antiquity of the 'nuclear' family, testing a well-worn sociological hypothesis against the parish records of births, marriages and deaths. As E.H. Carr put it in 1961, brilliantly anticipating, here as elsewhere, some of 'new wave' history's ruling passions, 'the more sociological history becomes and the more historical sociology becomes, the better for both.' Such precepts were still in the ascendant in 1976, when the opening number of *History Workshop Journal* fired an ill-directed salvo against them.

In the schools, under the influence of the comprehensive movement, the pressures against subject-based teaching were even stronger. In primary schools history was apt to disappear in integrated studies, or was subsumed in such epic titles as 'Man' (according to a recent HMI report, only 15 per cent of primary-school children do anything called history); in the secondary schools it was promoted, or protected, as a variant of 'Humanities' or World Affairs, while for the less able children it was smuggled in under the rubric of 'social studies'.

The status of history was also put in doubt by the insistent demand for 'relevance', which has been a leitmotiv of curriculum innovation and reform ever since the Robbins and Crowther Reports. In the early Sixties, with a prime minister promising to sweep the 'dead wood' from the boardrooms and subject venerable institutions to the 'white heat' of modern technology, history carried the stigma of being old-fashioned, and there was a concerned attempt to abandon earlier periods and drag the subject kicking and screaming into the twentieth century. As J.H. Plumb, that weathervane of the liberal establishment, put it, when writing of 'the crisis in the humanities', 'few hearts swell with pride in Mosley Road Secondary Modern School at the thought of Magna Carta or Waterloo'; the humanities 'must . . . adapt themselves to . . . a society dominated by science and technology'. 'What is needed is less reverence for tradition and more humility towards the educational systems of those two great countries – America and Russia – which have tried to adjust their teaching to the urban, industrial world of the twentieth-century.' The raising of the school-leaving age to sixteen and the lowering of the voting age to eighteen provided a further rationale for making the school syllabus more contemporary. 'It is surely far more important,' Edward Short, Labour's Minister of Education, told the Association of Education Committees in 1968, 'for young people to know the facts about Vietnam than it is to know all the details of the Wars of the Roses.'

These modernizing tendencies were very much to the fore in CSE, the school-leaving examination introduced in 1964 with the aim of giving every school-leaver some kind of qualification. Economic and social history constitute the record of 'industrial society', general history that of the modern world, a subject which happily elided history with the present. Similarly, 'Modern World History' had pride of place in the Schools Council History Project, while 'depth' studies, though taken from earlier periods, seem to have been chosen for the purpose of structured contrast or analogy with the present. Later versions of 'new history' have followed suit, offering a history of 'now' and 'then', or 'past' and 'present', rather than a chronological and developmental narrative of befores and afters. Tudors and Stuarts, firm favourites, as a period, in the days of the grammar schools, were reserved for the A-level syllabus, a last redoubt of traditionalism. Medieval history, the original groundwork for history as a teaching subject in the universities, was relegated to the junior schools, as a picturesque matter for projects rather than a testing ground for analytic skills or a source of serious knowledge.

The new methods of teacher-training instituted in the Sixties may also have helped to make historians uncertain about their subject. Under the PGCE, the graduate qualification required for those taking up posts in secondary schools, teachers were encouraged to think of themselves as 'educationalists' rather than specialists; to see their role as an enabling rather than a didactic one, and their subjects as adjuncts to the acquirement of cognitive skills. Content was subordinated to the learning process. The 'new' history, or what passes for new history in the schools (a phenomenon of the Seventies), was a product of these pedagogic enthusiasms. It owed its authority to neo-Piagetian notions of ages and stages of child development; it sidestepped the issue of content to concentrate on intellectual and perceptual growth. It did not matter so much what the pupils learned as how they learned it, and whether or not a subject developed 'concepts'. History was not about the past: it was a mode of ideation. It did not have a story to tell: it had a method to impart.

It is possible, too, that the increasingly hierarchical nature of the teaching profession and greater job mobility have had the effect of undermining the integrity of the subject and devaluing the status of the historian. The introduction of scale posts in 1961, under the Burnham agreement, with no fewer than thirty-nine different status levels 'each with a specific salary allowance', and the creation of departmental empires in the comprehensive schools, transformed the structure of the profession, making the knight's move a normal means of advancement. Instead of history being a job for life, or, to put it more grandly, a vocation, it became a mere stage in the teacher's career, leading to more indeterminate, but influential positions such as year leader, course co-ordinator, head of humanities, or (latterly) adviser to one of the burgeoning bureaucracies in an increasingly top-heavy profession.

History was attacked from a theoretical standpoint for being 'empiricist', or, in that favourite expletive of Sixties campus radicalism, 'positivist'. It suffered from 'arrested intellectual development' and was enslaved to a primitive faith in facts. It practised a naive realism, believing that the evidence spoke for itself, and that the historian had no higher task than to let the documents speak. Whereas sociologists tested hypotheses, refined concepts and offered a self-consciously theoretical analysis, historians remained wedded to the instance, accumulating endless examples and finding exceptions to every rule. Knowledge of the sources was the profession's substitute for thought. For the more outspoken radicals, and the more rigorous structuralists, knowledge itself, however its boundaries were defined, was suspect, both as an obstacle to systematic thought and as a form of social control. The great object of teaching, as they saw it, was not to transmit knowledge but, in the universities, to equip students with the means of 'demystifying' it; in the schools, through 'discovery' or child-centred learning, to enable pupils to construct it for themselves. Didacticism, however benevolent its intentions, was inherently authoritarian, knowledge 'élitist'.

The new history, though it has a long and honourable lineage in the progressive movement in English education, and in the idea of learning by doing, bears the traces of this negative pedagogy. It is deeply suspicious of any claim to teacherly authority. Ideally it would liberate the child from the encumbrances of scholarship, offering a naked confrontation with the sources in place of a history learnt at second or third hand. But since the sources themselves are radically flawed, not facts at all but statements, the object of 'source evaluation' is to enable children to see through them, to identify bias, to pinpoint guilty absences, to discover the repressed dialogue beneath the surface discourse, the hidden ideology which even the simplest wording conceals.

In this way, if one looked no further than the school classroom and the university seminar, it would seem that history in the Seventies, as in the previous decade, was progressively decentred to the point where its autonomous existence, as a teaching subject or a 'discipline', was in doubt. It was extramurally that new sources of energy were generated and notions of the historical enlarged: in the renaissance of local history and the remarkable growth of local 'amenity' societies; in the spread of the museums movement and of 'history from below'; and not least in Britain's gathering crisis of national identity.

The restoration of history to the school syllabus, though a testimony to the vitality of history from below, was engineered in the first place from above and as a result of pressure from traditionalists. It owes something to the personal enthusiasm of successive Conservative ministers of education, Keith Joseph, Kenneth Baker and now, it seems (though he is regrettably attached to the idea of famous names and dates), John MacGregor. It owes rather more perhaps to the HMIs, who in a series of reports have drawn attention to the devastating consequences of abandoning history in favour of such invertebrate programmes of study as those which go under the name of Humanities. History has no doubt been helped, too, by the fact that its graduates are so numerous in journalism and the arts, in government and the higher Civil Service, and that they retain affectionate memories of their undergraduate studies (the activities of the HUDG – History at the Universities Defence Group – may have helped to activate this constituency of opinion and to prepare a climate favourable to the claims of history in the schools). Finally, some reference ought to be made to the contribution of the Prime Minister, who, as in her invocation of 'Victorian Values' – or her strictures on the French Revolution – is continually calling up shades of the national past. Her interventions in the current debate are widely resented and interpreted in a sinister sense, but historians, while rejecting her precepts, might feel flattered and even encouraged by the attention given to their subject.

But if it is the Right, or traditionalists, who have led the return to subject-based teaching, and who have been most vociferous in affirming the worth of history as a distinctive form of knowledge, it is the Left – or at least the broad mass of historians, in the universities, in the schools and in society at large, dedicated to broadening the subject-matter of history – who have contributed more largely to the vitality of the subject and to its present popular appeal. The recovery of lost tradition – rescuing history's defeated from 'the enormous condescension of posterity' – has been for some thirty years a leading inspiration for what is inadequately called 'labour history': in the hands of Eric Hobsbawm, E.P. Thompson et al. it is more the biography of a class than a narrative or analysis of politics. A similar spirit has animated the study of the intellectual underworld, and the interrelationship of magic, religion and science. Women's history – in Britain, mostly in the hands of self-proclaimed socialist feminists – has challenged the priority traditionally given to the public sphere and put many of history's leading categories into question. Scholar-radicals too, in some cases worker-historians, like the printer John Gorman, or the Communist singer Ewan MacColl, pioneered the discovery of industrial folk-songs – a continuing component of British Pop as well as an important source for the study of mores – and the study of popular imagery. Above all, there has been the growth of oral history, a particularly pertinent influence on the schools. This has made 'living memory' a major historical resource and propelled a great deal of teaching towards the present. Oral history has been pioneered in this country largely by socialists (it has a rather different character in its country of origin, the United States); like women's history, it focuses on the politics of the personal and gives a privileged place to the study of everyday life, or what the German historians working in this vein call *Alltagsgeschichte*.

In the last thirty years the profession has been quietly but seriously radicalized. 'History from below', originally the enthusiasm of a handful of *francs-tireurs*, is now a central plank of higher research, and is indeed hardly less apparent in the work of the supposedly High Tory Jonathan Clark or the proto-Thatcherite Alan Macfarlane than in the Marxist historians whom they attack. There are now a dozen or more learned journals devoted to it – *Past and Present, Social History, History Workshop Journal, Llafur, Gender and History* to name but a few. (*Rural History*, due out shortly, promises to be a welcome addition.) In medieval history, the peasant land market has replaced seigneurial administration as the focus of research in studies of the agrarian economy, while the history of religion is more likely to start from parish wills than from the study of Church and state. John Vincent's *Poll-Books* pioneered a history of politics 'from the bottom up', though Vincent now seems to prefer the study of prime ministers. 'History on the ground', originally almost a personal obsession of W.G. Hoskins and Maurice Beresford, monitoring the lost villages of medieval England, is now a whole industry; it is the normal starting-point of local history, transforming it from a study of the manor and the parish – the form prescribed by the *Victorian Country History* – into one of the lived environment.

History has also been pushed in a more populist direction by exogenous influences, operating quite independently of the lecture-hall or the classroom. The preservation of the past, which thirty years ago was the province of small bodies of experts, is today a mass activity in which tens of thousands of people play some part. County Record offices, temples for the worship of the archives in the early days of their statutory existence, and the preserve of decayed gentlefolk, local antiquaries and a sprinkling of graduate researchers, are now in some sort popular institutions, with an out-reach to the schools and community groups. The manuscript Census returns, which only began to be widely used in the Sixties, are now among local historians' first ports of call. Family history societies have democratized the study of genealogy; though non-political in character, their sympathies are apt to be popular rather than aristocratic; plebeian ancestry is a matter of pride – not, as in the old days, something to be covered up for fear of losing caste.

In the study of the built environment there is an altogether new respect for vernacular architecture, with as much attention being given to the Victorian industrial terrace, and even to early council estates, as to the Tudor farmhouse or cottage. Do-it-yourself enthusiasms such as industrial archaeology (a term coined only in 1956) have vastly extended notions of heritage, turning the beam-engines of the industrial revolution into national monuments and putting warehouses and factories on a par with cathedrals and stately homes. Reference might also be made to the collecting mania, a by-product of, or a parallel development to, the antiques boom of the Sixties, which has elevated the humblest items of household life – the dolly mop, the birdcage or the firescreen – to the status of *objets d'art*. Each of these new sources has served to enlarge notions of the historical, bringing new avenues of inquiry within the ambit of teaching and research and progressively updating our notions of 'period'.

Although it is an influence which scholars and purists are loath to admit, the restoration of history to the school syllabus and the present vitality of the subject must owe something to the commodification of the past as a source of pleasure and enjoyment. On all sides, the future of history is debated in terms of its purposes: nation-building, character-formation, child-development, according to ideological taste. Yet one of the great arguments for history as a classroom subject is its popularity as a hobby, a holiday pursuit and a form of mass entertainment. The pioneers here were the railway preservationsists of the early Fifties, who not only rescued obsolete rolling-stock and narrow-gauge lines, but also – an early exercise in costume drama – dressed up as old-time railway servants. More recently, the vast development of historical or history-based tourism, and the multiplication of visitable shrines – for foreign visitors, Sunday motorists and school trips – has disseminated the idea of a more immediate past; an experience to be shared rather than a remote object of classroom study. Lessons can be learnt from display panels; souvenirs and survivals can give a tactile sense of the past.

It is perhaps symptomatic that the chairman of the History Working Party was neither an academic nor a schoolteacher but the owner of a Norman castle and founder of the Heritage Educational Trust, which uses historical buildings to bring children into a more direct encounter with the past. The most eloquent passage of the working party's interim report breathed the same spirit: 'The rough feel of woven cloth, the smell of the stable or of primitive sanitation, the taste of food smoked over an open fire, the sounds of horses' hooves on the cobblestone can evoke images as strong as the written or spoken word.' In a more opportunist and commercial vein – though one close to those 'marvellous stories' which were the stock-in-trade of nineteenth-century children's books – the promoters of 'Royal Britain', the exhibition now lodged at the Barbican, project the night side of 'living history'.

> Wicked stepmothers, executions, massacres and murders. Children will love it. Royal Britain. A great exhibition for people of all ages. From the dark ages to the modern age, 'Royal Britain' gives you the chance to experience the lives of all our kings and queens. And with a thousand years of wars, weddings, executions and empire-building, you'll discover the amazing truth about the most famous family in the world.

The restoration of history to the school curriculum could also be seen as a belated recognition of sea-changes in the national culture – in particular, the crisis of modernity which has afflicted both economy and society in the Seventies and Eighties. Thirty years ago 'new' was a word to conjure with, bringing the promise of a more open society, while the past was conceptualized in negative terms, as an incubus to be thrown off, a dead weight on the living, a byword for the dark. Today, with the apparent exhaustion of modernity as a principle of hope, the past typically evokes fears of separation and loss, recalling vanished stabilities or supremacies. The restoration of history to the school curriculum, on this view, is in keeping with the reversal of attitudes that has made conservation and preservation, rather than innovation, the major outlet of the reformist impulse in British life, and the preferred idiom for idealist visions of all kinds. In place of a better future, we use as our critical vantage-point a more immediately accessible past, and it is to make-believe identities in the past rather than the future that we look to find a home for our ideal selves. The return to history, under this optic, appears as a displaced expression of contemporary utopianism.

If there is a single issue which has made history seem more relevant, and more contentious, in recent years it is the emergence of the national question as a storm-centre of British politics. New Commonwealth immigration and settlement, the civil war in Ulster, the recrudescence of Celtic separatism, and Britain's increasing involvement in the EEC, have made any Anglocentric view of the national past quite untenable, while the increasing uncertainty about both personal and social identities has put a premium on the rediscovery of roots. At a stroke it has made topical and immediate such ancient episodes as the building of Hadrian's Wall, the conversion to Christianity and the separation from the Celtic Church. It has also made history into a front-line subject for issues of empire and race, and for the question of where the boundaries of Great Britain are to be drawn.

It would be a great misfortune if the return to history were to be accompanied by a revival of those sectarian and know-nothing attitudes to other disciplines and other fields of thought which were so prevalent before the cultural revolution of the Sixties. History has never been autarchic. In its early days the Oxford school was umbilically tied to law, and it was perhaps in deference to this that its central preoccupation was with constitutional developments. The Cambridge school, under the aegis of Sir John Seeley and Lord Acton, was almost as closely tied to political science. In the Edwardian schoolroom the study of history was a branch of 'Civics' and closely related to imperial geography. In the Twenties, when 'learning by doing' first made its appearance in junior classes, it was much influenced by the Art and Crafts movement, and by League of Nations idealism.

History owes its present vitality largely to forces generated outside itself. The history of the family, as pioneered by the Cambridge Group for the Study of Population, owed its initial procedures to demography and its problematic to sociology. In its more recent development it is being no less deeply marked by contemporary preoccupations with parenthood.

Foucault, a wayward cultural historian posing as a theorist, has provided an enormous impetus to work in the fields of medicine and crime, as well as producing new questions about the history of the state and sexuality. Edward Said's *Orientalism*, a work in which politics and aesthetics freely mingle, is having a comparable influence on the history of imperialism, and the constitution of Europe's Others.

It would be a misfortune if, in the interests of standardized attainment tests, the scope of history were to be narrowed. History has always owed its impetus, both as a classroom subject and as a scholarly pursuit, to the sense of discovery. Its truths, whether reached in the course of research, presented at the lectern, or arrived at on a project, typically present themselves as revelations, uncovering what has been hidden from the record. The subject would be cut off from its lifeblood if it were to contract to a uniform grid. New sources of knowledge are being brought into play; new lines of thought are providing research with its adrenalin. The last thirty years have seen a multiplication of sub-disciplines – each with its own subject-matter and time horizons – and a quite extraordinary proliferation of specialist journals. David Cannadine, in an influential but pessimistic article, has argued that this is a sign of the subject's decadence: that it involves knowing more and more about less and less. I prefer to see it as a sign of history's generosity, and its readiness to double back on its tracks. Twenty-five years ago, addressing a *Past and Present* conference not long before Peter Laslett published *The World We Have Lost*, Keith Thomas declared: 'The study of the family in English history has simply not begun.' Today it is an activity for tens of thousands of people. In the primary schools it competes with Norman castles and Saxon huts for the honour of introducing the youngest children to the idea of the past.

A history that was alert to its constituency would need to address not only the record of the past but also the hidden forces shaping contemporary understandings of it, the imaginative complexes in and through which it is perceived. Teachers, enjoined by ministers to regard themselves as custodians of 'heritage', might consider the past as a means of symbolic reassurance, as a source of borrowed prestige. Confronted with the phenomenon of 'period living' and the 460,000 houses now listed and statutorily protected as historic, they might point up the way in which the past – or make-believe representations of it – furnishes us with objects of desire. On school trips, negotiating a world of appearances, they might like to speculate on the deceptions of immediacy. And if, following the precepts of the new history, teachers saw their task as training children in the use of sources, they might find costume drama or romantic fiction more appropriate for critical viewing or reading than preselected documents or graphics.

If history is an arena for the projection of ideal selves, it can also be a means of undoing and questioning them, offering more disturbing accounts of who we are and where we come from than simple identifications would suggest. As an intellectual discipline, history requires a degree of detachment: the ability to draw contrasts and make connections, to discover a principle of order in the midst of seeming chaos, to explain, or attempt to explain, the whys and wherefores of apparently mysterious acts, to think the unthinkable. As a form of inquiry it is a journey into the unknown. As a classroom subject, it is supposed to broaden the mind, to challenge the commonplace assumptions of everyday life by showing the contingency of much that we regard as natural and permanent, the modernity of much that we mistake as traditional, the antiquity of much that passes for new.

One of the appeals of history is that it can allow an escape from self. In Carlyle's words, it gratifies an appetite for the wonderful; in Herbert Spencer's phrase, recalling his boyhood reading, it ministers to the 'epical' sense. All this is particularly relevant to children, who are much more used to imagining alternative worlds than adults. History may start from the known and the familiar, as it does in many primary schools today, where projects such as 'Grandmother's Washing Day' are classroom favourites. But children seem equally at home with, or excited by, the exotic: Christians thrown to the lions, slaves building pyramids. They have a morbid interest in the horrors and cruelties of the past – cruelties to children in particular – which, whether in the form of the Princes in the Tower, or the little hurriers down the mines, have long occupied a regular place in the outlines and primers. The popularity of *Blackadder*, cult-viewing for ten- and eleven-year-olds, testifies to the love of the comic and the grotesque. We may go to the past in search of ideal ancestors, but history would be a dull subject to teach if we peopled it with likenesses of ourselves.

The People with Stars in Their Eyes*

The 'great man' theory of history has been hugely controversial, ever since it was first propounded by Thomas Carlyle in the 1840s. It was fiercely challenged at the time. Some accused Carlyle of power worship, others of ignoring impersonal forces of development. H.T. Buckle, an embattled determinist, was contemptuous of what he called 'blind chance'. In his *History of Civilisation in England* (1857–58) he argued that history should be written as a branch of the natural sciences, taking 'social phenomena' as its subject-matter and interpreting them in the light of 'fixed and universal laws'. J.R. Green, the liberal-radical, was no less scornful of 'drum-and-trumpet history'. Not 'English kings' or 'English conquest' but 'the English people' were the subject of his landmark *Short History* (1874).

These ancient battles were resumed this week when Dr Nicholas Tate, the Government's chief adviser on the school curriculum, charged teachers with selling Britain short, arguing that Britain's sense of national identity was being eroded because history teachers were ignoring British heroes. Like his earlier plea for the teaching of the virtues of Britishness, Dr Tate's jeremiad invites derision, raising as it does the spectre of jingoism and the flag-waving enthusiasms of yesteryear. He quickly found an ally in Garry Bushell, who argued in his column in the *Sun*: 'Don't let teachers turn our heroes into zeroes', giving Dr Tate 'full marks' for his intervention. 'Children aren't taught about the great men and women who shaped our island any more,' he complained. 'The notion of great achievers doesn't fit the quasi-Marxist view of today's education "experts". Individual achievement has been downgraded in favour of learning about mass movements and the teaching of social history.'

Professional historians, who deal by preference with such aggregates as state formation or collective mentality, will hardly be sympathetic to Dr Tate's views. Toppling the great from their pedestals is a favourite scholarly sport. Alerted to 'the invention of tradition' and the theatricality of

* This essay was first published in the *Guardian*, 23 September 1995.

appearances, we see our job as that of exposing myth, puncturing legends or not conniving with them. Leaders, we will point out – drawing perhaps on Max Weber's theory of 'charisma' – are not causes but effects, authority figures on whom we project our fantasies of omnipotence. It is the job of the good teacher to cut them down to size.

Yet Dr Tate has a point. It certainly is the case that writers of school textbooks, and the devisers of the school curriculum, have wanted to escape from great man theories of history. In line with the deconstructive turn in contemporary thought, they have been centrally concerned not with personifying movements, or dramatizing heroic episodes, but rather with demystifying the procedures of historical inquiry. Not the foundations of national greatness, but the fragility of historical evidence and the contingency of interpretation are the animating dialectic of many of today's classroom exercises. As Nick Henshaw put it eloquently on Tuesday's Radio 4 *PM* programme, when discussing the fabrication of what he called 'the Nelson myth', the overriding preoccupation of the history teacher must be with the constituents of historical truth.

One pedagogic principle which this ignores is the power of example, which marks every stage in the learning process from the cradle to the grave. Following in the footsteps of others was fundamental to the whole literature of Victorian self-improvement, where the impulse to admire (greatest, wrote Samuel Smiles, in 'the season of youth') was seen not as a way of inculcating deference, but on the contrary as a means of what would today be called 'empowerment'. The imitation of greatness gave high ideals to strive for. What Edmund Burke called the 'school of example' is not less in evidence today, although its sources are promiscuous. Education, however libertarian, is inconceivable without mentors. It also involves an authority principle – indeed *educare*, the Latin original of the word, means literally to give a lead.

Another uncomfortable issue for those, like the present writer, committed to the practice of 'history from below' are the ambiguities attaching to the notion of 'ordinary people', a coinage of the 1930s, replacing older terms such as 'everyman' and 'the common people'. It was the flagship of the 'new wave' social history of the 1960s and 1970s, and in the schools widely canvassed as the alternative to famous names and dates. But it may be less democratic than it sounds. Imaginatively, it seems particularly unlikely to appeal to the young (if history from below nevertheless flourishes, it is perhaps because of the otherness of 'ordinary' people in the past, not because of their ordinariness).

Distressingly, from an egalitarian point of view – or a rationalist one – it is the romance of the past, the wonders and marvels, which seem always to have excited 'ordinary people' themselves. Not the poor labourer or the toiling spinster but Sir Guy of Warwick was the representative hero of those 'penny history' chap-books which for some three centuries were one of the great sources of knowledge about the past. The capacity to create legends is one of the primary forms of storytelling, confronting folklorists and anthropologists – the collectors of oral tradition – in whatever sphere they choose to work.

The existence of ideal types, whether in the person of great teachers, fearless warriors or earth-mothers, seems to be a cultural universal. The 'big hewer', an Atlas-like figure credited with performing Herculean feats of strength, was the miner's shield (albeit a purely symbolic one) against the terrors of his work, while the old trade union banners, with their portraits of local heroes and national leaders, remind one that the cult of personality has had as many devotees in British working-class movements as in those of Russia and Eastern Europe.

Like the phenomenon of stardom in the cinema, or mass idols on the concert stage, gods and heroes are an inescapable part of historical narrative, and it is not easy to see how they can be expunged from the record. Quite apart from the noble or terrible deeds attributed to them, they personify moral argument. The medieval monks knew this when they invented the episode of King Canute and the waves, a parable designed to show that kings and queens were made of the common clay. Hagiography – the Lives of the Saints – is one of the earliest forms of this country's written history. In a more secular vein, the outlaw hero was, from the sixteenth century onwards, a favourite subject for the chapbooks. Biography, though nowadays despised as an inferior form of the historian's art, is by far the most widely read. Even if it is expelled from the classroom it will stage a comeback through other spheres. Television biopics and drama-documentaries, such as Glenda Jackson's *Elizabeth R*, uninhibitedly present historical figures as larger-than-life characters. So do comics such as Asterix, in which great man theories of history enjoy a vigorous, if caricatural, after-life.

It is by no means clear that Nelson, one of the great heroes in the school readers of yesteryear, was the gung-ho figure which both Dr Tate and his critics believe him to have been. Desperately wounded in battle, blind in one eye, with his right arm amputated in 1797, he was depicted, even in his own lifetime – and not least by himself – as an intensely vulnerable man. Like the Jack Tars of nautical melodrama – the first proletarian heroes of the English stage – his life was continually at risk. It was his bloody sacrifice at the battle of Trafalgar rather than – or as well as – his naval victory which enshrined him in the hearts of his fellow countrymen, and it is that which perhaps accounts for the enduring admiration extended to him where the memory of the altogether more triumphalist Duke of Wellington (one of Mrs Thatcher's household gods) has faded. In Daniel Maclise's painting, *Death of Nelson* – endlessly reproduced in school prints – he is not so much a triumphant commander but rather a fallen Christ, pictured in the hold of the *Victory*, a languishing figure in a classically dying pose; behind him an upright mast and horizontal beams are the nautical equivalents of the cross.

The morbid preoccupation with death is also a recurrent strain in Victorian hero worship. It helps to account for the numerous portraits of Lady Jane Grey; and for the quite extraordinary popularity of Mary Queen of Scots, as a stage heroine, as a subject of court biography and of romantic portraiture in art.

Astonishingly, in the light of her well-known adulteries and her no less notorious Catholicism, she was, it seems, something of a school hero, among boys as well as girls (at Eton, the members of Pop, the school debating society, preferred her to Elizabeth I). The later Victorian enthusiasm for Joan of Arc, invented as a nationalist heroine by the historian Jules Michelet in the 1840s but adopted in England for her 'singularly sublime character', possibly owes something to the same cause.

A romantic and Gothic interest in the fate of the prisoner may also have played a part, as it did in such centre-pieces of 'Our Island Story' as the execution of Charles I and the murder of the little Princes in the Tower. As a writer in *The School And The Teacher* for March 1860 put it, discussing 'biography as a means of teaching and training':

> Do we not sometimes detect ourselves giving a very unwise prominence to plots, assassinations, and wars, thus engendering a feeling of romantic interest on behalf of the Guy Fawkes, the Feltons and the Napoleons of the world . . . while the really noble and sublime careers of a Newton, a Watt, a Hunter, a Wilberforce, or a Stephenson, are passed by with an indifference as unwise as it is ungraceful?

Even more remote from Carlylean power-worship was that vast corpus of Victorian popular biography – the stock-in-trade of the character-training manuals and the Sunday school prize-books – devoted to the triumphs of self-help. This was a literature plebeian rather than patrician in its sympathies, looking to the 'industrious sorts of people' for its subjects and making a gospel of work. As Stefan Collini has persuasively argued, it formed part of an emancipatory discourse, a repudiation of deference and rank. In the hands of Samuel Smiles, a Scottish radical by formation, and later a Chartist-sympathizing newspaperman, it was a celebration of honest worth, chronicling, in one version, the triumphs of the autodidact, in another the lives of the engineers.

The great man theory of history, as propounded by Thomas Carlyle, was bitterly contested by the evolutionary-minded, while the constitutional historians, such as Bishop Stubbs, the founder of the Oxford School of Modern History, attempted to bypass it entirely. But as a pedagogical device it was a brilliant success. It was adopted with enthusiasm in the school readers, as later in those early exercises in empathy where children were invited to take sides. At the Mechanics Institutes, the lecture halls, and the working men's 'mutual improvement societies', where history lessons normally took the form of a public debate, it found an immediate audience. It was no less popular in the great public schools, where debates, such as those on the rival merits of Mary Queen of Scots and Elizabeth I, were the only occasion in which Modern-side history got a look in.

Heroes and heroines cannot be willed into being, either by the chief executive of the School Curriculum and Assessment Authority or by anybody else. They will emerge, if they do emerge, as a byproduct of grand narratives. New movements bring new measures of significance.

Josephine Butler's moral crusades, challenging Victorian patriarchy in its lairs, takes on a new meaning in the light of contemporary feminism. Jeremy Bentham, a villain to students of the nineteenth-century Poor Law, may take on an entirely different character when he is seen as an early champion of animal rights. Edward II, vilified by the chroniclers and passed over in discreet silence by the old school history (so at least the Board of Education advised in 1908), becomes not a weak king but a victim of sexual politics.

If Dr Tate does want to engage children in moral argument – a worthy object, even if it is one which professional historians are wary of – he might find it profitable to concentrate on villains rather than – or as well as – heroes and heroines, or at any rate on those controversial figures who served nineteenth-century education rather well. He might start, perhaps, with Governor Eyre and the Jamaica atrocities – the subject of a momentous national debate in the 1860s, go on to Earl Haig, the butcher of Passchendaele, whose statue visitors to Whitehall will see between the Admiralty and Trafalgar Square, and end up with such near-contemporary figures as T. Dan Smith, the builder of tower blocks and throughways in 1960s Newcastle.

Or, taking a leaf from the new gay history, and from the pages of historical romance, he might invite classes to pay attention to the sexual politics of the English court, something familiar enough in the present day from the activities of the investigative journalists, but now being illuminatingly documented in the case of Renaissance England by literary scholars and art historians. Another possible line, taking a cue from *The Oxford Book of Villains* (now in paperback) or from Christopher Hill's forthcoming book on the subject, would be to ask children to make a special study of evil-minded judges, starting from the Wildeblood trial of the 1950s and moving backwards.

The leader principle is an offensive one to anyone whose politics and sympathies are libertarian. Yet regrettably, after three decades of cultural revolution, in which the authority figures have been under attack from all sides, it has shown itself to be remarkably resilient, not least in education, where masters, mentors and gurus offer models of emulation and achievement at every level in the scholastic hierarchy.

If heroes and heroines are myth, a projection of our longings, and if some of their most famous moments turn out to be apocryphal, they are nevertheless a necessary fantasy. We all need, at some stage in life, mentors. We all seek out people to believe in, patterns to follow, examples to take up. We take courage from those who seem stronger or more steadfast than ourselves. We glamorize stars and worship at the feet of gurus.

The world of popular entertainment is continually throwing up living legends. Rock music, in the space of thirty years, has created a whole Valhalla of posthumous fame, often tinged with tragedy. So far as 'Our Island Story' is concerned, the leader principle is something which confronts us at every turn. We cannot make society egalitarian by levelling its past.

Part IV

The War of Ghosts

Religion and Politics: The Legacy of R.H. Tawney*

Illustration by PETER CLARKE

* This article began as a letter to the *Guardian* and then grew. It was written when the newly formed Social Democratic Party (SDP) was winning a great deal of electoral support, attracting a stream of Labour defectors (among them a dozen or more MPs) and registering some 30 to 40 per cent support in the opinion polls. The first half was published in the *Guardian* on 29 March 1982, on the Monday after Mr Jenkins, an erstwhile Labour Chancellor of the Exchequer, won a notable by-election victory at Glasgow; the second half of the article reprinted here was published in the *Guardian* on 5 April 1982. The immediate provocation for the letter was the party's formation of a 'Tawney Society'. I was brought up on Tawney, both as a historian and a socialist, and the piece is correspondingly indignant. But it was also in some sort an act of exorcism, to get rid of the SDPer in myself. The companion piece, which follows in this collection, is a more considered one. I've resisted the temptation to tamper with either text. (Author's note)

The name R.H. Tawney, as recent correspondence in the *Guardian* suggests, is not one to be invoked lightly, least of all in the newspaper for which he wrote. And if the present controversy has the effect of encouraging people to read his work – a disturbing experience, whatever one's political persuasion – it may have done some good. Even so, the Social Democratic Party's claim to Tawney as a progenitor does look suspiciously like an afterthought, an exercise in generating fictitious moral capital rather than the acknowledgement of a spiritual debt. As a matter of literary tastes – Tawney was a master of English prose – it seems insensitive to yoke his name to that transatlantic neologism a 'Think-Tank', the SDP's alternative name for their Fabian Society; while on a point of political consistency, the talismanic use of Tawney's name sits uneasily with the oft-declared intention not to become a Labour Party Mark II, since that was the party, for good or ill, to which he gave some forty years of service.

Visually, the public image of the SDP – 'young, glamorous, dynamic' (according to Consumer Insight, the Mayfair firm of consultants); 'smartly-dressed, good-looking and forceful in appearance' like David Frost, Anna Ford or Sir Freddie Laker (according to a survey quoted in the *Guardian*) – could hardly be more different from Tawney, who was self-effacing to a degree, and notoriously shabby in dress (canvassers in his old constituency may recall him padding about Mecklenburgh Square in a worn-out khaki jacket).

As spiritual heirs, if that is what they now declare themselves to be, the SDP have been rather careless with their patrimony, going out of their way, during the first year of the party's existence, to pour scorn on Tawney's beliefs. There is only a single reference to Tawney in Dr Owen's *Face the Future*, and that by no means unequivocally complimentary: more notice is given to such luminaries of the contemporary political scene as Peter Jay and Henry Fairlie.

Shirley Williams has high praise for Tawney in *Politics Is for People*, but her characterization – 'pastoral, gentle and humane' – hardly does justice either to the intransigence of his socialist commitment. Roy Jenkins, as a part-time banker, can hardly find Tawney's writings on usury to his taste, and his activities as Common Market High Commissioner cannot have encouraged him to make *The Acquisitive Society* his bedtime reading. As for Mr Rodgers, he is not known ever to have said anything about Tawney, and his new book, *The Politics of Change*, does not rectify the omission.

Roy Jenkins is, however, a historian of stature. He has written two major political biographies and a number of interesting essays. But whatever their qualities, they are hardly Tawneyesque. His life of Sir Charles Dilke is an entertaining account of upper-class amours; and his life of Asquith a riveting description of Edwardian high politics; morally and historiographically (the range of sources and interest is narrow) they belong to a different world to that of the landless labourers and deprived cottagers evoked by Tawney in *The Agrarian Problem in the Sixteenth Century* (1912) or of the women blacksmiths whose sweated conditions at the time Tawney was investigating in *Minimum Rates in the Chain-making Industry* (1914).

The case of Asquith makes an instructive point of comparison. For Mr Jenkins he is a very beau ideal – 'the epitome of a Balliol man' (he got an effortless First); 'cultivated', 'brilliant'; a parliamentary performer with a natural 'front-bench' style. For Tawney, a Balliol man like Asquith (and Mr Jenkins) but cast in a very different mould, and a fervent supporter of the strike wave of 1911–12, Asquith belonged to the enemy camp. 'A. is like a halfpenny newspaper', Tawney noted tartly in his *Commonplace Book* (an attribution suggested by the book's editors), 'three parts advertisement and the rest sensation and misrepresentation'.

Again, Mr Jenkins is fascinated and charmed by that 'chatter of the lobbies' and 'lounging' in the clubs which Tawney so despised in the great and famous; his book conveys a sensuous delight in political infighting and parliamentary management, metropolitan dinner-parties and society gossip. He seems quite uninterested in (or ignorant of) labour history, even when it intrudes on the narrative (in the closing chapter Asquith's candidacy for the Oxford Chancellorship gets much more space than does his support for the government in the General Strike). Nor does he seem to have any historical sympathy for those Liberals with finer social consciences than Asquith who were brave enough to oppose the First World War; for social-liberals like Tawney's friends J.L. and Barbara Hammond; or for the liberal-progressives who made the London County Council a world model for city administration.

Mr Jenkins's life of Dilke is also exclusively concerned with High Society. The 'exciting menus' served at Dilke's house in Sloane Street (one of them is reproduced in full) are thought worthy of emphasis; not a word is said of Dilke's plebeian supporters – the Chelsea working men of the Eleusis Club – who, as Dilke himself handsomely acknowledged, kept him in his parliamentary seat. So narrow, indeed, are Mr Jenkins's sympathies that he is blinded to the one episode of real dignity in a story that would hardly otherwise justify the title *Charles Dilke, a Victorian Tragedy*: the steadfast support given to Dilke by the Free Miners of the Forest of Dean, who returned him to parliament after his disgrace. Not only are Mr Jenkins's sympathies not socialist, in Tawney's sense of the word; they are not even, in Mr Steel's terms, liberal – but rather patrician and Whig.

Rather than attempting to align the view of Tawney with those of the SDP, it might be more fruitful to contrast them, both in justice to Tawney's memory, and also as a way of taking a perspective on the SDP – and reflecting on some of the more subliminal components in its appeal.

I Past and Present

Tawney's life-work, both as a socialist and as a scholar, was to bring past and present into dialogue. His historical writing, as can be seen from his working notes (some of them are reproduced in *Tawney's Commonplace Book*, edited by J. Winter and D.M. Joslin), were framed as exemplifications of his Christian and socialist philosophy, and with contemporary events very much in his mind. He saw the acquisitive society of his own day as the culminating point in a very long-drawn-out historical process, whose stormy passage he charted from the class struggles of late medieval Europe to the homiletics of Archdeacon Paley. He traced the lineages of collectivism to the ideas and practices of the guilds, to medieval charity, and to what he calls, in a splendid phrase, the 'doctrineless communism' of the open-field village. His political writings also carry a very long view of the past. His yardstick for judging contemporary capitalism remained rooted in an imaginative conception of the moral economy of the pre-industrial village, while his watchwords for political action were consciously borrowed from the Puritan revolutionaries of the seventeenth century – during the 1912 strikes, he looked forward to the time when the 'industrial Lauds and Straffords' would meet their due. History provided Tawney with his conceptual categories, his compelling but idiosyncratic political vocabulary, his measures of tragedy and farce. In one register he was apt to represent the conflicts of labour and capital in terms of the age-old divisions between rich and poor – 'he hath put down the mighty from their seat and hath exalted the humble and meek' was a favourite biblical text. In another, he identified the fight for a socialist commonwealth with the Puritan 'Good Old Cause'. He looked back 'with pride' at the way in which the seventeenth-century revolutionaries had dealt with the Stuarts and subjected the Labour Party to a stream of unfavourable comparisons. 'How can followers be Ironsides if leaders are flunkies?', he wrote in an article on 'The Tasks Before the Labour Party'; and again: 'The Puritans, though unpleasant people, had one trifling merit. They did the job, or at any rate their job. Is the Labour Party doing it?'

The SDP has no such epic sense of the past. It acknowledges neither ancestral loyalties nor inherited beliefs, but takes its very title to existence from the breaking of traditional moulds. There are no towering figures to stand in awe of, as Tawney did when confronting the 'brooding melancholy' and 'glowing energy' of Milton and Cromwell; there are no great historical wrongs, such as the enclosure system, to recall. Apart from Dick Taverne, the St John the Baptist of the new dispensation, the party had no heroes in its Valhalla, no martyrs to commemorate in song. When the SDP advocates the 'market economy', as it does with increasing conviction, no rusting shipyards or abandoned pitheads rise in silent rebuke. When it advocates selective welfare services no folk memories of the Means Test stir. 'Never Again!', that most emotive of rallying cries on the Left, conjures up for the SDP nothing more frightening than the 'fudging and mudging' of the Wilson and Callaghan cabinets.

The SDP was marketed to the public as a brand-new product, a Phoenix risen from the ashes, 'a new beginning in British politics', 'the greatest opportunity for change for at least 60 years', 'something different', the herald of a bright new dawn. As the *Sunday Times* wrote, surveying the public launch: 'It had to have a modern, go-ahead, twenty-first-century ring about it . . .' Every step in the party's formation, even the private get-togethers of the leaders, was highly publicized, and treated as a momentous event. Its credit card membership, and computerized address list, were promoted as wonders and marvels. As the party gathered strength, the historical occasions proliferated: the Limehouse Declaration ('a liberation for millions of voters', 'a day for the . . . history books'); the public launch at the Connaught Rooms ('this historic occasion'); the Crosby by-election ('the beginning of a great movement in history, an idea that has found its time'); the Constitutional Convention. Not since H.G. Wells wrote *Tono-Bungay* has the country been exposed to so much puff (according to the party itself, the TV coverage given in the week after its public launch was worth some £20 million). The whole thrust of the party, as Dr Owen wrote in the secret memorandum which prepared the break, was that it was to be 'new, different, young and fresh-looking'. This inflation of the new was accompanied by a systematic devaluation of the past. Thus the history of the labour movement – miners' lockouts, *Ragged-Trousered Philanthropists* and all – was relegated to the limbo of what Dr Owen (borrowing from Professor Finer) calls 'adversary' politics; the idea of socialism to those 'outdated dogmas' and philosophies for which – as Mr Jenkins reassured the party's Constitutional Convention the other weekend – the new formation had no room. There was thus no 'good old cause' to champion, only the 'pointless conflict' engendered by the two-party system; there was no historic division between Left and Right, only a yah-boo ritual.

It is not surprising, then, that when it refers to its own prehistory, the SDP seems uncertain as to where to turn. Its immediate inspiration is variously attributed to Mr Jenkins's Dimbleby lecture; to Mr Taverne's by-election campaign; or (by Dr Owen) to an article written by himself and David Marquand in 1967. Further back, the ancestry seems more haphazard. Mr Rodgers, exploring new territory, got a big round of applause at the Perth conference when he stated his preference for the 'middle way' championed by Mr Macmillan in the 1930s. 'This is one reason why many people who once voted Conservative are going to vote SDP at the next election', he forecast. Mrs Williams offers us Kautsky, Owen and Tawney, 'the great philosophic exponents of social democracy', but since she has not a word to say about the first and little about the third, while of Owen we are given no more than a single quotation, decontextualized and made to refer to ecology, it is difficult to know how she came upon such an oddly assorted trio: none of them get as much space as what she calls 'a seminal article in *Accountancy Age*' which perhaps more accurately reflects the drift of her current preoccupations. Dr Owen, in *Face the Future*, offers some interesting passages on the Guild Socialists, but in the new preface to his book, added after the formation of the party, he turns to an electorally much more potent mix. 'Some will identify the Party with the post-war socialism of Clement Attlee, others may identify the Party with the "one nation" tradition of Conservatism, others with the radical Liberalism of Lloyd George. Certainly the Party must have its roots in the past . . .' This assortment (judiciously chosen to represent all three parties) has the merit of offering potential punters an ecumenically free choice, but it is not clear how the radical Liberalism of Lloyd George is consonant with an end to 'adversary politics' ('Peers vs People' was an archetypal 'two nations' issue), nor how Clement Attlee's 1945 socialism can be aligned to the 'decentralist tradition' which Owen espouses. David Marquand's oddly titled *Russet-Coated Captains: The Challenge of Social Democracy* (the reference is to the Cromwellian soldiers who 'knew what they fought for, and loved what they knew') also takes his lineage from each of the three main parties. Disraeli is summoned up as the Tory ancestor ('one of the most sensitive and creative political intelligences of the nineteenth century'); the Fabians as the Labour one (no mention is made of R.H. Tawney); Hobhouse and Keynes as the Liberals. As in Dr Owen's book, the historical credits are even-handed. 'The Tory Democrats' contribution to the social democratic traditions may have been less conspicuous than the Fabians' or the New Liberals', but it has been no less significant' (Professor Marquand omits to mention that well-known exponent of 'one nation' politics whom he has elsewhere treated to a full-length biography, Ramsay MacDonald; and the russet-coated captains of his title turn out to be not the Army agitators of 1647 but such reassuring figures as Professor Popper and Sir Isaiah Berlin, Evan Durbin and Hugh Gaitskell).

There is not much to be said for the ritual invocation of ancestors, but that of the SDP seems a peculiarly bloodless affair, undertaken more with an eye to electoral advantage than to coming to terms with the past. The party's populism – its claim to represent 'the people' against 'the politicians' – seems at first sight even more synthetic, a species of make-believe which allows insiders, playing the system against itself, to project themselves as outsiders, and career politicians to take on the protective colouring of the grass roots. The party's 'newness' is also in some degree cosmetic, allowing yesterday's moderates to appear in the guise of today's radicals, and permitting a party represented at conference mainly by middle-aged men to conjure up in the public mind the more pleasing images of youth. Nevertheless the SDP does have a serious claim to being a party of a new type, even if it has yet to emancipate itself from being an oligarchy with democracy's trappings. And the repudiation of the labour movement past, however regrettable to a historian, is surely a source of strength. It enables the party to define its struggle with Labour in terms of 'ancients' and 'moderns' and to identify the Labour Party with all that is traditional and archaic. It allows the party to explore new political territory unencumbered by hereditary obligations or historically conditioned fears; and to recruit, in the localities, what may turn out to be the nucleus of a new political class. Above all it corresponds to a sentiment which is to be found not only in Britain but also in Europe, and not only on the Right of the political spectrum, but also on the Left, that the political agenda of 1945 is in some sort exhausted, and that there is a vast range of questions waiting to be publicly agitated.

One hidden dimension in the SDP's make-up, which may help to explain both the novelty of its appearance and its strangeness as a political phenomenon, is its Americanism. The party's launch was pure Madison Avenue, right down to the logos on the teacups. Its leaders have been marketed, very much like American politicians, on the basis of their niceness and good looks, with Dr Owen as John F. Kennedy *redivivus* and Mr Jenkins in the more patrician role of Adlai Stevenson. The SDP's Fabian Society is called a 'think-tank'; its constitutional assembly a 'convention' (presumably on the model of the American Democratic Party rather than the Jacobin assembly in 1792 France). Many of the party's leading theoretical concepts are American importations, for example, the idea that 'post-industrial society' has made class divisions obsolete; or that of 'small is beautiful', a Californian cult. The ideological axes on which the party works, and its leading political terminology, often have in the first place an American reference. When, for instance, the SDP uses the word 'equality', which it does very frequently, the word seems to be used in its American rather than its French or English sense, the unspoken ideal being that of the American 'open' society, where everyone goes to the same high school, and there is a 'diamond-shaped' social structure (no working class, but a vast middle class, and a small substratum of the poor and deprived). The SDP also uses 'radical' in an American rather than English sense, divesting it of its historical associations with class, and using it in ways that seem close to that right-wing libertarianism which in America is one of the spiritual and ideological supports for Milton Friedman's monetarism.

Peter Hall, in the first of the Tawney Society's pamphlets (*Investing in Innovation* is its unTawneyesque title), writes that 'future historians may want to trace the influence of American sabbaticals on British Social Democratic thought', his own pamphlet owing much to 'incisive and expert advice' from colleagues at the University of Berkeley, California. The statement might be extended to refer to those Harkness Fellowships which numbers of SDP cadres seem to have benefited from; and it would certainly include Mrs Williams's *Politics Is for People*, some of which was written, as she says, at the Kennedy School of Government, Harvard. Much of what she writes seems to have an American frame of reference, just as her adoption of 'positive discrimination' for women seems to have been suggested by one of her trips to America rather than from any association with the women's movement in Britain. And it seems possible, on the evidence of an *obiter dictum* in her book, that one of the subliminal influences in the very idea of forming a new party was the notion of revolutionary changes of paradigm in Thomas Kuhn's *The Structure of Scientific Revolutions* (1962), a book which has been enormously influential in the field of the social sciences, but which has lacked, heretofore, a laboratory experiment in politics to test its truths.*

II Religion and Politics

Tawney's writings are inseparable from his religious outlook. He believed that politics should be addressed to 'noble and important emotions', and that economics raised issues of fundamental principle which could only be resolved by moral choice. History was a moral drama too, in which rival systems of belief contended for supremacy, and irreconcilable interests clashed. In *Religion and the Rise of Capitalism* and *The Agrarian Problem in the Sixteenth Century*, for all their scholarship and carefully qualified interpretation, we are offered, in essence, a secular version of the Fall, a reverse utopianism in which commercial forces accomplish the destruction of communal solidarities, and society as a spiritual organism gives way to the notion of society as an economic machine. Tawney believed that his socialism was an application of Christian doctrine to the circumstances of his time, but he interpreted it in a militant sense – 'to state that the social ethics of the New Testament are obligatory upon . . . the industrial organization which gives our society its character, is to preach revolution' – and he drew freely on the more wrathful books of the Old Testament to prophesy property's doom. Capitalism for Tawney was not only an inequitable economic system; it was also morally evil,

* One of the least pleasing of the SDP's Americanisms is its red-baiting. This seems to be far more a matter of the leaders than of the membership, and it fits uneasily with the party's proclaimed commitment to tolerance and reasoned debate. But it does show signs of becoming systematic. Thus, in the Hillhead by-election Shirley Williams was forecasting 'blood on the streets' if Labour was returned to power, and claimed that the SDP was 'the last chance for Britain to find a democratic, moderate but radical alternative to revolution'. Mr Rodgers in his new book warns of those who want to 'undermine democracy by looking for opportunities for confrontation'; while in another register, Mr Roger Rosewall, for some fifteen years a leading member of the Socialist Workers' Party, but now an SDP councillor, a member of its Industrial Policy committee, and an Oxford University lecturer in industrial relations, has produced an 'Aims of Industry' pamphlet which attempts to foist on to the Labour Party responsibility for the stratagems which he himself practised during his years as a full-time SWP organizer; and which concludes by offering expert advice to employers on how to sack obstreperous stewards.

something to be extirpated root and branch, and he believed that the Church should denounce it in much the same terms that medieval preachers had reserved for usurers: 'It must rebuke the open and notorious sin of the man who oppresses his fellows for the sake of gain as freely as that of the drunkard or adulterer'.

Tawney's Christianity makes his socialism different from a Marxist-derived socialism, and his idealized workman, Henry Dubb, was very different from the Marxian Prometheus – a captive giant – or that latter-day figure of socialist rhetoric 'the militant'. But his Christianity gave him a sense of the totality of social relations – including their psychic roots – which a Marxist might well envy; and it saved him from triumphalism. There was a sombre hue to Tawney's dialectic ('undoubtedly man walks between precipices'), and it not only allowed for but built upon a sense of unresolvable contradictions. Socialism involved a 'long and arduous struggle' and its work was never done; Puritanism was a historical tragedy, the story of a house divided against itself; individualism and collectivism coexisted in vigorous incompatibility within the same breast:

> In every human soul there is a socialist and an individualist, an authoritarian and a fanatic for liberty, as in each there is a Catholic and a Protestant. The same is true of the mass movements in which men marshall themselves for common action. There was in Puritanism an element which was conservative and traditionalist, and an element which was revolutionary; a collectivism which grasped at an iron discipline, and an individualism which spurned the senseless mass of human ordinances; a sober prudence which would garner the fruits of the world, and a divine recklessness which would make all things anew.

The SDP has no such sense of the numinous. It conceives politics in temporal rather than spiritual terms, as a pursuit of the arts of government rather than as a struggle between darkness and light. It is burdened neither by transcendental longing – a 'divine recklessness' – nor a metaphysical sense of loss, but cleaves, existentially, to the present. It is the child of a more secular age, faithfully reflecting its hedonism; and when Mr Rodgers, in his new book, writes of the electorate as being 'up for grabs', or speaks nostalgically of Mr Asquith's 'agreeable time' as Prime Minister (August 1914?), one is tempted to suggest that it shows some signs of becoming the first authentically post-Christian party. Mr Jenkins presents himself as the apostle of reason rather than faith, affirming (or as he believes reaffirming), 'the non-dogmatic tradition of conscience and reform'. Mrs Williams is a practising Catholic, but she tells us that what she likes about her Church is that it is 'a church of sinners', and in her book (which offers us some singularly lack-lustre pages on the history of Christian socialism) she implies that the 'legitimate concern' of the Church ought not to extend beyond 'moral and religious issues'. Dr Owen's *Face the Future* is wholly secular in character, and he is apt to subsume questions of political direction into those of administrative practicality, so that the discussion of industrial co-operation ends up with proposals for changes in company law (strikingly similar to those being discussed by F.D. Maurice in the 1850s), while the clarion call for decentralization issues in nothing more apocalyptic than a plea for implementing the Layard report on local government. Mr Rodgers's *Politics of Change*, though offered as a 'testament of personal conviction', is also wholly secular in character, and the 'enduring concern for man's relationship to man' promised on the dust-cover resolves itself into a scatter of homiletic asides which have less to do with the mysteries of the human condition than with economizing on welfare budgets. 'It is a denial of caring to say that money – including public money – will necessarily buy happiness and security or provide the stimulus to mind and spirit that is part of life.' 'We cannot buy our way into a just society.' He seems more at ease in the role of Mr Worldly Wiseman, and it is on a note of prudent realism that he brings his book to a statesmanly close:

> The successful management of the economy and a healthy environment for industrial recovery are central to the permanence of political realignment. So, too, is scepticism about the old shibboleths of Left and Right, combined with a sensible caution about radical solutions devised for the sake of being radical. The politics of change requires great skill if the balance is to be wisely struck. The vision and excitement that breaks the mould must be matched by the judgement and steadiness that can consolidate the achievement.

In SDP terms, Tawney was a fundamentalist. The Labour Party was a cause or it was nothing, and all its actions should be unified and informed by the pursuit of a single end – the supersession of the capitalist system and its replacement by what he called 'the Socialist commonwealth'. In government it should aim for the commanding heights of the economy ('An intelligent policy will start from the centre, not nibble at the outworks'); in opposition, it should refrain from promising 'smooth things'. Tawney was very much concerned with practical social politics; in Labour Party terms he was rather moderate or 'centrist', and mistrustful of what he called the 'heroics' of some of Labour's more radical middle-class recruits. Nevertheless, he believed that politics was the pursuit of higher ends than power, and that electoral advantage had to be strictly subordinate to the imperatives of structural change. Tawney never questioned the legitimacy of parliamentary government, but he despised the arts of electoral management and never dabbled in the Westminster mystique. The trouble with the Labour Party, he diagnosed in 1934, was the lack of a unifying creed. The Party should not offer 'cheaply won' benefits to its potential constituents, nor should it trim to opinion, or tack to the prevailing winds.

> New models are not won by being all things to all men . . . The business of making programmes by including in them an assortment of measures appealing to different sections of the movement must stop. The function of the Party is not to offer the largest number of carrots to the largest possible number of donkeys. It is . . . to carry through . . . the large measures of economic and social reconstruction . . . to secure that the key sectors of the economic system are under public control.

The SDP cultivates no such stoic virtues, nor does it believe that electoral advantage should be subordinated to higher ends. It presents itself in the role of a mediator rather than that of a protagonist, offering a historic compromise between labour and capital, Left and Right, individualism and the state. It promises to call off the 'futile' war between the public and private sector, to end the 'organized hypocrisy' of party strife. Its predominant appeal is that it is quietist, 'a party that . . . attempts consensus and conciliation rather than division and opposition', in the words of a Brent recruit. Social democracy, in the eyes of its founders, is less a unified creed and more a particular approach to society and its problems, now 'leaning' in one direction, now 'tilting' in another; by nimble administrative footwork balancing the different alternatives to find a just mean. There are no issues so intractable that they cannot be reduced to manageable proportions, no interests so irreconcilable that they cannot be administratively bridged. Thus where Tawney was apt to see violently opposed moral and ideological imperatives, the SDP argues that all the great questions are negotiable, if they can be defused of their ideological charge. It is thus possible to advance women's rights without raising the issue of feminism, to promote equality while treating the idea of socialism as old-hat, to bring the two sides of industry together while leaving the structure of ownership unchanged. Where Tawney saw the threat of the Leviathan state, the SDP sees nothing more menacing than a multiplication of 'nosey parkers'; where Tawney saw corporate power, the SDP finds nothing more offensive than the 'petty perks' of shopfloor managers.

One creed which the SDP does seem to subscribe to, albeit only half consciously, is that of administrative common sense – the ideology of the professional expert. According to this view, always popular among civil servants and planners, politics is a species of false consciousness which prevents sensible men from getting on with the job. Improvements can be effected without rhetoric or fuss, simply by making things work better. Thus incomes policies, an SDP Conference Paper tells us, have failed in the past 'not by some law of natural inevitability, but because Governments have made silly mistakes'. Failures in the field of economic policy are put down to a similar blind spot: 'Essentially, British governments of all persuasions have lacked a professional approach'. In a more utopian vein, the SDP explores the possibilities of accomplishing large-scale change by means of its favourite crotchets, as for example the use of random-sample surveys as a way of establishing a 'participatory' local democracy; or the introduction of proportional representation as a way of putting an end to 'adversarial' politics (for some reason, the SDP believes that a three- or four-party system is inherently less divisive of opinion than a two-party one). Another change in electoral mechanics, proposed in this case by Dr Owen, and winning loud applause when it was presented to the London conference, is that of calling the carpenters into Westminster and installing cross-benches. Apparently (such are the marvels of proxemics) it would make parliament 'a forum for the whole nation instead of a bickering cockpit'. In a similar vein, British insularity, it is thought, will succumb on the building of the Channel Tunnel – nothing, it was said, more perfectly realized the aims and aspirations of the SDP. Mrs Williams, like some latter-day nineteenth-century reformer, is full of such well-meaning 'improvements'. Thus the 'tragedy' of our highly segregated educational system might be countered by pupil swaps between public schools and comprehensives ('People from Eton might easily find themselves at comprehensive schools in Liverpool, which might seem rather a wild idea but we have to break down barriers'); the energy crisis might be partially resolved, and unemployment reduced, if youths were employed on double glazing; the problem of loneliness in old age could be countered by a revival of Voluntary Services (as in Kent County Council's 'Adopt a Granny' scheme); sexist ideas could be combated by having boys at school learn domestic science and parentcraft, 'with more emphasis on responsibility in relationships'; monotony at work could be relieved by industrial sabbaticals.

The SDP was launched as a 'great crusade' to change the face of British politics, but the predominant note in the party's building strategy has been not so much evangelical as narcissistic – a story of success. It launched itself with a whole battery of promotional aids, designed to flatter its self-image and project itself in the public mind as a fast-moving political force. It pitched its appeal to the prosperous, offering credit card facilities to attract the more affluent, but no special rates (so far as I know) to encourage membership from, say, the unemployed or old age pensioners. Who the SDP are, both at leadership and at local level, has always seemed more important than what they want (a year after the party's formation there are still many people who believe, wrongly, that the party is simply pragmatic and has no policies at all). At the party's autumn conferences, according to newspaper reports, delegates were continually saying how much they enjoyed themselves, and were congratulated by the leaders on being so 'nice'. There were no emergency resolutions to pass, no points of order to wrangle over, no tract distributions at the door, as there are at Labour Party conferences. In the localities, too, it seems that one of the principal appeals of the SDP is that it is a place where like-minded people can feel at home, and a good deal of its first year's existence seems to have been taken up with a species of social bonding. Here is the Brent SDP's evidently self-satisfied balance sheet:

> This is the nearest we can get to an advertisement for SDP T-shirts. Chairman Maurice Rosen is the spoilsport for not wearing one. The blonde is Eva Rose. The toothy grin is Madelon Dimont's. The smirk belongs to Lee Jones. The picture was taken at our Social Evening on July 16th, at which most of us made very merry indeed. It was enormous fun, and we thank the Social Activities Committee for organising it (next time, though, please avoid the 'Vino Blanco' from a certain supermarket chain. The morning after would have been very painful if we had not all been punch-drunk with the Warrington result). Our guest of honour, Bob MacLellan M.P., made a sincere and moving speech. Among other things we heard him say: 'Some of us who are more fortunate than our fellow citizens have a special responsibility to bring our message to people who are despairing at the time, in a language they can understand. We have to be relevant in all parts of Brent.' It was a sobering note, and we were grateful to him for saying it. Trivia have their part to play as well, however, and we are now open for business with SDP badges, T-shirts, sweatshirts, ties, scarves, lapel pins – and window stickers that really stick. Coincidentally, most of these goodies are manufactured by Bob MacLellan's own Area Party in West Scotland. And perhaps they are not so trivial. Those of us who have gone out shopping, say, wearing an SDP badge or T-shirt, have found that they attract both interest and sympathy. People are GLAD to see real live Social Democrats out in the streets. The more we can make our presence felt, the more credible we shall become as a political alternative . . . Do, please, become a Social Democratic clothes-horse if you can – or at the very least, a discreet badge-wearer. We are still so new that we need to dazzle the public with the message – SDP . . . SDP . . . SDP . . . SDP . . . SDP.

People do not convert to the SDP, as the newspapers tell us, they *defect*. The very word has a secular ring to it, and the manner in which the change is accomplished suggests less a spontaneous stirring of the spirit than a carefully orchestrated exercise in public relations. The statement faithfully echoes the current party line (there is usually a fearful reference to Mr Benn or to *Militant*), and it is timed to coincide with the run-up to a by-election, or a party conference. We are told that the decision has been preceded by weeks, even months of agonized indecision, but when the defector himself appears, he comes not as a repentant sinner, unloading his burden of guilt, nor yet as an old believer whose God has failed, but rather as the prodigal son entering into his full inheritance. There is usually a ritual expression of regret – 'associations of a lifetime', 'the pool of long-term friendships', 'the Party that I have loved' – but there is no doubt that for the defector himself the experience is intensely pleasurable and that it involves not so much renunciation of the world but rather a realization of self – a release from historically imposed obligation, the acknowledgement of long-repressed desire. He no longer has to mouth the word 'socialism', nor give utterance to sentiments in which he only half believes. He no longer has to thicken up his accent, or suppress untimely thoughts. At last he can be himself. His pet ideas for economic recovery will be listened to reverentially; his worries about the race question will be shared. He can complain about the telephone service, as Mr Rodgers did at the Perth conference, and get a round of applause for it; or poke fun at miners' delegates, as he did at the Bradford conference, and expect to raise a laugh. There are no more ideologues to be afraid of, no club stewards to humour, no ward secretaries to chat up.

As a self-proclaimed party of 'conscience and reform', recruited largely among the comfortably off, the SDP betrays few signs of that secularized sense of sin which, as Beatrice Webb tells us in *My Apprenticeship*, played such a large part in the moral make-up of an earlier generation of social reformers – among them of course Tawney himself. 'Good works' do not figure prominently in the party's local activities (it has steered well clear of community politics in order to concentrate on local elections and government). At national conference there is nothing philanthropic about the approach to welfare: in the spirit of the times, respecting cash limits occupies far more attention than evoking social need. References to the socially disadvantaged – 'our most vulnerable and needy citizens' – certainly appear, from time to time, in party rhetoric, but it cannot be said that in the first year of its existence social justice has been a leading plank in the party's platform. Party manifestos are more concerned with constitutional reform than with preaching the social gospels. At party conferences, questions of management–worker relations are lengthily discussed, but not, so far as I know, health and safety at work; trade union 'reform' but not job enrichment. There is much in the country that the SDP would like to change, and many things which it is against, but except for constituency activists in the Labour Party (and the 'zealocracy' in the trade unions) there seems little that makes them angry. Nor is humanitarian indignation a leitmotiv in the party's handling of day-to-day events. The party's response to the Toxteth and Brixton riots was conspicuously out of line with other sectors of opinion. Mr Heseltine may not be everyone's idea of Tory paternalism but he had the decency to extend his stay in Toxteth by a week, to listen to local opinion and to press for additional help to the neighbourhood. Lord Scarman openly questioned the police tactics. The Labour Party focused on the environment of need; the extra-parliamentary Left on the background of police harassment. Mrs Williams, however, used the occasion for an exercise in guilt-by-association. In a speech which lit up the Warrington by-election, referring to the current riots, she alleged that the Militant Tendency within the Labour Party had set up training schools in Toxteth and Brixton. 'It is perhaps not entirely strange that these areas had suffered great difficulties and violence over the past couple of weeks,' she said. She pointed out that only a week before the Labour Party Young Socialists were said to have distributed a pamphlet in Liverpool calling for a twenty-four-hour strike.

'I cannot imagine anything less likely to bring back order and sense to this country at a difficult time', she said. Nor was this a sentiment uttered in the heat of the moment. It reproduced a theme which she had already rehearsed a few days before. 'Socialist Pamphlet Added Fuel to Riot' ran the *Daily Mail* headline, followed by the story:

> Former Labour Cabinet Minister Mrs Shirley Williams last night accused the Labour Party's youth section of 'adding fuel to the flames of violence' in the weekend rioting in Liverpool. Mrs Williams, speaking at Risca, Gwent, said at the height of the riots the Labour Party Young Socialists distributed a 'provocative pamphlet' in Toxteth condemning the police and calling for a general strike. 'The Labour Party Young Socialists are the official youth section of the Labour Party' she said. 'The chairman of the party's youth committee is the far-Left MP Joan Maynard. The national officer is the militant Andy Bevan.

Tawney's version of Christian Socialism was in some sort peculiar to himself, but a Christian or Christian-derived ethic was a common property of the labour movement of his day, borrowing its terms from the transposed evangelicalism of Labour's well-born recruits; from High Church Socialism; and from the radical nonconformity which was part of its nineteenth-century inheritance. Tawney clearly felt morally at home in the Labour Party: more so, perhaps, than anywhere else except for the Workers' Educational Association. Despite the difference in life circumstances his outlook seems to have converged with that of the constituency stalwarts on a range of critical themes. Like them, he thought of socialism as a great and noble cause, to be pursued in a spirit of self-sacrifice and devotion; like them, too, he thought of labour as a 'movement', with historically appointed tasks. Another point of fundamental convergence was his sense of the world as a hostile place. Suspicion of worldliness, whether in the form of pomp and ceremony, airs and graces, opportunism or self-seeking, is one of the most deeply ingrained elements in the psychology of labour movement activists. It is a point at which evangelical fears of 'corruption' fuse with a class distaste for careerism, and dissenting hostility to power. Tawney gave it eloquent expression in his 1934 attack on the honours system, which may stand very well not only for his own feeling, but also for the 'common sense' wisdom of the constituency activists of the time:

> Talk is nauseous without practice. Who will believe that the Labour Party means business so long as some of its stalwarts sit up and beg for sugar-plums, like poodles in a drawing room? . . . It will not do. To kick over an idol, you must first get off your knees. To say that snobbery is inevitable in the Labour Party, because all Englishmen are snobs, is to throw up the sponge. Either the Labour Party means an end to the tyranny of money, or it does not. If it does, it must not fawn on the owners and symbols of money. If there are members of it – a small minority, no doubt, but one would be too many – who angle for notice in the capitalist press; accept, or even beg for, 'honours'; are flattered by invitations from fashionable

hostesses; suppose that their financial betters are endowed with intellects more dazzling and characters more sublime than those of common men . . . They have mistaken their vocation. They would be happier as footmen.

It is arguable that this fear of worldliness and corruption, with all its religious undertones, is one of the fundamental bones of contention in Labour's current crisis and the constitutional battles over the mandatory reselection of MPs – i.e. the whole sequence of events which led, among other things, to the formation of the SDP. It can certainly be seen, as an axis of division, in earlier Labour crises, and more generally as an unresolved and possible unresolvable tension in the very existence of Labour as a political force. Thus in the early 1950s the Bevanites stood out not only for welfare against rearmament, but also for the religion of the heart against that of the head. They championed the spirit of the pioneers against the compromises of the office-holders, and no epithet flung at their adversaries was more damaging than that which labelled Mr Gaitskell 'a desiccated calculating machine'. A similar line of division surfaces in the 1959–60 battles over Clause 4, with one side accusing the other of 'fundamentalism' – preferring purity of doctrine to the winning of government office – while the other accused their opponents of sacrificing principle for short-term electoral advantage. Tony Benn has drawn up the battle lines of the Seventies using very similar counters to those in use in earlier times:

After 30 years as a Labour MP I have good reason to know the value of dedicated local parties. They are made up of those who have, in the main, no personal ambitions to corrupt their judgement. Some may seek and win a seat on the Council. A very few may stand for Parliament but the vast majority of them work without any personal recognition because they believe in what they are doing. As a result their instincts are usually surer than those at the top in Parliament or government . . . Indeed the conflict between the rank-and-file on the one hand, and the leadership on the other is not usually susceptible to the crude analysis of 'extreme' versus 'moderate'. It is the difference between the principled stand of the party workers, and the compromises arising from the 'here and now' pressures and temptations of office to which those at the top are subjected.

On the other side of the divide, it is not difficult to discern the Worldly Wiseman, to whom the very idea of moral absolutes is anathema, and for whom politics is the art of the possible. Mr Taverne sarcastically attacks Mr Benn for having spent ten years in various government high offices 'without being in any way corrupted by the slightest taint of realism'; while Mr Rodgers, in his new book, elevates the 'day-to-day business of politics' into judge and jury in its own cause:

When the balance is struck between the competing claims of principle, compromise follows. Anyone who is unwilling to recognize this or face and resolve unpleasant moral dilemmas rather than be rendered helpless by them, ought

> not to be involved in politics at all. A political party that seeks to win power through the ballot box and exercise it widely cannot behave like a religious sect or enjoy the self-indulgence of the righteous.

More generally, one may recall that hostility to Puritanism was a unifying bond in Mr Gaitskell's Hampstead Set, one of the original nurseries for today's SDP leaders; and when one sees how consistently the Constituency Left is attacked for 'fanaticism' and 'dogma' one might speculate that, at the level of the political unconscious, it may not be so much the doctrine which is objected to, but rather the emotionalism which accompanies its advocacy – the warmth, enthusiasm and evangelical self-righteousness (or, as its opponents would experience it, intolerance) with which the Left advances its causes.

The religious element in English socialism has long been familiar to historians, and it has been given much prominence in accounts of the early labour movement. Once, however, the Labour Party is in place, it is quickly forgotten, and the party's subsequent progress is explained either in terms of organizational growth or else by purely class dynamic. Yet a study of political vocabulary, and of the subpolitical issues around which party feeling forms, might show that secularized versions of Christianity continued to play a large part in the moral make-up of Labour Party members, and that its residues have been reproduced from one generation of activists to the next. Many of the principal divisions in the party have been over ethical images, or over political questions which were argued out in ethical terms – most obviously on arms spending and militarism; and the moral component is no less striking in that range of subpolitical issues around which party feeling has formed – for example in Edwardian times, hostility to the drink trade, or, in the postwar years, the suspicions of hire purchase, advertising, commercial television and consumerism. Then again there are the recurring divisions between the claims of dissent and those of party loyalty, between pragmatism and 'principle', between the politics of conscience and that of common sense. Above all the question of government office is apt to produce the most explosive contradictions in the ranks of a party which is on the one hand thoroughly committed to electoralism, and on the other congenitally suspicious of office-holding (when Labour sits on the Treasury benches the experience is usually as traumatic as the loss of a general election is for Tories). Fears of worldliness are even more apparent on the revolutionary and sectarian Left, as it is on the extra-parliamentary Left today; and indeed there is a case for arguing that a secularized version of Christianity is even more important in their make-up than it is in such more obviously para-religious organizations as the ILP. Even British Trotskyism began as a splinter group from Conrad Noel's Catholic Crusade – that is, from the far left of 1920s Christian Socialism. It may not be accidental that the word 'militant', in such wide use by neo-Trotskyist groups today, is a word of Christian rather than Marxist provenance.

Conversely, one way of understanding right-wing revisionism, up to and including the SDP, would be to see in it a whole series of attempts to liquidate the religious legacy in English socialism. Mr Gaitskell believed he could do it by changing a crucial clause in the Labour Party Constitution. The SDP seem to have concluded that it can be done by dismembering the labour movement.

III The Free Market

For Tawney, capital, whether accumulated through land, industry or trade, was a species of immoral earnings, an increment on the back of labour, a tribute that rentiers drew. This was as much the theme of his *Land and Labour in China* (1932), a pioneering study of the process of immiseration in the Third World, as of his historical studies of enclosure, or his contemporary investigation into the conditions of domestic outworkers. In *Religion and the Rise of Capitalism* (1926), the controlling metaphor for exploitation is the market, which appears as the corrupting force undermining the solidarities of guilds and open-field villages. Tawney quotes with evident relish the medieval doctrine that trade, though necessary, was perilous to the soul, and he was no more tender to the early institutions of capitalist finance: 'an organized money market has many advantages. But it is not a school of social ethics or of political responsibility.' Tawney's target is the rentier class, and he is concerned to argue that there were no such things as property 'rights', only various degrees of usurpation. In *Equality*, the most systematic of his treatises against capitalism, his object of attack is irresponsible wealth. The industrial corporation was a species of modern feudalism which gave untold power to a handful of men. 'Lord Melchett smiles, and there is sunshine in ten thousand homes. Mr Morgan frowns, and the population of two continents is plunged in gloom.'

Tawney made his stand against capitalism not only in the name of social justice but also in that of freedom. Capitalism was a species of oligarchy, 'a pyramid in which power radiates downwards, from a tiny knot of bankers at the top, through intermediate layers of industrialists and merchants, to the mass of common men, who are twitched this way and that by the masters of the show, like puppets on a wire'. The control of the majority of the channels of public information was the monopoly of 'a handful of rich men'. Democracy was insecure so long as powerful vested interests could thwart a hostile government.

To the mechanisms of the market, Tawney counterposed the claims of collective life. As a Christian and a socialist he was concerned to argue that there was a principle superior to the 'mechanical play' of economic forces, that self-love and the social were *not* the same; and that competitive individualism – the indulgence of the 'egotistical' instincts, the pursuit of personal gain – was, like nationalism, inherently self-destructive. It was a condition of economic freedom 'that men should not be ruled by an authority which they cannot control'; the purpose of economic activity was not to maximize profits but to serve a social function. The first principle of socialism was that industry should be subordinated to the community, and in *The Acquisitive Society* he outlined six different ways in which – through what he called 'the extinction of the capitalist' – it might be accomplished. (Interestingly, nationalization, 'a word which is neither very felicitous nor free from ambiguity', was only one of them: his main hopes rested on worker-cooperation and self-management.)

The idea of what Tawney called 'industrial self-government' did not survive the decline of trade unionism and the shop steward movement in the interwar years, but the aim of putting industry 'in the service of the nation', and of eliminating the market as the arbiter of economic priorities, gained new force from the rise of planning ideologies in the 1930s. This was very much the spirit of Labour's 1945 programme, *Let Us Face the Future.* Nationalization, however limited it may retrospectively seem, was thought of at the time as the political economy of socialism, asserting itself aggressively against capitalism, and setting in train an irreversible process by which the private ownership of the means of production would become extinct. So much was this believed (at least in Labour ranks) that even the return of a Conservative government in 1951 did not immediately put an end to it. The authors of *New Fabian Essays* (1954), among them Mr Crosland and Mr Jenkins, firmly believed that England was a 'post-capitalist' society. Whatever the disputes about the pace of change there seemed no doubt about its direction. 'A mixed economy there will undoubtedly be,' wrote Mr Jenkins in his interesting book, *The Pursuit of Progress* (1953), 'certainly for many decades, perhaps permanently, but it will need to be mixed in very different proportions from this.' Nationalization came under increasing attack, with the 'revisionist' controversy led by Mr Gaitskell, but even so, *Signposts for the Sixties* (the then Labour programme) committed the party to taking over 'the commanding heights of the economy', while in another direction – that of welfare spending – Labour reasserted the primacy of the collective idea in making 'private affluence, public squalor' the watchword of its attack on Toryism.

To turn from this to the policy documents and writings of the SDP is to enter another world, one in which capitalism has been restored to a place of honour. The market, so far from being the seat of corruption, is 'unmatched' in its capacity for creating material wealth. It is no longer associated with corporate power, but has the advantage of being 'a highly centralized form of decision making'. Profits are a way of rewarding 'enterprise and effort', 'a measure of success and efficiency', while on the other side of the coin, labour appears in the negative form of a 'cost', to be subjected, where possible, to the disciplines of economic law, or what an SDP Conference discussion paper calls 'more market-related flexibility'. Mr Rodgers is the SDP leader who seems to have travelled furthest down this particular road, and in his new book he embraces the values of rugged individualism as though it were the newest line in ethics. 'A sense of personal achievement', he tells us, 'including an element of doing better than others – is vital in human motivation.' (Professor Friedman, the leading contemporary apostle of economic individualism, calls it 'instinctual'.) Elsewhere, in a passage which seems to confuse *The Origin of Species* with *Leviathan*, Mr Rodgers reassures us that 'the cut and thrust of a vigorous competitive economy . . . need not be equated with a Hobbesian tragedy in which only the fittest survive'. The competitive motif recurs in his discussion of fiscal policy, where the present tax structure is regretted because of the way it allegedly underwrites a timid approach to life: 'this is not the stuff of which successful entrepreneurs are made.' In the field of job protection, Mr Rodgers is suspicious of schemes which keep people in work 'for social rather than economic' reasons, and dislike of featherbedding moves him to a rare essay in metaphor: 'If the public spending budget is allowed to become a slush-fund for lame ducks, then there will be no money left to water the seedbed of sunrise industry.' Like Mr Whitelaw in the field of penal policy, or, earlier, Mr Heath in his advocacy of the Common Market, Rodgers seems to have high hopes in the therapeutic value of shocks. 'A radical solution to Britain's industrial problems is certainly not to be dismissed simply because of the upheaval in attitudes, habits and policies that it involves. A traumatic shake-up – of whatever kind – could be precisely the shock that British industry required by 1979, given almost twenty years of disappointment.' And again, 'A sense of shock has been coupled with a recognition that the easy-going ways have changed for good. The survival of the fittest has resulted in a trimmer and more viable manufacturing base and less dependence upon the Whitehall begging bowl.'

The SDP is still in favour of the 'mixed' economy, as, in one form or another, are all the major parties, but it privileges the place of market forces in the mix, and tilts state intervention towards encouraging them. The point of such intervention should be to restore market incentives and widen the sphere in which they can operate. Thus in the field of regional policy, the SDP calls for 'an intelligent strategy for attracting multinational and multiregional companies to the regions'. In housing policy it hopes to see a revitalization of the inner city by releasing urban land from county planning schemes, vesting it in the hands of private developers, and encouraging various combinations of private sector initiative and public sector finance. In economic policy it declares it 'a major priority of the Social Democrats to make government an understanding partner of industry', and wants government-financed capital projects, such as the Channel Tunnel, to be undertaken by private corporations. In the nationalized industries, the public corporation would be free to act as commercially as the private sector and external commercial competition would be encouraged, not restricted.

The rupture here with Tawney is obvious, but it seems worth pointing out that it marks a real break with the SDP's previous political mentors. Mr Crosland and Mr Gaitskell were not partisans of the market. They accepted it as an inescapable component of the 'mixed' economy and looked to state-promoted welfare measures and redistributive taxation as a way of neutralizing its biases. The SDP, by contrast, speak quite often of the 'market' rather than of the 'mixed' economy and they expound its virtues with a good deal more enthusiasm than many Liberals or Tory 'wets'. Mr John Horam MP, the SDP spokesperson on regional affairs (an ex-leader writer for the *Financial Times*), registered the change with refreshing candour in a guest column which he contributed last July to that nursery of laissez-faire thought, *The Journal of Economic Affairs*:

> The state needs to create the sort of framework within which the market can work to our advantage. In this country this means developing a coherent industrial strategy which gives the businessman the feeling that the state is trying to help rather than hinder them at every turn . . . It is recognized that unalloyed market forces lead to inequality. I believe that Tony Crosland was wrong to elevate equality into the major objective of socialism. Since I am not a socialist I cannot say how socialists should restate their aim, but I believe that the Social Democrats should have freedom as their main aim, while appreciating that more freedom does involve at least a minimum of equality: the freedom of the very poor is very restricted.

For the SDP, the market is not only economically necessary, a condition of material wellbeing, it is also morally good. As in Chicago economics, the free market is synonymous with consumer free choice and consumer free choice is the guarantor of personal liberty. It is also a very precondition for the existence of a 'pluralist' democracy, the economic counterpart to the principle of electoral choice. Consumer free choice is also invoked by the party as setting limits on its social options. Thus 'support for freedom of parental choice in education and health' was recommended at the October conference of the SDP not, it seems, from any affection for either the public schools, or private medical schemes – Dr Owen went out of his way to express a distaste for the latter – but because any attempt to restrict them would violate consumer sovereignty. 'They could not possibly in justice interfere with the rights of anyone to use their tax incomes as they saw fit.' The conference spokesperson on housing put a similar argument: 'Housing policies should be approached from the point of view of the consumer. The problem should be treated in commodity terms, and Victorian paternalism should be eradicated.'

The SDP and the New Middle Class*

The rise of the Social Democratic Party has been largely discussed in relation to the crisis in the Labour Party and the decline of working-class politics. But it may be that changes in the middle class are more pertinent to the appearance of the new party, both in accounting for its distinctive moral temper – in particular, its narcissism – and in explaining the emergence, both locally and nationally, of what looks to be, at least in embryo, a new political class.

The middle class before the Second World War was less a class than a society of orders, each jealously guarding a more or less self-contained existence, and exquisitely graded according to a hierarchy of ranks. The clergyman's widow, in reduced circumstances, would not make friends with the elementary school teacher, though she might have her round to tea. The vet's daughter, if she had pretensions to being county, would not go dancing with the articled clerk. The dentist's wife lost caste if she asked a favour of the grocer's wife.

The academic in cap and gown would hardly mix with the shirt-sleeved, chain-smoking journalist; nor the public servant with the racing driver. Barristers and solicitors inhabited different universes, the one a refuge for the impecunious sons of gentlemen, the other a summit of ambition for the shopkeeper's brightest son. Public schools looked down on grammar schools. Men and women lived in separate social spheres, symbolized by such all-male preserves as the Rotarians, and the virtual purdah to which the spinster was confined.

Middle-class identity was constituted amid a sea of social fears, with hidden reefs on which the frail barque of respectability could only too easily be wrecked. In a limited social landscape, all kinds of spectres loomed – 'rude' language, 'vulgar' clothes, 'coarse' looks. There was a servant you couldn't trust, the daily who was sullen and resentful, the Jews who had moved in round the corner, the 'sergeant-major' type who was

* This essay was first published in *New Society*, 22 April 1982.

throwing his weight about at the office. Keeping up appearances was a very condition of middle-class existence, snobbery a way of life; a vast amount of energy was expended on the management of social distance and keeping intruders at bay. Class distinction became the articulating principle of British political life.

Fear of losing caste within the middle class was accompanied by real terror at the thought of falling out of it. For a hundred years and more the masses – 'the dangerous classes' as they were known in early Victorian England – constituted the menacing 'other' in middle-class existence, the open-mouthed abyss waiting to swallow up those who lost their foothold in society. Individually the members of the working class were conceived of as pollutants; collectively they constituted the beetle-browed figures who lurked at the street corners, the harridans who fought in the pubs.

In the epoch of the October Revolution and the General Strike, such fears crystallized around the threat of the organized labour movement. Thus it was that, notwithstanding a certain lessening in economic differentials between the wars, class division became the articulating principle of British political life. Arguably it remained so up to the general election of 1959.

Class guilt – 'the conscience of the rich' – was the obverse side of class fear, conditioned by the same set of contrasts. In some it was associated with a notion of moral duty – *noblesse oblige*; in others with a deliberate rejection, or partial rejection, of class identity, and an attempt to put one's talents at the service of the masses.

The middle-classes of today are much more occupationally diversified, with the multiplication of professional and managerial hierarchies, and the proliferation of salaried employments. But it may be that culturally they are more compact. The vastly expanded universities have given their children a common education, subsuming the antique divisions between public school and grammar school, men and women, Anglican and Nonconformist, North and South. The lower professions, like journalism and public relations, have been economically and culturally upgraded. Scientists and technologists have stepped out of their small back rooms to serve on the boards of public companies. Even the arts are organized more like businesses, and business is a principal sponsor for them.

This newly unified middle class distinguishes itself more by its spending than its saving. The Sunday colour supplements give it both a fantasy life and a set of cultural cues. Much of its claim to culture rests on the conspicuous display of good taste, whether in the form of kitchenware, 'continental' foods, or weekend sailing and cottages. New forms of sociability, like parties and 'affairs', have broken down the sexual apartheid which kept men and women in rigidly separate spheres. The fear of mixing with the wrong set has given way to a positive eagerness to make new friends.

The new middle class are outward-looking rather than inward-looking. They have opened up their homes to visitors, and exposed them to the public gaze. They have removed the net curtains from their windows, and taken down the shutters from their shops. They work in open-plan offices and establishments, with plate-glass windows and see-through partitions and doors. In their houses they make a fetish of light and space, replacing rooms with open-access living areas and exposing the dark corners to view. They turn servants' attics into penthouses and make basements into garden flats. Back yards blossom out as patios; kitchens are aestheticized; even the lavatory is turned into a miniature folly.

The new middle class do not aspire upwards, aping the speech of their betters, imitating their furnishings, or reproducing their manners.

They dress down rather than up, for parties, in tight trousers rather than dinner jackets, pinafores rather than gowns. They go hatless to work and spend long and expensive hours at the hairdresser's, to cultivate a windswept look. They make a show of peasant pots in their kitchens. Their homes are imitation farmhouses rather than miniature stately homes, with stripped pine rather than period furniture, linens rather than chintz, and concealed lighting rather than cut-glass chandeliers.

The new middle class are much less snobbish than their predecessors. They positively welcome those who have made it from nothing, as confirming instances of their own classlessness and the openness of the society in which they move. They show few signs of envy, since they believe themselves to be in the thick of things and are broadly content with their lot. Their manners are open and relaxed. They do not blush in public or stammer in their speech. They no longer worry about dinner-table etiquette. At parties, they are less concerned with creating a favourable impression than making the most of the tasty bites.

The new middle class are not, in the conventional English sense, snobs, because they don't feel anyone can threaten them. They have little sense of being privileged. Even if they are second-generation meritocrats, like the sons of Labour MPs, and have been expensively educated at the ancient universities, they believe that they owe their position not to the advantages of birth or wealth, but rather to personal excellence. And since they gain their livelihood, in most cases, by salaries or fees – through access to corporate or institutional wealth, rather than drawing a dividend or making a profit – they believe that, however inflated their incomes might appear to outsiders, they earn every penny that they get. *Quantitatively* they may be better off than wage-earners; but *qualitatively* they feel the same, and indeed in some ways – because of the taxes they pay – rather harder done by.

Class hardly enters into the new middle-class conception of themselves. Many of them work in an institutional world of fine gradations but no clear lines of antagonism. Distinctively working-class people have only walk-on parts – like cleaners, porters, maintenance men. Even the giving of orders, as between, say, professional men and their secretaries, will sometimes appear in the guise of asking for a favour. Lines of seniority in the workplace, though real enough, are mediated by the relative unimportance attached to work identities socially; while in business and the professions themselves, influence is built up on horizontal rather than vertical lines, by activating inter-professional networks and cross-professional contacts.

The new middle class have a different emotional economy than that of their prewar predecessors. They go in for instant rather than deferred gratification, making a positive virtue of their expenditure, and treating the self-indulgent as an ostentatious display of good taste. Sensual pleasures, so far from being outlawed, are the very field on which social claims are established and sexual identities confirmed. Food, in particular, a postwar bourgeois passion (an SDP admirer has called it 'the opium of the centrist classes'), has emerged as a crucial marker of class.

The 'liberal hour' of the 1960s may turn out, retrospectively, to be the moment at which the repressed energies of this class were released, when it began to move freely across the face of society, and to see in itself, culturally if not politically, society's natural leaders. This was perhaps the moment, too, when it was released from the thraldom of some of its more ancestral class fears. The middle class were the great beneficiaries of the moral and social reforms of the 1960s, most obviously in the sphere of higher education, but also in that of public morals – those Home Office reforms with which Roy Jenkins was associated.

The influence of 1960s lifestyles can be seen right across the political spectrum, but it does seem that the SDP has given them a peculiarly concentrated expression. The 'notables' and 'eminences' who signed the Declaration of a Hundred were heavily drawn from the alternative establishments swept to power under the 'winds of change' of the 1960s. The inner circles of the party leadership, such as those on its national steering committee, have been recruited from the greyer end of the liberalized middle class – administratively-minded intellectuals, educational technocrats, faint-hearted feminists, career politicians with a reputation for 'heart', one-time progressives and ideas men enjoying a second youth. The advisory panels of the party are drawn from a constellation of interprofessional networks, administrative think-tanks, pressure groups, and policy-making kindergartens which are very much a product of the past twenty years.

Some of the party's leading ideas, as I have tried to suggest elsewhere, could be seen as transpositions of consumerist ideas from the sphere of retail trade into that of national politics. The influence of consumerism can be seen not only in specific panaceas – such as proportional representation – but also more generally in the value attached to novelty, imagery and style, and the equation of the old with the obsolescent. The SDP was marketed, like a new product, by a leading form of consultants. It has made a fetish of travel. High-speed journeys were a feature of its public launch. More subliminally, one may wonder how far the gastronomic enthusiasms of William Rodgers (an early contributor to the *Good Food Guide*) or of Roy Jenkins (whose taste in fine wines must be as familiar to contemporary newspaper readers as was Keir Hardie's cloth cap to those of the 1890s) may have influenced the increasingly favourable direction of their views on the market economy; or speculate on the way in which Dr Owen's role, as a pioneer white settler in Limehouse, may insensibly have influenced his ideas of political leadership, just as those of Attlee and Tawney, in the very different East End of the 1900s, were shaped in the crucible of the Toynbee Hall settlement.

Despite its commitment to decentralization, and its appeal to 'the people' against 'the politicians', the SDP – at least in this early phase of its existence – is very much an insider's party, recruited from people who, even if they are novices to political organization, are certainly not strangers to public life. It seems to have a special appeal to those who are used to working with the decision-making process, people who enjoy planning, who are familiar with the language and procedures of administration, and who like to see things hum.

The party headquarters at Cowley Street is snugly within the sound of the division bells at Westminster, closer even than the Conservative Party headquarters in Smith Square, and very much closer than the Labour Party in Walworth Road. The leaders of the party are people who have spent most of their adult lifetime in politics. They clearly enjoy government, if not the political process itself. Their books, though written as political testaments, read like nothing so much as civil service briefs, full of ambitious plans for every department of national life, and marked by an unusual attention to particulars.

Locally, too, the SDP seems to draw its activists from those who, within their own particular circuits, are used to being at the centre of things – the busy medical practitioner who is also a member of the regional board of health, the executive's wife who is also a magistrate and a school governor. The SDP seems to appeal especially to frustrated professionals, who would like to exercise their energies on a wider public stage.

Lawyers, mainly barristers from the Inns of Court, were the first special interest group to organize within the party. Well before its public launch, they had formed themselves into a group variously reported as some 200 or 350 strong – 'very high-powered non-stuffy lawyers', according to one of them.

The more recently formed Women for Social Democracy seems to bear a kindred character. 'The group looks quite unlike the old stereotype of militant women's collectives', the SDP journalist, Polly Toynbee reports:

> It includes senior lecturers, teachers, a managing director and other managers, doctors, physiotherapists, lawyers, journalists, housewives and a rabbi . . . Many . . . were already members of the 300 Group, the all-party campaign to

> get more women into the House of Commons. Most had had little to do with the broader women's movement since that is, for the most part, mixed up with the extra-parliamentary politics of the left.

The party was, from the start, well connected in the business world. In particular, it seems to enjoy excellent links with the one sector of capitalism to have emerged relatively unscathed from the recession – the City of London. The party's Chief Executive is Bernard Doyle, who was chairman of Booker-McConnell Engineering. Among the party's illustrious recruits is the new chairman of ICI, and it also seems to have recruited vigorously among middle managers and industry's young cadets.

Business was well represented in the industry debate at the party's Perth conference, in October. Speakers were reported to include a woman lecturer on microbiology, an advertising executive, an economic researcher, an industrial psychologist, and the holder of the title Scottish Young Businessman of the Year.

A remarkable number of SDP leaders and activists served their apprenticeship as student politicians, either at the university Labour clubs, in the case of those who went to Oxford and Cambridge, or, for those who went to university in the provinces, the caucus politics of the National Union of Students. Among the younger parliamentarians there is a whole crop of men in their late thirties who came up through the National Union of Students machine (then dominated by the Labour Right) in the early and middle 1960s: Ian Wrigglesworth, Mike Thomas, Dickson Mabon, Tom McNally.

Then there is that curious bloc of ex-Communist and ex-Conservative students who formed the leadership of the NUS in the mid-1970s, in an alliance against the further Left. Students like this don't seem to be the kind to spend long years in doctoral research, that Slough of Despond; nor to atone for the relative privilege of their position by going into social work; still less are they the drop-outs or those who suffer from graduate unemployment.

When the eight Conservative students (among them six ex-presidents of student unions) made their well-publicized collective defection to the SDP in August 1981, their occupations, a bare three or four years after going down from the university, were recorded in the party press release as: commercial conference director, commercial manager, student accountant, management consultant, stockbroker, TV presenter, commercial banking and production manager.

Individual party membership in the SDP is heavily recruited from the professional and managerial classes – some 57 per cent, compared with 7 per cent of manual workers, according to an Opinion Research Centre poll of November 1981. And it may be that, within the professions, it is the more comfortable professions which are taking the lead – doctors and dentists, say, rather than clergymen.

The party pitched its membership appeal at the successful, with a whole battery of promotional devices to suggest an environment of prosperity rather than need. Its largest local branch, with a membership of more than 700, is reported to be in the extremely opulent London suburb of Richmond and Twickenham. All the evidence suggests SDP members are far more socially homogeneous than those of other parties.

One of the subliminal appeals of the party may be that it offers a political identity and field of action to those who feel themselves to be the beneficiaries rather than the victims of recent social change. They are a 'concerned' middle class, the products of an expanded higher education and occupationally upgraded by technology. Though they may indeed be 'concerned' with how the country is going, they are not personally frightened by it, or angry about it, or personally alienated from it.

The SDP's electoral support is drawn from a much wider spectrum than the membership. No doubt different groups support it for different reasons, but it may be that the party has a particular appeal to those who, whatever their particular station in life, feel that the country has served them well – home owners, say, who have seen the value of their property appreciate, newly-settled commuters who can measure the distance which separates them from the inner city, old-time Labour voters who have seen the hopes of earlier years fulfilled.

Politics can never be reduced to the interests of its most active supporters, nor is it ever an unmediated expression of social being. But it can correspond, in some ultimate sense, to a class *unconscious*, and in the case of the SDP, the fetishization of the uncontentious seems at least to be congruent with, even if it cannot simply be explained by, an unalienated social state.

The social complexion of the SDP's membership may not account for its policies, and the party deliberately eschews the representation of sectional interests. But the nature of the party's recruitment might help to account for its distinctive moral temper. The party's greatest merit in its own eyes, and that of many of its supporters, is that it is quiet, and stands for consensus and conciliation against both Right and Left 'aggro'.

'Calm, reasoned argument' was the hallmark of the party's October conferences. There were no wrangles over points of order, no emergency resolutions to be moved, no fervent paper-sellers at the door. At Perth some of the voices were so quiet that the chairman had to ask them to speak up, 'an injunction unheard of among the ranters and bellowers at a Labour party conference'. The same equanimity appears to prevail at SDP public meetings – 'reverential' was one of the terms used to describe the atmosphere at those held during the Crosby by-election. The SDP may be the recipient of a protest vote, but there is nothing Poujadist about its appeal nor even, by comparison with present-day Conservatism, anything rancorous about its populism.

It is not only the Labour Party which, by contrast to the SDP, sounds strident, but also the Tories. Mrs Thatcher, by comparison with Mrs Williams, has a shrill voice. Norman Tebbit, by comparison with Roy Jenkins, sounds bitter. In parliament, the Conservative Party seethes with repressed grievances, such as those which, in its current crisis, have broken round the head of Lord Carrington. At conferences the members seem angry and disturbed, at odds both with their own traditions and even their own class inheritance. The Tories seem to have a very strong sense that society is moving against them, that time is not on their side. As many Tories seem to see it, the moral order is under siege, and it is from their own most cherished institutions that the threat of a sell-out comes – Home Secretaries who are 'soft' on crime, the Foreign Office riddled with traitors, an Establishment in the hands of 'do-gooders', the BBC showing terrible things on television.

It is possible to suggest that the conservatives speak increasingly in the name of small business people, while the SDP represent those who are more integrated with the worlds of capital and bureaucracy. But the differences seem to have to do as much with culture as with class, and in particular with access to (or exclusion from) symbolic capital and power. And it is in these terms, rather than the more conventional measure of birth and wealth, that the SDP, during the first year of its existence, has made the Tory Party seem provincial and almost plebeian.

One of the features of the new middle class which the SDP reproduces is its narcissism – the delight which it takes in itself. In their own eyes at least, they are the beautiful people of politics, representing a force for civilization and refinement. They are flexible where others are rigid, clear-thinking where they are dogmatic, sensible where they are prejudiced. In the idiom of Shirley Williams, they are 'the fun people's party'; in that of William Rodgers, they are 'a representative cross-section of thinking people'. At the SDP's October conferences, the members were being continually congratulated by the leaders for their niceness, while the delegates responded in kind by expressing a huge satisfaction at the contemplation of themselves.

The SDP electorate is flattered in no less fulsome terms: the thinking part of the population as opposed to those who obey the atavistic appeals of traditionalism. Locally, the party is recommended as a place where like-minded people – 'radical . . . but reasonable', as a Brent recruit puts it – can feel themselves at home.

The rapid progress of the SDP during its first year, and the party's success in attracting a mass membership, could be seen as a delighted act of self-recognition by a new class coming out and discovering its common identity. At by-elections, the teacher will get together with the garage owner to prepare a coffee morning and join a company director at the late-night party to celebrate the result. In the run-up to the local elections, the verger's wife will prepare a questionnaire with the greengrocer, the university lecturer will plan a spot of fundraising with the Volvo dealer, the lady journalist will exercise her flair for publicity by pushing T-shirts.

The party brings a touch of high life to the suburbs while providing metropolitan sophisticates with an agreeably 'civilized' and (at least in the first year) highly deferential 'grass roots'. It allows those who are already stars within their own orbit to glitter on a wider stage. It is a democracy of the well-placed, a natural extension of the new middle-class capacity for sociability.

Or you could interpret the rise of the SDP as a political counterpart to the phenomenon of gentrification, with the SDP as the imaginative 'modernizers', taking on the national equivalent of a rundown street. On this view, its rise could be seen as a movement of home colonization by a newly self-confident class (or of a distinct cultural stratum within it) taking on the role of society's natural leaders, and transposing into the field of politics some of those innovative capacities which, in the 1960s, made them leaders in national taste. The working class, which the SDP sees as the chief obstacle to modernization in British society, would then represent a class equivalent to the unregenerate houses in a newly refurbished street, living in dark and poky rooms ripe for property development. The SDP wants not so much to improve as to abolish them.

From the 1920s to the 1960s, a large bloc of the middle classes voted Tory and accepted upper-class hegemony, simply because they were afraid of Labour, not only on account of specific threats to their interests and privileges, but also because of that whole complex of fear and anxiety for which Labour, by its name and its constituency, was the symbol. Since the by-elections of the early 1960s, this bloc has shown signs of disintegration, and its historical rationale has increasingly come into question.

Internationally, the spectre of working-class insurrection has been exorcised both by the success of postwar welfare capitalism and latterly by the growing crisis in, and evident debility of, world Communism. The Sino-Soviet split; the containment and then fragmentation of the Third World liberation movements of the 1960s; the repression of the Prague Spring; the emergence of Euro-communism; the military takeover in Poland – all these seem to reinforce the belief that, as the Italian Communist Party put it in a recent statement, the historical epoch which opened with the October Revolution is coming to a close.

Domestically, the direction of postwar social change, and the shape of postwar politics – notwithstanding occasional alarums about a 'sick' or 'ungovernable' society – have been of a kind to neutralize the residues of class fear. In terms of occupational structure, and even more in that of social cohesion, it is the newly unified middle classes who seem to be growing, while the working class are diminishing, not only in numbers but also – through physical dispersal to out-county estates and the increasing privatization of working-class life – in social visibility. The working class may still pose many problems to society, but from the point of view of their would-be improvers, as dangerous classes they seem for the moment dispersed.

By comparison with the pleasure they take in themselves the SDP is unmistakably hostile to the working class, wanting both to disperse it as a cultural presence (in the name, it must be said, of 'equality') and to deconstitute it as a political force. As modernizers, heralding the advent of a 'post-industrial' society, they see its very existence as in some sort anachronistic. In their more euphoric moments they have come to believe that it may not be there at all, except as a mirage in the minds of the militants, or else as the artificial byproduct of 'adversarial' politics.

The working class, in the imagination of the Social Democratic Party, is the cynosure of all that is backward-looking – 'tribal' in its allegiances, insular in its preferences, suspicious of progress and change. Thus the Labour Party appears as an institutionalized force for conservatism, 'out-of-date, inward-looking, restrictive', and its followers are political primitives. They vote Labour because their fathers did, and their grandfathers before them, 'all the way back to Keir Hardie'. The trade unions, in SDP eyes, are if anything even more fossilized, antiquated in their structure, 'deeply sunk in lethargy', 'Canute-like' in their attitude to job protection, Luddite in relation to new technologies. 'To be radical,' Lord Vaizey writes in *Capital and Socialism*, 'is to be against them.'

As protagonists of consensus, the SDP see working-class consciousness as an obstacle to social peace. Indeed for William Rodgers a main reason for worrying about class difference is that a society marked by them 'can be manipulated by those . . . looking for opportunities for confrontation'. The Labour Party, by its mere existence, is dangerous, artificially dividing the country into two camps, and in its present phase of existence it is wide open to 'bovver boys', and 'wreckers' and 'yobs'. As Mike Thomas, the improbable apostle of consensus politics, put it in a comment on last year's unemployment demonstration in Glasgow: 'Labour is fast becoming the demo party – the party of the slogans, chants and clenched fists'. The trade unions, 'who thrived on a simple "them" and "us" philosophy,' are an even greater source of potential 'aggro'.

The working class is no less offensive to the SDP's notion of egalitarianism, and to their vision of society as a frontierless open space. Electorally, it is interest-bound rather than issue-orientated. Economically, it is sectionalist. Culturally, it is closed. It is the very separateness of working-class life which seems to constitute the offence, and in this light almost any manifestation of the working class becomes suspect.

Where others have found warmth and comradeliness, the SDP sense claustrophobia; where they have celebrated solidarity, the SDP see only tyranny; where they have known community, the SDP find ghettoes. Even beer and tobacco, those last vestiges of old-time working-class sociability, are deprecated on the grounds that they are injurious to health. Rodgers, arguing that 'No to smoking, no to alcohol' has more to recommend it as a slogan in the field of welfare than 'Restore the cuts', points out that 57 per cent of unskilled manual workers smoke, compared with 29 per cent of professional men. (Interestingly in the light of the SDP's gastronomic enthusiasms, no such campaign is proposed against over-eating.)

Housing estates seem to lurk in the SDP imagination roughly as the city slum did in that of earlier generations of reformers. The negative value attaching to them goes far beyond its ostensible occasion. It is difficult to avoid the conclusion that they represent moral and physical eyesores, first and foremost because they are largely inhabited by one class. The SDP want to end the 'terrified apartheid' of housing estates and to substitute instead mixed developments 'where owners and tenants could become indistinguishable'.

Much the same ideal of openness is held out as the panacea for the inner city where 'ghettoes which house the unwanted and those on the margins of society' would be replaced by 'genuine neighbourhoods where people of different classes and backgrounds can live harmoniously together'. Dr David Owen's remedy (hardly one that needs any canvassing in inner London) is gentrification: 'inner-city areas have an attraction for some people, and with the very high cost of commuting caused by the ever increasing public transport fares, more and more suburban dwellers might be persuaded to return to the inner city'.

It is recognized that one of the major causes of the defection of the SDP's parliamentarians was the Labour party's continuing hostility towards the EEC. However, it seems possible that after the Wilson government's humiliating defeat over *In Place of Strife*, and then the industrial unrest from 1969 to 1974, a culminating resentment and eventually outrage at what William Rodgers calls the 'deferential habit' of the Labour governments of the 1970s in consulting the trade unions provided the underlying dynamic which actually propelled them from dissidence to defection; while discomfort at what Professor Marquand (*Encounter*, July 1980) recalled as the

> strange, inward-looking proletarianism . . . increasingly prevalent in the parliamentary party and in the party headquarters in the late 1960s and 1970s may have been as deep-seated a source of unease, for at least some of the defectors, as the more publicized demand of the constituency activists for 'accountability'.

The suggestion is necessarily speculative, but it perhaps casts some light on the fact that, when the new party was launched in 1981, it seemed to have little use for its working-class recruits. So far from making the most of them in its well-orchestrated publicity, the party may be said rather to have rendered them, as near as possible, invisible. Lord George Brown, the right-wing Labour candidate for party leader in 1963 (he was backed by, among others, Roy Jenkins), was not added to the Gang of Four, or elevated to the dignity of elder statesman, but was rather treated as a spectre at the feast.

The Social Democratic Association, a pre-existing grass-roots grouping of dissident ex-Labour councillors and others, who combined right-wing views with an aggressive proletarianism (*The Times* described them as 'the new movement's rough trade'), were consistently marginalized. Even though they were incorporated in the new party, the local election campaigns which they undertook in May 1981 were officially disowned. The defection to the SDP of the Islington Labour councillors – 'working-class, middle-aged men, locally born and bred' – has been a source of real embarrassment to party headquarters and the more gentrified elements in the local party, and four of them have now been expelled.

Note, too, the way in which Tom Bradley, an MP with long trade union connections, has been consistently upstaged by Rodgers in debates on industrial relations at party conferences or in the House of Commons.

Hostility to the trade unions – or as the SDP would prefer to put it, trade union power – is a persistent undercurrent in party thought, surfacing in conference addresses and public meetings; in books and pamphlets; and in policy documents outlining the party's long-term perspectives. It says something of the suspicion in which the trade unions are held that though a Society of Social Democratic Lawyers was soon set up, a proposal for a similar body of trade unionists ran into heavy opposition when it was presented to the Bradford conference last October. Tom Bradley, speaking from the platform, was forced to withdraw in the face of shouts from the floor of 'No' and 'We want a joint body'. References to the 'barons of the TUC' or 'the Moguls of Congress House' trip off the tongues of the SDP leaders as easily as the 'Gnomes of Zurich' used to do for Harold Wilson when he faced a run on the pound. A survey of SDP members in November 1981 showed that there was a larger percentage of SDP members in favour of outlawing the closed shop than there was for any other measure. And it is only fitting that the party's first significant parliamentary vote (albeit divided) was for Norman Tebbit's anti-union Employment Bill.

The SDP's hostility to the trade unions is based in the first place on their political role as 'kingmakers' and 'paymasters' of the Labour Party. But it is in fact no less radical in the industrial sphere. Here the party challenges the liberal social democratic consensus represented, in the 1960s, by the Donovan report. The report recognized that the collective expression of grievances was an inescapable feature of industrial life. Trade unions and employers should adjust to it, according to Donovan, by shifting from national agreements to individual plant bargaining. The participation of shop stewards in day-to-day decision-making should be positively encouraged. The SDP, however, have come to conclude, like Mrs Thatcher (and Michael Edwardes of British Leyland), that there is a 'silent majority' of workers who have no grievances at all.

Industrial disputes only take place because of what an SDP document calls 'the zealocracy,' small groups of unrepresentative militants, who operate in outdated structures and keep a politics of confrontation alive. As Roger Rosewell, a member of the SDP industrial policy committee, puts it in a recent pamphlet, 'grievances can be fanned . . . strikes can . . . be engineered'. 'Marxists often play a key role in this process' (*Dealing with the Marxist Threat to Industry*).

But it is not only shopfloor agitators who come under attack. The entire structure of lay and full-time organization is regarded as being unrepresentative and out of touch with membership feeling. The SDP propose bypassing the trade unions in every possible way, by avoiding the kind of high-level government–trade union agreements which prevailed in the period of the social contract; by encouraging direct worker representation on boards of management; and by appealing to members over the heads of the leadership and shop stewards by means of compulsory postal ballot. The SDP also want to depoliticize the trade unions by persuading them, where possible, to disaffiliate from the Labour Party, and to confine themselves, on the model of American business unionism, to a purely bargaining function – or what Roy Jenkins calls 'their proper industrial job'.

The SDP's discomfort with the working class makes a striking contrast to the proletarian sympathies of earlier generations of right-wing Labour leaders. Among the 1950s revisionists, for instance, both Hugh Gaitskell and Anthony Crosland enjoyed excellent and, indeed, sentimental relations with their constituency parties. In their battles with the Left, it was one of their strengths that they could speak for the men on the football terraces and the women in the Labour Party rooms.

Gaitskell was a genuine social reformer who had come into politics, like Tawney, to help the oppressed. His sympathies had been 'instinctively' on the side of the miners during the General Strike, and he joined the Labour Party under its impact ('Henceforth,' he wrote to an aunt, 'my future is with the "working classes"'). It was his experiences as a Worker's Educational Association tutor in Nottingham, 'especially in the coalfields', which turned him to active politics. He found the people there, among them girlfriends and dancing partners, 'more honest and natural than the middle class who are always trying to be something they aren't and who are never quite sure whether they are saying the right thing'.

In the aftermath of the 1959 election defeat Gaitskell wanted the Labour Party to divest itself of its 'cloth cap' image, but he did not doubt that it should remain a party, nor that it was his mission to serve the working class. 'We as middle-class socialists have got to have a profound humility', he is reported as saying. 'We must feel humble to working people . . . We've got to know that we can lead them because they can't do without us.'

In the old Labour Party of the 1920s and 1930s professional people got the same kind of respect which Tories gave to military men and landowners. There were not too many of them, but they brought knowledge, skills, contacts, learning and, not least, motor transport (Gaitskell's first service to the party was as a driver). At election times, or when there were marches, demonstrations or strikes, their services, their homes and their telephones were indispensable. The alliance of professional people and workers, pivoted on the exchange of service and respect and premised on a clear sense of separate social identity, held good at every level of the party, in the constituencies, on the Labour benches at Westminster, in Labour governments and cabinets. It was also reported in the relationship between Labour MPs and their constituency parties.

The right wing in the Labour Party was umbilically linked to working-class and trade union loyalism during its years of dominance from 1935 to 1960. The Left, during the same period, had its heartland in the soft suburbs which read the *New Statesman* and subscribed in the 1930s to the Left Book Club, and in the Tory shires, and country and seaside towns, of southern and western England when little groups of beleaguered socialists gathered around such people as left-wing school masters.

Hampstead had a role in left-wing politics somewhat akin to Hackney and Islington today; and in the early 1950s a hostile press was apt to pour scorn on the extremist resolutions emanating from such tranquil places as the Merton and Morden CLP.

The Left were, broadly speaking, those who might be described as 'progressives'. They descended in one line (via the Union of Democratic Control) from Gladstonian 'Little Englandism'; in another, from pacifism; in another, from solidarity with the movements for colonial freedom. In the terms which Frank Parkin uses to describe the first CND they were engaged, very often, in 'symbolic protest', 'expressive' rather than 'instrumental' in character. They seldom offered a serious threat to the dominant right-wing leadership, and it was only too easy to dismiss them either as impractical idealists or else as 'intellectuals', 'cranks' or, that most withering of Labour Party expletives, levelled against the Bevanites in the early 1950s, 'frustrated journalists'.

The basis of this political complex, and of the cross-class alliances which supported it, was undermined by changes which it is beyond the scope of this article to discuss. One might refer, summarily, to change in material culture (like the spread of car ownership and the telephone) which undermined some of the cultural monopolies of the professional middle class. Or to the increasingly domestic character of working-class life, of which the decline in working-class politics is an aspect. Or one might consider the increasingly deprivatized and social character of middle-class life, and the openings which this gave to autonomous middle-class, or semi-middle-class radical movements. From this point of view – distressing though it must be to an old Aldermaston marcher, and hardly a lineage which the ultra-Atlanticist and pro-bomb SDP would like to own – the remote origins of the SDP might be sought in the first CND, just as, in a perverse way, and notwithstanding Mrs Williams's implacable hostility to it at the time, the student movement of 1968 could be seen as a more immediate source.

One way of approaching the phenomenon of the SDP would be to see it as middle-class radicalism gone sour, just as in its more strictly economic aspect, where its hard edge is turned against trade unionism and 'lame ducks', it could be seen as Wilsonism fallen on hard times. In the field of housing and welfare, it seems to reflect nothing so much as the disenchantment of architects and planners at the results of their handiwork (Peter Hall, who in 1960 was influentially dreaming up a motorway future for London, is the author of one of the SDP's first research pamphlets).

Still more important for changing class relations within the Labour Party, and therefore ultimately for the breakaway of the SDP, was perhaps the rise in trade union membership, which began in the late 1950s and was only checked at the trough of the depression in 1979–80. With it came the unionization of white-collar and professional workers; the extension of union spheres of influence and recognition in welfare, local government, university and other public sector employment; improved shop steward facilities; and increased trade union influence on dismissals and disciplinary procedures. The phenomenal rise of ASTMS in private industry and commerce, and of NUPE in the public sector, brought the issue of trade unionism into the heartland of professional and managerial prerogatives.

The stunning victory of the miners' strike of 1973–74, which put an end to the Heath government, and the social contract with which Wilson was returned to his fourth term of office brought trade union power into the innermost recesses of the Cabinet. One way of accounting for the rise of the SDP, and of its belligerent hostility to trade unionism, would be to see it as a delayed reaction to the trauma of the middle class when confronting trade unionism on their very own doorstep. The revolt of low-paid workers in the 'winter of discontent' of 1978–79 – an event which, on his own testimony, still haunts Rodgers – appeared not as a movement of the underprivileged, but rather as a revolt by upstart bully boys. Reading between the lines of Rodgers's new book, it seems that some Labour cabinet ministers felt the same when forced to parley on equal terms with Jack Jones, Hugh Scanlon and Alan Fisher.

The SDP leaders are quite differently constituted from the older right-wing Labour leadership. They are recruited neither from the great public schools, nor from people who have risen from the ranks. They come characteristically from nowhere and positively rejoice in the absence of regional or local ties. They seem to find their most natural home in free-floating administrative mafias. They are not popular educators like, say, Dalton or Gaitskell, not proselytizers, like Tawney and Cripps, not 'do-gooders' nor philanthropists, but rather reformers gone sour.

They do not have the sense of privilege – or the guilt which sometimes accompanied it – of the old service upper middle class, nor do they have the self-hatred of the 'ivory tower' intellectual, seeking an escape from a cloistered condition by 'going native'. Many would falsely regard themselves as classless. The very existence of a self-conscious working class constitutes an affront to their self-esteem. It is also the chief obstacle to the open society of their particular dreams – a gigantic empty space filled with socially mobile, outward-looking people.

The SDP's hostility to the organized labour movement has superficial resemblances to that of the Tories. But its sources are quite different from the Conservative Party. However much it might like to be rid of the Labour movement, it cannot really be said to be anti-working class. Traditionally, the Tories have lived in an organic relationship, albeit hierarchical, with working people, as landlords to labourers, masters or mistresses to servants, employers to employed, officers to men. Politically they have courted a working-class support since the 1830s. Far from being embarrassed by 'rough diamonds', they have been only too happy to condescend to them (in last summer's Warrington by-election, they even adopted one as a candidate).

The SDP, on the other hand, though tolerant to machine operators, are much too fastidious to touch a man who is beery. They do not want to represent or help the working class in the manner of the Labour Party; nor, in the manner of the Tories, to win its loyalty and support. They want to abolish it. In their mind's eye, with a speculative gaze fixed on the microchip revolution, and the impact of 'sunrise' technologies, the day does not seem far distant when the country may be inhabited by people as radical and reasonable, as up-to-date and mobile, as themselves.

Ancestor Worship*

Ancestor worship, as Aneurin Bevan warned us in *In Place of Fear*, is the most conservative of all religions. It invites us to take a sentimental view of our weaknesses and a heroic view of our strengths. It is also a bounty on what Marxists call 'false consciousness', offering us a retrospective sense of belonging – what used to be called 'lineage' and today is known as 'roots' – to compensate for the uncertainties of the here and now. It gratifies our need for household gods, offering us a source of symbolic gratification and a transcendence of, or escape from, ourselves.

Ancestor worship usually involves a double misrecognition, both of our own qualities and those of our predecessors; each, by a process of osmosis, is apt to take on the idealized character of the other. Ancestor worship is premised on a *necessary* falsification of the past. Nothing is more chameleon than tradition. We all have half a dozen possible ancestries to chose from, and fantasy and projection can furnish us with a dozen more. It necessarily involves selectivity and silence – valorizing a prestigious great uncle, forgetting the family black sheep.

Conservatives, irrespective of their particular policy – free trade or protectionist, paternalist or laissez-faire – invariably pose as the guardians of the British people's 'traditional way of life' (the words are those of the 1955 election manifesto); and Mrs Thatcher, during the 1983 election, demonstrated the mileage to be made from 'old-fashioned' Victorian Values.

Mr Benn, in the volumes under review, seems to be making a comparable play with what Sidney Higgins calls 'his radical non-conformist background . . . the cause that the Benns have for four generations pursued'. Both, interestingly, converge on that potent figure of national

* This essay was first published in the *Guardian*, 4 October 1984. The books mentioned in it are by Tony Benn (ed.), *Writings on the Wall: A Radical and Socialist Anthology 1215–1984*, London 1984; and Christopher Hampton (ed.), *A Radical Reader: The Struggle for Change in England 1381–1914*, Harmondsworth 1984.

myth, the 'free-born Englishman': for Mrs Thatcher it is a merchant adventurer in every counting house, a village Hampden in every store: for Mr Benn, the embattled moral crusader.

Mr Benn's conversion to 'tradition' is comparatively recent, and can be dated with some precision to the first of the Leveller anniversary celebrations at Burford in 1975. He does not have the historical turn of mind which made the past so continuously present in the imagination of many of his left-wing predecessors: it has been rather a matter of an additional string to his bow.

Mr Benn made his appearance on the public stage as an ardent iconoclast, tacking to the winds of change, keen on the application of the media to politics: he managed Gaitskell's television appearances in the 1959 election and Harold Wilson's in 1964. Like Mr Wilson, whose speechwriter he became in 1963, he was an ardent modernizer: 'The most distinguishing characteristic of a vigorous society', he wrote in the *Guardian* in April 1964, 'is one in which the future becomes more real and important than the past'.

This was the spirit of his time at the Ministry of Technology, as apostle of managerialism; it was also the spirit in which he set about *divesting* himself of his family inheritance, renouncing his peerage and eventually even his name, or most of it. If there was a single target of his attack in the 1960s it was the 'hereditary principle', whether in the form of the honours system, the House of Lords, or outdated and restrictive practices. But now here is *Writings on the Wall*, a splendid collection of texts, and, thanks to the diligent (and insufficiently acknowledged) researches of Andrew Franklin and Suzanne Franks, both ecumenical in spirit and full of unexpected pleasures. From the reign of Henry III we have 'Where money speaks, there all law is silent', and in a song of the times (*c.* 1400), this:

> At Westminster Hall
> They well enough know the laws;
> Nevertheless for them all
> The mighty bear down the right cause.

It also has a hard edge which makes it, though slighter, more satisfying than Christopher Hampton's *A Radical Reader*; and it gives proper space to those causes which Mr Benn has shown both foresight and courage in championing – notably women's rights and anti-militarism. But precisely because of the power of these texts, readers should beware of treating them – as Mr Benn wants us to – as an unproblematic whole. The continuity, or 'tradition', is in the eye of the beholder.

The social doctrines of the Levellers and Diggers are probably better understood in relation to medieval categories and thought – or to what Tawney called the 'doctrineless communism of the open field' – than as the testament of the original ancestors of labour (the symbolic space they occupy in Mr Benn's notion of tradition).

The 'free-born Englishman' has gone through many appropriations in the course of a long career and was arguably more at home in the patriotic bombast of Hanoverian times – or in Hogarth's 'Beef and Liberty' club – than in any distinctively socialist tradition.

Again, the 'non-governmental society' which is the evident inspiration of the more libertarian texts in this collection consorts uneasily with Mr Benn's (and Mr Kinnock's) enthusiasm for a state take-over of the 'commanding heights' of the economy or indeed with the overwhelmingly collective spirit which informs the volume's Labour Party offerings.

There is in fact no unitary radical or socialist tradition which can be cobbled together in the manner of an annual conference composite resolution. Mr Benn's notion of tradition – or at least his presentation of it – is essentially additive: new causes are given their historical lineage as they loom on the contemporary horizons: the old ones stay unchanged.

But feminism – to take the example of this anthology's strong points – cannot simply be appropriated as a Labour 'tradition' even though the Independent Labour Party was one of the original nurseries of the women's suffrage movement, and Labour, once upon a time, established itself as a national party on the basis of women's and welfare issues. Socialism, after all, was conceived as a movement of working *men*, and it is evident that male bonding, and the exclusion of women, was one of the very principles of trade unionism.

Then one of the distinguished features of war resistance, notably in the ILP opposition to the First World War, was its cross-class character; it owed more to Christian humanism, Free Trade universalism, or even Gladstonian Little Englandism, than it did to proletarian internationalism.

To say this is not to demand a stricter sense of tradition, but a more contingent one, and to recognize that Labour's own inheritance is far more promiscuous than a reading of these texts would suggest. There is indeed a dissenting component in the Labour tradition, fairly represented in the present day by Mr Benn, as it is by Michael Foot and E.P. Thompson. But it is arguable that High Church socialism, as represented, say, by Attlee, Tawney and William Temple, played as great a role in the making of the Labour Party; or occult religion (Keir Hardie and Lansbury were spiritualists, Ramsay MacDonald a Swedenborgian, numbers of pre-1914 Fabians Theosophists); or those secular cults and material mysticisms of which Marxism is only the best-known example.

Again, Tory socialism, and those chivalresque ideas of noblesse oblige and public service brilliantly pieced together by Mark Girouard in *Return to Camelot*, may have loomed larger in the mental universe of Labour's pioneers than liberal dissent. John Ruskin, the Tory socialist, was a towering influence on the autodidact: it is no accident that the first trade union college was named after him; or that in W.T. Stead's survey of the 1906 intake of Labour MPs, he figured alongside Carlyle as the main source of intellectual inspiration.

Ruskin is one of the more conspicuous absentees from *Writings on the Wall*; Ramsay MacDonald, supreme exponent of ethical socialism, another. Above all, curiously underplayed here, there is the spirit of working-class combination, deeply *conservative* in its attachment to 'custom and practice', deeply hostile to individualism and – as the miners' strike is showing once again – amazingly tenacious in the defence of threatened collective rights.

Conceptual space should also be given to those sub-political currents which are apt to be overlooked because there are no canonical texts to sacralize them. Ken Livingstone perhaps owes as much to the traditions of popular theatre and music hall as to Marx, and not the least of his services has been to release the pent-up forces of irreverence in the metropolis.

Labour can make no proprietary claim to traditions as various – and as contradictory – as these. Nor is it the privileged bearer of oppositional and dissenting currents in British society, though it can be the beneficiary of energies generated outside itself to which it may be more or less hospitable.

There is no law of the Medes and Persians which says that Labour should be a champion of minority rights, something which, historically speaking, has been more a preoccupation of liberalism than of socialism. If it shows signs of becoming a Labour cause it is not because of something imminent within the socialist tradition but because the self-activity of groups like the Vauxhall Caribbeans and the Spitalfields Bangladeshi are forcing it on to the Labour agenda.

Traditions, as Eric Hobsbawm and Terence Ranger have argued (in *The Invention of Tradition*), are not inherited: they are a name given to something which is constantly being made.

The Discovery of Puritanism, 1820–1914: A Preliminary Sketch*

I

'Puritan' is an unstable term, or, to put it more generously, it is a prodigal one, capable, at any given moment, of accommodating wildly discrepant meanings.[1] Today, as a journalistic trope, it is freely applied to such disparate phenomena as Islamic fundamentalism,[2] 'new wave' American feminism, and the charismatic communities of New Ageism – not to speak of President Clinton's promised 'covenant' with the American people,[3] or the 'Puritanical Tradition' in English design, traced back to the Arts and Crafts movement of the 1880s, and held responsible, in more recent years, for Laura Ashley and early Habitat style.[4] It is subject to startling reversals, such as those which, in the space of the last twenty-five years, have moved it from Left to Right in the political spectrum. It changes colour and complexion when it crosses or recrosses the Atlantic, a source, one might suggest, of mistaken identity as well as of semantic confusion, as in the current association of Puritanism with the sexually repressive. It has quite different histories in the four nations of Britain. It is also subject to a double dialectic in which nineteenth-century oppositions between Church and Chapel, Aesthetes and Philistines, Hellenes and Hebrews are reproduced; and nineteenth-century usages, when the term 'Puritan' was subject to a vast metaphorical inflation, count for more than the utterances of the Civil War sectaries or the Elizabethan divines. In another register, current equations of Puritanism and prudery, where not the byproduct of twentieth-century modernism's revolt against the Victorian, seem to date no further back than the 1880s and 1890s, when the 'Nonconformist Conscience' so dramatically overreached itself and seemed for a brief period to be the arbiter of public life.[5]

* This essay was first published in *Revival and Religion Since 1700: Essays For John Walsh*, Jane Garnett and Colin Matthew (ed.), London 1993.

Surfacing, as a term of reproach, in the ecclesiastical disputes which followed the Elizabethan settlement, given a new turn by the pamphleteers of the 1600s, and another by the playwrights and wits, the word Puritan had a vertiginous existence during the first seventy years of its career,[6] when it was at the mercy of both satirical invention and polemical excess. Singled out by the orthodox as a malignant growth, treated as a generic term for dissidence, but owned up to by none, it is difficult to disentangle from what historians have taken to calling 'hot Protestantism'.[7] As a party label, it was superseded, at the outbreak of the Civil War, by 'Presbyterian' and 'Independent', while as a negative signifier or nickname it was lumped together with those 'sectaries' and 'schismatics', Anabaptists, Socinians and Ranters whom the more conservative denounced as 'despisers of government', 'disturbers of the public peace' and 'destroyers of all civil relations and subordinations'.[8] The army agitators, in the Putney Debates, were wont to speak of themselves as representatives of the 'communion of saints';[9] Oliver Cromwell, in his correspondence and addresses, when referring to those whom nineteenth-century historians were to call 'Puritan', prefers the more inclusive 'people of God'.

'The name of Puritan is from this time to be sunk', remarks the editor of Neal's *History of the Puritans* (1732–38), the only work on the subject to be published before the nineteenth century. 'They are for the future to be spoken of under the distinction of Presbyterians, Erastians, and Independents, who had all their different views.'[10] He was referring to the Westminster Assembly of 1644. By this time 'Puritan' was being overtaken, as a portmanteau term, by 'Nonconformist' and 'dissenter'; in the 1650s it was already beginning to be referred to in the past tense;[11] in *Reliquiae Baxterianae* it is a volcano that had become extinct. J.R. Green, in his *Short History of the English People* (1874), wrote that the 'real victory' of Puritanism was posthumous, and that it was only after the defeat of 1660, and the ejection of the Nonconformist clergy under the Clarendon Code, that it began to embody itself in lifestyles (he credited it with the creation of the domestic ideal of the home), and that its deeper influence on civil society began to be felt.[12] More recently Christopher Hill, N.H. Keeble and others have been at pains to argue that Puritanism's greatest literary monuments came from 'the experience of defeat'.[13] Yet the term 'Puritan' itself barely survived, either as a 'reproachful name' or as a synonym for the Good Old Cause. It hardly figures in eighteenth-century denunciations (or advocacies) of religious enthusiasm. Hume, in his well-known essay on Enthusiasm and Superstition, refers to the Independents ('the . . . nearest to the quakers in fanaticism'), the Levellers and (in Scotland) the Covenanters.[14] Adam Smith in his plea for popular education, and his remarks on the baleful effects of fanaticism, speaks of 'the Independents' of the Civil War period ('a set no doubt of very wild enthusiasts') but notes that the provisions made by dissent for education 'seem very much to have abated the zeal and activity of those teachers'.[15] 'The people called Methodists', denounced as enthusiasts and practising a religion of the heart rather than one of the head, initially derived their doctrinal framework, as is well known, more 'from a High Church than from a Calvinist environment'.[16] When not attacked as 'Ranters' they were apt to be reviled, in their early days, as crypto-Catholics or 'papists'.[17]

Nor does Puritan seem to have entered eighteenth-century literary discourse. Humble virtue is not called 'Puritan' by Gray in his *Elegy*, even when he is invoking 'mute, inglorious Miltons' and 'village Hampdens'. The 'Puritan' novels of Defoe and Richardson, which literary scholars have taught us to read as exemplifications of a Calvinist aesthetic, carry no sectarian message.[18] Toland made Milton into a Whig;[19] Dr Johnson, in his *Lives of the Poets* – passing lightly over the Civil War years, and noting with satisfaction that Milton's last tract (a *Treatise of True Religion*) was 'modestly written, with respectful mention of the Church of England, and an appeal to the Thirty-Nine Articles' – speaks of Milton's political notions as 'those of an acrimonious and surly republican'.[20] It was the nineteenth century which turned Milton back into a Puritan.

On the other side of the Atlantic, too, it seems, Puritanism was in eclipse, as a trope if not as a family of beliefs, until, as literary scholars argue, it was 'reinvented' in the 1830s and 1840s by the writers of the American Renaissance.[21] 'Presbyterian' rather than 'Puritan' was the generic name given to the gathered churches and it was also the polemical term bandied back and gathered forth in the controversies leading up to the Revolution. The Declaration of Independence took its language from the eighteenth-century Enlightenment rather than the seventeenth-century divines.[22] Religious energy, after the Great Awakening of 1739–40, took direction and shape from Revivalism and Methodism.

Before the nineteenth century, Puritanism was given little more than a walk-on part in histories of the Civil War. As Caroline Robbins and others have shown, the eighteenth-century 'Commonwealthmen', though taking their inspiration from the writings of the Interregnum, were secular in spirit, harking back to the Civil War republicans rather than to the Saints, and the histories written under their influence – such as Catherine Macaulay's – reflect this.[23] The eighteenth-century Nonconformists, a people apart, surviving on the rugged peripheries of national life, or in obscure town meeting-houses, whilst their American and Scottish co-religionists had the authority of 'lawful ministers' or a kirk, were eager to live down their regicide past. In the earlier part of the century, when their numbers were if anything in decline, they were only too anxious to prove their loyalty to the Crown;[24] the 'Revolution principles' to which, like the Whigs, they clung, were not the antinomian ones of the Civil War, but those of 1688, the 'grand event' when 'despotism' drew its last breath; the

Revolution which had given them 'religious liberty'.[25] Those who did nurse memories of the Good Old Cause, like the beleaguered group of Cromwellians affectionately remembered in one of Crabbe's *Tales*, seem to have done so as an almost private passion.[26]

Thomas Fuller, the first historian of the Civil War, had wished that the word 'Puritan' could be 'banished', so many were the confusions attached to it.[27] His successors gave it short shrift. Clarendon, famously rebuked by Sir Charles Firth for writing the history of a religious revolution 'in which the religious element is omitted',[28] makes no mention of Puritanism either in his character sketches or his narrative of the Civil War, though he refers darkly to 'seditious' preachers who stirred up trouble in 1642. Cromwell, in his religion, was a great dissembler: 'whilst he looked upon the Presbyterian humour as the best incentive to rebellion, no man was more presbyterian; he sung all psalms with them to their tunes, and loved the longest sermons as much as they'.[29] David Hume, in his luminous *History of England*, blames religious fanaticism for what he believed to be a disaster; credits 'the Presbyterian religion' with responsibility for the outbreak of the Civil War; in his account of the Commonwealth and Protectorate he pays tribute to Cromwell's cunning in dealing with 'the pretended saints of all denominations' and playing on 'Protestant zeal'. Like other pre-nineteenth-century historians, monarchical or republican, Whig or Tory, he treats Cromwell as a usurper, a soldier or a statesman rather than a soul-striver – the character which was so to captivate the readers of Carlyle's *Letters and Speeches*.[30] Like other eighteenth-century historians, too, Hume held the Civil War in low esteem, not as that heroic event which was accorded status in the Victorian and Edwardian schoolroom, but rather as a melancholy, if instructive, record of failure. Hume's *History* held the stage for nearly a hundred years: it was perhaps under its influence that, in the late 1830s, the Commonwealth remained for many a military usurpation, and Cromwell the arch-dissembler whose 'religious as well as . . . republican professions had been mere baits to catch men's opinions'.[31]

In the nineteenth century the word 'Puritan' was rescued from near oblivion and was subject to a vast metaphorical inflation, without which it would be difficult to account for its subsequent versatility, or its salience in present-day historical and sociological thought. It reentered the field of religious and political controversy, providing a newly awakened and increasingly militant Nonconformity both with a symbolic inheritance and a source of borrowed prestige. Transposed from the field of doctrine to that of personal conduct, it provided the self-help manuals with their exemplars, housemasters and Sunday School superintendents with their character-training ideals. In the hands of Bible-carrying sergeants and town missionaries, it helped to Christianize the British Army. As represented by the self-sacrificing, high-minded heroines of George Eliot (she is insistent on the 'Puritan' character of Dorothea Brooke, though giving her an Anglican upbringing and marrying her off to a clergyman), or such soul-strivers as Hardy's Clym Yeobright and Jude Fawley,[32] it offered alternative ideas of masculinity and femininity to those associated with the worlds of rank and fashion.

The effect on historiography, particularly at the level of pedagogy, was momentous. The Puritans, no more than anonymous, 'factious' clergymen or preachers in the pages of Clarendon and Hume, were now represented by the towering figures of Cromwell, Milton and Bunyan. The Civil War, elevated from an Interregnum into an epic, became 'the Puritan Revolution', the rubric under which it has been studied by generations of undergraduates; it is now so deeply ingrained that even the most erastian and iconoclastic of seventeenth-century scholars finds it impossible to dispense with.[33] 'Puritan Revolution' was a neologism coined, it seems, by Guizot,[34] popularized (though he did not use the phrase) by Carlyle, and assimilated to the constitutional proprieties (as well as domesticated for the university examination syllabuses) by Gardiner and Firth. In the schools, where, as Valerie Chancellor notes in *History for Their Masters*, the tone of textbooks became markedly more parliamentary in sympathy as the century advanced,[35] it replaced the 'Glorious Revolution' of 1688 as the central event in the national past, allowing for and even encouraging a two-camp interpretation of English history, where previously there had been something closer to a consensus, and positively inviting the use of history for moral argument.[36] In adult education, where debate was the chief medium through which history was learned, and in the public schools, where the debating club was one of the few arenas where 'modern' history had some place, the rights and wrongs of the Civil War were earnestly rehearsed: 'Was the revolution under Cromwell to be attributed to the tyrannical conduct of Charles, or to the democratic spirit of the times?' This was the subject chosen by the Oxford Union Society, in 1829, for its first debate.[37] Twenty years on, in the nearby town of Wallington, after what the enthusiastic secretary declared was the most momentous debate which had ever taken place in the town's history (it went on for seven successive nights), the young men's Mutual Improvement Society, after taking a vote (in the most advanced manner of the day) by ballot, decided by a large majority that 'with the exception of sometimes allowing his religion to degenerate into enthusiasm and consenting to the death of the king . . . a better Christian, a more noble-minded spirit, a greater warrior, a more constant man (than Oliver Cromwell) has scarcely ever appeared on the face of the earth'.[38] The following meeting at St Thomas's Institute, Hackney, E. London, was minuted in 1876:

> Nov. 28. The elocution class met for an evening's discussion 'Oliver Cromwell' being the subject. The chair was taken by Mr Stoddart and the proceedings opened by a short sketch of the life of Cromwell. Mr Moore then laid several

> charges against Cromwell and Mr Ford at great length answered most of the charges and it was put to the Meeting whether Cromwell murdered Charles for his own aggrandisement or whether he did what is laid to his charge from inspired motives. 11 were for Oliver and 4 against. One of the latter Mr Moore afterwards said that he had taken his place that evening against Cromwell for the sake of argument but in reality he upheld his actions.[39]

The discovery of Puritanism, in Britain as in North America, was in the first place a literary phenomenon. It owed a great deal, no doubt, to what one might call the resurrectionist turn in historical thought in which 'philosophy teaching by example' was underpinned, or overlain, by a vivid sense of the past as a historical present. The Lake poets made some contribution to it. Coleridge was one of the first literary voices to be raised in favour of Bunyan. Southey's 1830 edition of *The Pilgrim's Progress*, carrying the imprimatur of the poet laureate, marked Bunyan's entry into the literary pantheon after a century and a half of well-bred put-downs – among them David Hume's. A more indirect echo of Bunyan (it has been argued) were Wordsworth's pilgrim-like wanderers and solitaries.[40] A late Ossianism might help to account for Macaulay's 'Battle of Naseby' (1824), a favourite recitation piece for schoolboys.[41] Byronism has a part to play in another favourite recitation piece, Felicia Heman's 'Landing of the Pilgrim Fathers': 'the heavy night hung dark . . . on the wild New England shore'.[42] Hawthorne's *Scarlet Letter*, set in seventeenth-century new England, is a Gothic narrative of entrapment.

In Britain the discovery of Puritanism was prepared by a much more widespread revolt against the politeness and polish of eighteenth-century literature, a positive appetite for the unruly, the spontaneous and the stressful. Macaulay, hailing Southey's edition of *The Pilgrim's Progress*, used it as an occasion to settle old scores: 'the dialect of plain working men', Bunyan had shown, was perfectly sufficient 'for every purpose of the poet, the orator and the divine':

> Cowper said forty or fifty years ago, that he dared not name John Bunyan in his verse, for fear of moving a sneer. To our refined forefathers, we suppose, Lord Roscommon's *Essay on Translated Verse*, and the Duke of Buckingham's *Essay on Poetry*, appeared to be compositions infinitely superior to the allegory of the preaching tinker. We live in better times; and we are not afraid to say, that, though there were many clever men in England during the latter half of the seventeenth century, there were only two minds which possessed the imaginative faculty in a very eminent degree. One of these minds produced the *Paradise Lost*, the other *The Pilgrim's Progress*.[43]

Linda Colley, in her otherwise splendid discussion of eighteenth-century Protestant nationalism (in *Britons: Forging the Nation*), says of *The Pilgrim's Progress* that it was, like Foxe's *Book of Martyrs*, a 'canonical' text. She points out that it had reached its 57th edition by 1789.[44] But, as

N.H. Keeble has shown, Bunyan's *literary* reputation was almost non-existent before the Romantics, even among those who recommended *The Pilgrim's Progress* for religious instruction.[45] Joseph Addison cited Bunyan as evidence that anyone could gain a popular following, regardless of merit. David Hume, with his fastidious Enlightenment taste, regarded Bunyan as beneath contempt.

> Whoever would assert an equality of genius and eloquence between . . . BUNYAN and ADDISON, would be thought to defend no less an extravagance, than if he had maintained a mole-hill to be as high as TENERIFE, or a pond as extensive as the ocean.[46]

The years from 1820 to 1920 might fairly be described as Bunyan's century. In New England, where *The Pilgrim's Progress* reached a peak of popularity in the 1840s, it was exploited to strengthen millennial ideas, to arouse hopes of raising utopia in the wilderness (such as the disastrous project which Louisa May Alcott's father engaged in), and to supply imagery for the antislavery movement. In Britain, it supplied the original for whole new classes of children's literature, such as the 'waif' stories which figure so prominently in Sunday School prize books; while a secularized version of it enjoyed immense popularity in the brief lives which make up Samuel Smiles's *Self-Help, Character* and *Thrift.* The working-class autobiography, a literary subgenre, born in the 1840s, which chronicled the pursuit of 'learning under difficulties', and pictured life as a succession of struggles, is another secular analogue. Thus the autobiography of Joseph Arch, the farm workers' leader, is cast as a progress from darkness to light. It starts with a series of parables illustrating the harsh lot of the farm labourers ('like the children of Israel waiting for someone to lead them out of the land of Egypt'). 'Sore at heart', he writes, commenting on the divisions which appeared in the union ranks, '. . . never – no not when the storm was at its highest, or the fight waxed hottest and fiercest – did I lose heart altogether, and fall a prey to the ugly old Giant Despair'.[47] Robert Tressell's *The Ragged Trousered Philanthropists*, British socialism's one serious contribution to English literature, is cast in the form of a Bunyanesque allegory, likewise ending with a mystic vision of the Celestial City.[48] At the very end of the period (as Paul Fussell shows in *The Great War and Modern Memory*), *The Pilgrim's Progress* took on a new lease of life as the soldier's comforter.[49]

Historiographically, the rehabilitation of Puritanism may be said to have begun with the Whig revival in post-1809 Scotland, when after the long night of Tory hegemony, radicals began to put their heads above the parapet. Thomas M'Crie's *Life of John Knox* (1812), eagerly promoted by the new *Edinburgh Review*, rehabilitated a figure who, to the historians of the Scottish Enlightenment, as to kirk 'moderates', was the very embodiment of gloomy fanaticism. The book, Halévy remarks, signalled the opening of a new epoch in Scottish thought.[50] M'Crie, reared in the 'primitive strictness' of the secessionist branch of the kirk, which he later served as a minister, was a lifelong liberal. As a student in the early 1790s he took a 'warm interest' in French political movements; in 1822 he mobilized Scottish opinion in support of the Greek struggle for independence; in 1830 he took part in antislavery agitation.[51]

He entered historical controversy to vindicate the Covenanters against the strictures of Sir Walter Scott.[52] His histories are marked by a strong national feeling and an even stronger republican one (after Knox he went on to write a biography of Andrew Melville). His Knox is a man of inflexible principle; he is also a political reformer, making monarchy quake before his will. Scottish Chartists accepted M'Crie's reading of Knox with enthusiasm. Knox, to the Glasgow-based *Chartist Circular*, was 'a zealous Radical Reformer – a Democrat – a Republican', even a 'physical force Chartist . . . Let us honour his name – respect his ashes, and pray God, *soon to send* us another John Knox.'[53]

M'Crie's *Knox*, which preceded Carlyle's *Cromwell* by some thirty years, anticipated some of its most genial features – above all the biographical approach to the study of the past and the belief that the historian's subjects should be able to speak in their own words. Knox's correspondence, taken from a hitherto unused manuscript, was one of the substantial bases of his work. M'Crie uses it, as Carlyle did with Cromwell's letters, to make his subject humanly credible, and indeed admirable. Where the philosophic historians of the Enlightenment were delighted to measure their distance from the past, treating history as a record of the 'crimes, follies and misfortunes of mankind', he on the contrary reverenced it and conceived himself in some sort as the medium who allowed it to voice its faith.

M'Crie also anticipates the talismanic importance which nineteenth-century writers – the novelists, historians and poets no less than the moralists and the pedagogues – were to attach to the idea of 'character'. The work of a clergy man and a doctor of divinity, passionately engaged in the ecclesiastical controversies of his own time, as well as in those of the Reformation, M'Crie's *Knox* is nevertheless more concerned with moral qualities than with doctrine. What makes Knox heroic is his simplicity. Faithful unto death, he carries a two-handed sword to defend the martyr Wishart against would-be assassins. Despising worldly advancements, he refuses a bishopric 'for conscience's sake'. Humble to God and haughty to man, he refuses to bow the knee to his monarch. M'Crie's Knox, in short, is one of those 'pattern-men' (to take the phrase used by Carlyle in his *Cromwell*) by which the nineteenth-century literature of self-improvement set such store.

The discovery of the 'Puritan' Milton, and his rescue from 'that elaborate libel on our great epic poet',[54] Dr Johnson's *Life*, preceded Carlyle's discovery of the 'Puritan' Cromwell by some twenty-five years. Indeed Carlyle, who read through Milton's prose works with great enthusiasm in

1822, originally seems to have intended to write a biography of the first rather than the second.[55] The publication of the *De doctrina Christiana*, discovered in 1823 and printed two years later, was an important moment here, showing Milton as a passionate and heterodox religionist, not making his peace with the Anglican Church (as Dr Johnson had persuaded himself) but, on the contrary, in the last year of his life, making secret preparations to publish his heretical views in Holland.[56] Macaulay, in his 1825 article on Milton in the *Edinburgh Review* (the essay which made him famous), was wary about where to place Milton theologically, but his enthusiasm for the Puritans – 'the most remarkable body of men, perhaps, which the world has ever produced' – as also for Milton as a religious poet and as a radical, was unbounded.[57] The 1830s saw a flurry of 'Puritan' lives of the poet. Still more pertinent for the radical rereading of Milton was the discovery of his pamphlets and prose. Popular publication followed and by the early 1840s, it seems, the *Areopagitica* was establishing itself as a radical classic. One of those who took it up was the young Edinburgh-educated, Chartist-sympathizing editor of the *Leeds Times*, Samuel Smiles. For Smiles, Bob Morris tells us, the seventeenth century *was* Milton:

> He accepted with great fervour the Miltonic belief that in free discussion truth would prevail, and each week the *Leeds Times* carried as its headpiece the quotation from *Areopagitica*, 'Give me the liberty to know to utter and to argue freely according to conscience above all other liberties'. Smiles identified with Milton in his campaigns against abuse and privilege. The opposition of the privileged to popular suffrage became 'scrannel straw voices', an echo from 'Lycidas' which neatly merged attacks on bishops, church establishments and monarchy from seventeenth- and nineteenth-century radicals: 'Would we have a revival of the fine old Puritan spirit of the days of Cromwell, Hampden, Pym, Elliott and others. Milton thou shouldst be living at this hour.'[58]

Masson's *Life of Milton*, published in six volumes between 1859 and 1880 and dedicated to reclaiming Milton as a revolutionary, as a radical religionist, and as an enlightened spirit, carried this work to new heights. The work, a vast undertaking, seems to have begun with the idea of contextualizing Milton's poetry, but it swelled, by degrees, into 'a continuous History of his Time'.[59] Masson has some claim to being a founding father of English literary scholarship (his edition of De Quincey, like the *Life of Milton*, is still a standard work). He was also, by the standard of his own days, or ours, a remarkable historical scholar, and a pioneer of archive-based research. He made use, for the first time, of Milton's academic essays, 'written while he was a student at Cambridge'; inspected parish registers for Milton's 'pedigree'; consulted the British Museum manuscripts for Milton's relations to the literature of the reign of Charles I; and the Milton manuscripts at Trinity College, Cambridge, to attempt to determine, by the handwriting of the original drafts, 'dates and other particulars'. Above all, as he records in the preface to volume III, there were the manuscripts at the State Paper Office, all of them, for the period he was researching, 'utterly uncalendared'.[60]

Masson was a great democrat, an enthusiast for the revolutions of 1848, a lifelong friend of Mazzini and the first secretary of the Society of Friends of Italy. He was a champion of women's rights and a pioneer of higher education for women.[61] His literary and historical work bears the reflection of these causes, and at various points in the commentary he is at pains to align Milton with more contemporary radical causes: temperance agitation; the movement for divorce law reform; popular education; minority rights. But on the central issue of religion, there is no faint attempt to corral his author or to rewrite his thoughts on party lines. On the contrary, as a good scholar and one who seems to have taken some delight, albeit vicariously, at the expression of antinomian views, he positively rejoices at Milton's heterodoxy, and the impossibility of pinning him down. Here is the considered conclusion of his work:

> Milton cannot be identified . . . with any of the English sects or denominations of his time. A professed Congregationalist in Church-polities, though with a tendency to absolute Individualism, a strenuous Protestant in the main principle of reverence for no other external authority in religion than that of the Bible, and a confirmed anti-Prelatist and Anti-State-Church-man, he had manifest points of sympathy theologically with several of the massive sects of English Nonconformists, but complete agreement with none of them . . . It would be a mistake to say of Milton, on any of these accounts, or on account of his Anti-Sabbatarianism and Latitudinarianism generally, or on account of the extreme boldness and heterodoxy of some of his speculations, that he did not belong most truly and properly to the great Puritan body of his countrymen. We have seen sufficiently in these pages what English Puritanism really was, through what phases it passed, what multiform varieties of thinking and of freedom it included. Only an unscholarly misconception of Puritanism, a total ignorance of the actual facts of its history, will ever seek, now or henceforward, to rob English Puritanism of Milton, or Milton of his title to be remembered as the genius of Puritan England.[62]

Carlyle's *Letters and Speeches of Oliver Cromwell* (1845) arguably had a greater effect on the nineteenth-century imagination – anyway the historical and political imagination – than any other scholarly work for, though it could not compete in popularity with Macaulay, Green or even Hume (let alone with *Mangnall's Questions*), it turned history into a moral drama; not so much 'philosophy teaching by example', but rather character revealing, or betraying itself, by the words on the printed page. In place of grand narrative it offered a politics of the personal, in which spiritual economy – or what Carlyle (and after him, Masson), drawing on German transcendentalism, called 'soul-effort' or 'soul striving' – replaced constitutional progress as the measure of worth. In the process it also brought Bunyanesque themes to the very centre of the historical stage, turning the simple life into the nursery of virtue, making the refusal of worldly honour – in Cromwell's case, the grand subject of Carlyle's third volume, the refusal of the English Crown – the crucible in which character revealed its true gold.

Carlyle, though he subscribed to the cult of genius, was at great pains, in his *Cromwell*, to stress, indeed to make a poetic of ordinariness. He addresses his hero familiarly as 'Oliver' or, playfully, when he has become Lord Protector, as 'your Highness'. He domesticates the great state occasions, puncturing the official solemnities with 'Amen', 'Here!' and 'Hum-m-m', inserting inspired and sometimes hilarious stage directions (italicized and in brackets, to preserve verbatim speech); and adding whispered grimaces and asides.[63] There are no great crowds, as there are in his *French Revolution*, but knots of men engaged in earnest converse. Carlyle shares in the intimacies of Cromwell's family circle and calls his pedigree 'kindred'. He loves the plainness and informality of Cromwell's letters, the urgency, the awkwardness, even the silences of the speeches. 'Cromwell, emblem of the dumb English, is interesting to me by the very inadequacy of his speech'.[64] The brilliantly chosen, but quite arbitrary starting-point of the narrative is the boggy grassy fields where Cromwell, 'the Farmer of St Ives', was engaged at harvest-work.[65] He is not the country squire, as he might have been in a more English or aristocratically-minded account, nor mounted on horseback, as he was to be in Ford Madox Brown's Carlyle-inspired portrait of him as a country visionary,[66] but rather 'a solid inoffensive farmer' engaged in humdrum tasks – mowing, milking, cattle-marketing.

Carlyle had set out to write an epic,[67] with a warrior in the leading role (he was undecided at first whether it should be Cromwell or – for the Convenanters' wars in Scotland were then equally in mind – Montrose),[68] and with set-piece descriptions of the battles. But the documentation imposed itself until in the end Carlyle gave himself up to it, reproducing individually each of the letters and speeches, as well as lengthy exchanges, and reducing the authorial role to that of an 'elucidator'. The effect, and indeed the intention, was to produce a kind of historical *Bildungsroman* which charted a mind in the making or what Carlyle thought of as the progress of a human soul, 'the largest soul in England'.[69] In place of grand narrative, the reader is invited to be an eavesdropper, listening in to Cromwell's soliloquies, and measuring his outward performance by reference to the inner man. Events were relegated to the background, while character (as Carlyle's critics sometimes complained) was put 'in boldest relief'.[70] Perhaps this explains why a mere five pages of the book are given to the Battle of Naseby, though Carlyle made an early visit when gathering material for the book, while no fewer than sixty pages are given up to Cromwell's refusal of the English Crown – a protracted negotiation, in which, as Carlyle saw it, the Lord Protector's selflessness was put to the test. Maguire's painting of this, *Cromwell Refusing the Crown of England*, was a sensation when, in 1859–61, it was taken on a tour of the Northern cities.[71]

Puritanism was one of Carlyle's discoveries in preparing the book. He had approached the subject with a Covenanter's eye, as one brought up in a warrior-church, and he was amazed to find that there had been an English analogue. Cromwell ('poor Cromwell'), he wrote in a letter of 23 May 1840, after attempting to lecture on him in Chelsea, was 'the valiant soldier in England of what John Knox had preached in Scotland'; he was a 'believing Calvinist soldier and reformer'.[72] In the course of writing the book, which he undertook in part as a way of getting acquainted with England ('a great secret to me always hitherto'), he seems to have shifted ground; Calvinism became Puritanism and he himself, in some sort, English. In *Cromwell* he refers freely to 'our English character', [73] and opens the book with the resounding and famous declaration that 'Puritanism was the last of all *our* Heroisms' (my italics).[74] It has also crossed the border. Presbyterianism was 'Scotch Puritanism'[75] and the Scottish people 'the first beginners of this grand Puritan Revolt'.[76] Carlyle is intoxicated not only with the idea of Puritanism but also with the word itself. He uses it both ecumenically and talismanically – rather as the Civil War sectaries used 'godly' – to dignify whatever it touched. The parliamentarians of the Long Parliament were 'Puritan men'; the Barebones Parliament (to which he showed some sympathy) was a 'Puritan Assembly of Notables'.[77] Oliver Cromwell was 'the soul of the Puritan Revolt',[78] 'the most English of Englishmen, the most Puritan of Puritans – the Pattern Man . . . of that Seventeenth Century in England'.[79]

The impact of Carlyle's work, which can be documented from many different sources, was palpable, immediate and, in the recorded cases, revelatory. How much was this due to the fact that it was written by one who was nationally, socially and confessionally, in English terms, a rank outsider? He had no political affiliations or even – after the break with John Stuart Mill – political friendships to keep up, no loyalty to the idea of representative government (the reason why Commonwealthmen and republicans had been so hostile to Cromwell), but on the contrary a sovereign contempt for the 'quiblings and vacillatings and constitution-pedantries' of parliamentary routine.[80] He was equally hostile to the 'frothy cant' of Exeter Hall evangelicalism.[81] Nor does he seem to have had any interest in or sympathy for English Nonconformity. The Puritanism of his book, he wrote in the opening chapter, was 'not of the nineteenth century, but of the seventeenth'.[82] His relations with the Scottish Church – where the national Church was Presbyterian – were difficult: those of 'lad o'pairts' learned in Scripture and destined for the ministry, who had broken with Calvinist orthodoxies. His only admitted loyalty was a generic one to what he called 'Gospel Christianity'. Like Cromwell he had no theology, only a simple faith. His notion of seventeenth-century Puritanism was correspondingly non-sectarian, at once more national and more plural than it might have been in one who owed some loyalty to an English Church or Chapel; more unqualified in his revolutionary enthusiasms, so far as the Civil War was concerned, than those who pinned their faith in constitutional development. Rescuing Cromwell from the 'enormous condescension' of posterity, his sympathies were also stirred by the Levellers, shot down at Burford, and the Diggers at St George's Hill.

Carlyle projected his *Cromwell* as a grand act of *restitution*, giving back a character to one whom posterity – and history – had vilified and traduced. He championed Cromwell as an *underdog*, and it is this which perhaps accounts for the immediate sensation which followed publication of his work and the fervour with which its message was spread in public lecture and debate. The lecturers presented themselves, like Carlyle, as *vindicators*, standing up for a man of integrity on whom 'historians . . . had thrown their slime'.[83] George Dawson adopted this stance in 1846, blaming the 'lackey ages' which followed the Restoration for having blackened the name of 'this giant'.[84] Charles Bradlaugh, the secularist leader, was using the same idiom twenty years later:

> Oliver Cromwell has few or no monuments. The country to which he devoted his virility has seen his bones rattle in gibbet chains, and for two hundred years has, on its knees, thanked God that hollow, tinsel, lying, lustful Stuart was restored to rule England, in lieu of this fierce, sturdy Puritan man, whose soul inbreathed power only because the power carried England's standard higher.[85]

Carlyle gave history a moral mission, that of rescuing the past from obloquy or oblivion – cleansing the record (or clearing off the dirt) to reveal things in their primitive beauty. The role of the scholar in this was simultaneously humble and heroic – heroic because it meant taking up a new stand, humble because Carlyle's method in *Cromwell*, where pride of place is given to the letters, while the 'elucidator' remains in the background (as in *Past and Present*, where he is a mere commentator on Jocelin de Brakelond's *Chronicle*), is that of the servant rather than the master of the evidence, one who, like R.H. Tawney in the face of the 'towering' figures of Milton, Cromwell and Bunyan, is in awe at what he sees.

Carlyle's *Cromwell* might also be said to have elevated politics into a species of moral theatre, prefiguring a whole series of later Victorian dramas, no less common in the Nonconformist pulpit than on the Liberal front bench at Westminster, in which a prophet, 'criticized' and 'misunderstood' although he enjoys the consolation of a loyal following, wrestles with his own conscience, suffers spiritual crises, yet withal engages in a life of ceaseless strife. John Vincent credits Gladstone with creating this in the Midlothian campaign, but one could with equal justice point to the great Cromwellian leaders of metropolitan Nonconformity – Spurgeon at the Metropolitan Tabernacle, who liked to boast that he had Puritan blood in his veins, Hugh Price Hughes at the West London Mission (the man who invented the term 'Nonconformist

Conscience') and John Clifford, the presiding figure at the Cromwell Tercentenary celebrations of 1899, who in 1922 was making his fifty-seventh court appearance for non-payment of the educational rate.

In mid-Victorian England, enthusiasm for the seventeenth-century Puritans moved from the peripheries of society to the very centre of the national stage. It registered itself at the Palace of Westminster, where in 1856 a picture celebrating the Pilgrim Fathers, showing them embarking in the *Mayflower* with a flag bearing the motto 'Freedom of Worship', was put up on the walls of the Houses of Parliament.[86] Perhaps it played some subliminal part in the 1859 legislation which discontinued the Day of National Humiliation commemorating the execution of Charles I. In the 1860s it began to make its mark on the built environment, with the first Milton Roads and Cromwell Avenues (in the current London A–Z there are thirty-six Cromwells, almost as many as the streets dedicated to the Duke of Wellington). 1862 marked the bicentenary of Black Bartholomew, when many Nonconformist churches put up busts, bas-reliefs and friezes, or installed stained glass windows, to commemorate their ejected forebears. The Memorial Hall, Farringdon Road, where later, in 1900, the Labour Representation Committee held the founding conference of the Labour Party, was one such effort: another was the obelisk to Defoe at Bunhill Fields, subscribed to by the readers of the *Christian World*. When Alfred Waterhouse's Assize Court went up in Manchester – a neo-Gothic extravaganza built between 1859–64 – Oliver Cromwell figured among the crowned heads, along with the kings and queens,[87] as he was to do in the new Town Hall opened at Leeds in 1874. In 1875 a full-scale statue of Cromwell was erected near the cathedral in Manchester 'on the spot where the first man was killed in the civil war'. It made the name of the sculptor, Matthew Noble.[88]

So far as history teaching was concerned (matters are very different if one turns from the textbooks to historical romance), a 'Puritan' interpretation of the seventeenth century, or at the very least a parliamentary one, could be said to have become in some sort the 'common sense' of the lecture hall and classroom. It is not less apparent in Dorothea Beale's addresses to her sixth form at Cheltenham Ladies College[89] than in the lectures of George Dawson[90] or Goldwin Smith on the platforms of the Mechanics Institutes. 'The Puritan Revolution' as it was routinely called by the 1880s – S.R. Gardiner's volumes began publication in 1876 – established itself as the high point in the history syllabuses, not only in University Extension[91] with its strongly Nonconformist following, but also in the ancient citadel of high Anglicanism, the University of Oxford, where Bishop Stubbs in the 1860s had tried to keep it out of the Schools, on the grounds that it would excite too much party feeling.[92]

A particularly striking testimony to the change is Charles Dickens's *Child's History of England* (1852), the work of one described at the time as an 'anti-Puritan'[93] and the novelist more responsible than any other for the low repute of nineteenth-century evangelicalism.[94] It is instructive to compare it with Keightley's *History of England* on which (Dickens scholars tell us) it was based.[95] Keightley's book, published in an 'elementary' children's version in 1841,[96] speaks of the eleven years of Charles I's personal rule as a 'despotism', and rebukes Laud with having cruelly treated Prynne, Bastwick and others, who were 'gentlemen and men of education'.[97] But Charles I was 'grave and decorous in his manner, a lover and patron of the fine arts, and sincerely attached to the Protestant religion'.[98] Keightley is very sympathetic to Strafford and notes that at his trial 'the ladies . . . were all captivated by his manly and graceful eloquence'.[99] Charles I's 'main fault' was failing to save him, but there is otherwise no criticism of the king. His execution in 1649 was a 'solemn mockery'. Keightley gives some pages to a mainly royalist narrative of the Civil War; the period of the Commonwealth and Protectorate is dispatched in three. At the Restoration, a short paragraph on Charles II ('a slave to pleasure')[100] is followed by a sober account of the First Dutch War, the Great Plague, the Fire of London etc.

In Dickens's *History* Charles is still 'grave and dignified in bearing', but he is no longer either a patron of the arts or 'sincerely attached to the Protestant religion'. Instead he has 'monstrously exaggerated notions of the rights of a king'. His 'taint' was that he was untrustworthy and 'evasive'.[101] It recurs through the subsequent narrative (the outbreak of the Civil War is attributed to his 'plotting'). Dickens almost approves of the execution in 1649: 'With all my sorrow for him, I cannot agree with him that he died "the martyr of the people", for the people had been martyrs to him and to his ideas of a King's rights.'[102] A great deal of space is given to the Commonwealth and Protectorate. Cromwell 'ruled wisely' and 'The whole country lamented his death'. Where in Keightley Charles I is patron of the arts, in Dickens it is Cromwell: 'he encouraged men of genius and learning, and loved to have them about him. Milton was one of his great friends'. He was 'good humoured' and a loving *paterfamilias*, being particularly attached to his eldest daughter.[103] The Restoration, in Dickens's account of it, is the very pit of English history, one long winter of national humiliation culminating in the execution of Russell and Algernon Sydney. The whole court was 'a great laughing crowd of debauched men and shameless women', indulging in 'vicious conversation' and committing 'every kind of profligate excess' (the only person of whom he has anything good to say is Nell Gwyn).[104] On Charles's sale of Dunkirk to the French he recalls Cromwell's strengths and wishes the new king might have met the fate of his predecessor. Dickens is indignant at the explusion of the Nonconformist clergy from the Church (Protestantism was supposed to be about religious freedom) and quite Gothic about the Five Mile Act of 1665 which, he says, 'doomed' Nonconformist ministers 'to starvation and death'.[105] His silences are no less remarkable than his rages. The author credited with 'inventing' Christmas does not say a word about the Puritan attempt to abolish it (Keightley has them turning it into a national fast); nor does the thespian in him feel moved to upbraid them about the closing of the theatres.

Carlyle's *Cromwell*, with its psalm-singing soldiers and generals communing with Providence, anticipates, prefigures and possibly had some influence on the rise, during the second half of the nineteenth century, of what Olive Anderson calls 'Christian militarism'.[106] The seventeenth-century analogy is well documented for the 1890s when the term 'soldier saint' (a neologism of 1892, according to *OED*) spread like wildfire.[107] The *Soldiers' Pocket Bible* of 1643 was reprinted in 1895 with a foreword by Lord Wolseley,[108] and the example of the 'plain russet-coated captains' who 'knew what they fought for and loved what they knew' was, it seems, as appealing to younger, reform-minded officers, as it was to be again in the Second World War.[109] Earlier the term 'Ironside' was much invoked, as it seems to have been during the disasters of the Crimean War; according to a local newspaper report: 'Many have dwelt upon the days of the Protectorate, when a man, unfettered by routine and sprung from the people, made England's arms both feared and respected'.[110] Another Carlylean figure much in evidence during the second half of the nineteenth century was the General next to God. An influential incarnation was Sir Henry Havelock ('every inch a soldier and every inch a Christian . . . a Puritan of the true Cromwellian stamp')[111] – the martyr-general of the time of the Indian Mutiny and a Baptist, whose statue still stands on the eastern side of Trafalgar Square.

Matthew Arnold, in *Culture and Anarchy* (1869), treats 'Puritanism' and chapel Nonconformity as interchangeable terms, targeting its militants as the enemies of 'sweetness and light'. Liberal politicians were apt to make the same equation, although of course they did so in a positive sense, instrumentalizing the example of the seventeenth century for party ends.[112] In the aftermath of the 1867 Reform Act, when Nonconformity in one or other of its national varieties – Welsh, English or Scottish – emerged as the principal basis of their electoral support, they grew adept at playing the Puritan card,[113] while in intra-party struggle, as for example between the radicals and the Whigs, to claim Puritan blood, or better still, like Bright or Chamberlain, to boast direct descent from one of the ejected ministers of 1662, was a standard trope. In local politics, where Anglicans and Nonconformists clashed over issues like church rates and education, the term 'Puritan' was used as a Nonconformist conceit, and more occasionally a Liberal one, although it was not until the 1890s that 'Municipal Puritanism' surfaced as an explosive issue in metropolitan politics. A precocious example is Blackburn, where, according to the town historian (himself at the time a member of the majority group on the Liberal Council), a Puritan regime was initiated between 1853 and 1861: 'Puritans were its Mayors and acting Magistrates . . . Puritans a number of its officials . . . Even the Police took to reading religious tracts in their spare moments . . .' At the time of the 1868 election, the trade union newspaper *The Beehive* invoked a collective ancestry:

> Can any man of dispassionate mind doubt as to how Milton would vote, were he alive in England next week or Cromwell, or almost any other of our forefathers who were devoted to freedom and progress, and whose memories we are proud of? We cannot conceive Milton as voting against Mr Gladstone and for the unscrupulous politician whom fate has ironically made Premier of England.[114]

The seventeenth century analogy was very much to the fore in the Bulgarian Atrocities campaign of 1876, at least in the mind of its orchestrator, W.T. Stead – a lifelong Cromwellian (in 1899 he produced a popular digest of Carlyle's *Letters and Speeches*). 'Cromwell, Milton and the Vaudois' were the central themes of his first appeal, and he returned to the example when urging Mr Gladstone in the wake of his famous pamphlet to propose a 'Bulgarian Sunday'.[115]

The past-present dialectic worked the other way round for the liberal historians of the period who drew on the analogy of the nineteenth century (or the unspoken example of it) when engaged in seventeenth-century work. The point of reference, however, was not a 'godly politics', as it was for the Nonconformists and as it had been for Carlyle, but rather seventeenth-century anticipations of the democratic idea. In line with a rhetoric which pitted 'the people' against privilege, and pictured the increasingly radicalized Liberal Party as the historically-appointed vehicle of the English 'Democracy', the Puritans, even though their minority character was admitted, became the ambassadors of the future. Thus J.R. Green, an 'advanced' liberal though also an Anglican clergyman, argued in his *Short History of the English People* that, 'great as were its faults', Puritanism 'may fairly claim to be the first political system which recognised the grandeur of the people as a whole – Shakespeare knew nothing'.[116] S.R. Gardiner, an ardent Gladstonian Liberal, as J. Adamson has recently reminded us,[117] and one whose Nonconformist affiliation had kept him out of Oxford in his earlier life, made strenuous efforts to keep party spirit out of his multi-volume history, but the very word 'Puritan', which he insists on, functions both as a party rallying cry and a label: 'Puritanism not only formed the strength of the opposition to Charles I, but the strength of England itself. Parliamentary liberties, and even parliamentary control, were worth contending for'.[118] Sir Charles Firth, acutely aware that the political activity of the Cromwellian army was the reverse of popular, nevertheless saw it as propagating 'democratic principles' which would be more fitly realized in the future by others. The Putney Debates, which he discovered, transcribed and published, became a kind of dress rehearsal for modern politics.[119]

The syncretism of new and old can also be seen in the novel, as in

Middlemarch, where Dorothea Brooke doubles in the part of a Puritan and a Lady Bountiful. Louisa M. Alcott's *Little Women* turns *The Pilgrim's Progress*, of which it is quite explicitly a modern reworking, into a family romance, making a whole universe of domesticity, investing the March family with the trappings of gentility, even though they are hard up, and turning the father – in the real-life original a failed utopian and struggling scholar – into the altogether more manly figure of a soldier. Here home is the Celestial City, at once the arena of the children's trials, and the site of their spiritual triumph. Just as, in their play, the cellar is the City of Destruction, so in their real-life travails, the Victorian sick-room is the Valley of the Shadow of Death. Superadded to this, and one reason, commentators have suggested, for the book's enduring popularity in the United States, are the elements of the American dream. 'Meg's Horatio Alger-like Mr Brooke applies himself to his accounts and ultimately provides her with servants. Amy marries the grandson of a millionaire and loves to bestow her largesse upon the less fortunate; and Jo inherits Plumfield, Aunt March's estate'.[120]

The domestication of Puritanism can also be followed in the pages of *Black Beauty*, the *Pilgrim's Progress* (or *Book of Martyrs*) of the animal rights movement. Coming from a very heartland of English Nonconformity, and written by a bedridden Victorian Miss, the book unfolds in a succession of parables, now demonstrating the cruelties of the 'bearing rein' (the arching of the horse's head to give it a showier appearance), now rebuking a great lady for her improvident housekeeping, now attacking the careless brutality of the ignorant master or the heavy Victorian father. Puritan-humanist in its emphasis on kindness to animals, and resuming the ancient Puritan opposition to blood sports, the book is at the same time quite attentive to the Victorian proprieties. Indeed the opening chapter, in which Black Beauty's mother takes the pony to one side to warn of the perils of frisking with the rough young colts in the meadow – 'You have been well bred and well born; your father has a great name in these parts, and your grandfather won the cup two years at Newmarket' – must have provided generations of English girls with one of their elementary lessons in class and gender comportment.

Enthusiasm for the seventeenth-century Puritans was distinctly a minority affair. Indeed it derived much of its energy from this, being taken up most ardently by those who were at some sort of odds with society or – like the young Ben Tillett, in his apprentice days as an agitator, 'spellbound' by the 'dark fury' of Carlyle's prose – up in arms against the corruptions and injustice of the world. The leaders of the 'Revolt of the Field', the farm labourers' movement of the 1870s, perhaps fall into this category. The *Labourers Union Chronicle*, edited by Liberal sympathizers, claimed that 'puritanism and non-conformity' were supplying the motive power, and the 'moral earnestness' which gave them the courage to take on the parson and the squire.[121] Joseph Arch himself, the farm labourers' leader, a village Hampden, or 'mute, inglorious' Milton finding a national voice, set great store by this, believing, as he wrote in his autobiography, that some of his Warwickshire forebears fought with Cromwell at Edgehill, 'against tyranny and oppression and for the liberation of the people'.[122] There must have been others who liked to picture their seventeenth-century ancestors as fighting on opposite sides to the local squire – we know from his daughter's biography that Joseph Ashby of Tysoe did.[123] It was in this spirit that the Labourers' Union in Northamptonshire held an annual demonstration and gala at Naseby, concluding the proceedings with an original song relating to the battle. But at the farm labourers' conferences and rallies, where sympathizing newspapermen were amazed at the outpouring of the spirit, it was not people's history which gave first-time orators the strength to speak, but sacred history: Old Testament examples of how tyrants met their doom. At Lark Rise where, to follow Flora Thompson's memoir, the farm labourers in the 'Wagon and Horses' were Gladstonian to a man, naughty children were still being threatened: 'If you ain't a good gal, old Oliver Crummell'll have 'ee!'[124]

Metropolitan Nonconformists, with their vast Sunday congregations, at places like Spurgeon's Tabernacle, their prosperous suburban churches, and their vivid political life, acquired a quite inflationary notion of their numbers and strength. Their children were brought up, like the radical journalist Howard Evans, 'to regard Cromwell and Milton and Bunyan as the great heroes of the Primitive Apostolic and Puritan faith'.[125] In their homes not only Mr Gladstone but even (Leah Manning recalls of her fervently radical Wesleyan grandfather) the by-elections were included in the family prayers.[126] If one was a visitor at Spurgeon's new house in the suburbs, one might be invited to play 'at the old Puritan game of bowls'. It is not surprising that when the Nonconformists found themselves in power, in the newly created London County Council of 1888, they treated their majority as a mandate not only for municipal collectivism but also for 'municipal puritanism'.[127]

II

Historians seem generally to be agreed that the 1890s and 1900s, when Nonconformity reached some kind of zenith of political influence, also marked the onset of secular decay.[128] The progressive removal of civil disabilities, such as the abolition of University Tests, opened Nonconformists to assimilation from above; while emancipatory measures such as the Burials Act of 1880, which allowed them to conduct their own funeral services, made the cry of 'religious equality' sound increasingly shrill. Nonconformity was also threatened, more dangerously, it is argued, than the Church of England, which required less strenuous commitment, by the secularizing tendencies of the age.[129] Already in the 1850s worldly prosperity was exposing the more successful to the temptations of what the Quakers called 'gay' dress; to the attractions of worldly amusements and to the lure of 'vain' sports.[130] Fireworks displays 'in which some of the younger members were preparing to indulge' were one of the 1850s troubles of the Birmingham Quakers;[131] Samuel Morley, the millionaire philanthropist, was outraged when two of his children, visiting the home of a local minister, were inveigled into joining a game of charades.[132] Things got worse when outdoor games, such as lawn-tennis and later golf, were taken up by the middle class; and when the seaside holiday, 'which had been previously considered slightly raffish', was adopted as a normal part of middle-class life.[133] As for popular culture, the cricketing teams, which by the 1890s some chapels were running,[134] could not compete with the footballing excitements of the Saturday half-holiday, while the Pleasant Sunday Afternoons which they put on, to insulate their congregation from the Sabbath-breakers ('an Evangelistic service, with instrumental and vocal music, hymns, solos, and a short address'), were no match for the shooting brakes laden with pleasure-seekers, the 'streams of bicyclists', or the crowds assembling round the bandstand in the parks.[135]

Under the influence of an extravagant chapel-building programme, Nonconformity was becoming an increasingly hereditary affair, transferring its energies from evangelizing work to consolidation, and locking them up in its suburban fastnesses. The chapels themselves, with their cathedral-like towers and spires, the visible signs of Nonconformity's prosperity, were also a testimony to its decadence, exhibiting a love of ornamentation and ostentation which a simpler and more passionate faith had held in check, and making the survival of poorer congregations, left behind in the rage for ornamentation, increasingly untenable.[136] Politically, the voluntary principle, nineteenth-century Nonconformity's grand specific for social ills, was eclipsed by a growing belief, not least within radical Nonconformity itself, in the power of collective provision, while economic and social questions came to count for more than those issues of status and rights by which Nonconformists had set such store. The Liberal landslide of 1906, in which Nonconformists made up almost half the new majority, was a Pyrrhic victory: the Church versus Chapel issues on which (at least in the eyes of passive resisters and those who had campaigned against the 1902 Education Bill) it had been won were speedily displaced by such welfare measures as Old Age Pensions. As Richard Helmstadter puts it: 'Free churchmen, in spite of their active press and increasingly efficient central organisation, faded into a religiously indifferent landscape.'[137]

Yet if Nonconformity was decaying, or stationary, in its denominational fastnesses, secularized versions of it were flourishing and discovering new fields of endeavour in the world outside. One was municipal enterprise, which emerged, in the late nineteenth century, as one of the leading outlets for the reformist spirit in national life as well as a springboard for collectivism. Pioneered by Nonconformists and still, in the 1900s, very largely in their hands, it was regarded by the moving spirits – on the borough councils of the 1900s they included such characteristic figures as the Sunday School teacher, the school attendance officer, and the 'concerned' general practitioner and health worker – as a matter of Christian duty, bringing light into dark places, giving a helping hand to the weak.[138] In this spirit, it extended the notion of public utility from the provision of cheap gas and pure water to the running of municipal trams;[139] to the feeding of schoolchildren; and the supply of municipal milk. By degrees, too, councils began to involve themselves in cultural politics, turning free libraries into flagships of municipal progress,[140] opening up recreation grounds and parks, with bandstands for the performance of municipal music and playgrounds for children's swings and slides. The missionaries of the civic gospel also engaged in those acts of moral policing which earned them the title of 'municipal puritans'.[141] 'Fresh, bright and clean pleasures', such as those represented by municipal concerts and municipal swimming baths, were promoted as a sovereign remedy for intemperance and vice. In London the Progressive majority on the newly formed LCC, under the influence of such temperance zealots as the 'Methodistical Puritan' J. McDougall of Poplar – 'a representative municipal statesman of the type of the serious English middle class' – used their licensing powers to curtail drinking hours and reduce the numbers of beerhouses and pubs; while the Theatres and Music Hall Committee, under the vice-chairmanship of Richard Robert, the member for South Islington, a 'radical nonconformist' who did 'not regret the revival of Puritan sentiment which has always characterised English Liberalism in its best days', attempted to 'check indecency and gilded vice', to stop the performance of 'objectionable' songs and – as John Burns, the member for Battersea put it in an election address of 1895 – to prevent art and artistes 'from being made mere accessories to drink and debauchery'.[142]

It is interesting that some of the strongest 'municipal Puritans' were not Nonconformists at all but those secularist radicals or free-thinkers who worked in tandem with them. John Burns, 'an unwavering preacher of righteousness, though in a conventional meaning of the term he is not a religious man', in the words of a 1908 hagiographer, is an interesting and influential example.[143] A martinet for discipline during the great dock strike – one of the reasons why, though famed as the man with the Red Flag, he won the plaudits of the public press – and already, as his diary for 1887–88 shows, apt to scrutinize working-class pleasure-goers for tell-tale signs of degeneracy, he had trained himself from boyhood, it seems, to do without, refusing to 'coddle himself'.[144] It was one of his proud boasts, when elevated to a position where he was on intimate terms with the highest in the land, that he had never had to wear an overcoat in his life.[145] A rigid and lifelong abstainer, known as 'Old Coffee-Pot' by his workmates in his early engineering days, 'on account of his refusal to touch spirits or beer',[146] he gave wholehearted support to the LCC's temperance reforms.[147] As candidate for Battersea in the 1895 LCC election he was no less vociferous in supporting Mrs Ormiston Chant's crusade against the music-halls.[148] 'In the real meaning of the word John Burns is a Puritan to the depths of his being', wrote the hagiographer of 1908,

> a twentieth century incarnation of those prophets of Israel who arraigned monarch and meanest subject alike in burning words for national sins, and of those stern-visaged men of their bands who in the seventeenth century hurled a perjured king from his throne to save the liberties of the English people. No Puritan pulpiteer thundered against the vices of his time more vehemently than John Burns has denounced the drinking and gambling habits of the working-man of today. No face has been set more sternly against slackers and moral flabbiness; no austerer moralist could be discovered in the Long Parliament of 1649 than is the president of the Local Government Board . . .[149]

In another sphere, that of state intervention rather than civics, a secularized version of the Calvinist notion of the 'calling', and a vocational and professional one of the gospel of work, were a fundamental component of the public service ethic as it emerged in the reformed universities of the 1870s. One might refer here to those notions of *noblesse oblige* which captivated the undergraduates who sat at the feet of such charismatic teachers as A.J. Toynbee.[150] Or to those theories of social obligation, stressing duty, discipline and the subordination of the self in the service of a higher cause, associated by J.R. Seeley, the historian, with the practice of enlightened statecraft;[151] by T.H. Green, the philosopher, with the pursuit of moral and temperance reform;[152] and by Alfred Marshall, the economist, with legislative action on behalf of the 'residuum'. Or to those more aristocratic notions of leadership which found expression in the settlement houses where budding empire-builders such as Alfred Lord Milner found their vocation. At a lower level, and at a slightly later date, one might refer to the young idealists, turned out in such numbers by the teacher-training colleges of the 1890s, who found their parish and their lifelong vocation in the elementary schools;[153] to the apostles of university extension and 'fellowship' who discovered in tutorial classes a whole new missionary field (Albert Mansbridge, the mystically-minded founder of the Workers' Educational Association, and R.H. Tawney, its most distinguished tutor, are representative types);[154] or to those civil service recruits, some of them drawn from industry, who took positions of responsibility in the burgeoning welfare bureaucracies – 'a new model army of vigilant administrators, supplanting property by organisation', as those who manned the newly formed Labour Exchanges were called in 1910.[155]

A Puritan idea of service and sacrifice gave a rationale for late Victorian overseas settlement, burdening the British diaspora with a tremendous task – nothing less than that of conjuring order out of chaos.

It provided some of what Martin Green calls (in relation to *Robinson Crusoe*) the 'energising myths' which gave the empire-builders the courage to take up their appointment with destiny.[156] Kipling, the poet laureate of Empire, a lifelong Cromwellian, descended, on both sides of the family, from what he chose to call 'puritan blood' (both his grandfathers had been Methodist ministers) pictured the task as a thankless one, with many dangers and few rewards.[157] The terrain was hostile – an Old Testament landscape, cursed with pestilence and exhibiting nature red in tooth and claw; the very plants (Darwin taught) only survived by cannibalizing one another. 'Jungle' emerged, towards the end of the century, as a key metaphor. It was originally a Hindu word, but was little used by H.M. Stanley in his narratives; yet by the 1890s, when Conrad wrote *Heart of Darkness,* it had been transplanted to tropical Africa. The Empire was rich in martyrs (Keir Hardie called Gordon of Khartoum 'the most Christ-like man this country has ever seen'),[158] it also provided a wide new field for the combination of those qualities which (as was often said in eulogies of Cromwell)[159] united the 'Man of Action' and 'the Mystic' – the 'practical mystic' as Lord Rosebery called Cromwell in his tercentenary address, 'a man who combines inspiration . . . apparently derived . . . from close communion with the supernatural and the celestial'.[160] Personified in the district officer bringing the rudiments of order and justice to some wild hill tribe or in the missionary braving impossible difficulties to carry the Gospel to the heathen, it made every act of colonization a spiritual triumph.

The socialist movement, to follow autobiographical accounts of the period, was rich in saints and martyrs, 'noble-minded' men and women – women especially – who sacrificed life and health for the cause. Within a very few years of the foundation of the Independent Labour Party the roll-call of the 'martyred dead', commemorated in the Red Flag, extended from Chicago's vaults to such indigenous figures as Carolyn Martin and Enid Stacey, who had given their all to the itinerant propaganda, and met with an early death.[161] Embracing the socialist cause was regarded – at least by those who joined it from the comfortable classes – as an act of renunciation, one which made its votaries indifferent to physical wellbeing. In their own eyes, they were 'social saviours' standing up for justice and right, shielding the downtrodden and oppressed.[162] Socialism was not only historically inevitable, it was also (Annie Besant wrote) 'ethically beautiful'.[163] Those who were its appointed missionaries exhibited a sublime indifference to material things. Margaret McMillan, a leading spirit in the Bradford ILP and a pioneer of the kindergarten movement and of open-air nurseries, was a hugely admired example: in the urgency of writing she would allow her fingers to grow blue 'without thinking that she could put a match to the fire'.[164] Charlotte Despard, the Queen of South London Socialism, and in later years a famous tribune for the Irish, is another example, as her recent biography records:

> She had begun to read Thoreau and Walt Whitman, the prophets of simplicity and naturalism, and under their influence her preference for the uncomplicated way of life she had enjoyed as a girl quickly revived. Living alone, she was able to follow Shelley's advice and become a vegetarian, and in the poverty of Wandsworth she could adopt a plainer form of clothing than a more formal class of society would have approved. A simple, habit-like black dress without ornamentation became her invariable garb, set off by the eccentricity of a black lace mantilla. In that bustled, stayed and busty age her refusal to lace her spare figure into corsets, or to cover her head with an extravagant hat, rendered her distinctive to the point of oddness. By the time she began to wear open sandals instead of narrow shoes, it seemed quite in keeping with the rest.[165]

As the foregoing may have suggested, late Victorian Britain offered many new fields for the exercise of what T.H. Green called 'ascetic altruism'.[166] The Puritan virtues of plain living and high thinking may have been under siege (as ministers complained) in the Nonconformist heartlands, but an aestheticized version of them was the very basis of the Arts and Crafts movement – 'England's modernism' as it has been called – which had as its starting-point a revolt against Victorian opulence. 'Simple Lifeism', its secular analogue, was ardently practised in those communities of the alienated (fellowships as they were often called) where spiritual vagrants found a refuge from religious doubt. It is not difficult to find echoes of Puritanism in those late Victorian ethical movements which served as a platform for 'advanced' ideas. They were very much in evidence in the Fellowship of the New Life, the original seedbed of Fabianism. Members took as their object 'the cultivation of a perfect character in each and all'; as their guiding principle 'the subordination of material . . . to spiritual things'; and, as a condition of membership, 'single-minded, sincere, and strenuous devotion to the cause'.[167]

The need for, and the possibility of, a grand purification of life was one of the major themes of early socialist propaganda, which pictured the society of the future as a leaner, fitter one, purged of superfluity and excess. It targeted luxury as the main enemy, arguing that it was only the insatiable demand for comfort by the wealthy few that condemned the many to a life of toil. Edward Carpenter, the sandal-making sage of Millthorpe who was the great exponent of Simple Lifeism, drew his inspiration from the American transcendentalists and community-builders. In the rhetoric of the Fabians, lecturing to middle-class audiences on the virtues of the servantless home,[168] or launching their philippics against unearned increment and wealth,[169] a more traditional vocabulary came into play. It is perhaps indicative of this that one of their 1890s tracts was *A Word of Remembrance and Caution to the Rich*, a reprint of a 1773 pamphlet by the New England Quaker and pioneer of negro emancipation, John Woolman.[170] Robert Blatchford, in *Merrie England* (1894), the booklet which did more than any other to domesticate the socialist idea – it sold some two million copies – linked 'opulence of mind' with 'frugality of body'.[171] In place of luxury he argued for a return to the production of primary necessaries:

> Robinson Crusoe's first care was to secure food and shelter. Had he neglected his goats and his raisins and spent his time in making shell-boxes he would have starved . . . But what are we to call the delicate and refined ladies who wear satin and pearls, while the people who earn them lack bread?[172]

'Luxury', a young worker-scholar of 1900 would have learnt in his 'Elementary Sociology', went 'hand in hand' with vice and stifled 'high endeavour'.[173] The true wealth of a nation lay in the character of its people. The 'primary wants' were few – love and marriage, companionship and books; all the rest was 'secondary' and 'derivative'. (The lesson, one may imagine, was peculiarly appealing to the impecunious young bachelor, pressing his claims on doubting in-laws.)

> I want to get married to John or Eliza Jane. This is a primary want, because people must marry or the world would stop. But I want a big wedding in the church, a grand wedding-cake, a trousseau, and a wedding-ring with three sparking diamonds on it, these are secondary wants . . . We all want to eat, but . . . such a strong hold does mere taste obtain over some people that they would prefer a pretty dish served daintily to them, even if it were empty, to the largest amount of steaming food in a more direct way.[174]

Simple Lifeism, or a feminist version of it, calling for a new spiritualization of the household and a new emotional economy, was quite central to the *fin de siècle* ideas about 'companionate' marriage, as they were practised (or canvassed) in the advanced circles of the time, 'a comradeship . . . rather than a state where the woman was subservient to, and dependent on the man'.[175] The wife, instead of being a male plaything or a suffering Madonna, would enjoy relations of solidarity and respect. The husband – a helpmeet rather than a lover – would renounce, or restrain, the sexual passion. Absence of physical attraction, so far from being an inhibition, might be the passport to marital happiness, as it was for Beatrice Potter when she entered her lifelong partnership with Sidney Webb, or Virginia Stephen when Leonard Woolf began to court her.[176] The 'Platonic' friendship, another *fin de siècle* ideal which had a large following among the emancipated, was of a piece with this: it was only be the reining in of the passions that 'holy sweetness' could remain pure.[177]

The 'New Woman' as she appeared on the stage of the Little Theatres, in the feminist and anti-feminist novels of the 1890s, and in the misogynist caricatures of *Punch*, was one who put self-development first.[178] She is pictured in austere surroundings, struggling to keep her independence intact or, like Nora in *A Doll's House*, preparing to abandon creature comforts in the search for an ideal state. She dresses plainly: in sensibly hygienic or rational dress, in the *Punch* caricature; or more romantically in free-flowing, loose-fitting 'aesthetic' dress; or, nun-like, in a habit. She regards what Millicent Fawcett (in a letter to Thomas Hardy) called 'the physical element of love' with distaste,[179] believing that sexual advances are an invitation to self-surrender. Marriage is the result of female guile or male lust. When entered into for the sake of security, it is 'the uncleanliest traffic in the world'; 'A mere mouldering branch of the patriarchal tree'.[180]

Olive Schreiner, a soul-striver, attempting to storm the heavens yet doomed to wander homeless in the world, was a living incarnation of this feminized version of Puritanism, alike in her passionate, unfulfilled being and in her evangelically-charged writings. *The Story of an African Farm,* though written by a free-thinker who had rejected the religious teachings of her missionary parents, is full of religious echoes. Biblical references abound. The soul is orphaned, the terrain bleak. It was perhaps in acknowledgement of these qualities that her London admirers included not only free-thinkers such as Eleanor Marx (with whom she lodged), but also two of the leading Nonconformists of the day – Hugh Price Hughes, the self-appointed custodian of the Nonconformist Conscience, who wanted to use her evangelical powers for Wesleyan Methodism, and W.T. Stead, who enlisted her support for his 'Maiden Tribute of Modern Babylon' crusade.[181] In Arnoldian terms, Schreiner was a 'Hebraist'. Her tastes (writes a biographer) 'were intellectual rather than artistic'.[182] There are few references in her correspondence to any other art than music. Clothes gave her no pleasure: she was careless of her personal appearance and a zealous advocate of dress reform. She had little or no taste for the minor pleasures of life. Her whole mode, as a feminist or a socialist, a war-resister or a social reformer, was that of the yearning soul. Like Carlyle, with whom she shared a taste for Old Testament prophecy, she attached a religious meaning to work, picturing labour– 'earnest, independent labour' – as the divine instrument of female emancipation, a deliverance from the house of bondage.[183] She also had a religious view of love, looking for one that was 'great' and 'pure', yet a brooding melancholy told her that such a love would burn up like parchment in the fire, leaving only ashes.[184]

More distant echoes of Puritanism, crossed with nature mysticism and more sinisterly with late Victorian notions of race and class, might be seen in the idea of 'clean living', as it was propagated by the food reformers and faddists, the fresh-air fanatics and the community builders, or the pioneers of Callisthenics and Swedish Drill.[185] In one idiom it was a short-hand expression for working-class respectability and the lines of division which separated the aristocracies of labour from the Great Unwashed. In another, adopted by the purity campaigners of the 1880s and 1890s – those agitations to which the 'Nonconformist Conscience' owes its name – it was a watchword for moral hygiene. In yet another, anxiously suggested by the Social Darwinists and the Eugenicists, it was bound up with fears of 'race degeneration'. By the 1900s, when go-ahead municipalities such as Battersea were establishing pure milk depots, or, like St Pancras, a School for mothers, it was becoming an integral part of the Civic Gospel.[186] When Margaret McMillan, in 1906, persuaded Sir Robert Morant, the very Cromwellian Chief Secretary of the Board of Education, to adopt a programme of medical inspection of the schools, it also became the cutting edge of state intervention in the lives of the poor.[187]

In terms of body politics, the New Hygiene has most recently been discussed as a sinister force. For the Foucauldians it represents a new stage in the ambition to establish medical strategies of surveillance and control. Historians of sexual politics associate it with the medicalization and criminalization of homosexuality.[188] Students of nineteenth-century eugenics remind us that in one direction it points forward to the compulsory sterlization of the unfit – even, via ideas of 'race preservation', to the gas chambers. In the light of this it seems worth pointing out that, quite apart from its obvious contribution to the reduction in mortality rates (which fell steeply after 1870), the New Hygiene was associated in its time with movements that were forward-looking and progressive. From 'Hygieia' onwards (the vision of the smoke-free city presented to the National Association for the Promotion of Social Science in 1875)[189] it was absolutely central to utopian community-building projects; in organizations like the Clarion League, where vigorous exercise was in some sort the physiological counterpart to freedom from convention, it was no less central to New Life ideals.

The emancipatory side of the New Hygiene was very much to the fore in the new girls' high schools of the 1870s, where Callisthenics or Swedish Drill replaced exercises in ladylike deportment. Frances Mary Buss's schools at Camden Town, 'a rather Bohemian quarter where artists and actors abounded', were the pioneers here.[190] Early prospectuses and timetables noted that a college garden was available for gentle Callisthenics 'under the tutelage of Captain James Chiosso'. In the early 1870s, Miss Buss succeeded in gaining access for students to the St Pancras Baths, engaged a swimming instructor, arranged for the students who made the most progress to receive a prize, and encouraged mistresses to give up free time to supervise.[191] Sophie Bryant, who succeeded Miss Buss as headmistress, was both a keen supporter of hockey and the founder, in 1890, of the 'Healthy and Artistic Dress Union'.[192]

The New Hygiene attached a talismanic importance to the use of 'pure' water, not only as a cleanser but also as an invigorator, bringing listless limbs to life, and in the case of swimming – one of the New Hygiene's most genial enthusiasms – forcing clogged-up lungs to engage in deep breathing. As Peter Beilharz interestingly observes, the Fabian London programme, like William Morris's *News from Nowhere*, makes a great deal of the purification of the River Thames:

> Water, for Webb, is for cleaning; drinking water ought to be as pure and as soft as from a Welsh lake. London ought to provide its citizens with free public baths, railway stations with drinking fountains and hand-basins; parks should offer bathing and skating ponds. More, water should be supplied to every floor [of model dwellings] . . . and gas and hot water laid on.[193]

Fresh air, vigorously promoted by housing reformers such as Octavia Hill, was another of the New Hygiene's great enthusiasms: in the model dwellings built under her influence, doors and windows were kept deliberately ill-fitting in an attempt to force the rooms to breathe, and later adopted as a prophylactic against TB. Like pure water, or bacteria-free milk, 'the pure air of heaven' was credited with both moral and thaumaturgical powers. 'More air, less alcohol'[194] was one of the watchwords of the Garden City Movement and one so persuasive to those who took up residence at Letchworth – the *Ultima Thule* of Edwardian Progressivism – that they consistently voted to keep the town dry.[195] For the children in McMillan's open-air nursery in Deptford, it opened the way to the stars:

> Here the little girls gathered each evening, as the sweltering day turned to twilight; pale faces brightened at the sight of the sweet-williams and white fox-gloves which 'I can look at after I'm in bed'. Here, sleepy eyes looked from their pillows at points of starry fire in the indigo blue depth; the night wind cooled their little heated bodies, and a primrose dawn called them awake. Will these children ever forget the healing joy of such nearness to the earth spirit as is possible even in Deptford?[196]

The influence of the New Hygiene is nowhere more apparent than in the field of dress reform. The idea of 'rational' or minimalist dress goes back at least as far as Rousseau's *Emile*, and it had been an unofficial feminist enthusiasm ever since Mary Wollstonecraft in *The Vindication* (1792) took up arms against the mind-numbing frivolities of fashion. Among the Quakers, ancient protagonists of plainness of dress, the gravitational pull had been in the other direction, as Elizabeth Isichei reports. If *Felix Holt* is to be believed, something of the same may have been a threat to the Congregationalists of Treby Magna. The 1851 movement inspired by the American women's rights campaigner, Amelia Janks Bloomer, was a failure, as was an attempt to revive it in the 1860s.[197] 'Aesthetic' dress, fashionably promoted in the 1870s by Arthur Liberty's new shop in Regent Street, seems to have been an affair of the culturally privileged. In the 1880s, however, under the banner of 'Sanitary . . . Clothing' and 'Hygienic Wear' (and finding expression in a series of

'Rational Dress' societies), loose-fitting, simplified garments, in the form of tweeds and jerseys, blouses and shorts, came into their own.[198] Sweat, it seems, was one of the bugbears on which the woollens movement fed. At Abbotsholme, first of the new Progressive Schools, established by a disciple of Edward Carpenter and a follower of the Fellowship of the New Life, 'as little' clothing as was compatible with health, comfort and decency was the school rule. Underwear was forbidden; for their outer garments the boys were to wear 'as so far as possible' nothing tight and nothing but wool 'which keeps sweet and will not burn'.[199] Similar fears seem to have prompted Baden-Powell in his choice of Boy Scouts uniform (in *Scouting for Boys*, as at Abbotsholme, 'sleeping on the back . . . with too many blankets on' was counted as a sin, on a par with 'eating rich food').[200] The hygienic argument was also very much to the fore when dress reform was adopted by *The Young Woman*, a Nonconformist illustrated monthly, addressed to work-girls and domestic servants. Reports on Nonconformist good works were combined with serial stories by romantic novelists and practical articles on such matters as 'easily made, but useful . . . gifts'. Heavy clothing, readers were taught, was responsible for undue fatigue, for overheating and for afterchills. Corsets enfeebled the muscles and produced round shoulders. Superfluous petticoats impeded freedom of movement:

> From the point of view of health the modern woman is far ahead of her grandmother . . . although she is still far below the ideal hygienic standpoint. She dresses more sensibly, more hygienically and more appropriately . . . The frills and furbelows of the early Victorian period would never be tolerated in these days of out-door girls and business young women . . . The gospel of cleanliness – medical cleanliness – has been preached to such purpose that we are beginning to learn the lesson that the less durable and the more frequently washed our clothing the better . . . The modern blouse, for example, is a hygienic garment, because it can be frequently changed and frequently washed. Compare it with the heavy polonaise of five-and-thirty years ago, a garment as ridiculous, artistically speaking, as it was undesirable, hygienically speaking, because of its weight, and the fact that it was generally made of unwashable material.[201]

In the case of food reform, where the 1880s saw the start of a widespread revolt against Victorian gluttony and the birth of the vegetarian movement, gastronomic arguments, developed by the New Hygiene, and animal rights ones propagated by Henry Salt's Humanitarian League seem to have merged with 'New Life' and feminist arguments about companionate marriage.[202] Plain food was not only more nutritious than delicacies and dainties, it was also labour-saving, freeing the woman of the house from the servitudes of elaborate cooking, and giving her time for the pursuit of higher things. It seems to have been adopted, for this reason, as one of the unofficial causes of the Garden City Movement.

Letchworth, that 'New Jerusalem' of Ann Veronica's artistically-minded socialist suitor,[203] was a veritable show-case of food faddism, with a 'Food Reform Restaurant and Simple Life Hotel', a 'Health Food Store' ('under the personal supervision of . . . a life vegetarian') and a galaxy of bakers selling wholemeal bread.[204] Baillie Scott, one of the architects of the Garden City Movement, had dreamed of a dining-room table no longer 'disfigured' by the family joint, 'but adorned, instead with piles of luscious fruit and nuts'.[205] To judge by the number of herbivores and teetotallers who settled in the town (it remained dry, by popular vote, down to 1920) his dream may well have been realized.

In the 1890s and 1900s, as in earlier periods of the nineteenth century, Nonconformity presented itself, in one aspect at least, as a *modernizing* force, on the side of progress and change. Havelock Ellis, the sexual radical, argued (in 1907) that in England 'the vital movement of Reform' and that of what he called 'Puritanism' were umbilically linked and historically coterminous. It was out of Puritanism 'as represented by Milton' that the first 'genuinely modern' conceptions of the marriage relationship had emerged. Milton, in his *Doctrine and Discipline of Divorce*, published in 1643, 'proclaimed the supremacy of the substance of marriage over the form of it', and the spiritual autonomy of the individual in the regulation of that form. He had grasped the meaning of that conception of personal responsibility 'which is the foundation of sexual relationships as they are beginning to appear today'. The Puritan influence was transferred to America 'and constituted the leaven which still slowly works on producing the liberal though too minutely detailed divorce laws of many states'. In England, sadly, the spirit of 'blind conservatism' had reasserted itself.[206]

The progressivism of nineteenth-century Nonconformity is particularly apparent in the sphere of women's rights. As Ray Strachey wrote in *The Cause*, the chapel-based antislavery agitations of the 1840s and 1850s were the first in which women's right to an independent political voice had been acknowledged.[207] It was largely, though not exclusively, from the ranks of old dissent – the Quakers and Unitarians especially – that the Langham Place circle formed in the late 1850s; the first feminist pressure-group.[208] At a later date the Salvation Army, whose phenomenal late Victorian growth might serve to put in question current chronologies of secularization, was the first national movement, religious or political, in which women appeared not as auxiliaries but as principals. Ray Strachey, who was closer to these things than we are, argued that the Army, which came into formal existence in 1875, 'exerted a most tremendous influence upon the position of women' and that the 'practical example of sex equality' which it displayed 'did more than millions of arguments to destroy the suspicion and prejudice of the poor'. In 1880s London, as Judith Walkowitz remarks in *City of Dreadful Delight*, the Hallelujah lasses were amongst the most conspicuous epresentatives of emancipated womanhood to brave the streets of the metropolis.[209] They were also, as *Major Barbara* reminds us, certainly amongst the most audible.

British feminism was not as closely linked as its American counterpart to the temperance cause,[210] while the Edwardian franchise agitation drew its followers from many different spheres. But recent research has highlighted the close links between the suffrage movement and the purity crusades of the 1880s and 1890s, where numbers of suffragists served a political novitiate. The tactics of the suffrage movement – militant acts, by-election interventions, extra-parliamentary mobilization – were those brilliantly initiated by Josephine Butler in her campaign for the repeal of the Contagious Diseases Acts.[211] So far as consciousness-raising is concerned, these movements (some historians have been at pains to argue) were more important in challenging male supremacy than the legal and parliamentary campaigns which produced divorce law reform and the Married Women's Property Acts. Josephine Butler's campaign 'destroyed the conspiracy of silence surrounding sex'; the White Slavery agitation served as a dramatic, if extreme, example of the fate of women in a male-defined and male-controlled society.[212] Cumulatively these 'Puritan' campaigns, radical–Nonconformist in the constituencies on which they drew and running in tandem with an increasingly politicized and powerful temperance movement, had the effect of highlighting domestic tyrants, violent drunks, aristocratic libertines; and of picturing women as the symbolic victims of male animality. These themes, it is argued, formed part of the Suffragette unconscious, giving a tremendous moral authority to its claims. They became publicly visible when, as a result of the split between the National Union of Women's Suffrage Societies, with its strong labour movement roots, and the direct-actionists of the Women's Social and Political Union, anxious to court 'those frail hot-house blooms, the Conservative supporters of women's suffrage', the militants transposed the field of battle from politics to sexuality.[213] As Christabel Pankhurst, in the notorious article which claimed that 70 per cent of the male population were the carriers of venereal disease, urged: 'Votes for Women and Chastity for Men'.

The discovery of the 'social question' – the name given to the Condition-of-England question when, in the 1880s, it reemerged at the centre of public debate – also owed a great deal to Nonconformity. In one aspect – the symbolic centrality which it gave to the idea of the 'slum' (a term coined in 1880–81 which spread like wildfire)[214] – it could be seen as a counterpart, in the sphere of public provision, to those rescue movements launched by the Salvation Army which had as their object the reclamation of the lower depths. In another, the fear of race or urban 'degeneration', it had obvious affinities to the purity movements of the time, and the moral panics associated with sexually transmitted disease. In a third, 'bourgeois guilt' or what Beatrice Webb calls 'social compunction', the way for it had been prepared by the hugely popular 'waif' novels of such socially conscious Sunday School prize book writers as Hesba Stretton and Silas K. Hocking. It was a Congregational minister, Andrew Mearns, whose 1883 pamphlet *The Bitter Cry of Outcast London* put housing reform on the agenda of national politics.[215] And it was the Nonconformist Settlement houses, such as Mansfield House in West Ham or the Bermondsey Settlement – much more involved in local politics than their high Anglican or broad-church counterparts – which agitated the social question in the school boards, the poor law guardians, and the borough councils.[216]

It is perhaps indicative of this that the social question was so frequently conceptualized, or perhaps one should say visualized, in biblical or Bunyanesque terms, as it was to be, almost irrespective of politics, right down to 1942, when Sir William Beveridge prefaced his revolutionary proposals for national insurance by invoking the five giants – Want, Disease, Squalor, Ignorance, Idleness – which stood between the citizen and social security.[217] Andrew Mearns, in *The Bitter Cry of Outcast London,* pictures a people living in the Valley of the Shadow of Death. General Booth, in his *In Darkest England* (co-authored with the sensation journalist W.T. Stead), is even more phantasmagoric.[218] The sombrely coloured frontispiece, modelled on those beehive models of *The Pilgrim's Progress* which were so popular with the Victorian illustrators, depicts London as a shipwreck where three million souls are perishing in a storm-tossed sea, 'the unemployed', 'the homeless', and 'drunkards' sinking into 'starvation'. 'Envy', 'Covetousness' and 'Avarice' are the pillars on one side of the picture; 'Uncleanness', 'Adultery' and 'Fornication' the other. Salvation Army officers with arms outstretched – the men in red-coats, the women in bonnets – are trying to bring survivors to the shore, while near at hand are those more immediate palliatives recommended by the best progressive opinion of the day: 'Labour Bureau'; 'Lodging for Single Women'; 'Suburban Villages Twelve Miles from Town'. In the middle distance there is the Promised Land of 'the Farm Colony'; and on the far horizon that great white hope of the time, bathed in a sunset glow, 'the Colony across the Sea'.

For the young Beatrice Potter, a rent collector for the Charity Organisation Society in the neighbourhood of St Katharine's Dock, East London was a vortex, dragging the population down with it, some contriving to keep their heads above water, others giving themselves up to the whirlpool.[219] Margaret McMillan pictures her open-air nursery in Deptford as an oasis of light while its surroundings are a Slough of Despond, 'a black ooze, a deep sinking bed', very deep and steep, 'the soft black yielding mass under the black waters of Poverty. At every step one goes down and down'.[220]

Another extremely potent idiom, in this case drawn directly from the radical-Nonconformist 'purity' crusades of the 1880s, but applied to industrial conditions rather than slum housing, was 'White Slavery'. W.T. Stead reintroduced the term into political rhetoric when mounting his 'Maiden Tribute of Modern Babylon' campaign of 1885. Three years later, when Stead joined hands with Annie Besant, he acted as her co-editor on the *Link* and promoted 'Ironside Clubs' for her Law and Liberty League. In the aftermath of 'Bloody Sunday' white slavery was famously applied to the Bryant and May match girls whom Annie Besant led in their strike – the spark which set fire to the Thames and brought about the huge upheaval of metropolitan labour.[221] In the labour press of the 1890s industrial atrocities, whether in the form of pit explosions, 'sweating', or the malodorous conditions of 'the dangerous trades' were the staple fare of socialist propaganda. The *Labour Leader* devoted a weekly column to them, and alongside the telling local reportage, there were also the more emotive appeals, couched in the melodramatic idiom which Stead had so flamboyantly pioneered in the cause of the child-prostitutes:

The Industrial Shambles

Huddled and blindfold to the shambles driven,
These are the deaths that human cattle die,
Flung headlong to the ghastly jaws that ply
At pain's unending banquet – God in Heaven!
Are not the Devil's tithes most justly given
With blood and bone and fibred flesh weighed out?
Here's Britain's balance righteously made out –
So many thousands risked, some six or seven
Swept daily by the croupier Usury's rake
Into the mounted mound of wasted lives.
This is the tax of tears on widowed wives
And children orphaned – Up ye men and wake,
(A murrin that this mammon's dance survives!)
Some flint of action strike for Freedom's sake! – *J.R.T.*[222]

The British Labour Party was proclaimedly secular in intention. Before 1914 it was limited in aim, restricting its brief to the representation of the legal and economic interests of the trade unionists. It eschewed sectarian religious affiliations and took no part in the campaigns for religious equality, or the disestablishment of the Anglican Church. It placed its emphasis on state intervention rather than self-help, social provision rather than moral reform. Yet the party was founded at the Memorial Hall, Farringdon Road, a monument to the bicentenary of 1662, and in its early years it displayed the strongest possible affinities to its radical-Nonconformist predecessors.[223] The Independent Labour Party was famously chapel-bred, drawing many of its early recruits from the young men's 'mutual improvement societies' and finding its early electoral constituencies in such strongly Nonconformist parts of the country as the West Riding of Yorkshire, Scotland, County Durham and South Wales.[224]

Meetings – indoor or open-air – were conducted with all the fervour, and many of the rituals, of a religious mission, prefaced or punctuated by a choir, 'singing for socialism' and winding up with what Philip Snowden described as 'Come to Jesus' appeals.[225] The Fabian Society, though avowedly 'modern' and composed 'chiefly' of 'the younger people of middle class', was no less wedded to guilt-tripping, arguing that it was only by a grand act of renunciation that the comfortable classes could purge themselves of their unearned wealth.

The socialism of the 1880s and 1890s had very strong affinities to the purity movements of the time. Socialists may not have denounced the music halls as 'temples of Beelzebub', the position they occupied for General Booth,[226] but they were forever taking issue with the 'coarseness' of working-class life. 'Materialism' was one of their great enemies;[227] the corruptions of mass entertainment another; the 'gambling spirit' (epitomized by capitalism) a third. The early socialist movement recruited itself from self-consciously minority elects who derived much of their adrenalin from the belief that they were a people apart. Working-class adherents were apt to pride themselves on being 'clean livers' and on that account gave a heartfelt support not only to temperance (one of Labour's unofficial causes) but also to such New Life crotchets as vegetarianism.[228] Middle-class converts were no less apt to insist on the ways they had renounced worldly advantage and material comfort to wipe the slate clean.

The religious impulse was very strong in Keir Hardie, Labour's best-known public figure. He was closely associated, in the 1890s, with the Labour Church movement, which he supported not only as a means of spreading the socialist word, but also as a way of keeping the infant movement up to the mark. If the ILP was made up 'chiefly of great men and women inspired by a great ideal, it will be irrepressible'; if it fell 'into the hands of drinking, card-playing, worldly-minded folk, then it had better never been born.'[229] Hardie was never happier than when expounding the social gospel in religious terms. He presented himself to the public as a Christ-like figure, and indeed Caroline Benn, in her new biography, suggests that so close was the identification that he may actually have believed himself to be the Messiah.[230] He was also not averse to taking on the mantle of an Old Testament prophet when the occasion demanded it, as during an address to support a railway strike:

> Oh, men and women, in the name of God whom ye profess to believe in . . . Come out from the House of bondage, fight for freedom, fight for manhood, fight for the coming day when in body, soul and spirit you will be free to live your own lives, and give glory to your Creator.[231]

Hardie was a lifelong purity campaigner. Abstinence was his first political cause; he served his political apprenticeship as a full-time temperance worker and even when he transferred his allegiance to the ILP he remained hopeful that the temperance and socialist movements could march together hand-in-hand.[232] He supported the anti-music-hall policy of the London County Council and argued strongly for the municipalization of the drink trade, believing that public houses under municipal ownership could be transformed from drinking dens 'associated with all kinds of demoralizing influences' into healthy places of public resort.[233] In a similar spirit he supported vegetarianism, 'as an attempt to secure a cleaner standard of living'.[234] In parliament, in 1912, Hardie seized on the Queenie Gerard case – a high-society scandal of the time – in an attempt to revive the White Slavery agitation. Invoking the spectre of 350,000 'fallen women', he accused the Home Secretary of making himself the cover for 'rich scoundrels', and pledged that he would not rest until the land had been cleansed of the 'filthy brood'.[235]

Hardie was no less preoccupied with cleanliness in inner-party life. He refused to have anything to do with Robert Blatchford after seeing him in the company of theatricals.[236] When it came to his attention that John Trevor, the respected founder of the Labour Church movement, had married for a second time, he wrote at once to say that this conduct had 'given the movement . . . a blow . . . it will not recover from in a hurry' and asked Trevor to resign. He was similarly severe with Tom Mann when he was found to be attending meetings in the company of a woman other than his wife, forcing him to step down from the ILP secretaryship.[237]

Ramsay MacDonald, the secretary of the Parliamentary Labour Party, was an altogether more secular figure than Keir Hardie, and a more administratively-minded one. But the fellowship of the New Life, of which he was for some years the Secretary, had been his initiation into politics and he retained from it a very strong taste for ethical propaganda.[238] When he fought his first election in 1894, as ILP candidate for Southampton, he tried to establish a branch of the Labour Church, sending his agent the Labour Church Hymn Book ('I have marked those that seem to be the favourites') and urging that in the forthcoming campaign 'the ethical side of the movement' should be kept well to the front, with 'music, singing, exhortative readings and short discourses'.[239]

As Secretary of the Parliamentary Labour Party and later as party leader, MacDonald amplified this rhetoric, infusing it with his readings from the moralists and the poets, charging it with the melancholy of the Highland mists. It enabled him to take the high ground when facing down party enemies or dealing with divisions and splits. A most interesting example – very *à propos* for the present essay – is the 'Plea for Puritanism' which he published in 1912. The unspoken targets of attack were the rebellious spirits – among them Robert Blatchford – who had recently formed a rival organization, the British Socialist Party:

> Puritanism is not popular. It has been associated with hypocrisy and cant, with spiritual gloom and self-righteousness, with eyes turned up to heaven and black mittens. And these things are not popular . . .

But the Labour movement must welcome Puritanism if it is to be any good, or even if it is to last. And the reasons are these amongst others:

> Our young men who join us full of enthusiasm against the present crushing order of society will never be disciplined and hardened for the fight, made wary against its difficulties, and sobered in preparation for its triumphs by the vanity and mental exhilaration of tall and smart talk, of platform bravado, of literary swashbuckling. The man who is to do anything in the Labour and Socialist movement must begin by getting himself in hand. He has to serve an apprenticeship in mental and moral discipline . . .
>
> Then the Puritan spirit protects the movement against rascals of all types. With the Puritan, character must always count. The Puritan can no more ask what has private character to do with public life than he can ask what has theft to do with honesty. The Puritan view is that personality does count, and that sterling qualities count in personality. A man who has been unfaithful to a woman may be a fine mob orator, but he is untrustworthy as a representative of men, and is unworthy of any position of public trust and responsibility.[240]

Reference might be made, finally, to the persistent interplay – so evident in Ramsay MacDonald's own brand of evolutionary socialism, with its Darwinian, nature-derived theodicy – between Puritan soul-striving and more secular and (or scientistic) mysticisms. The overlap between spiritualism and socialism – or in the case of W.T. Stead spiritualism and radical Nonconformity and 'Cromwellianism' – has been well documented.[241] It was interestingly represented on the Labour benches at Westminster by Frank Smith, the long-serving MP for Nuneaton, and for many years Keir Hardie's right-hand man and closest confidant. A part-time evangelist for the Salvation Army in 1879, and later a leading Commissioner – the editor of the newspaper the *War Cry*, leader of the Social Reform wing of the Army and according to some the original author of its social programme – Smith later became a fiery propagandist and resourceful organizer for the ILP. Returning briefly, in 1901, to service in the Salvation Army he finally settled for Socialism and a version of spiritualism which he practised until his death.[242]

Then one could refer to those more modernist mysticisms – such as Nature cures, play therapy or, in *Sons and Lovers*, the early stirrings of the sacramental view of the sexual act – which were such a feature of ethical movements in *fin de siècle* and Edwardian England. Theosophy – the bridge which carried Annie Besant, the erstwhile wife of a mid-Victorian Anglican curate, to presidency (in 1917) of the Indian National Congress[243] – would be worth a particular mention, if only because of its influence, through Rudolf Steiner's books on the 'child-mind', on the 'Progressive' movement in English education, and because it prefigured those many different versions of 'One-Worldism' which were to exert so powerful an imaginative appeal in the wake of the Great War.

Inaugurated, in New York, by Madam Blavatsky, an expatriate and peripatetic Russian visionary, Theosophy claimed to subsume, in its Secret Doctrine, the core teachings of the religions and philosophies of the world. For all its Kabbalism, theosophy presented itself as a futurism, in harmony with the advanced scientific thought of its day. As a revisionist Darwinianism it promised evolution to a higher consciousness and a higher state of being. In its vegetarianism it brought Nature and Culture together and offered a new harmony of body and soul. In its neo-Eugenicist concern with the perfection of the species, it put birth control – the neo-Malthusian cause which Annie Besant had championed in her Secularist days – on a spiritual plane. As she wrote in 1896, explaining why she had abandoned the advocacy of contraception:

> Theosophists should sound the note of self-restraint within marriage, and the restriction of the marital relation to the perpetuation of the race . . . passing from Materialism to Theosophy, I must pass from neo-Malthusianism to what will be called asceticism.[244]

In Edwardian times, Theosophy established a strong following among the Fabians, appealing especially, it seems, to those 'practical mystics', such as health workers, doctors and teachers, who seized on whatever could give cosmic significance to their work.[245] It was a vivid presence among the Simple Lifers of Letchworth Garden City, where the Brotherhood Church of the Rev. Bruce Wallace subscribed to it, and the semi-monastic artistic colony of 'The Cloisters' was dedicated to 'Eternal Reality' and 'The Perfect Inviolable Whole'. It was also, it seems, a presence in the women's movement. Charlotte Despard, 'the famous exponent of Woman Suffrage, and the untiring toiler among the working girls of London', was one of those who embraced it. *The Theosophist*, in 1911, called her 'one of the Saintliest of women-Theosophists',[246] and she herself, in the chapter which she contributed to *The Case for Women's Suffrage* (1907), invoked Isis of Egypt, Pallas Athene of Greece, Juno of Rome, the Virgin Mother, the medieval abbesses who sat on state councils, and great saints such as Catherine of Siena and Teresa of Avila. (By contrast Mrs Pankhurst 'kept strictly to the political points in hand', while Christabel Pankhurst's summary of female civil disabilities was 'brisk'.)[247]

Gandhi, in his remarkable syncretism of Eastern and Western religion, gave global significance and political weight to ideas and undercurrents which might otherwise seem to be the sectarian property of the wilder and more antinomian fringes of Anglo-American progressivism. It was a reading of Ruskin's *Unto This Last* and Edward Carpenter's *Civilisation: Its Cause and Cure* (he called Carpenter 'a great English writer') which converted him to that version of Simple Lifeism, which, in Hind Swaraj, the movement for Indian Home Rule which he launched in South Africa in 1909, became the great argument for rejecting Western Civilization. His student years in London, 'crucial for his intellectual growth', introduced him to the philosophy and practice of vegetarianism (his first publication was an article in an 1892 issue of *The Vegetarian*), and most significantly of all (through a meeting with Madam Blavatsky and Annie Besant of the Theosophical Society) to the world-historical importance of Hindu religion and philosophy. Four years later it was in attempting to produce a Sanskrit translation for some Theosophical friends in South Africa that he first discovered the Bhagavad-Gita – the foundation of his life's work.

Gandhi's passionate advocacy of cleanliness – like the practice of arts and crafts, it was built into his campaign for national regeneration – has also been attributed to his student days in London. It seems legitimate to wonder whether his personal rejection of sexuality may not have owed something to that preference for 'spiritual' union which was such a feature of Theosophy, as of New Life circles of all kinds. In any event, if one wanted to look for twentieth-century inheritors of *fin de siècle* notions of 'purity', the overseas diaspora might turn out to be as rewarding, even inspiring, to inquire into as more indigenous progeny.

Notes

1 Thanks are due to Jane Garnett and Colin Matthew, for their patience with a piece which has had to change colour and shape more times than its subject; to Brian Harrison, for some excellent references; to Jonathan Clark, for advice on American sources; to Christopher Smout for help on Scottish history; and to Jon Cook, Christopher Hill, James Obelkevich and Alison Light.

2 Ernest Gellner, who in *Muslim Society* (Cambridge 1981) devotes a chapter to what he calls the 'generic Puritanism' of Islam, offers an entirely different perspective; in a dense and fascinating argument, the 'Puritans' are the modernizing elites pitting learning, philosophy and rationality – as well as austerity in personal conduct – against the flamboyance and messianism of popular religion.

3 D. Selbourne, 'After the Illusion, a New Covenant', *Independent*, 17 February 1993.

4 A. Sebba, *Laura Ashley: A Life by Design*, London 1990.

5 R. Helmstadter, 'The Nonconformist Conscience', in P. Marsh (ed.), *The Conscience of the Victorian State*, Hassocks 1979, pp. 135–72, argues interestingly that the Nonconformist conscience took to the public stage at precisely the moment when Nonconformity lost its bearings and began its secular decline. D.W. Bebbington, *The Nonconformist Conscience: Chapel and Politics, 1870–1914*, London 1982, is a more descriptive account. There is a rapidly growing literature on the purity movement of the 1880s and 1890s, identifying it, disconcertingly, with both the emancipatory movement of feminism and the repressive one of homophobia. See L. Bland, 'Feminist Vigilantes of Late-Victorian England', in C. Smart (ed.), *Regulating Womanhood: Historical Essays on Marriage, Motherhood and Sexuality*, London 1992; Frank Mort, *Dangerous Sexualities: Medico-Moral Politics in England since 1830*, London 1987. According to OED the first coupling of 'prude' with 'puritan' occurs in a novel by Mrs Braddon. Before the 1880s, 'prude' seems to have been a kind of sexual identity rather than a name given to purity campaigners. Among other things it was a derogatory word for 'spinsters' and 'old maids' though *Habits of Good Society* (London 1858) uses it as a synonym for the 'bluestocking'. Inquiry into earlier phases in what is today called prudery might lead one back to such distinctly un-Puritan figures as Beau Brummel (so fastidious that he would not speak to a girl whom he had once seen eating cabbage) or Lord Chesterfield or even Adam Smith, and those republican ideas of virtue which an influential school of historians likes to call 'civic humanism'.

6 For some revisionist attempts to expel 'Puritan' from the scholarly lexicon, see C.H. George, 'Puritanism as History and Historiography', *Past and Present*, 41, 1968, pp. 77–104; C.H. and K. George, *The Protestant Mind of the English Reformation, 1570–1640*, Princeton

1961; B. Hall, 'Puritanism: the Problem of Definition', *Studies in Church History*, ii, 1965, pp. 283–96; Michael J. Finlayson, *Historians, Puritanism and the English Revolution: The Religious Factor in English Politics before and after the Interregnum*, Toronto 1983.

7 P. Collinson, *The Elizabethan Puritan Movement*, London 1967. In this account 'hot Protestanism' was part of a general forward movement which came to a well-organized climax at the Hampton Court Conference of 1604. More recently, when there has been a determined attempt to expel the word 'Puritan' from the historian's lexicon, and to bypass it in the Civil War, 'hot Protestantism', like everything else in seventeenth-century studies, seems to be looking more and more conservative. Collinson, *The Religion of Protestants: The Church in English Society, 1590–1625*, Oxford 1985.

8 From the *Large Petition of the Levellers*, a Thomason tract reprinted in A.S.P. Woodhouse, *Puritanism and Liberty: Being the Army Debates (1647–9)*, London 1951.

9 *The Clarke Papers*, ed. C.H. Firth, Camden Soc. (1891), i, pp. lxxiii–lxxiv.

10 D. Neal, *The History of the Puritans*, 5 vols, London 1822, II, p. 116.

11 *Images of English Puritanism*, ed. L.A. Sasek, Baton Rouge, LA 1989.

12 J.R. Green, *A Short History of the English People*, 2 vols, London 1960, II, pp. 589–94, 434.

13 C. Hill, *The Experience of Defeat: Milton and Some Contemporaries*, London 1984; N.H. Keeble, *The Literary Culture of Nonconformity in Later Seventeenth-Century England*, Leicester 1987. For a more Augustan interpretation, D. Davie, *A Gathered Church, the Literature of the English Dissenting Interest*, London 1978.

14 David Hume, 'Of Superstition and Enthusiasm', *Essays, Moral, Political and Literary*, London 1875, pp. 114–20.

15 Adam Smith, *The Wealth of Nations*, London 1895 ed., pp. 619–20. For Smith's attack on the newer (unnamed) fanatic sects, ibid., pp. 625–7.

16 J.D. Walsh, 'Origins of the Evangelical Revival', in G.V. Bennett and J.D. Walsh (ed.), *Essays in Modern Church History*, London 1966, p. 155.

17 Bishop Lavington, *The Enthusiasm of Methodists and Papists Compared*, London 1749; Robert Southey, *The Life of Wesley*, 2 vols, London 1925, II, p. 293, repeats the old canard.

18 I. Watt, *The Rise of the Novel: Studies in Defoe, Richardson and Fielding*, Harmondsworth 1981; M. Butler, *Jane Austen and the War of Ideas*, Oxford 1987, pp. 50, 64, 70, 72, 74.

19. John Toland, *The Life of John Milton*, London 1741.

20 Samuel Johnson, *Lives of the Poets*, 2 vols, Everyman ed. 1925, I, pp. 89 and 93.

21 L. Buell, *New England Literary Culture from Revolution through Renaissance*, Cambridge 1986.

22 G. Wills, *Inventing America: Jefferson's Declaration of Independence*, London 1980.

23 C. Robbins, *The Eighteenth-Century Commonwealthman*, Cambridge, MA 1959; B. Hill, *The Republican Virago*, Oxford 1992.

24 Neal, *History of the Puritans*, II, pp. xi–xiii, for an egregious example.

25 ibid, V, p. 279. This is taken from an afterword by Neal's editor. The Toleration Act (1690), wrote the first historians of eighteenth-century dissent, 'may be considered the Magna Carta of the dissenters': David Bogue and James Bennett, *History of Dissenters from the Revolution in 1688 to the Year 1808*, 4 vols, London 1808–12, p. 122. For eighteenth-century dissent's talismanic use of Locke, Roger Thomas, 'Philip Doddridge and Liberalism in Religion' in *Philip Doddridge: His Contribution to English Religion*, ed. G.F. Nuttall, London 1951, pp. 125–9.

26 George Crabbe, *Tales*, London 1812.

27 Thomas Fuller, *The Church History of Britain*, ed. J.S. Brewer, Oxford 1845, pp. 86–7, quoted in C.H. George, 'Puritanism as History and Historiography', *Past and Present*, 41, 1968, p. 93.

28 C.H. Firth, *Essays, Historical and Literary*, London 1932, p. 119.

29 Edward Hyde, Earl of Clarendon, *The History of the Rebellion and Civil War in England*, 6 vols, Oxford 1888, IV, p. 305.

30 David Hume, *The History of England*, 16 vols, London 1824 ed., III.

31 W. Smyth, *Lectures on Modern History*, 2 vols, 1840; London 1854 ed., I, p. 451; S. Maunder, *The Treasury of History*, London 1839, p. 388.

32 For a brief but illuminating discussion, see V. Newey, 'The Disinherited Pilgrim: *Jude the Obscure* and *The Pilgrim's Progress*', *Durham University Journal*, new series, xlix (i), December 1987.

33 H.R. Trevor-Roper, 'The Continuity of the English Revolution', *Transactions of the Royal Historical Society*, 6th series, i, 1991, pp. 121–35.

34 I owe the Guizot reference to Christopher Hill.

35 V. Chancellor, *History for Their Masters: Opinion in the English History Textbook, 1800–1914*, Bath 1970, p. 52.

36 A Board of Education guide to teaching history in Secondary Schools (1908) runs as follows:

> It will be desirable to pass over with the very briefest notice those periods, the history of which is merely a record of bad government, as e.g. the reign of Edward II, or those which are occupied with complicated and often squalid political intrigues, which interesting and instructive as they may be to mature historical students, offer little that is useful to younger pupils. . . For this reason it will often be desirable to pass over almost without mention much of the internal history of the eighteenth century (e.g. the struggles between the different sections of the Whig Party, or the whole of the Wilkes episode), much of the political history of Charles II's reign, the internal history of the Lancastrian period, the civil war of Stephen's reign . . . in order to secure more time for a fuller treatment of events such as the Crusades, the Civil War, the reign of Elizabeth, the great wars for Colonial supremacy.

This is quoted in R. Samuel, 'Continuous National History', in R. Samuel (ed.), *Patriotism: The Making and Unmaking of British National Identity*, 3 vols, London 1989, I, p. 13.

37 H.A. Morrah, *The Oxford Union, 1823–1923*, London 1923, p. 10. I am grateful to Brian Harrison for this reference.

38 *Oxford Chronicle*, 14 February 1852.

39 Hackney Reference Library, *St Thomas's Institute Magazine*, December 1876; for some other examples at this time, see also *Warrington Guardian*, 24 February 1877; ibid., 14 March 1877.

40 V. Newey, 'Wordsworth, Bunyan and the Puritan Mind', *English Literary History*, 41, 1974, pp. 212–32.

41 Lord Macaulay, *Lays of Ancient Rome*, London 1892 ed., pp. 95–8.

42 *The Poetical Works of Mrs Felicia Hemans*, London n.d.

43 Lord Macaulay, 'John Bunyan' (1831), in *Critical and Historical Essays*, 2 vols, Everyman ed., London 1907, II, p. 410.

44 L. Colley, *Britons: Forging the Nation, 1707–1837*, London 1992, pp. 28–9.

45 N.H. Keeble, 'Bunyan and his Reputation', in N.H. Keeble (ed.), *Bunyan Tercentenary Essays*, Oxford 1988, pp. 243–51.

46 David Hume, 'Of the Standard of Taste', in R. Sharrock (ed.), *The Pilgrim's Progress: A Casebook*, London 1976, p. 50.

47 *The Life of Joseph Arch by Himself*, London 1898, pp. 252–3.

48 Robert Tressell, *The Ragged Trousered Philanthropists*, London 1965, p. 584.

49 P. Fussell, *The Great War and Modern Memory*, Oxford 1977, pp. 137–44, 152, 168–9.

50 E. Halévy, *History of the English People in the Nineteenth Century*, 6 vols, London 1961, I, p. 465.

51 *Life of Thomas M'Crie, D.D. by his Son, the Rev Thomas M'Crie*, Edinburgh 1840, pp. 19, 276–7, 417.

52 T. M'Crie, *Vindication of the Convenanters in a Review of The Tales of My Landlord*, Edinburgh 1845.

53 'Literary Sketches: John Knox' in the *Chartist Circular*, 80, 1841, p. 338. I am grateful to my student Alan Weaver for this reference.

54 G.O. Trevelyan, *The Life and Letters of Lord Macaulay*, Oxford 1978 ed., p. 109.

55 J.G. Nelson, *The Sublime Puritan: Milton and the Victorians*, Madison, WI 1963, p. 82.

56 John Milton, *A Treatise on Christian Doctrine*, trans Charles R. Sumner, London 1825.

57 Macaulay, 'Milton', *Critical and Historical Essays*, pp. 150–94, at p. 185.

58 R.J. Morris, 'Samuel Smiles and the Genesis of *Self-Help*: The Retreat to a Petit Bourgeois Utopia', *Historical Journal*, 24, 1981, pp. 89–109, at p. 94.

59 David Masson, *The Life of John Milton*, 6 vols, London 1859–80, I, p. xiii.

60 ibid., III. Masson, whom George David, *The Democratic Intellect: Scotland and Her Universities in the Nineteenth Century*, Edinburgh 1961, characterizes as 'a representative Scot if ever there was one', was an Aberdonian-born Edinburgh-educated 'generalist' and by English standards a polymath. As well as being a prince of editors, and a pioneering researcher, he was also an innovative teacher of English, first as professor of

literature at University College, London, then as professor of literature and rhetoric at Edinburgh.

61 David Masson, *Memories of London in the 'forties, Arranged and Annotated by F. Masson*, Edinburgh 1908; Edinburgh Ladies Educational Circle, *Report*, Edinburgh 1869. For her mother's enrolment at Bedford College, Flora Masson, *Victorians All*, London 1931.

62 Masson's conclusion to his *Milton*, vol. VI, pp. 839–40.

63 Thomas Carlyle, *Oliver Cromwell's Letters and Speeches*, London 1895, III, pp. 142, 186, 307; see also IV, pp. 15–77.

64 ibid., I, p. 78.

65 ibid., I, pp. 85f.

66 R. Strong, *And When Did You Last See Your Father? The Victorian Painters and British History*, London 1978, pp. 146–51.

67 He still speaks, in the book itself, of a 'Cromwelliad', Carlyle, *Cromwell* I, p. 5.

68 J.A. Froude, *Thomas Carlyle: A History of His Life in London, 1834–1881*, 2 vols, London 1897, I, pp. 164–5.

69 Carlyle, Cromwell, II, p. 74.

70 T.H. Green, 'The English Commonwealth', in *The Works of Thomas Hill Green*, ed. R.I. Nettleship, 3 vols, London 1888, III, p. 276.

71 *Leeds Mercury*, 12 November 1859; *Wigan Observer*, 11 January 1861.

72 Froude, *Thomas Carlyle*, I, pp. 194–5.

73 Carlyle, *Cromwell*, IV, p. 18.

74 ibid., I, p. 1.

75 ibid., II, p. 245.

76 ibid., II, p. 169.

75 ibid., III, p. 73.

76 ibid., I, p. 120

77 ibid., IV, p. 15.

78 ibid., IV, p. 16.

79 ibid., II, p. 53.

80 ibid., I, p. 8.

81 ibid., II, p. 53.

82 ibid., I, p. 8.

83 PRO, HO 45/3136: Henry Vincent, lecture at Oldham Town Hall, 11 May 1850, reported by a police spy.

84 G. Dawson, 'The Genius and the Works of Thomas Carlyle', reprinted in *Biographical Lectures*, London 1886, pp. 426–7.

85 Charles Bradlaugh, *Cromwell and Washington: A Contrast*, London 1877.

86 Strong, *And When Did You Last See your Father?*, p. 151. The picture, by the genre artist Charles West Cope, is a very Victorian one: the 'Fathers' are a family group, with children and a pet spaniel to the fore, and the 'ship' is a rowing boat that looks as though it would be lucky to get as far as Margate.

87 B. Read, *Victorian Sculpture*, London 1983, pp. 237–8.

88 ibid., pp. 112–13.

89 Dorothea Beale, *Great Englishmen, Short Lives*, London 1881.

90 George Dawson was an advanced Birmingham radical, son of a London schoolmaster, Baptist and later Independent minister.

91 See *The Oxford University Extension Gazette*, 8 August 1890, for an example.

92 W. Stubbs, *Two Lectures on the Present State and Prospects of Historical Study*, Oxford 1876.

93 D. Masson, *British Novelists and Their Style*, London 1859, p. 245.

94 Cf. V. Cunningham, *Everywhere Spoken Against: Dissent in the Victorian Novel*, Oxford 1975, pp. 203–5, 228–30.

95 P. Hobsbawm, *A Reader's Guide to Charles Dickens*, London 1981, pp. 288–91.

96 This is the edition I have used for comparison, since it is aimed at the same age group as Dickens's book.

97 T. Keightley, *An Elementary History of England*, London 1841, p. 199.

98 ibid., p. 194.

99 ibid., pp. 202–3

100 ibid., p. 262

101 Charles Dickens, *A Child's History of England*, 3 vols, London 1852–4, III, p. 171.

102 ibid., p. 223.

103 ibid., p. 249–50.
104 ibid., pp. 254–93.
105 ibid., pp. 265–66
106 O. Anderson, 'The Growth of Christian Militarism in Mid-Victorian Britain', *English Historical Review*, 86, 1971, pp. 46–72.
107 The soubriquet is said to have been applied to the celebrated W.T.. Stead after he went down in the *Titanic*.
108 See the discussion in Sir Charles Firth, *Cromwell's Army*, London 1902, pp. 331–5.
109 J.P.D. Dunbabin, 'Oliver Cromwell's Popular Image in Nineteenth-Century England', in J.S.. Bromley and F.H. Kossman (ed.), *Britain and the Netherlands* v, The Hague, pp. 141–63, at pp. 160–1 (reference unlocated).
110 *Oxford Chronicle*, 24 February 1855.
111 J. Marshman, 'Brief Sketch of the Career of the late Major-General Sir Henry Havelock, K.C.B.', *Baptist Magazine*, April 1858, p. 209.
112 J. Vincent, *The Formation of the Liberal Party, 1857–1868*, London 1966, p. xliii.
113 Janet Howarth, 'The Liberal Revival in Northamptonshire', *Historical Journal*, xii, 1969, pp. 78–118, at pp. 99–100.
114 P.T. Phillips, *The Sectarian Spirit*, Toronto 1982, pp. 128–30; *The Beehive*, 14 November 1868, p. 4. For Solly's editorship, see H. Solly, *These Eighty Years*, London 1893.
115 R.T. Shannon, *Gladstone and the Bulgarian Agitation, 1876*, 2nd ed., Hassocks 1975, p. 137.
116 Green, *Short History*, I, p. 412.
117 J.S.A. Adamson, 'Eminent Victorians: S.R. Gardiner and the Liberal as Hero', *Historical Journal*, xxxiii, 1990, p. 641.
118 S.R. Gardiner, *History of the Great Civil War 1642–1649*, 4 vols, London 1893, I, p. 9.
119 Firth, *Essays*, p. 385.
120 D.E. Smith, *John Bunyan in America*, Bloomington 1966, p. 100.
121 See Nigel Scotland, *Methodism and the Revolt of the Field*, Gloucester 1981, p. 37.
122 *Joseph Arch: The Story of His Life Told by Himself*, London 1898, pp. x–xii, 2–4, 10–12, 15–19.
123 M.K. Ashby, *Joseph Ashby of Tysoe, 1859–1919*, Cambridge 1961.
124 P. Horne, *Joseph Arch: The Farm Workers' Leader*, Kineton 1971, pp. 127–8; F. Thompson, *Lark Rise to Candleford*, 1939; Harmondsworth 1987, pp. 65–6, 215.
125 H. Evans, *Radical Fights over Forty Years*, London 1913, p. 17.
126 L. Manning, *A Life for Education*, London 1970, p. 20.
127 *C.H. Spurgeon's Autobiography: Compiled from His Diary, Letters, and Records, by His Wife [S. Spurgeon), and His Private Secretary*, 4 vols, London 1897–1900, III, pp. 189–90.
128 J. Kent, 'Hugh Price Hughes and the Nonconformist Conscience', in G.V. Bennet and J.D. Walsh, (ed.), *Essays in Modern Church History*, London 1966, pp. 181ff; John Gay, *The Geography of Religion in England*, London 1971, pp. 112–13, 123–5.
129 A.D. Gilbert, *Religion and Society in Industrial England: Church, Chapel and Social Change, 1740–1914*, London 1976.
130 E. Isichei, *Victorian Quakers*, Oxford 1970, p. 45.
131 A. Peckover, *Life of Joseph Sturge*, London 1890, p. 15.
132 E. Hodder, *The Life of Samuel Morley*, London 1887, pp. 177–8.
133 J. Marlowe, *The Puritan Tradition in English Life*, London 1956, p. 123.
134 J. Cox, *The English Churches in a Secular Society: Lambeth, 1870–1930*, New York 1982, p. 183.
135 Charles Booth, *Life and Labour of the People in London*, 17 vols, London 1902, final volume, 'Notes on Social Influences and Conclusion', pp. 48–9. For a more affirmative account of the PSAs, H. McLeod, *Class and Religion in the Late Victorian City*, London 1974, pp. 65–9 and K.S. Inglis, *Churches and the Working Classes in Victorian England*, London 1963, pp. 79–85.
136 Gilbert, *Religion and Society in Industrial England*, pp. 170–1.
137 Helmstadter, 'The Nonconformist Conscience', p. 171.
138 See Cox, *English Churches in a Secular Society*.
139 For F.B. Meyer, the Lambeth Baptist, the construction of LCC tram lines over Westminster Bridge, against the objections of the House of Lords, was a local manifestation of a worldwide, 'divinely inspired' advance for democracy. 'The Revolution in Russia', he told the Baptist Union, 'is symbolic of a world-wide movement which is destined to have a

profound effect on the lives of obscure dwellers in our slums. It is not without significance that Westminster Bridge is being seamed with tram lines for working girls.' Quoted by Cox, *English Churches in a Secular Society*, pp. 174–5.

140 For the phenomenal growth of public libraries in London during the years 1893–1920, T. Kelly, *History of Public Libraries in Great Britain, 1845–1965*, London 1973.

141 For municipal Puritanism in London, Penelope Summerfield, 'The Effingham Arms and the Empire: Deliberate Selection in the Evolution of Music Hall in London', in S. and E. Yeo (ed.), *Popular Culture and Class Conflict, 1590–1914*, Hassocks 1981, pp. 216–21; Cox, *English Churches in a Secular Society*, pp. 153–63; Chris Waters, *British Socialists and the Politics of Popular Culture, 1884–1914*, Manchester 1990, pp. 139—52; S. Pennybacker, 'It Was Not What She Said, but the Way She Said It: The London County Council and the Music Halls', in P. Bailey (ed.) *Music Hall: The Business of Pleasure*, London 1986; I. Britain, *Fabianism and Culture: A Study in British Socialism and the Arts, 1884–1918*, Cambridge 1982, pp. 139–60.

142 W.T. Stead, *The London County Council Election, 1892*, London 1892, pp. 49, 52, 63.

143 Arthur Page Grubb, *The Life Story of the Rt Hon. John Burns*, London 1908, p. 272.

144 W. Kent, *John Burns: Labour's Lost Leader*, London 1950, pp. 50–3.

145 Grubb, *Life Story of John Burns*, p. 28.

146 ibid., p. 276.

147 Cf. John Burns, *Brains Better than Bets or Beer*, Clarion pamphlet no. 36, London 1902, p. 12, where he regrets that among the poor 'The ancient Puritan reserve is being abandoned' through 'lack of a decent home life', 'town-bred conditions' and a 'cheap-and-nasty Press'.

148 Chris Waters, 'Progressives, Puritans and the Cultural Politics of the Council, 1889–1914', in A. Saint (ed.), *Politics and the People of London: The London County Council, 1889–1965*, London 1989, p. 67.

149 Grubb, *Life Story of John Burns*, pp. 271–2.

150 A. Milner, *Arnold Toynbee: A Reminiscence*, London 1901.

151 D. Wormell, *Sir John Seeley and the Uses of History*, Cambridge 1980.

152 M. Richter, *The Politics of Conscience: T.H. Green and His Age*, London 1964, is a splendid book which age does not wither. C. Jenks, 'T.H. Green, the Oxford Philosophy of Duty and the English Middle Class'. *British Journal of Sociology*, 28, 1977, pp. 481–97, interestingly attempts to subsume Green's supposed neo-Hegelianism in a more diffuse 'philosophy of duty'. Green was an active Liberal, on Oxford City Council, and a strong temperance advocate. He was also, from his Rugby schooldays onwards, a passionate Cromwellian. Cf. his 'Four Lectures on the English Revolution' in Nettleship (ed.), *Works of Thomas Hill Green*, III, pp. 276, 364.

153 For autobiographical accounts, F.H. Spencer, *An Inspector's Testament*, London 1938, and Jessie Chambers, *D.H. Lawrence: A Personal Record*, Cambridge 1981, pp. 73ff. Clara E. Grant, *From 'Me' to 'We' (Forty Years on Bow Common)* (privately printed 1940), pp. 1–10, is an appealing memoir by one of the first generation of teacher-idealists.

154 A. Mansbridge, *The Kingdom of the Mind: Essays and Addresses, 1903–7*, London 1944; *The Trodden Road, Experience, Inspiration and Belief*, London 1940.

155 J. Harris, *Unemployment and Politics: A Study in English Social Policy, 1886–1914*, Oxford 1972, pp. 352–3, quoting the Fabian idealist and activist, later killed on the Western Front, Ben Keeling.

156 M. Green, *Dreams of Adventure, Deeds of Empire*, London 1980, pp. 75–83.

157 D. Davie, 'A Puritan's Empire: The Case of Kipling', in Harold Bloom (ed.), *Rudyard Kipling: Modern Critical Views*, New York 1987, pp. 45–56.

158 K.O. Morgan, *Keir Hardie*, London 1975, p. 40.

159 G.W.E. Russell (ed.), *Sir Wilfred Lawson: A Memoir*, London 1909, p. 266.

160 Quoted in M. Pollard, 'A Plea for Mysticism', *Theosophist*, November 1911, p. 226.

161 Sylvia Pankhurst, *The Suffragette Movement*, London 1977, pp. 127–8; S. Yeo, 'A New Life: The Religion of Socialism in Britain, 1883–1896', *History Workshop Journal*, 4, Autumn 1977, pp. 5–56.

162 *Our Corner*, xi, February 1888, p. 119.

163 Annie Besant, *An Autobiography*, London 1908, p. 304.

164 C. Steedman, *Childhood, Culture and Class in Britain: Margaret McMillan, 1860–1931*, London 1990, p. 200.

165 A. Linklater, *An Unhusbanded Woman: Charlotte Despard; Suffragette, Socialist and Sinn Feiner*, London 1980, p. 62.

166 Richter, *Politics of Conscience*, p. 256.

167 There are good accounts of this in W. Sylvester Smith, *The London Heretics, 1870–1914*, London 1967, pp. 132–41; W. Wolfe, *From Radicalism to Socialism: Men and Ideas in the Formation of Fabian Socialist Doctrines, 1881–1889*, New Haven 1975, pp. 153–63, 239–45; Britain, *Fabianism and Culture*, pp. 27–41.

168 Fabian Society, *Lecture List*, 1891, p. 8.

169 See Fabian Tract no. 1, *Why Are the Many Poor?*, London 1884; Tract no. 30, *The 'Unearned Increment'*, London 1892.

170 Tract no. 79, London 1897.

171 R. Blatchford, *Merrie England*, London 1894, pp. 15, 46.

172 ibid., p. 174. For other passages carrying this message, see pp. 41–3, 87–91 and chapter xxiii, 'Luxury', pp. 172ff.

173 'The Advantages of Simpler Living', by a corresponding student, *Young Oxford*, i, February 1900, p. 20. *Young Oxford* was the journal of the Ruskin Hall movement.

174 'Elementary Sociology', ibid., pp. 9f.

175 *The Hard Way Up: The Autobiography of Hannah Mitchell, Suffragette and Rebel*, London 1977, p. 88. Hannah's disillusion with her husband, and her discovery that 'these Socialist young men expected Sunday dinners and huge teas with home-made cakes, potted meats and pies, exactly like their reactionary fellows', is recorded ibid., pp. 96–7.

176 For Virginia Woolf, see P. Rose, *Virginia Woolf: Woman of Letters*, London 1986, pp. 81–9. One way of interpreting and contextualizing those celebrated literary and political unions (the marriage of Havelock Ellis and Edith Less is another well-known example of the period) is to see them as extreme cases of a limitation of fertility which had become general among sections of the middle class before the advent of modern methods of birth control. On this, see A. McLaren, *Birth Control in Nineteenth Century Britain*, London 1978; J.A. Banks, *Prosperity and Parenthood: A Study of Family Planning Among the Victorian Middle Class*, London 1954.

177 Olive Schreiner to Havelock Ellis in D.L. Hobman, *Oliver Schreiner: Her Friends and Times*, London 1955, p. 73.

178 V. Gardner, Introduction, in V. Gardner and S. Rutherford (ed.), *The New Woman and Her Sisters: Feminism and Theatre, 1850–1914*, London 1992, pp. 1–17, for a striking overview; P. Boumelha, *Thomas Hardy and Women: Sexual Ideology and Narrative Form*, Brighton 1982, pp. 135–54 for the ambiguously named Sue Bridehead.

179 Boumelha, *Thomas Hardy and Women*, pp. 135–36, quoting 'To Millicent Garrett Fawcett', 14 April 1892, in Thomas Hardy, *Collected Letters*, ed. R.L. Purdy and M. Millgate, Oxford 1978.

180 Olive Schreiner, *The Story of an African Farm*, Harmondsworth 1980, pt II, ch. iv. S.K. Kent, *Sex and Suffrage in Britain, 1860–1914*, Princeton 1987, p. 84, quoting from M. Cairol's *Daughters of Danaus*.

181 Samuel Cronwright Schreiner, *The Life of Olive Schreiner*, London 1924, pp. 181, 265, 289–90.

182 Hobman, *Olive Schreiner*, pp. 5–6.

183 Oliver Schreiner, *Women and Labour*, London 1923

184 Olive Schreiner, *Story of an African Farm*, pt II, ch. iv.

185 For the introduction of Swedish Drill into the Board Schools, S. Fletcher, *Women First: The Female Tradition in English Physical Education, 1880–1890*, London 1984, pp. 17–24.

186 A. Davin, 'Imperialism and Motherhood', *History Workshop Journal*, 5, Spring 1978, pp. 9–65.

187 Steedman, *Childhood, Culture and Class*, pp. 54–7; B.B. Gilbert, *The Evolution of National Insurance in Britain: The Origins of the Welfare State*, London 1966, pp. 117–58.

188 J. Weeks, *Sex, Politics and Society: The Regulation of Sexuality since 1800*, London 1981; F. Mort, *Dangerous Sexualities: Medico-Moral Politics in England since 1830*, London 1987; David Armstrong, *Political Anatomy of the Body*, Cambridge 1983.

189 Benjamin Richardson, 'Address on Health', *Transactions of the National Association for the Promotion of Social Science* (1875).

190 Sara A. Burstall, *Retrospect and Prospect: Sixty Years of Women's Education*, London 1933.

191 K.E. McCrone, *Sport and the Physical Education of Women*, London 1988, pp. 65–9.

192 J. Marsh, *Back to the Land: The Pastoral Impulse in Victorian England from 1880 to 1914*, London 1982, p. 193.

193 P. Beilharz, *Labour's Utopias: Bolshevism, Fabianism, Social Democracy*, London 1992, p. 54. For Margaret McMillan's belief in water as the great awakener of the child's body, and swimming as the answer to poor breathing, Steedman, *Childhood, Culture and Class*, pp. 198–9.

194 The phrase is Ralph Neville's, presiding over the 1901 Garden City Conference at Bourneville. Michael Day, 'The Contribution of Sir Raymond Unwin and Barry Parker', in Anthony Sutcliffe (ed.), *British Town Planning: The Formative Years*, Leicester 1981, p.173.

195 R. Beevers, *The Garden City Utopia: A Critical Biography of Ebenezer Howard*, London 1988, pp. 121–2.

196 Steedman, *Childhood, Culture and Class*, pp. 84–5.

197 For Bloomerism, A. Ribeiro, *Dress and Morality*, London 1986, pp. 132–4, 139, 143–5.

198 See R. Strachey, *The Cause*, London 1978, pp. 386–9, for the contribution of dress reform to feminism, and D. Rubinstein, *Before the Suffragettes: Women's Emancipation in the 1890s*, Brighton 1986, pp. 216–19. See *The Rational Dress Gazette*, 1888–89, for the progress of the movement.

199 Marsh, *Back to the Land*, pp. 210–11.

200 M. Rosenthal, *The Character Factory: Baden-Powell and the Origins of the Boy Scout Movement*, London 1986, p. 186.

201 E. Chesser, 'Health and Clothing', *Young Woman*, xvii, 1908–9, p. 165. See also 'Dress and the Real versus the Ideal', ibid., pp. 408–10.

202 H.S. Salt, *Seventy Years among Savages*, London 1921; S. Winsten, *Salt and His Circle*, London 1951, for the 1890s campaigns of the Humanitarian League who were pioneer defenders of animal rights.

203 H.G. Wells, *Ann Veronica*, London 1910.

204 Marsh, *Back to the Land*, p. 233.

205 M.H. Baillie Scott, *Houses and Gardens*, London 1906, p. 21.

206 Havelock Ellis, *Sex in Relation to Society*, London 1937, p. 353.

207 Strachey, *The Cause*, pp. 43–4; Isichei, *Victorian Quakers*, pp. 252–5, for Quaker support.

208 S. Alexander, 'Why Feminism? The Women of Langham Place', in *Becoming a Woman, and Other Essays in 19th and 20th Century Feminist History*, London 1994.

209 Strachey, *The Cause*, pp. 212–16; J.R. Walkowitz, *City of Dreadful Delight: Narratives of Sexual Danger in Late-Victorian London*, London 1992, pp. 76–9.

210 For the connections between feminism and prohibitionism in the United States, A.S. Kraditor, *The Ideas of the Woman Suffrage Movement, 1890–1920*, New York 1981, pp. 57–62, 72–3.

211 J.R. Walkowitz, *Prostitution and Victorian Society: Women, Class and the State*, Cambridge 1980.

212 S.K. Kent, *Sex and Suffrage in Britain, 1860–1914*, Princeton 1987.

213 Pankhurst, *The Suffragette Movement*, pp. 522–3, quoted in L. Tickner, *The Spectacle of Women: Imagery of the Suffrage Campaign*, London 1987, p. 224.

214 See *OED*. The term 'black slum' is an earlier one. *OED* attributes 'slumming' to 1884, and 'slumdon' to 1882.

215 Mearns had been appointed secretary to the London Congregational Union in 1876. *The Bitter City* was actually written by W.C. Preston, a Congregational minister who had held a pastorate at Wigan during the Cotton Famine and had been active there in relief work. He also had experience as a journalist. Mearns, assisted by the Rev. James Munro, did the field work on which the pamphlet was based. S. Mayor, *The Churches and the Labour Movement*, London 1967, p. 56. It was W.T. Stead, the editor of the *Pall Mall Gazette*, who turned *The Bitter City* into a sensation; he did so by deliberately linking its revelations about housing conditions with dark suggestions of incest.

216 For the Browning Settlement, Lambeth, which included prayers for Progessive victories in LCC elections in its services, Cox, *English Churches in a Secular Society*, p. 171, and for Scott Lidgett's political activism at the Bermondsey Settlement, Fenner Brockway, *Bermondsey Story: The Life of Alfred Salter*, London 1949, pp. 13, 17, 23, 39, 26–7.

217 *Social Insurance and Allied Services: Report by Sir William Beveridge*, London 1942, p. 6.

218 W. Booth, *In Darkest England and the Way Out*, London 1890.

219 'Alas for the pitifulness of this ever-recurring drama of low life – this long chain of unknowing iniquity, children linked on to parents, friends to friends, ah, and lovers to lovers – bearing down to that bottomless pit of decaying life', Beatrice Potter, 'The Docks', in C. Booth, *Life and Labour of the People in London*, I, p. 29.

220 Steedman, *Childhood, Culture and Class*, p. 115.

221 A.H. Nethercot, *The First Five Lives of Annie Besant*, London 1961, pp. 263–75; Besant, *Autobiography*, pp. 329–38; Walkowitz, *Dreadful Delight*, pp. 76–9.

222 *Labour Leader*, 2 June 1894, p. 7 (and also 'The Industrial Shambles' column in the *Labour Leader* issues of 5, 12 and 19 May 1894). See R.H. Sherard, *The White Slaves of England*, London 1897.

223 For some dramatic encounters between Labour and Nonconformity in the earliest days of the ILP and the Labour Church movement, see *Labour Prophet*, November 1892 (J. Keir Hardie addressing, and then being shouted down at the Horton Lane Chapel, Bradford); D. Howell, *British Workers and the Independent Labour Party, 1888–1906*, Manchester 1983, p. 182, for the stormy divisions in the Bradford Nonconformist Association and the Bradford Temperance Confederation when Ben Tillett stood as Independent Labour candidate in the election of 1892.

224 Laycock's Temperance Hotel was the original nursery of Bradford socialism. Fenner Brockway, *Socialism over Sixty Years: The Life of Jowett of Bradford, 1864–1944*, London 1946, p. 30.

225 P. Snowden, *An Autobiography*, 2 vols, London 1934, I, p. 82.

226 H. Begbie, *The Life of William Booth, the Founder of the Salvation Army*, I, London 1920, p. 451.

227 Opening the William Morris Labour Church at Leek, Staffs, Dr Russell Wallace praised 'a great man [who] . . . strove with all high might to convince this materialistic age, whose only real God is Mammon, that there was a better way than that which they were following'. *Labour Leader*, 9 January 1897, p. 3, col. 4.

228 Tom Mann, finding his feet as a young engineer in 1880s London, was one of the many who came under the spell of food reform: 'When I came to recognise limitations to the temperance movement, I extended my activities to embrace food reform . . . That which weakened my ardour in this direction was the recognition that however widely food reform might be diffused, it would never prove a cure for the economic evils I deplored'. Tom Mann, *Memoirs*, London 1923, pp. 54–5.

229 Quoted in *Labour Prophet*, March 1895, p. 36.

230 C. Benn, *Keir Hardie*, London 1992, p. 18

231 ibid., p. 259.

232 Keir Hardie, 'The Temperance Question', *Labour Leader*, 17 April 1897.

233 Waters, 'Progressives, Puritans and Cultural Politics', p. 65.

234 Keir Hardie, 'Towards Municipal Socialism', *Co-operative Wholesale Society Annual for 1901*, p. 304.

235 *The Queenie Gerard Case: A Public Scandal. White Slavery in a Piccadilly Flat. An Exposure*, by Keir Hardie MP is the title of a penny pamphlet issued by the National Labour Press. For an account of Hardie's conduct in parliament over the case, Benn, *Keir Hardie*, pp. 305–6.

236 ibid., p. 84.

237 ibid., pp. 143–4.

238 MacDonald also lived at 'Fellowship House', the 'Utopia' which the Fellowship set up at 29 Doughty Street, Bloomsbury, in 1891.

239 J. Cox (ed.), *A Singular Marriage: A Labour Love Story in Letters and Diaries*, London 1988, p. 20.

240 'A Plea for Puritanism', *Socialist Review*, v, no. 48, February 1912.

241 L. Barrow, *Independent Spirits: Spiritualism and English Plebeians, 1859–1910*, London 1986.

242 K.S. Inglis, *Churches and the Working Classes in Victorian England*, London 1963, pp. 201ff, 298ff; E.I. Champness, *Frank Smith, M.P. Pioneer and Modern Mystic*, London 1943.

243 For the later stages of Annie Besant's life, A.H. Nethercot, *The Last Four Lives of Annie Besant*, London 1963; and the very good recent monograph, R. Dinnage, *Annie Besant*, Harmondsworth 1986.

244 Annie Besant, 'Theosophy and the Law of Population' (1896), repr. in S. Chandrasekhar (ed.), *'A Dirty, Filthy Book': The Writings of Charles Knowlton and Annie*

Besant: Non-Reproductive Physiology and Birth Control – an Account of the Bradlaugh-Besant Trial, Berkeley, CA 1981. I owe this reference to Suzanne Raitt.

245 Thus for instance one finds Dr L. Haden Guest, in later years Labour MP and a leading spirit in the Socialist Medical Association, writing on 'Theosophy and Social Reconstruction' in the August 1911 issue of the *Theosophist*, while the journal itself, both editorially and through the articles of Annie Besant, engaged intensely with the national railways strike of August 1911 and the industrial unrest of that time.

246 *Theosophist*, xxiii, 1911–12, p. 391.

247 Quoted in M. Mulvihill, *Charlotte Despard: A Biography*, London 1989, p. 76.

The Tory Party at Prayer*

The Conservative Party has decided to combat the progress of left-wing views in the Church by holding a conference to put the case for Conservative Christianity. The conference, which is being organised by officials at Conservative Central Office and a group of MPs of all denominations, will take place next week . . . The organizers say the timing of the conference just before the discussion of a church report advocating unilateral disarmament, is 'a happy coincidence'. Mrs Thatcher knows of the conference and is said to 'thoroughly approve' . . . Mr Mervyn Kohler, an assistant director at Central Office, said: 'We want people to wake up to the fact that there are Christians in the Conservative party.'

Observer, 23 January 1983

It is some measure of the weakening hold of the Conservative Party on one of its traditional components, Anglicanism, that Central Office is now reduced, rather in the manner of the Communist Party or the Militant Tendency, to holding a fraction meeting in preparation for the Church of England's general synod next month; and that threatening sounds of disestablishment are now coming from the Right rather than, as in the nineteenth and early twentieth centuries, from the dissenting and radical Left.

All this, from the point of view of a historian, is startling. 'Throne and altar' was the original Tory rallying cry in the reign of Queen Anne, and the mobilization of 'Church and King' mobs in the 1790s (in Birmingham they sacked the houses of the dissenting intelligentsia, in Lancashire they burnt effigies of Tom Paine) was perhaps the earliest experiment in Tory democracy. 'Church defence' was the one unifying theme of the Conservative policy in the nineteenth century, and the 'hereditary alliance' with the Church, as T.E. Kebbel put it in 1886, 'one of the chief titles of the Tory Party to the confidence of the English people'. For a politician like Lord Salisbury, whose name graces the

*This piece originally appeared in the *New Statesman*, 28 January 1983.

theoretical journal of today's New Right (the first issue has an article by a Cambridge don arguing that West Indians are 'structurally' unfitted to be British), religion was (as Paul Smith tells us) 'the main sheet anchor of his mind', the Church of England (as he declares) 'the main beam' of 'the ancient fabric of constitution' and Church defence 'the dearest matter upon the whole field of political controversy'.

It provides him with a touchstone not only on matters of high politics but also on manners and morals. He disliked the godless Jowett at Balliol as much as he feared a 'wave of infidelity' sweeping over the land, and opposed university education for women not only out of fear of them 'suffering permanently in health' ('in consequence of attempting to study at an age when men can safely do it and they cannot'), but also on the grounds that (as he had been told), 'young ladies . . . instead of going to Church . . . assembly on Sunday mornings at the rooms of a free-thinking Don, and . . . discuss all conceivable forms of unbelief'. (On the other side of the political divide, it was Nonconformity more than any other interest or issue which held the Liberal ranks together, as in later years it was to be the cement of the Liberal–Labour alliance.)

These historical associations were not forgotten when Mrs Thatcher assumed the Conservative Party leadership. In an early address she reminded members that it had originated as a Church party, and the appeal to religion could be said to be an unspoken premise in her pleas for a return to 'traditional' values. Christian doctrine still finds occasional echoes in the Conservative platform rhetoric (Nigel Lawson, as Energy Secretary, has suggested that the discovery of North Sea oil was a 'divine providence'), and it can also be found in those Augustinian reflections on man's innate depravity with which, it seems, in the still watches of the night, the more philosophically inclined Conservatives are apt to console themselves.

As the otherwise cheerful Mr Lawson put it in a recent pamphlet '. . . Conservatism is founded on the basic acceptance of the ineradicable imperfection of human nature'. Dr Edward Norman, the high priest of Thatcherite theology (though he is not a theologian but a historian), put it more severely, '. . . What is permanent in human nature is . . . moral frailty and . . . the universal incidence of sin'.

In the Tory psyche, however, there has been a simmering anger against the Church, which – like the analogous feeling against the BBC – came to the boil with the Falklands War. Hostility to the Church has, it seems, become the standard form among delegates at Tory Party conferences. Last October carping references to the Church received an eager hearing.

A crescendo of rage was registered at the time of the Falklands Thanksgiving Service when the Archbishop of Canterbury courageously refused to recognize that God was British. Sir John Biggs-Davison spoke of 'cringing clergy' who were 'misusing' St Paul's to call the war in question; Julian Amery MP – the son of a well-known imperialist – complained of the absence of martial hymns; the Prime Minister was variously reported as 'hopping mad' or 'spitting blood' at the insult to national honour. A new wave of indignation followed the Church working party's report on nuclear disarmament. The *Sunday Telegraph* editorialist raised the spectre of secession:

> The Church of England would be very wrong . . . to accept the report of its working party on defence policy, which in effect condemns nuclear deterrence as unchristian. It would be wrong to do so, in the first place because such a conclusion is grossly to oversimplify the ethical and moral problems involved . . . But, more importantly, it would be wrong to do so because many of its faithful would be so scandalised by such a decision as to be forced out of the Church.

The discomfort now attending the Conservative Party's relations with the Church is in striking contrast to the interwar years. Then, government took the Church seriously as the major symbolic expression of national unity, while the Church saw itself as keeper of the nation's conscience. A leading minister, like Sir Edward Wood (later Lord Halifax), could be regarded as being as active a churchman as he was a politician. The bishops, for their part, did not hesitate to put themselves in the limelight: their representations were tolerated, even if their advice was not followed, when they intervened against government policy during the General Strike, and later against cuts in the dole. High Church socialism and 'social' Christianity, in its flourishing subvarieties, enjoyed a substantial following; William Temple – later Archbishop of Canterbury – was a widely admired leader and the massive COPEC conference he organized in 1924, though strongly radical and even anti-capitalist, excited none of the alarums which Conservatives are directing today against the Church of England Board for Social Responsibility (the very name seems to be enough to send shivers down a Thatcherite spine).

The recent outbreak of hostilities may have to do with the relative values which Conservatives attach to the issues at stake (industrial questions are in the end negotiable: war is sacred), but it seems more likely to be due to metabolic changes both within the Conservative Party and the Church. Speculatively one could point to the degentrification of the party, both at parliamentary and constituency level, and the decline in deference to every species of authority, except that of party leader: the cloth no more commands an automatic reverence than does a university education or a 'blue chip' voice.

More tangible would be the changes in the means of persuasion. Whereas for Disraeli the Church was 'the best, if not the only agency, for evangelizing the masses', today's Tory leaders have got far more mileage out of nursing the *Sun*. In the field of public order, there seems to have been a comparably seismic change. Whereas, in the nineteenth century, education and religion were the grand specifics for social disturbance, today more faith seems to be placed in the police (readers will recall that Mrs Thatcher's first act on taking office was to increase police pay). The symbolic space which the police occupy in the contemporary Conservative imagination can be gauged by the rapturous applause at party conferences when any proposal is made to increase police numbers or strengthen police powers.

Within the Church the metabolic changes, if less immediately visible, may be more profound. Here too one could point to a process of degentrification, following, in some sort, the fall in the value of Church livings, or the decline in the proportion of Oxford-educated ordinands – a process whose remote origins can be traced back to the Great Depression of the 1870s and 1880s. (It is remarkable how quickly the English gentleman lost interest in the Church when the money went out of it.)

Or one could refer to 'South Bank theology' and the questioning of established orthodoxies and received social identities in the cultural revolution of the 1960s. A more momentous change however, and a more radicalizing one, was surely the internationalization of the Church, as a result of the ecumenical movement, the growth of the black churches in Africa, and the way in which – at a decisive moment of choice – the churches in the metropolitan countries began to take their lead from those in the Third World. It occurred in precisely the epoch when the overseas preoccupations of the Conservatives were limited to the fate of their 'kith and kin' in white Rhodesia, and its disturbing effect on the Conservative psyche can perhaps be gauged by the attacks directed against the World Council of Churches in Dr Norman's Reith lectures. In the same period, the 'new wave' charities, such as Oxfam, brought the condition of the Third World to the heart of Christian consciousness, while domestically, the Conservative Party's long flirtation with racist sentiment, inaugurated by Peter Griffiths's by-election victory at Smethwick in 1964, brought its rank and file into increasing dissensus with Church teachings. Whereas the professions and the media were liberalized in the Sixties, the churches seemed to have been seriously radicalized, and to judge by the strength of Christian opposition to the Falklands War, and of support for CND, the movement of opinion and loyalties was both more distinctive and more enduring than elsewhere.

The Tory attack on the Church forms part of a wider discourse which opposes hard-nosed 'realism' to high-minded 'do-gooding', and which looks on any public interference in the private sphere as both economically wasteful and morally debilitating. It goes with a sniggering contempt for 'namby-pamby' teaching in the classroom, judges who are 'soft' on criminals, 'bleeding heart' liberals who hawk their consciences to the world. As a political commentator remarked in July 1982, 'if you want the quickest route to the heart of the Conservative party conference, make a cheap joke about the Commission for Racial Equality'. The anger is directed less at Labour than at the *via media* of the liberal and social democratic consensus and more specifically at what Arthur Marwick has recently (and aptly) described as the 'secular Anglicanism' which has dominated the postwar welfare state. Paul Johnson, an erstwhile Wilsonian modernizer now turned salon traditionalist, gave characteristically forceful expression to this kind of feeling in an article in *The Daily Telegraph*:

> One of the great interpretive problems of twentieth-century history is the analysis of the substitutes which the high-minded have found for a vanished religious faith. All that human need to believe has to go somewhere . . . A century ago Ken Livingstone would have been a Low Church clergyman, a cunning, scheming Rev. Obadiah Slope, getting his clutches on the Chapter . . . In Victorian times most members of the ecological lobby . . . would have been filled with a more conventional missionary spirit. They would have been hard at work in Africa or the Pacific, forcing perfectly decent naked savages to wear ill-becoming cotton dresses and trousers, to cohabit solely within the bonds of matrimonial monogamy and to make love in what the French still call 'the missionary position . . .'. The missionaries were backed up by gunboats. The ecologists have Unesco and the media . . . A hundred years ago, the natives occasionally hit back and popped a missionary in the pot. Today alas there's not much chance of an ecologist being eaten.

His historical analogy with the missionaries seems close to the mark, and he would no doubt take it as supporting the 'Conservative Christian' conference – his absent adversary is indeed a missionary's son, E.P. Thompson. But the verbal violence of the passage – and the distinct ambivalence about conjugal fidelity – may suggest something of the unease which contemporary Conservatives feel at the spectre or shadow of their forebears.

Mrs Thatcher, too, seems to experience peculiar discomfort at the notion of 'do-gooding'. She belongs to a whole new breed of first-generation Tories who make a positive virtue of the absence of social conscience. West Indian immigrants are not to them, as they might be to the historically minded, descendants of those who survived the Middle Passage, but rather an alien stock who threaten, in Mrs Thatcher's word, to 'swamp' us, whoever 'us' may be. Those who are in receipt of public assistance are liable to be 'wastrels' or 'no goods' living off the welfare state. The unemployed are those who lack initiative. As one of Mrs Thatcher's admirers, Mr Biffen, put it: 'There are no Stockton-on-Tees skeletons in the Grantham cupboard'. (The reference is to Mr Macmillan's constituency whose 1930s sufferings are said to have impelled him towards support for state intervention.) What Mrs Thatcher has called 'bourgeois guilt' – 'that sense of . . . self-criticism which affects those . . . who cling to a relatively comfortable life while feeling a troublesome pang of conscience because there are others less well off' – is not only a psychological deformation from which she seems singularly free, but one she has deliberately set out to extirpate within her party's ranks.

The Conservative anxiety about the state of the Church corresponds to a deep-seated craving for authority, both in the maintenance of domestic order and the conduct of public life. It is also fuelled by a sense of betrayal. Even if politics is moving their way (Conservatives seem to feel) society is not. The values they were brought up on are vilified. Here the Church is blamed not only for weakness and 'woolliness' – accommodating itself to the new moral order instead of castigating it – but for giving positive encouragement to those who are questioning traditional moral standards. As perhaps the most public national forum in which the moral issues raised in the 1960s still present themselves as matters of painful choice, the Church attracts to itself the anxieties which reflection on them arouses and, discomfortingly for Conservatives, to whom the 'New Morality' is simply 'clap trap', it argues cases out on their merits, forever widening, as it seems, the area of dissensus.

Against such unpalatable dilemmas as these Mrs Thatcher offers a moral world in which there are precepts which can be repeated with dogmatic precision and rules to be honoured and obeyed. The religion which she offers – defending orthodoxy against the shifting sands of permissiveness – is one which emphasizes sin rather than grace, law rather than charity. It is the religion of the Ten Commandments, rather than of ethical complexity. It offers self-acting principles which, in the sphere of morals as in that of economics, will by themselves dispose of painful choice. Scriptural injunction is invoked both as an agenda for personal conduct and as a species of moral police. It is perhaps indicative of this that when she wants to evoke the glories of Victorian philanthropy, it is not to the Night Refuges and Asylums for the Houseless Poor that she turns, nor to the parochial soup-and-blanket funds, nor yet to the activities – by their own lights heroic – of the Bible Women and City missionaries, but rather to that great engine for bringing sinners to repentance, and inculcating behaviour according to rule, the Victorian penitentiary.

Mrs Thatcher constitutes religions orthodoxy with the same confidence that, in other discourses, she will evoke that mythopoeic category, 'old-fashioned' law and order, assuming that her Christianity is 'traditional' because (as she remembers it) it was the way in which she was brought up. There is no notion that Christianity might be a revolutionary religion, as it has been so often in the past and as it is in many parts of the world today; nor yet of the way it has been used in the past by her own party, as an ideology for defining the status quo.

Nor does she allow space for the way in which beliefs can be conditioned by their time. Yet her own case might provide an instructive example. At the heart of her beliefs is an entirely individualist notion of salvation which seems remarkably close to the 'truths' she teaches in economics. The Church too, in her view of it, should be in some sort privatized, being concerned with personal holiness rather than social causes or public affairs. Even the notion of sin, on which she lays a heavy emphasis, like others in her party, seems homologous with a wider party view, being invoked as the impassable barrier to utopian schemes of improvement.

The primacy which Mrs Thatcher gives to self-help – or at least her gloss on it – seems to owe as much to business liberalism as to belief in personal responsibility. The tremendous leap which she makes from biblical text to a highly ideological conclusion can be shown in the following passage, where 'self-love and social' are not only connected with each other, but in some sort treated as interchangeable terms, and 'self-regard', from being a *starting*-point for service or help to others, becomes the final end.

> The admonitions 'love they neighbour as thyself' and 'do as you would be done by' . . . do not denigrate self, or elevate love of others above it. On the contrary, they see concern for self and responsibility for self as something to be expected, and ask only that this can be extended to others. This embodies the great truth that self-regard is the root of regard for one's fellows . . .

It is an exegesis which might have been designed to flatter the privileged of this world in the enjoyment of their good fortune, whether in the sphere of material wealth or cultural capital – but it is quite unclear what obligation (if any) it imposes upon them towards those less fortunately placed. Like a number of Mrs Thatcher's recent statements, it reads very much like a high-minded cover-up for narcissism; or in simpler language, 'looking after number one'.

However revisionist Thatcherite theology (the Jubilee Group's booklet, *Christianity Reinterpreted*, argues that one main branch of it is indistinguishable from Gnostic heresy), there seems no doubt that it corresponds to many people's expectation of what a religion should be about. It has the potent appeal of great simplicity. It offers clearly marked boundaries between good and evil, right and wrong. Translated into terms of childhood experience and upbringing, Mrs Thatcher's favourite idiom, it offers the poignant, if illusory, promise, of a return to a security that has in later years been lost. As Mrs Thatcher put it in an early interview: 'I want decent, fair, honest, citizen values, all the principles you were brought up with. You don't live up to the hilt of your income; you respect other people's property, you save, you believe in right and wrong; you support the police'.

Mrs Thatcher and Victorian Values*

I

'Victorian' was still being used as a routine terms of opprobrium when, in the run-up to the 1983 election, Mrs Thatcher annexed 'Victorian Values' to her party's platform and turned them into a talisman for lost stabilities. It is still commonly used today as a byword for the repressive just as (a strange neologism of the 1940s) 'Dickensian' is used as a shorthand expression to describe conditions of squalor and want. In Mrs Thatcher's lexicon, 'Victorian' seems to have been an interchangeable term for the traditional and the old-fashioned, though when the occasion demanded she was not averse to using it in a pejorative sense. Marxism, she liked to say, was a Victorian (or mid-Victorian) ideology;[1] and she criticized nineteenth-century paternalism as propounded by Disraeli as anachronistic.[2] Celebrating, at one moment, the achievements of Victorian philanthropy and quoting the example of Dr Barnardo, she was ready, at the next, to strike at one of its taproots, and to proclaim her freedom from what she derisorily termed, in an early address as party leader, 'bourgeois guilt'.[3]

Mrs Thatcher's traditionalism was perhaps more a matter of style than of substance. If in one voice she regretted lost stability, in another she seized on what was new and developing. Monetarism was the 'modern view' of the role of government rather than (or as well as) a revival of 'old-fashioned laissez-faire'. Privatization was hard-nosed realism. For all

*This essay was originally read as a paper at a Joint Symposium of the Royal Society of Edinburgh and the British Academy, 12 December 1990; it was first published in *Victorian Values*, proceedings of the British Academy 78, ed. T.C. Smout, Oxford 1992. Thanks are due to Jonathan Clark and Christopher Smout for a critical reading of the first draft of this piece; to Fran Bennett of Child Poverty Action Group for advice on the 'Scroungermania' scare of 1975–76; and to the historians taking part in the 'History Workshop' symposium on 'Victorian Values' in 1983: Gareth Stedman Jones, Michael Ignatieff, Leonore Davidoff and Catherine Hall.

her denunciation of permissiveness and 'TV violence', Mrs Thatcher felt no compunction about licensing Cable TV (in the name of free consumer choice), or conferring a knighthood on that pioneer of 'bubbly' journalism, the editor of the *Sun*. Her well-advertised attachment to the work ethic did not exclude an enthusiasm for hi-tech industry or a willingness, indeed eagerness, to contemplate the robotization of the motor-car factories, or the substitution of nuclear power for coal. 'Enterprise culture', the flagship of Mrs Thatcher's second term of office, probably owed more to the inspiration of contemporary America (or Japan) than to the railway mania of the 1840s. BUPA, Mrs Thatcher's preferred alternative to the National Health Service, was modelled on Medicare, the corporation-funded medicine of the United States; the great working-class friendly societies of the nineteenth century, the Buffaloes, the Oddfellows or the Foresters, though monuments to the spirit of self-help, might have existed on another planet for all the attention they received.

In her modernizing moments, Mrs Thatcher had a radical contempt for the antiquated and the out-of-date. Restrictive practices were a relic of nineteenth-century industrial relations. Government subsidies or 'handouts' were a throwback to the past 'protecting yesterday's jobs and fighting off tomorrow's'.[4] Manning agreements, though supported by unions and management, were a recipe for industrial decline, ossifying labour where it should be mobile, strangling innovation at birth.[5] Mrs Thatcher believed that 'traditional' British industries, unless they adopted advanced technology, would vanish, and that without a radical restructuring of the labour market, enterprise would wither.[6] Whatever the pain associated with redundancy and the return of mass unemployment, she feared entropy more, a Britain (as she warned the Institute of Directors in 1976) 'living in the nostalgic glories of a previous industrial revolution', a 'Museum Economy' dedicated to obsolete practices and wedded to the production of uncompetitive goods.[7]

Mrs Thatcher's attitude to traditional institutions, so far from being reverent, was iconoclastic. She deregulated the City of London and destabilized (or abolished) the County halls. She attacked by turns those erstwhile pillars of the Establishment, the Higher Civil Service, the Church of England, the House of Lords, the Universities and the Bar. She was even impatient, it seems, with monarchy. Nor did she demonstrate any particular regard for things Victorian. As one who made a fetish of never using public transport, her attitude towards that 'typical illustration and symbol of the nineteenth century, the railway train'[8] was the reverse of nostalgic, and she was equally unsentimental about such relics of Victorian achievement as free libraries and the penny post. Above all, identifying it with jobbery and bureaucracy, extravagance and sloth, she attempted to put an axe to what is arguably the most substantial twentieth-century legacy of the Victorian era, the public service ethic.

Yet it was as a traditionalist that Mrs Thatcher set out her stall as party leader, and made a pitch for the minds and hearts of her followers. She presented herself as a conviction politician, standing up for old-fashioned values where others were apologetic or shamefaced. In a climate of permissiveness – or what many Conservatives thought of as moral anarchy – she called for a restoration of the authority principle in society. She denounced those who were 'soft' on crime. She defended the family as the bedrock of national life. She advocated 'parent power' in the schools. Economically, she declared her faith in the principles of laissez-faire, quoting John Stuart Mill on the perils of over-government, Adam Smith on the need for the unfettered pursuit of wealth.[9] She appeared concerned to vindicate nineteenth-century capitalism and rescue it from the opprobrium of posterity. She argued that 'the heyday of free enterprise in Britain' was also 'the era of selflessness and benefaction'. She complained (in 1976) that 'the Victorian Age' had been very badly treated in socialist propaganda. 'It was an age of constant and constructive endeavour in which the desire to improve the lot of the ordinary person was a powerful factor'. She quoted with approval Samuel Smiles, a joke figure to generations of progressives, enlisting him to support the proposition that 'the sense of being selfreliant, of playing a role within the family, of owning one's own property, of paying one's way, are all part of the spiritual ballast which maintains responsible citizenship, and provides the solid foundation which people look around to see what they might do for others and themselves'.[10]

Mrs Thatcher aimed at the modernizing programme to restore business to a place of honour in national life, and reverse a century of denigration by those, in her party's own ranks as well as among its opponents, who affected to despise money-making and who wanted to keep commerce and trade at arm's length. She adopted business maxims as her watchwords – e.g. 'Value for Money' – drafted in businessmen as her advisers, watchdogs and troubleshooters; advocated business patronage for the arts and the appointment of businessmen as governors of schools and colleges. 'The discipline of market forces' was government's sovereign remedy for social ills; the revival of enterprise the object of its policy. Historically, Mrs Thatcher was concerned to identify business with the creative forces in national life, the risk-takers and the innovators, the doers and the makers. She gave it a heroic pedigree, offering an alternative version of the national epic, in which there was a merchant-adventurer in every counting-house, a village Hampden in every store. In place of constitutional development – the traditional basis of Whig narrative – or its Tory counterpart, statesmanship and the rise of government, she offered, as the national epic, the romance of trade, conjuring up an age of primitive virtue where nothing was easy and everything had to be earned.

Mrs Thatcher seems to have stumbled on the phrase 'Victorian Values' as a rallying cry by accident, conjuring the phase out of nowhere, and launching it on its public career in the course of an interview with 'Weekend World' (16 January 1983).[11] Only those who are privy to the secrets of the television studio will know whether it was an inspiration of the moment, or a premeditated plant. However that may be, it was a rhetorical trope which seemed both to thematize her causes and to give them a retrospective dignity. In the following weeks she elaborated it, invoking on the one hand 'the Puritan work ethic',[12] on the other a leitmotiv of the election campaign – 'family values'. Her followers added inflections of their own. Thus Mrs Winterton, the candidate for Congleton, who 'agreed wholeheartedly' with Mrs Thatcher's Victorian Values, interpreted them benignly as 'thrift, kindness and family values'.[13] On the other hand, Dr Rhodes Boyson, Minister of State for Education, and himself an ex-headmaster (and an ex-historian), argued that they meant a return to strictness.

> He said parents did not want their children to be taught 'deviant practices by proselytising homosexuals'. What parents want is for their children to learn discipline, self-discipline, respect, order, punctuality and precision . . . Parents expect their children to be punished when they step out of line . . . No discipline, no learning. Good old-fashioned order, even Victorian order, is far superior to illiterate disorder and innumerate chaos in the classroom.[14]

It seems possible that, as so often when speaking her simple truths and advertising her hostility to the postwar social settlement, Mrs Thatcher was deliberately courting outrage. If so, she was duly rewarded by the chorus of indignation which greeted her remarks. For Labour, already convinced that the Tories were planning to destroy the National Health Service and dismantle the welfare state, it was proof positive that they wanted to turn the clock back. It showed yet again that the Tories were 'uncaring' and was of a piece with their 'callous indifference' in other spheres. Just as, in the sphere of family policy, the Tories supposedly wanted to return women to the kitchen sink, and were even toying (it was believed) with eugenics, so in welfare they wanted to go back to the Poor Law. 'Victorian Values', we were told by the opposition, meant each man for himself and the devil take the hindmost. Some invoked the spectre of the workhouse, some of child labour, some of the Dickensian slum. 'Victorian Britain was a place where a few got rich and most got hell', Mr Kinnock, then shadow minister of education, told the Labour Club at Workington. 'The "Victorian Values" that ruled were cruelty, misery, drudgery, squalor and ignorance'.[15]

Victorian Values, though a latecomer to Mrs Thatcher's political platform, had been anticipated in a whole series of prior tropes. She had come to the leadership of the Conservative Party, in 1975, on a gospel of 'self-reliance and thrift'.[16] In government she liked to say that her monetarist policies were inspired by 'an old-fashioned horror of debt'. The 'work ethic' was her favoured idiom when arguing for fiscal reform.

'Privatization' was her tonic for energizing the economy and 'rolling back the frontiers of the state'. 'Personal responsibility' was the mantra of her addresses on moral questions, 'parent power' her grand specific for schoolroom disorder and youth unrest.[17] It was not hard to slot 'Victorian Values' into this continuum.

'Victorian Values' were also of a piece with Mrs Thatcher's personal mythologies. She presented herself to the public not as a scholarship girl who had found her vocation in the city of dreaming spires, nor yet as a successful tax lawyer and denizen of Chelsea, but as a grocer's daughter from Grantham who was still living, metaphorically speaking, above the shop. Her father, as she portrayed him in countless interviews, was a very personification of the Victorian worthy, a self-made (and self-educated) man who had left school at thirteen and who had pulled himself up by the bootstraps, ending up as an alderman on the town council and a lay preacher at the chapel. In Mrs Thatcher's account of Victorian Values, as also when she spoke of 'traditional' Christianity, there was a conflation between the precepts of her Grantham childhood there and those of an earlier past. 'I was brought up by a Victorian grandmother' she told an *Evening Standard* reporter:

> we were taught to work jolly hard. We were taught to prove yourself; we were taught self-reliance; we were taught to live within our income. You were taught that cleanliness is next to godliness. You were taught self-respect. You were taught always to give a hand to your neighbour. You were taught tremendous pride in your country. All of these things are Victorian values. They are also perennial values.[18]

In another and earlier interview, she describes these values as follows: 'You don't live up to the hilt of your income; you respect other people's property, you save; you believe in right and wrong; you support the police'.[19]

If the call for a return to Victorian Values struck a chord in 1983, it was perhaps because it corresponded to widespread disenchantment with the modernizations of the 1960s, together with a post-1960s awareness of the limits of economic growth, and also to transformations in the perception of past–present relations. Perhaps, too, it drew subliminal strength from the revival of period styles and the rage for the restoration of 'period' interiors. A concurrence of different influences could be hypothesized here. In the property market, the conversion of run-down Victorian terraces and the elevation of Victorian mansions to the status of 'period' residences; in marketing, the mushroom growth of what came to be known, in the 1980s, as the 'Laura Ashley' look; and in heritage, the proliferation of open-air and industrial museums. All of them had the effect, so far as popular taste was concerned, of rehabilitating the notion of the Victorian and associating it not with squalor and grime, but on the contrary with goodness and beauty, purity and truth.

Victorian Values also created a metaphorical space for the expression of moral anxiety. As a rhetoric, it spoke to those who felt bewildered or alarmed by the shape of cultural change. It ministered to the belief, widely canvassed in the public press, that Britain was becoming ungovernable, in Mrs Thatcher's words, 'a decadent, undisciplined society'. It played on fears that the family was in crisis and marriage falling apart. In one aspect, the invocation of Victorian Values was a counterpart to Conservative demands for a 'crack-down' on crime; in another it was perhaps an alarmed response to the coming out of previously stigmatized (and criminalized) sexual minorities. It could be seen as a late echo of the purity campaigns of the 1970s and the mass mobilizations of the Festival of Light.[20] Affirming the need for clearly defined standards of right and wrong, it questioned the wisdom of past reforming Home Secretaries. Against the pleasure principle, it counterposed the worth of self-control and self-restraint.

One aspect of moral anxiety was fear of 'welfare scroungers', seen as early as 1975–76, when a whispering campaign against welfare state 'spongers' swelled into a chorus of newspaper complaint (even, it has been argued, an orchestrated campaign) against those who were allegedly living it up on the dole.[21] With the acknowledgement of unmarried mothers and single-parent families as categories in need, numbers dependent on social security payments had risen to new heights. At the same time the extension of 'supplementary benefit' to take account of previously unrecognized contingencies (e.g. rent, mortgage payments, clothes and more generally 'child poverty') narrowed the gap between waged and unwaged almost to vanishing point at the bottom of the social scale. Those caught in the 'poverty trap' (it was then argued) had little or no inducement to get out. Welfare was producing the very condition it was supposed to alleviate, reducing its recipients to a state of dependence and calling new classes of idlers into being.

Mrs Thatcher appealed directly to this sentiment, indeed anticipated its public expression by some months, when, campaigning for the leadership of the Conservative Party in January 1975, and addressing the annual conference of the Young Conservatives, she appealed to the party to 'back the workers and not the shirkers'; she coupled this, in a five-minute credo, with a ringing declaration of faith in the individual as earner. 'The person who is prepared to work hardest should get the greatest rewards and keep them after tax. It was not only permissible but praiseworthy to want to benefit your own family by your own efforts'.[22] In the years of opposition these were her constant themes. People wanted to be left to get on with their own lives 'and have more of their own pay packets to spend'.[23] Welfare hand-outs sapped initiative.[24] Food subsidies 'had gone to people who did not need them',[25] housing benefits unfairly advantaged the Council tenant:

> The Britain I want is a land where a man can know that if he works hard and earns money for his family, he will be allowed to hold on to most of what his efforts have brought him rather than have it seized to build Ministerial empires . . . The Britain I want is a land where people are not ground down in the name of false equality to the point where a man is better off on the dole than at work.[26]

In the leadership election, Mrs Thatcher opined (presciently as it turned out) that these sentiments would have as much resonance on the working-class council estates as in the dormitory towns and suburbs. In the following years she was to deploy them with singular effect, discovering, or creating, a new constituency of Tory voters, many of them working-class. They were quite undeferential to the rich but had a considerably developed hostility to those further down the social scale. Here is a letter in 1983 from one of them, a real-life original, it may be, of that 'Essexman' who, by the end of Mrs Thatcher's term in office, was to be recognized as her most faithful supporter.

> Returning to Britain after a five-year absence, I have noticed a wonderful transformation. People are tired of featherbedding for those too lazy or inadequate to fend for themselves. They want an end to our sick, inefficient welfare state. They realise the nation is not a charitable institution and has no business running free hospitals and soup-kitchen benefits, or interfering with private enterprise. They applaud the curbing of the unions and want to see our nation great once more. Who has brought about this change? Mrs. Thatcher, of course. Her resolution in rebuilding our country after decades of mismanagement is awesome. A new spirit walks abroad – and this is only the beginning. Well done, Maggie. It's great to be back.
> Alex Thirle
> Colchester, Essex.[27]

II

When, in the early days of her party leadership, Mrs Thatcher called for a 'restoration' of parental authority, as later when she took up the call for a return to Victorian Values, what mattered was less the words themselves than the character she projected of one who was not afraid of sounding reactionary, but on the contrary gloried in old-fashioned ways. As a piece of symbolic reassurance it was magnificent, convincing her party followers that Conservatism was returning to the paths of faith. It enabled her to magnify differences with her predecessor – always, it seems, a consideration with Tory leaders – and further to distinguish herself not only from Mr Heath but also from Mr Wilson and Mr Macmillan. Where they made a fetish of tacking to the winds of change, she was by contrast sternly inflexible.

One of Mrs Thatcher's strengths, and not the least of the reasons why she was able so frequently to wrong-foot her opponents, was that of translating policy issues into questions of what has been called, in another context, 'moral economy'. Even the Poll Tax, the wildly unpopular reform which helped to bring her down, was conceived as an act of justice, applying nineteenth-century principles of fair play and fair shares to local government taxation, and bringing home a sense of personal responsibility to the local electorate. Private enterprise, Mrs Thatcher argued, was not only economically efficient, it was also ethically beautiful, harnessing the self-regarding virtues to the higher good. Protectionism, whether in the field of trade unionism, state intervention or local government, bred monopoly; welfare was enervating; bureaucracy was an invitation to extravagance and sloth. Competition on the other hand was bracing, putting workers and employers on their mettle. The market generated an equitable distribution of the available goods, making producers directly accountable to consumers. Job-shedding was a way of losing weight and producing a leaner, fitter labour force. Monetarism was an exercise in frugality, applying the principles of household budgeting ('living within your means') to the management of the national economy. 'Some say I preach merely the homilies of housekeeping or the parables of the parlour', she told the Lord Mayor's banquet in November 1982, when anger about monetarism was at a peak, 'but I do not repent. Those parables would have save many a financier from failure and many a country from crisis'.[28]

Mrs Thatcher used 'Victorian Values' as a way of conjuring up lost innocence. Against a background of inner-city disturbances, such as those which swept the streets of Toxteth and Brixton in 1981, she pictured an older Britain where parents were strict, children good-mannered, hooliganism (she erroneously believed) unknown. At a time when both the struggling and the prosperous were mortgaged up to the hilt, she recalled the virtues of penny saving. In a contracting economy, where, under the shadow of microchip technology, every occupation was under actual or potential threat, she looked back to a time when labour was a means of self-fulfilment, when occupations were regarded as callings, and when jobs – or businesses – were for life. In the face of multiculturalism, she resurrected the mythology of a unified national self.

In all these instances, Victorian Britain was constituted as a kind of reverse image of the present, exemplifying by its stability and strength everything that we are not. The past here occupies an allegorical rather than temporal space. It is a testimony to the decline in manners and morals, a mirror to our failings, a measure of absence. It also answers to one of the most universal myths, which has both its left-wing and right-wing variants, the notion that once upon a time things were simpler and the people were at one with themselves. Like the small-town America of Mr Reagan's rhetoric – God-fearing, paternalistic, patriotic – Mrs Thatcher's Victorian Britain is inhabited by a people living in a state of innocent simplicity. Instead of nationalized industries there are small business and family firms. Work is accorded dignity, achievement rewarded rather than taxed. Families hold together and put their savings by against a rainy day. People know right from wrong. By a process of selective amnesia the past becomes a historical equivalent of the dream of primal bliss, or of the enchanted space which memory accords to childhood. By metaphorical extension, Victorian Values thus passed from the real past of recorded history to timeless 'tradition'. They were, Mrs Thatcher assured us, like those of Christianity, 'perennial', the values which had made Britain great.[29]

Other people of Mrs Thatcher's generation and earlier, it is worth noticing, recall things with a different emphasis. In working-class accounts of the 'good old days', as recorded in oral history and written memoirs, it is the images of sociability that prevail – the sing-songs in the pubs, the funeral processions, the 'knees-up' street parties, the summer outings. The canvas is crowded with characters; street performers will sometimes get a page or two to themselves and there may be a whole chapter for Whitsun or Bank Holiday. Shopping is remembered for its cheapness – 'a packet of fags and a pint of beer and you could still bet change from two bob'. People are forever in and out of each other's houses: 'everyone was in the same boat together', 'everyone was the same'. Children make their own toys, stage their own theatre, invent their own games. The street is their playground, waste lots their battlefields, bunkers their lairs. Pleasures, though simple, are treasured. As Lionel Bart put it, both sentimentally and sardonically, in his musical *Fings Ain't What They Used to Be:*

> It used to be fun
> Dad and ole Mum
> Paddling dahn Southend
> But now it ain't done
> Never mind chum
> Paris is where we spend our outings.

Mrs Thatcher's version of the 'good old days' is altogether more severe. Her lost Eden is one where resources were scarce and careful husbandry was needed to ensure survival. She remembers her childhood not for its pleasures but for its lessons in application and self-control. Reading is not a form of escape but a means of improvement; library visits are compulsory.[30] There are no outings or beanos, though she goes to chapel three times a day on Sunday, no remembered holidays (though at Guides she learnt the lifelong motto 'be prepared'),[31] no secret gardens or ways of playing truant. 'Was she happy?' a journalist asked in an interview. 'We didn't take happiness as an objective. We did a lot. Our parents worked. Our home was always spotless. Cleanliness and hard work were next to Godliness'.[32]

Mrs Thatcher's values, as many commentators have pointed out, were Puritan values. A literal belief in the devil[33] may help to account for her readiness to discover 'enemies within', while a Puritan alertness to backsliders might be seen in the vigour with which she attacked fainthearts and waverers in the ranks or, worse, in her immediate Cabinet entourage. As a political leader, Mrs Thatcher was happiest in the role of an evangelist confronting the country with uncomfortable truths. She despised 'soft' options:[34] she used the word 'easy' in a consistently pejorative sense – 'a generation of easy liberal education has accustomed many to suppose that Utopia was soon to be achieved';[35] 'freedom is not synonymous with an easy life';[36] 'the world has never offered us an easy living'.[37] She made a fetish of plain speaking, 'calling things by their proper names'. She prided herself on never flinching from making 'painful' decisions, following unpopular courses, or speaking up for unfashionable truths. She relished the idea of struggle, picturing herself romantically as travelling rugged roads, navigating shoals and rapids, braving stormy weather. Even after eleven years in office she still pictured her life as a succession of uphill fights. 'Work is the ethic', she told an interviewer shortly after her resignation:

> ... Decide what you think is right to do and try to persuade other people to try *your* way. That was instilled in me in childhood ... That's my life. If you believe something passionately and do something that is really worthwhile you will get opposition from people who believe differently, so my life will always be uphill all the way ... I have never been worried about being unpopular if I thought I was doing right.[38]

In nineteenth-century terms, Mrs Thatcher spoke in the accents of chapel rather than the church. Brought up a Methodist and a provincial, with a father who had left school at thirteen and started his own business, she seems to have felt an elective affinity with the culturally underprivileged, and a corresponding suspicion of those who used to be called 'the comfortable classes'. Her version of Victorian Values reflects this, invoking the plebeian virtues of self-reliance and self-help rather than the more patrician ones of chivalry and *noblesse oblige*, and in her radical contempt for paternalism, and her suspicion of philanthropically-minded 'do-gooders', whether in the socialist or the Conservative ranks, it is not difficult to find echoes of her Northamptonshire shoemaker forebears – 'the radicallest set of fellows in the radicallest town in England', as one of their number told the *Morning Chronicle* Commissioner when he visited Northampton in 1850.[39] If, as Arthur Marwick has interestingly suggested, the postwar social consensus was sustained by a kind of 'secularised Anglicanism',[40] and if the Attlee welfare state was, as Gareth Stedman Jones has eloquently put it, 'the last and most glorious flowering of late Victorian liberal philanthropy',[41] then Mrs Thatcher's revolt against it might be seen as nineteenth-century Methodism's revenge.

Mrs Thatcher's values were also grammar school values, those of a scholarship girl who had come out top of the form. Hence, it may be – the matter is speculative – her insistence that she had been born with 'no privilege at all', and had had 'precious little' of it in her early years[42] – a distinctive note in her leadership campaign of January 1975, as it was to be in that of her successor, John Major – and her fierce resentment of those who, whether by reason of hereditary title and wealth, or expensive education, or, as in the case of one of her adversaries, Mr Wedgwood Benn, both[43] – had started life with unfair advantages. Hence, too, one could argue, her belief that the failures in life were the lazy. Like that other grammar school star to whom she has some uncanny resemblances, Mr Wilson, she made a great point of having all the facts and figures at her fingertips, of being prodigiously industrious and well-prepared. Her economics, too, has a distinctively prefectorial tang. Competition kept people up to the mark; 'merit' and 'distinctions' spurred them onwards. Success was a recognition of ability: progress was achieved by diligence, application and efforts. The virtues ascribed to Mrs Thatcher's Methodist upbringing – 'order, precision and attention to detail'[44] – were, of course, also grammar school values. It was Mrs Thatcher's originality to project them out to the national stage.

All this has some political relevance if, rather than seeing the cultural revolution of the 1960s as an outcome of the campus revolt (which followed rather than preceded it), one were to seek its roots instead – as I have tried to argue elsewhere[45] – in a prior sixth-form dissidence. It may be that at the heart of the 1970s call for a return to 'standards' was outraged grammar school sentiment, the bewilderment and anger of those who found that the very qualities which had served them so well in life were, under the impact of the counter-culture, deliberately transgressed. It is strikingly the case that, from the publication of *The Black Papers on Education* (1969) down to current calls for a return to the three Rs, the crusade for the defence of 'standards' has been voiced most urgently by right-wing scholarship boys, Professor Cox, the editor of *The Black Papers*, Mr Boyson, an erstwhile Lancashire lad, Paul Johnson, a Merseyside Catholic and by his own account a youthful swot, being striking cases in point. Mrs Thatcher, from the moment she was elected party leader, weighed in on their side. 'Our schools used to serve us well', she told Party Conference in 1975. 'A child from an ordinary family, as I was, could use it as a ladder, as an advancement. The socialists, better at demolition than reconstruction, are destroying many good grammar schools. Now this is nothing to do with private education. It is opportunity and excellence in the state schools that are being diminished.'[46]

Mrs Thatcher's Victorian Britain, like that of Asa Briggs – one of the 'new wave' social historians who, by their scholarly work, prepared the way for the rehabilitation of Victorian Values – is an 'age of improvement'. There is space for the Mechanics Institute, but hardly for the free-and-easy, nor yet for that class who are so inescapable a presence in the novels of the period, the shabby genteel. While not exactly filled by grammar school types, it is peopled by humble, striving, God-fearing folk who might be thought of as their spiritual ancestors. They are artisans and tradesmen rather than carriage folk, the industrious sorts of people rather than those who were called, in the literature of the time, the Upper Ten Thousand. People rise, but they do so in a modest way, advancing socially by degrees, rather than meteorically, by flying upward leaps. Tradesmen prosper not by speculation (or the adulteration of goods) but by punctilious attention to their ledger books. School leavers learn to educate themselves, in the manner of Mrs Thatcher's own father. The self-made men whom she celebrates are not the commercial adventurers, like Mr Merdle, nor the fraudulent projectors, like those presiding over the Anglo-Bengalee company in *Martin Chuzzlewit,* nor the stock jobbers attempting to corner the market in cotton on Manchester or Liverpool 'Change. They are rather the patient who better themselves, moving up in the world without losing their family roots.

III

Mrs Thatcher's rhetoric of Victorian Values was, on the face of it, a remarkable example of 'a political attitude' struck for purely symbolic rewards. Except for the restoration of hanging – something for which she voted consistently whenever the issue of Capital Punishment came before the House of Commons – Mrs Thatcher showed no signs of wanting to translate it into legislative enactment or administrative practice. No attempt was made to impose any modern equivalent of the workhouse test on welfare claimants (during Mrs Thatcher's period of office the number of those depending on supplementary benefits rose by leaps and bounds, from 3.4 million in 1979 to 5.6 million in 1988). For all her well-advertised horror of debt, Mrs Thatcher made no attempt to curb consumer credit; indeed if her precepts had been taken seriously, the economy would have been in ruins. In the consumer-led boom of the 1980s, when credit facilities multiplied, outstanding debt (excluding home loans) grew in real terms by 3 per cent a quarter between the end of 1981 and the first quarter of 1988, rising from 8 per cent of annual household disposable income in 1981 to 14 per cent in 1987. In the same period personal savings (excluding life assurance premiums) fell from 16.3 per cent in 1980 to a mere 1.3 per cent in late 1988. Frugality and thrift, in short, so far from staging a come-back during Mrs Thatcher's period in office, all but disappeared.[47]

If one turns, however, from the real to the imaginary, and from literal to figurative meanings, then it can be seen that, if short on legislative pay-offs, the metaphor of Victorian Values was a rich political source of psychic satisfactions. It confirmed misanthropists in the belief that the country was going to the dogs, while rallying traditionalists to the defence of 'standards'. In a more egalitarian register, it peopled the past with familiars, picturing Britain as a nation given over to honest toil. As an allegory of the bourgeois virtues, it celebrated ordinariness, treating humble origins as a mark of distinction and family fortune as the sign of grace. It gave serious money a pedigree and offered class exiles – among them, one might suggest, Mrs Thatcher – an ideal home, a little commonwealth where birth and breeding counted for nothing, and character was all.

Victorian Values also helped the Conservatives to turn the tables on their opponents by presenting Labour as ossified and sclerotic and the Conservatives as the true radicals, destabilizing the Establishment. Where its opponents kept whole armies of wage-earners in thrall, Conservatism was emancipatory: Victorian Values also released the more utopian strains in Conservative thought, and in its more exalted moments, seizing on privatization as a token of the shape of things to come, the party could even appropriate the old Marxist dream of the 'withering away' of the state. They pictured the new Britain which 'enterprise culture' made possible as a capitalism without classes and a society without the state. Equipped with the precepts of self-help, claiming the protective mantle of tradition for a born-again radical individualism, and evoking that archetypal figure of national myth, the free-born Englishman, Conservatives could thus present themselves *both* as the party of the future, championing what was new and developing where their opponents were stuck in a time-warp, *and* as the party of precedent, restoring a spirit of republican independence to national life and character.

Within the Conservative Party, Victorian Values gave a voice to the Tory unconscious, licensing the public expression of sentiments which would have been forbidden in the liberal hour of the 1960s. It also provided an idiom or code within which intra-party differences could be fought out. For Conservative loyalists, adopting laissez-faire economics as though it was a long-lost Tory creed, monetarism was a test of stamina; state intervention, however benevolently intended, a confession of weakness; Conservative dissidents, the high Tories or 'Wets', plucking up courage to speak for the unemployed, or, during the strike of 1984–85, for the miners, but fearful of being tarred with the brush of postwar 'consensus' politics, invoked the counter-tradition of nineteenth-century paternalism and philanthropy. In the coded meanings that, in the 1980s, seemed *de rigueur* at party conferences, they invoked a Disraelian notion of 'one Nation' against the laissez-faire 'dogma' of the government. The rhetoric of Victorian Values could be seen as an example of what the post-modernists call 'double-coding' and sociologists 'cognitive dissonance' – i.e. of words which say one thing, while meaning another and camouflaging, or concealing, a third.

Mrs Thatcher's traditionalism allowed her to act as an innovator – arguably the most ruthless of our twentieth-century prime ministers – while yet sounding as though she were a voice from the past. By turns radical and reactionary, modernizing and atavistic, she moved from one register to another with the dexterity of a quick-change artist. Her political career exhibits the same paradoxes. At one moment she was the Little Englander, proclaiming the virtues of splendid isolation, or speaking up for old-fashioned sovereignty; she was a globetrotter at the next, making the world her oyster, and trying out the part of statesman on an international stage. In one role, sniping at the mandarins of Whitehall and Westminster from her Downing Street redoubt, she was the insider playing the system against itself; in another, speaking up for 'ordinary people', she was the great outsider, rallying the country against the court. Victorian Values were similarly double-coded, a programme for the future disguised as a narrative of the past. The watchwords may have been conservative, but they were used for subversive ends, to destablize established authority; to mobilize resentment against the status quo; to give historical precedent to what was essentially a new turn. She could thus appear simultaneously as a fierce iconoclast and a dedicated restorationist, an avatar of the future, pointing the way forward, and a voice from the past, calling on the British people to return to its traditional ways.

In each of the different phases of her career, Mrs Thatcher, taking up the age-old radical cry of corruption in high places, pictured herself as at war with an *ancien régime*. In a remarkable inversion of the Marxist theodicy not capital but labour appeared as the fetter on the forces of production, the feudal integument which had to be broken if capitalism was to resume its forward march. There were in the first place the trade unions, with their privileged immunities, and oligarchic government, strangling innovation by restrictive practices and over-manning. Their leaders were accused of being overmighty 'barons', holding the country to ransom, as in the 'winter of discontent' which did so much to bring Mrs Thatcher to power. Shop stewards, too, were overmighty subjects, with their flying pickets intimidating the public and defying the forces of the law. Then there was the Labour Party, with its vested interest in the extension of public sector employment, its 'client' vote, its state monopolies, its town hall 'czars' and regional fiefs. It was, Mrs Thatcher argued, a paternalism turned sour, a benevolent despotism whose day was done, protecting dying occupations, shoring up declining industries, multiplying benefits to hold on to a contracting electorate. It fed on the weakness of its constituency, levelling down rather than up in the schoolrooms, maintaining claimants in a state of dependence, lording it over council house tenantry and preventing individuality and excellence from leaving their mark.

> It is now our turn to take a major step towards extending home ownership to many who have until now been deliberately excluded. Councils, particularly

> socialist councils, have clung to the role of landlord – they love it because it gives them so much power – so that more than 2 million families have seen themselves paying rent for ever. Petty rules and restrictions, enforced dependence. There are the marks of this last vestige of feudalism in Britain.[48]

The Welfare State, under this optic, appeared as Old Corruption writ large, a gigantic system of state patronage which kept its clients in a state of abject dependence, while guaranteeing a sheltered existence for its officials and employees. A hundred years of collectivism (one of Mrs Thatcher's new circle of intellectual advisers argued) had produced powerful interest groups and influential lobbies whose privileges were bound up with the extension of the public service. 'Every reform ends up by increasing the number of jobs for the boys.' The Whitehall world of 'big government' was a Dracula devouring an ever-increasing quantity of both human and financial resources, and insatiable in its appetite for more (public expenditure consumed 40 per cent of the national product in Mr Macmillan's premiership; under Mr Callaghan the proportion had risen to 55 per cent). In office, Mrs Thatcher translated these precepts into practice, abolishing at least a token number of quangos, the advisory bodies of the great and good which had grown up to serve the machineries of state intervention; deprivileging the higher civil service; attempting to restrict supplementary benefits, and to disqualify whole classes of claimants; imposing cash limits on health and hospital authorities; slashing education budgets; ratecapping local councils; cutting off the life support for ailing industries; selling off state assets. But the 'nanny state' turned out to be a many-headed hydra, with Establishments in every reach of public life, and sympathizers in the highest circles of the land. Professional bodies, such as the British Medical Association and the Royal College of Nurses, sprang to its aid; the House of Lords and the Church of England came to its defence; the universities and the polytechnics, notwithstanding the attempt to introduce business patronage, remained wedded to the idea of public service, the schools to the principles of universalism, the town halls to the provision of welfare. One adversary was no sooner slain than others rose in their stead.

Victorian Values formed part of a wider discourse in which Mrs Thatcher sought, with remarkable success, to replace the antique divisions between capital and labour, or class and class – 'pernicious relics' of the nineteenth century as she called them – with a whole set of new 'Us' and 'Them' antitheses which pitted private sector against public sector employment, business against the professions, 'enterprise culture' against 'the dependency' state. Consciously or otherwise, she brought into requisition the age-old radical opposition between the 'productive' and the 'unproductive' classes, the 'industrious sorts of people' and the idle rich. 'Business' – a term which by metaphorical extension included both workers and employers – was cast in the role of the wealth-producing sector of the community. The professions, by contrast, with the privileged exception of the Army and the police, were treated as social parasites, feeding off the country's 'trading base', running up inflationary costs. The 'caring' professions, with their heartland in the Welfare State, and their outriders in the churches and the charities, were particularly suspect, protecting their privileges and comforts while pretending only to be concerned with others. In another frequent opposition the free-market economy was contrasted to the dependency state, the one a democracy of strivers, the other a protectionist racket. In either case business, like the agricultural interest of the nineteenth century, was 'the backbone of the country', the doers rather than the talkers, the hardheaded rather than the soft-hearted, the active rather than the passive. As in other matters where 'tradition' was at stake, Mrs Thatcher was able to relate these antinomies to her own family history. She told a TV interviewer:

> . . . My father [was] a grocer . . . he employed some people in the shop and in another small shop at the other end of town. So he having left school at thirteen provided employment for other people. There was a great fashion in that time that [the] next generation should go into the professions because quite honestly in our town the people who had the greatest security were in the professions. So I took a science degree and I was employed in a scientific job and then I came into law and politics. I with much higher education have not actually created jobs. And I often think of my father when I hear some academics pontificating about how to solve the unemployment problem . . . I'm tempted to say to them well if you find it so easy to solve why don't you go out and start a business by your own effort and employ – five, ten, fifteen, twenty, a hundred, two hundred. Why don't you? I will tell you why – because you can't. It's easier to tell other people what to do about it than it is to sort it out for yourself. But in the end we have to provide the kind of society where people who can do this who can build up a business are prepared to start . . . Of course . . . you've got to have the good administration in government . . . you've got to have good education – you've got to have good health – don't think you can do without the professions . . . But in the end we rely on those who say . . . 'I've always wanted to build up a business' . . . because they are the people who spot what you and I will want . . . – and they are the people who create the jobs.[49]

Politically, Victorian Values may have made some contribution to the degentrification of the Tory Party, a process which Mrs Thatcher's successor, with his declared attachment to 'classlessness', shows no sign of wanting to reverse. It offered an alternative tradition to that of the Altar and the Throne, or for that matter of Empire 'Kith and kin'. It had no place for the great public schools (though many of them were Victorian foundations), no room for stately homes, not even those such as Hatfield which had been the country seats of Tory leaders. The parson and the squire were not there, nor were the Upper Ten Thousand, i.e. the world of rank and fashion, the metropolitan rich, or those whom Mrs Merdle called 'Society'. The most interesting absentee of all was the nineteenth-century Tory Party itself. Perhaps because of its nineteenth-century association with protection and paternalism, Mrs Thatcher was happier to invoke the liberal-radical John Stuart Mill and the ex-Chartist Samuel Smiles. She has a good word for the nineteenth-century trade unions, quoting them as an example of public-spiritedness, none at all for the Marquess of Salisbury.

After her own fashion, Mrs Thatcher was offering her party 'a history from below', one which gave pride of place to those whom she called 'ordinary people'. Mrs Thatcher had no feel for the traditions of the British governing class, or perhaps, despite the Falklands War, for the imperial dimension of British history. She did not, like her rival, Mr Heseltine, set herself up as a country gent; and a lifetime spent in politics seems to have insulated her from, rather than drawn her towards, the mystique of Westminster and Whitehall. She reached out instead to the provincial England of her childhood and constructed out of it a family saga. In the process she domesticated the idea of tradition and feminized it. Her narrative concentrated on the small details of everyday life. It was exclusively concerned with the private sphere, omitting such traditional ingredients as wars and diplomacy, monarchy and government, the nation and the state. As she put it in perhaps her best-known aphorism: 'There is no such thing as society, only individuals and their families'.

Victorian Values, if the argument of the foregoing is accepted, was modernization in mufti. It marked a historic check to the collectivist idea which had been gathering strength, almost unopposed, ever since the discovery (or rediscovery) of the social question in the 1880s. It signalled a sea-change in attitudes to poverty and welfare. It dramatized public disenchantment with the cult of planning. It registered the exhaustion of a programme of state-led modernization, an idea which has been on the agenda of British politics ever since the Safeguarding of Industries Act (1922) and the formation of the National Grid; which had been vigorously canvassed by 'middle opinion' in the 1930s; and which the 'comprehensive redevelopment' and state-engineered amalgamations of the 1960s had seemed to carry to new heights.

In economics, the call for a return to the market cloaked a rationalization of British industry more ruthless than ever before. It put trade unionism on the defensive and heralded a remarkable erosion of those craft practices which had survived and indeed flourished in the interstices of modern industry; it heralded the emergence of 'flexible' work-forces and the spread of part-time employment. Most interestingly of all – for the term 'Victorian Values' was coined in the pit of a recession – it seized on what were to be some of the leading strengths of 'born-again' capitalism, in particular the new vitality of small-scale enterprise, and the emergence of the market as a universal panacea for political and social skills, a phenomenon not less marked, at time of writing, in Russia and

Eastern Europe than it is in Britain. 'Back to the future', in a word, has proved a more convincing paradigm for change than 1960s gigantism or 'going-for-growth'.

In education, the call for a return to the traditional standards, though framed, by the *Black Papers* of 1960s, as an anguished plea by traditionalists in the humanities has now broadened out into a covert, concerted assault on its predecessor – the idea of a 'liberal education', campaigned for in Matthew Arnold's *Culture and Anarchy*. When the Minister of State attempts to resurrect 'Payment by Results' it is not Matthew Arnold who is the presiding spirit, but if one were to look for Victorian Values in the current revival of the idea of 'useful' knowledge, and the talismanic importance currently being attached to 'performance indicators', it is Mr Gradgrind who is the presiding spirit.

As one who traced a line of descent from the Northamptonshire shoemakers, whose father was a lay preacher and who had herself a strict chapel childhood, Mrs Thatcher has better credentials than most for speaking about Victorian Values. Historians, however much they might want to qualify or question her version of the nineteenth century, ought to acknowledge their indebtedness; as those who assembled last December for the British Academy conference on the subject acknowledged, we would be envious of one of our colleagues who, ten years on, was still able to kindle the fires of scholarly controversy. But it is a sad irony of our time that Mrs Thatcher, though espousing the work ethic, presided over a decade which saw more job losses than at any other time in twentieth-century British history, and which witnessed (or confirmed) a decisive shift from a manufacturing to a service economy. There is no reason to doubt the sincerity of Mrs Thatcher's professions of faith, but if one were to look for those who, during her period of office, most obstinately stood out for Victorian Values generally, whether one interpreted them in terms of family solidarity, the dignity of work, the security of the home, or simply the right of the free-born Englishman to stay put, it would not be the Prime Minister, but the miners defeated in the strike of 1984–85 – her 'enemy within' – who would have the stronger claim.

Notes

1 Margaret Thatcher, Address to the Bow Group, 6 May 1978, reprinted in Bow Group, *The Right Angle*, London 1979.

2 'The Healthy State', address to a Social Services Conference at Liverpool, 3 December 1976, in Margaret Thatcher, *Let Our Children Grow Tall*, London 1977, p. 81.

3 Address to the Institute of Socio-economic Studies, New York, reprinted in ibid., p. 4. As she acknowledges, she owed the phrase to Helmut-Schoeck, *Envy*, London 1969.

4 Margaret Thatcher, *The Revival of Britain*, London 1989, p. 98.

5 Speech to the Conservative Party Conference, *The Times*, 17 October 1981.

6 The *Guardian*, 9 October 1982.

7 Address to the Institute of Directors, 11 November 1976, in *Let Our Children Grow Tall*, p. 70.

8 Havelock Ellis, *The Nineteenth Century. A Dialogue in Utopia*, London 1900, p. 144.
9 For Adam Smith, *Let Our Children Grow Tall*, pp. 15, 98, 212; for J.S. Mill, *Sunday Times*, 6 February 1975.
10 *Let Our Children Grow Tall*, p. 101.
11 Interview with Brian Walden, *Weekend World*, 11 January 1983. Typescript in the writer's possession.
12 *Daily Telegraph*, 29 January 1983; *Guardian*, 29 January 1983.
13 *Daily Telegraph*, 25 April 1983.
14 *Daily Telegraph*, 23 April 1983.
15 *Daily Telegraph*, 23 April 1983.
16 Russell Lewis, *Margaret Thatcher*, London 1975, p. 113; *Let Our Children Grow Tall*, p. 34.
17 *The Times*, 8 May 1977.
18 'The Good Old Days', *Evening Standard*, 15 April 1983.
19 Reference temporarily mislaid.
20 For the Festival of Light, Dallas Cliff, 'Religion, Morality and the Middle Class', in Roger King and Neill Nugent (ed.), *Respectable Rebels, Middle Class Campaigns in the 1970s*, London 1979.
21 For an excellent account of this 'moral panic' and the very effective political campaign which followed in its wake. Peter Golding and Sue Middleton, *Images of Welfare: Press and Public Attitudes to Poverty*, Oxford 1982.
22 Lewis, *Margaret Thatcher*, p. 129.
23 *Sunday Express*, 8 February 1976.
24 *Let Our Children Grow Tall*, p. 108.
25 *Financial Times*, 18 July 1976.
26 The *Sun*, 2 May 1979.
27 The *Mail on Sunday*, 24 April 1983.
28 Speech at Lord Mayor's Banquet, November 1982, reported in Hugo Young, *One of Us*, London 1989, p. 5.
29 *Evening Standard*, 15 April 1983.
30 Young, *One of Us*; Margaret Thatcher, *The Revival of Britain*, London 1989, p. 63.
31 *Sunday Mirror*, 31 July 1972.
32 Interview with Jilly Cooper, *Sunday Times*, 19 September 1976.
33 Address at St Lawrence, Jewry, 30 March 1978, reproduced in *The Revival of Britain*, pp. 67–8.
34 Speech to Conservative Party Conference, *Guardian*, 7 October 1981; *Sunday Express*, 8 February 1976.
35 *The Right Angle*, p. 4.
36 *The Revival of Britain*, p. 70.
37 ibid., p. 98.
38 Interview in *The House Magazine*, reported in the *Independent*, 15 December 1990.
39 'The Manufacturing Districts . . .', *Morning Chronicle*, . . . , 1850.
40 Arthur Marwick, *British Society Since 1945*, Harmondsworth 1982.
41 Gareth Stedman Jones, *Languages of Class, Studies in English Working Class History, 1832–1982*, Cambridge 1983, p. 246.
42 Lewis, *Margaret Thatcher*, pp. 112, 115.
43 Patricia Murray, *Margaret Thatcher*, London 1980, p. 178.
44 Young, *One of Us*, p. 6.
45 Raphael Samuel, 'Born-again Socialism', in Robin Archer and others (ed.), *Out of Apathy, Voices of the New Left Thirty Years On*, London 1989.
46 Speech at Conservative Party Conference, *Guardian*, 11 October 1975.
47 Ivor Crewe, 'Ten Years on', *Daily Telegraph*, 4 May 1989; Sarah Hogg, 'How Did We Do under Thatcher?', *Sunday Telegraph*, 25 November 1990; Vivien Goldsmith, 'Thatcher's Legacy to Homeowners', *Independent on Sunday*, 25 November 1990; Christopher Huhne, 'From the Horn of Plenty to the Poisoned Chalice', *Independent on Sunday*, 25 November 1990.
48 Speech to the Conservative Party conference, *Guardian*, 7 October 1981.
49 TV interview with Gill Neville, reproduced in Sheila Harding, *Orderly Freedom: The Common-Sense of Margaret Thatcher*, Sheffield 1985, pp. 7–8.

Appendix

Reading the Runes*

I Historical Associations

The built environment gives materiality to the idea of history. It offers clues to the forensically-minded, asking us to pay attention to the historical associations of the writing on the walls – inscriptions, where the original names of premises can still be picked out in the brickwork; dedication panels (a feature it seems of the eighteenth-century London street); datestones; old-time parish boundaries. It invites us to see history not as a chronological gallop from point to point, but rather topographically, as a sediment of geological strata, a multi-layered reality in which the physical layout of the original settlement – the fields beneath the street – shapes patterns of subsequent occupancy. It makes us more alert to changes in the idea of public space; to retail revolutions, such as the one currently producing 'edge' cities; to human ecology and the competing claims of different housing classes.

In school practice, the use of buildings as a way of introducing children to the idea of the past – fundamental to project work today – seems to have been given a first airing in Edwardian times, when it was adopted by go-ahead teachers along with such precocious exercises in 'learning by doing' as school visits and nature walks. The new social history adopted it as a flagship, too, along with the drawing of 'period' costume and 'period' dress. By 1927 it was sufficiently well established in junior schools to appear in the Board of Education's *Handbook of Suggestions for Teachers*:

> Without any attempt to define precisely such terms as feudalism, chivalry, the Church or the manor, it will frequently be possible to bring home to the children's minds by concrete examples how these institutions of the Middle Ages

*This is an early draft for a section to be called 'The Built Environment' which had been left unfootnoted.

> influenced the lives and actions of men of that day . . . The names of streets, roads, buildings, e.g. Watling Street, Greyfriars, Friargate, Priory Lane, Abbey Street, Jury Street, Old Jewry, Old Bailey, Guildhall should become names with meaning. Similarly the most striking differences from age to age in the style of architecture, e.g. the change from Norman to Early English, and in the methods of building, e.g. the change from wood to stone and brick, can sometimes be shown by local churches and other buildings.

The extension of this pedagogy from the drawing of scale-models of Norman castles or medieval guildhalls to barns and cottages, and to such favourite school exercises as the building of Saxon huts, could be described as a late offshoot of the Arts and Crafts movement and the burgeoning interest in the vernacular. Marjorie and C.H.B. Quennell, two ardent disciples of William Morris, introduced it to the junior schools with their four-decker *History of Everyday Things*, which began publication in 1919, later giving it a new dimension when Marjorie became first curator of the Geffrye Museum, an old-established charity which in 1931 turned itself into a 'living history' exhibition of the English domestic interior. By the 1930s, modelling a half-timbered house was a normal part of 'education through art', while in nursery teaching, the four- or five-year-old's fledgling efforts at mimesis were proudly displayed on classroom and corridor walls in crayon drawings of 'my house'.

Eileen Power, a pioneer of the new social history, and one who contrived to combine a scholarly career with the popularization of knowledge through the medium of the BBC and children's books, made the cause of building history her own, using it to establish a more domestic and affectionate relationship to the objects of her inquiry, the merchants and manufacturers of the medieval wool trade. In *Medieval People* she amplified the argument into a more generalized advocacy of the visual:

> It is the greatest error to suppose that history must needs be something written down; for it may just as well be something built up, and churches, houses, bridges, or amphitheatres can tell their story as . . . plainly as print for those who have eyes to read. The Roman villa, excavated after lying lost for centuries beneath the heel of the unwitting ploughboy – that villa with its spacious ground-plan, its floors rich with mosaic patterns, its elaborate heating apparatus, and its shattered vases, brings home more nearly than any textbook the real meaning of the Roman Empire, whose citizens lived like this in a foggy island at the outermost edge of its world. The Norman castle, with moat and drawbridge, gatehouse and bailey and keep, arrow slits, instead of windows, is more eloquent than a hundred chronicles of the perils of life in the twelfth century . . . The country-manor-house of the fourteenth century, with courtyard and chapel and hall and dovecote speaks of an age of peace once more when . . . the great mass of Englishmen went unscathed by the Hundred Years' War . . . Then began the merchants' elaborate Perpendicular houses in the towns and villages of the fifteenth century, standing on the road, with gardens behind them, and carved beams, great fire-places, and a general air of comfort;

they mark the advent of a new class in English history – the middle class, thrust between lord and peasant and coming into its own.

Professor W.G. Hoskins, another historian who was at least as influential outside the university as within, and the leading figure in the postwar renaissance of English local history, carried this line of argument a great deal further. Believing that, in the countryside, every hedge has a history, which pollen counts could date, and that field-names could yield the secrets of changes in agrarian practice, he proposed the making of the English landscape as the unifying theme for any grand narrative of the national past. More locally he made the 'great rebuilding' of rural England, in the century preceding the Civil War of the 1640s, the hinge on which the political and social upheavals turned, mapping the rise of the yeoman class by means of probate inventories, and measuring the increase in domestic comfort by the advent of such humble items as bed-linen and table-ware.

In the town, the built environment serves in some sort as the equivalent of field-systems. It preserves the visual evidence of prior states of being – the canal basin, the butchers' shambles, the market cross. It offers us vivid reminders of vanished supremacies – triumphal arches, stately drives, ceremonial squares, military parade grounds (the Honourable Artillery Company's one at Finsbury goes back to Elizabethan times). Bridges, straddling the river and mildewed with age, offer panoramic views of worlds that we have lost, while at the same time silhouetting the newest additions to the townscape. The bonded warehouses of the waterfront, now subdivided into studios, offices and computer terminals, remind us of the great overseas trading companies – deliberately so in the case of Cutler's Gardens, the 'business village' at Houndsditch, where the clock of the old East India Company has been given pride of place. The marble-columned halls of the City banks recall the glory days of the London discount market. Obelisks, such as the Chilianwala Memorial, Chelsea, built in the grounds of the Hospital to honour the 255 officers, non-commissioned officers and privates who met their death there, give a ghostly after-life to what would otherwise be forgotten battles. Statues like Sir Henry Havelock's in Trafalgar Square – the Christian hero of the Indian Mutiny – commemorate the gods and heroes of yesteryear.

The built environment preserves, as in aspic, ancient shapes, incorporating, after its own fashion, the hamlet and the village, the common and the green. Traffic junctions, such as the Angel, Islington, take us back to coaching days, when it was customary for travellers approaching London to stay overnight at the inn, rather than running a gauntlet of footpads. Twisted, narrow streets, the very reverse of the French boulevard, follow the circuitous routes of ancient cart-tracks, the case with one of London's newest ethnic high streets, Brick Lane, Spitalfields, as with such more obviously venerable thoroughfares as Carter Lane. The medieval criminal sanctuary, such as Devil's Acre, Westminster, or Whitefriars, Strand, contrived to sustain a fitful but continuous existence right down to the 1840s, when they figure prominently among the 'rookeries' of Mayhew's London; street markets have been hardly less tenacious (as 'Rag Fair', Petticoat Lane originated, one hundred or so yards to the north, in Jacobean times). The 'old town', under an optic like this, can be seen to retain a medieval sense of enclosure, however often it may have been built over; new towns such as Edinburgh's, built in the aftermath of the Porteous riots, appear as monuments to civic order, replacing what John Evelyn derisorily called 'crinkle crankle' with regularity, symmetry and space.

Street-names serve in some sort as almanacs, registering those personalities and events – mythic or real – which have imprinted themselves on popular consciousness. They can also serve as archaeological indicators of some more ancient past when there was a haymarket in St James's, when pheasants were dressed in Poultry, loaves baked in Bread Street and flour ground in Windmill Street, Piccadilly. Lombard Street reminds us of the time of the Bardi and the Peruzzi, when Italians replaced the Jews as the king's moneylenders. In another common register, streets take their nomenclature from the speculative builder, the property developer and the urban landlord, while the Harley estate – eighteenth-century Toryism's reply to 'Whig' Bloomsbury – gives posthumous renown to the country seats of the noblemen who financed the development. In the nineteenth century, politics enters the lists, with 'Wellington' a runaway favourite for the Tories, while Liberals tried to construct an alternative pantheon of writers, thinkers and poets.

Pubs, always on the look-out for ways of currying favour with their clientele, will occasionally rename themselves in the light of current events. In seaports, write Larwood and Hotten in their *History of Signboards*, they favoured famous men of war 'in honour of some brilliant feat or to solicit the patronage of the crew'; more recently, the 1982 expedition to the South Atlantic produced a small crop of 'Falklands Arms'. More interesting are the time-warped. Signs like the 'Battle of Minden', a pub in Portsmouth, or the brilliantly sited 'King of Prussia', which commands the estuary crossing at Fowey, Cornwall, bring us a whiff of eighteenth-century grapeshot; while 'Admiral Vernon', one of the most frequent of old-time pub names, immortalizes the memory of the commander who instituted the sailor's allowance of grog. Pub signs also perpetuate a legendary history, in which King Lud, the alleged conqueror of Roman London, still stalks the purlieus of the Fleet Ditch, while mythical beasts, such as griffins and unicorns, keep intruders at bay.

Almshouses are among the most architecturally beautiful of urban relics, and also, though adapted to other uses, the best-preserved. A monument to merchant munificence, they were originally, it seems, a byproduct of the Reformation, a Protestant alternative to monasteries, chantries, and Masses for the dead. In some cases they were medieval hospitals 're-edified'. In London almshouses are a striking feature of the metropolitan landscape. Some of the best-known, like Sir Christopher Wren's Trinity almshouses, in Mile End Road, built for 'Decayed Masters and Commanders of Ships or ye widows of such', were put up by the City Livery Companies. The Geffrye Almshouses in Kingsland Road, Hackney – erected in 1715 and now a much-loved museum of the English domestic interior – were maintained by the Ironmongers in deference to the will of one of their dignitaries. Many more, however, seem to have been a legacy of quite obscure local philanthropists and vestrymen. The architecture and layout of these almshouses, quadrangular or terraced as the case may be, but in any event set in their own cloistered precinct, was to a remarkable extent unchanging. Puma Court, Spitalfields, built in 1860 'for the inhabitants of the Liberty of Norton Folgate' to replace a group of almshouses which had been demolished nearby, is a kind of miniature Inns of Court, built in the style of the seventeenth century, though with heart-shaped peepholes to the shutters to emphasize the cottage-like character of the buildings.

Estate development, as practised by urban landowners, a kind of town equivalent of the model village, has been a later source of time-warps. Here strict covenants forbid alien intrusion, and preserve the original grid intact. The Grosvenor estate, which has done so much to preserve the eighteenth-century layout of Mayfair, is a prestigious West End example, the Lloyd Baker estate, Pentonville, built in the 1820s to provide superior terrace housing for the artisan, another. As David Cannadine has shown in *Lords and Landlords, The Aristocracy and the Towns, 1774–1967* such procedures were fundamental to the nineteenth-century development of greenfield sites, giving speculative builders their head while using restrictive covenants to preserve the unity of the whole. At the seaside more eccentric examples abound, sometimes as a result of municipal intervention, sometimes of proprietorial whim. The Dame of Sark, a feudal autocrat, famously forbids travel by anything except a horse and cart, while Clovelly, north-west Devon, owes its 'irregular quaintness' and picturesque preservation to the efforts of the lords of the manor (as the date plaques suggest, many of the houses were Georgianized in the aftermath of the Great War).

More recently, conservation areas, which have served for some thirty years as a flagship for environmental improvement and urban renewal, pursue a quite self-consciously historicist quest. Giving a new lease of life to run-down property, they nevertheless contrive to look old-fashioned. The whole effort here is to restore buildings to what is fancifully imagined to be their original state, stripping them of alien intrusions, purging them of additions drawn from modern times. The effect, if not the intention, is to produced a mummified version of the past, in which every feature conforms to type and architectural good manners override all other considerations. Newly built-housing and infilling will often play quite as large a part in giving a unified character to such an area as the preservation of the old, while modern antiques, such as 'Victorian' lamp-posts, will often count for as much as 'period' features.

The suburban villa of the nineteenth century, the 'ornamental' villa as it was sometimes called in the builders' copy-books, was a great site for historicist fantasy. Dickens, who himself had a dream of an Arcadian cottage where everything remained unchanged – the epiphany which closes *Nicholas Nickleby* – has left us a memorable account of one of them, Mr Wemmick's baronial fantasy of 'Walworth Castle', his suburban home where the drawbridge is raised each evening, and cannon fired, to enhance the effect of the make-believe medieval turrets. Mr Meagles's creeper-hung cottage in Twickenham, filled with *objets d'art,* is a picturesque equivalent, cultivating an air of total rusticity. The revolt against what was thought of as the monotony of the Georgian terrace, and the belief that houses should reflect individual tastes, produced a riot of revivalist styles. As Robert Fishman argues in *Bourgeois Utopias,* 'suburbia was to become the characteristic terrain for such eclectic mixtures of period architecture'. Already in John Nash's Park Village East and Park Village West, 'ancestors of all picturesque suburbia' according to Sir John Summerson, and supposedly London's first semi-detached development, the houses were deliberately variegated. 'Some are "Italian", some "Gothic", some affect a Chalet style'. The nearby suburb of St John's Wood, 'a forest of villas, of nearly all sorts and sizes', was even more historically promiscuous. An 1857 report in the *Building News,* tartly told it off:

> Here we have one [house] in the pseudo-Greek style, there, another in very indifferent Italian; at the next turn the feudal castle is represented in miniature, with its central tower carried up to a most preposterous height, and surmounted by frowning battlements; again, the quaint Elizabethan rises, with its eccentric peculiarities . . .

No less insistent, as a utopian strain, was the attempt to reproduce a countrified air, whether by means of restrictive covenants which forbade commercial development, parklike gardens or thickly planted shrubberies. Long before the advent of the garden city, ambitious suburban developments, such as Edgbaston, Birmingham, where making a fetish of their rural associations, while the more ambitious mansions, with their elaborate driveways, were modelled on the country seat.

Even when they were doing modernist or futurist things, Victorian architects and designers believed that they were returning to some more ancient past. Railway tunnels were castellated almost as a matter of course, and the juxtaposition of functional train sheds and massive historicist architecture – as, famously, with the Euston Arch or Bristol

Temple Meads – remained characteristic throughout the nineteenth century. Philip Webb's 'Red House', with its revolutionary use of undressed brick, its disdain for ornamentation and facade, its simplicity and straightforwardness, was praised by William Morris – for whom it was designed – as being 'in the style of the thirteenth century'; while the white-panelled rooms and white-framed windows of Norman Shaw and J.J. Stevenson – avatars of an aesthetic of light – claimed to be a revival of Queen Anne.

Perhaps the most enduring of these historicist enthusiasms, because it prefigures the current vogue for neo-vernacular, was that which came to be known as 'Old' or 'Early' English. As a phrase, it made a precocious appearance in John Claudius Loudon's 1833 *Encylopedia of Cottage, Farm, and Villa Architecture and Furniture,* 'the principal copy-book for builders all over the country for at least fifty years after it was first published'. Here it was treated as a more or less interchangeable term for the Gothic. And indeed in the 1830s, the Gothic and the Elizabethan seem to have been regarded as *the* national styles (in the competition for the new Houses of Parliament, after the fire of 1834, they were specified as the only possible styles for the new building). In Loudon as in Cobbett and Carlyle, Old English was essentially medieval; by the 1860s, when Frith painted his picture of marriage frolics in the olden days, the idea of 'Merrie England' had moved on to the more Protestant terrain of the Elizabethan and the Jacobean.

It was in the 1860s that 'Old English' came into its own, albeit in the sphere of domestic architecture rather than public building. One crucial element in it was the discovery or rediscovery of red brick, and its vigorous promotion as an alternative to stucco. For Philip Webb, whose Red House, in Bexley, Kent was the prototype of the tile-hung, vernacular revival residence, red brick was 'quintessentially English'. Voysey, twenty years onwards, was using it quite self-consciously to develop a national style, and it was adopted in this spirit by the architects of the London School Board, some of whom served their apprenticeship in the office of Philip Webb. The vogue for Elizabethan half-timbering – a related enthusiasm – came a little later, though it seems that as early as 1820 Lord Carnarvon, a Tory ultra, when building a country house, expressed a strong preference for Elizabethan brickwork and half-timbering over 'Whig' or 'Italianate' stucco, the Prince Regent's favourite.

The interwar semi, with its half-timbering and bay windows, was not less historicist in appearance. Indeed it was in the period of postwar reconstruction that 'old English' established itself as the dominant idiom in domestic architecture, covering the broadest spectrum of housing classes, from the stockbroker's Tudor favoured by the white settlers of the Surrey hills, to the Tudor Walters houses built as homes fit for heroes. On the private estate, where they were named rather than numbered, it was boasted that no two houses were alike. Council house developments cultivated a rustic air. At Dagenham, the London County Council architects adopted what they fondly thought of as an East Anglian vernacular; in Bermondsey Labour laid out its alternative to the slum in cottage estates. The interwar semi was an avatar of modernization, marking the advent of the labour-saving, servantless home. But it was marketed to the public in a variety of Arcadian disguises. 'Fine example of a modern house built in such a manner that it has the appearance of age', runs the caption to the frontispiece of P.A. Barrow's *The House Desirable* (1929). Externally, the battle of styles in the outer suburbs was between Georgian, Tudor and vernacular, joined in the 1930s by the 'Moderne'. Internally the houses were rich in historical allusion, with Elizabethan galleons putting up their prows in stained-glass fanlights, oak-panelled walls, and 'Jacobean' reproduction furniture giving a baronial touch to the hall.

II Follies

Another focus of historicist enthusiasms, even more eclectic than those of the suburbs, would be what might be termed 'holiday architecture'. It is a broad category, which would need to include the eighteenth-century spa town, one of the great originals of the neo-classical revival, as well as its more Cockneyfied nineteenth-century successors. Reference might be made to the ice-cream kiosk, the Edwardian bandstand, and the pier-head pavilion, as well as, a little later, in the Coney Island pleasure parks, to the water chute and the scenic railway, those singular monuments to what John Betjeman called 'seaside Baroque'. Fairground architecture, now lovingly preserved and restored by the steam traction engine fanatics, is a second cousin; so are the Moorish picture palaces of the 1930s, those build for Granada in particular. Earlier, reference might be made to the cricket pavilions, boathouses, and 'Corinthian' football grounds which in the heyday of Old Boy networks and public school athletics pioneered the advent of spectator sports; and to the appearance of what Mark Girouard in *Sweetness and Light* calls 'holiday Queen Anne', a fun architecture which played with the idea of Elizabethan half-timbering, anticipating the bypass Tudor of the 1920s roadhouses, and of Arthur Liberty's rebuilt Regent Street store.

Follies, one of the commonest eighteenth-century forms of holiday architecture, contrived to be both experimental and atavistic, playing on the appeal of antiquities and reproducing them in replica, while at the same time cultivating an appetite for the exotic. Revivalism here was definitely cosmopolitan, at one moment cultivating a taste for Chinoiserie, at the next, playing with the Zodiacal or the Druidical. At Stowe, William Kent's Temple of British Worthies (1735) is a semicircle of niches 'with a stepped pyramid in the centre', while the Congreve Monument which he designed in the following year is a small tall pyramid, sprouting masks and panpipes, and presided over by a carved monkey. Alton, Staffs, was landscaped as an English Rhineland, Hakstone Lake as a Dutch still-life. As Hedley and Meulenkamp write of the gentleman's park:

> The circuit of the grander gardens began to resemble a miniature world tour, with architecture from every nation and every period . . . The Temple of Virtue, in the severest Greek Doric, would remind promenaders of the democracies of the Ancients, just as a hermitage would recall the purity and innocence of the devotional life of the anchorite.

In the form of mock castles and abbey ruins such follies anticipated the Gothic Revival, albeit in the character of a visual joke rather than, as in the nineteenth century, an attempt to return to the Christian architecture of the high Middle Ages. Likewise the Temple of Theseus (1758), designed by 'Athenian' Stuart after his return from Greece, was the first Greek Revival building in Britain – Lord Lyttelton, who had it erected on his Hagley estate, called it truly 'Attick'. The garden statuary of the eighteenth century, taking its subjects from the gods and heroes of the ancient world, was, if anything, even more influential in establishing a taste for neo-Classicism.

Grottoes, cultivating an air of melancholy and ministering to nostalgia for the primeval, are the oldest form of folly. They are frequently cited in the literature of the ancient world as sanctuaries or as sites of mystery, and in the Holy Land they are connected to Christian miracles. They were powerfully renewed in Renaissance imitations of antiquity, often to evoke the fantastic and the grotesque. They were comparatively speaking latecomers to England, being adopted by the landscape gardeners of the eighteenth century. They figured largely in the Hon. Charles Hamilton's follies at Painshill, as also in Henry Hoare's precociously romantic landscape at Stourhead.

Follies are usually discussed as though they were an aristocratic plaything, a privilege of the idle rich, even though it was a commoner, Alexander Pope, who in his celebrated garden at Twickenham brought the grotto to perfection, and the artists of Renaissance Italy who rescued it from oblivion. Even Barbara Jones, the great chronicler and discoverer of what she called, in her Festival of Britain exhibition at the Whitechapel, the 'unsophisticated arts', had eyes only for the follies of the country estate – her 1955 book, the inspiration for all subsequent work in the field, is very largely an inventory of them. Yet it is an open question whether the pleasure gardens of the eighteenth century, the resort of the prentice, the sempstress and the tradesman as well as of the world of rank and fashion – London was girdled by them – did not have as much to show by way of legendary and grotesque statuary, or make-believe Roman and Greek remains, as the great landed estates. The great Rotunda, or 'ring of folly' as the satirists called it, was the central attraction at Ranelagh, in Chelsea, 'a splendid place for dancing . . . masquerades and ridottos' as well as a favourite promenade; a Chinese

House and a Venetian Temple, set beside a canal, were among its lesser delights; fireworks displays, re-enacting the siege of Gibraltar – an entertainment introduced in 1786, widely imitated in the pleasure gardens of the nineteenth century – were among its nocturnal sensations.

Grottoes, too, were very much a feature of the pleasure gardens. The New Wells in Lower Rosoman Street, Clerkenwell, a popular London tea-garden, had a Merlin's Cave in 1740, some five years after Queen Charlotte had constructed one in the Royal Gardens at Richmond; there was a 'Gipsey's Cave' at the Cremorne, sold off when the gardens were closed down in 1878; Egyptian pyramids and an Egyptian sphinx at the Spaniards Inn, Hampstead, then as now a much frequented pleasure resort, and a self-styled 'Folly' – 'a sort of castellated houseboat' – moored during the summer months opposite Somerset House (in Pepys's time, it was resorted to by the ladies of the town; later it became notorious as a gambler's hell).

Grottoes had a great fillip from the development of the seaside holiday, and indeed some of the best-known nineteenth-century ones, such as Margate's, were associated with the seaside resort. Geologizing and fossilizing were, for the historically-minded, one of the great delights of the seaside holiday, and related to them was the craze for making shell mosaics (in one of Leech's 1850s *Punch* cartoons, the entire beach population seems to be engaged at it). Very much lower down the social scale, grottoes also made a ubiquitous appearance as a street Arab's resource. In London where, as readers of Dickens will recall, 'poverty and oysters' went together, St James of Compostela's day, 25 July, served as an alternative or complement to 5 November, 'Please, sir, remember the Grotto' or 'A Penny for the Grotto' being the children's plea, backed up by a makeshift shrine – oyster shells, stones, earth, and sometimes clinker from the gasworks, 'ornamented with flowers, moss, and bits of broken or coloured china'.

Coming much more up-to-date, something should be said about the phenomenon of garden gnomes. Universally ridiculed because of their association with the suburb – and latterly, with the business ventures of John Major's father – they nevertheless have a venerable lineage. In Germany, where according to Huygen and Poortvliet's *Gnomes*, they originated in the gnome gardens of the Black Forest, and where today they are as much a feature of the suburban garden as they are in Britain, they took their inspiration from fairy lore, establishing a link with magical beliefs older than Christianity. In Britain, where they have been dated back to the 1880s, their introduction is attributed to Sir Charles Isham's famous gardens and rockery at Lamport Hall in Northamptonshire. (Isham, a believer in 'earth spirits', as well as an inventive gardener, believed that they were occult agencies.) But they have a family resemblance to so many other domestic icons, from the stone figurines who have served as gatepost statuary – lions, jackals, dragons as well as guard dogs – to such chimney-piece grotesques as Uncle Toby. The authors of *Dunroamin*, in their brave attempt to vindicate suburban taste, assert that garden gnomes function as phallic symbols (there are no female goblins). But they could as plausibly be characterized as priapic. Walt Disney, in *Snow White and the Seven Dwarfs*, desexualizes them, making them into harmless old men who are fit objects for the heroine's motherings. In any event, it seems possible, as with so many other household icons, to hypothesize multiple origins.

Brighton Pavilion, the Prince Regent's pleasure palace, 'transformed the country gentleman's private conceit of the "folly" into an acceptable form of public building', writes Kenneth Lindley in *Seaside Architecture*. With its Turkish dome and Arabian Nights turrets it was as much Orientalist as historicist in inspiration, and indeed owes its charm to a reckless profusion of styles, Gothic at one moment, Regency at the next, and never taking itself too seriously. Ninety years on, its domes and minarets were an inescapable element of fun architecture, whether in the shape of the ceiling nymphs and goddesses who danced with reckless abandon around the dome of Frank Matcham's palaces of variety, the orientalist kiosks which stood as sentinels on the seaside promenades, or the Indo-Moorish observatories and watch-towers. 'Scores of crude, miniature Royal Pavilions were build for concert parties and fortune tellers at the ends of piers.' Brighton Chain Pier (1823) was built with towers in the Egyptian style, Margate's (1853–56), an early work of the great pier architect Eugenius Birch, had a tiny octagonal pavilion. The grand hotels of the 1870s – a boom period in seaside architecture – had an altogether heavier touch, positioning themselves, in the manner of the Scottish baronial castle, on precipitous escarpments (the 'Grand', Scarborough, is a famous example which could have come straight out of the spookier illustrations to *Waverley* or *The Bride of Lammermoor*). A still more spectacular Victorian seaside folly is the one created by George Burt at Swanage. Using the good offices of John Mowlem, a local boy made good, who had become a leading building contractor in London, Burt masterminded a mass transfer of architectural salvage, including an archway from Hyde Park Corner, a Chinese pavilion complete with dragons, floor tiles from the Houses of Parliament, and assorted iron columns from Billingsgate. The magnificent Clock Tower had originally been erected on London Bridge as a Wellington testimonial.

An alternative seaside which grew up in the later nineteenth century, more perhaps in marine painting and sentimental prints than in actuality, though it had its real-life analogues, was much more atavistic, exchanging novelties for antiquities, and taking its cue, so far as souvenirs and style were concerned, from the vernacular of Mr Peggotty rather than that of Kubla Khan. It preserved, where it could, the culture of oar and sail, and made a fetish of the irregular and the quaint, whether in the form of fishermen's cottages, ship figureheads or harbourside quays. The discovery of the Cornish coast – England's Mediterranean according to the enthusiasts – a phenomenon of the 1870s, was one straw in the wind; the multiplication of seaside resorts in North Devon, most famously Clovelly, was another; a little later came the development of yachting on the Norfolk Broads, and the cognate invention of 'Poppyland' – the North Norfolk littoral which the feats of the Cromer lifeboatmen helped to make heroic.

Reference should be made finally, and most generally, to what might be called 'imitation vernacular', arguably, along with picturesque, to which it is so closely related, the most enduring of this country's historicist enthusiasms. *The* style of the 1980s, so far as domestic housebuilding is concerned, and a major component of postmodernism, both in British commercial architecture and abroad, it harks back, like the Gothic revival, to the eighteenth-century folly. Sutherland Lyall, in his illuminating book, *Dream Cottages*, finds one original in the hermitages and primitive garden huts of the newly landscaped gentlemen's estates of the second half of the eighteenth century, ramshackle wooden piles which made a feature of their improvised character. In France, where it was believed they first saw the light of day, the cottage *ornée* remained an aristocratic sport, most famously represented by the make-believe village, Le Hameau, where Marie Antoinette and her ladies-in-waiting played at being milkmaids and shepherdesses, even while Madam Defarge and her *tricoteuses* prepared their deadly work. In Britain, by contrast, or at any rate in England, where old-time peasant life was on the wane, ornamental cottages were taken up in a big way, first by Humphrey Repton and the great John Nash, who built a whole village of them, then by J.C. Loudon in his Encyclopaedias of domestic architecture.

As with other folly-originated architectures, imitation vernacular was given a particularly hospitable reception at the seaside. The vernacular cottage, 'with stout tree-trunks supporting the porch and various additions attached in the approved Picturesque manner', was a favourite in early nineteenth-century Isle of Wight. Swiss-style chalets were also, it seems, a feature of the 1920s new-build properties on the Essex coast, a kind of upmarket equivalent of those poor people's villas which Colin Ward has written about so movingly in *Arcadia For All.* Clough Williams-Ellis's Portmeirion, which began life in 1926, and was progressively extended for the following fifty years, is generally put down as an example of English, or Anglo-Welsh eccentricity. Hedley and Meulenkamp describe it as 'the finest, most elaborate and sustained piece of folly work in Great Britain'. Purpose-built to look like the Italian fishing village of Portofino, it was also an *omnium gatherum* for distressed buildings – often themselves follies – transplanted from other parts of the country – for instance the eighteenth-century Bath-House of Mr Reeves of Bristol. But with the building, in the late 1960s, of François Spoerry's Port-Grimaud, in the Var, an imitation French fishing village 'complete with cobbled square . . . old cottages, irregular pantile roofs, faded painted stucco and the occasional classical column', it established itself as a kind of model, with dozens of imitations on the European coast – *le style Club Méditerranée* as it is sarcastically referred to by critics.

The seaside resort, writes a recent commentator, is a 'living museum' of popular taste. Its novelties, like those of the fairground, are subtly out of date. Slot machines, projecting such venerable spine-chillers as 'The Haunted Graveyard' and 'Madame Guillotine', perpetuate the humours of the Gothic, while the 'Ghost Train', a great favourite with the courting couple, draws on even more venerable frights. *(Continue paragraph)*

III Mnemonics

Buildings have been from the earliest times showcases of the commemorative arts. Rulers have used them as display boards to magnify their greatness, to celebrate their victories and to record the detailed incidents of their campaigns. The religious have turned them into miniature temples and shrines, allotting niches for the household gods and inscribing fascia with the precepts of their faith. The early Christians, according to St Cyril of Alexandria, manifested their faith by engraving the cross on the porches of their houses. The merchant class of medieval London, Sylvia Thrupp tells us, were fond of texts that expressed confidence of divine approval, displaying such mottoes as 'I trust in God', '*a Domine factum est istum*'.

The idea of getting buildings to tell a story, and of using them as mnemonic devices, to teach history, mythologize rulers and commemorate great events, is as old as the Pharaohs of Egypt. Hieroglyphics were miniature pictures and their distinct purpose, when inscribed on monuments, funerary stelae and tombs, was to 'make to live' for eternity the things depicted. We know the names of the first kings from them, and sometimes the biographical details of their careers.

It is not only drum-and-trumpet history which can be extracted from early inscriptions, but also representations of high officials and even, on occasions, artisans, such as the skilled workmen who made and decorated the royal tombs in the Valley of the Kings. At the very dawn of civilization, the Sumerians, it seems, used inscriptions and pictorial representation not only for the record of high politics but also for that of quite humble reaches of everyday life. As S.N. Kramer tells us:

> Whenever a building was erected, a new door made or any other alteration, it was dated by a clay plaque . . . in which public and private events were recorded . . . In this way the first rendition of written history was as a visual display. On the important buildings of the city states of Sumeria were written the histories of the glorious rulers and their military successes but a door in

a private dwelling might be dated by the time grandfather lost his goats outside the city walls.

The pictorial chronicles of the Assyrians, one of the first historical narratives we have, are a more elaborate exercise in mnemonics, giving a blow-by-blow, albeit heavily mythicized, account of famous battles, preserving the memory of legendary warriors, and giving corporeal form to origin myths. The building inscription for Darius I at Susa, celebrating the achievements of Persia's greatest monarch, goes much further, focusing on the arts of peace as well as those of war:

> A great god is Ahuramazda, who created this earth . . . who made Darius king, one king of many, one lord of many.
>
> I am Darius, great king, king of kings, king of countries, king of this earth . . . what was done by me, all that by the will of Ahuramazda I did.
>
> This is the palace which at Susa I erected. From afar its ornamentation was brought. Down the earth was dug until rock-bottom I reached. When the excavation was made, rubble was packed down, one part 40 ells in depth, the other 20 ells in depth. On that rubble a palace I erected.
>
> And that the earth was dug down, and that the rubble was packed down, and that the brick was moulded, the Babylonian folk, it did that.
>
> The cedar timber, this – a mountain named Lebanon – from there was brought; the Assyrian folk, it brought it to Babylon; from Babylon the Carians and Ionians brought it to Susa.
>
> The Yaka wood from Gandara was brought and from Carmania.
>
> The gold from Sardis and from Bactria was brought, which was used here.
>
> The stone – lapis lazuli and carnelian – which was used here, this from Sogdiana was brought.
>
> The stone – turquoise – this from Chorasmia was brought which was used here.
>
> The silver and the copper from Egypt were brought.
>
> The ornamentation with which the wall was adorned, that from Ionia was brought.
>
> The ivory which was used here, from Ethiopia and from Sind and from Arachosia was brought.
>
> The stone pillars which here were used – a place named Abiradush, in Uja – from there were brought.
>
> The stone-cutters who wrought the stone, those were Ionians and Sardians. The goldsmiths who wrought the gold, those were Medes and Egyptians. The men who wrought the *ishmalu*, those were Sardians and Egyptians. The men who wrought the baked brick, those were Babylonians. The men who adorned the wall, those were Medes and Egyptians.
>
> Says Darius the king: At Susa, here, a splendid task was ordered; very splendidly did it turn out.
>
> May Ahuramazda protect me; and Hystaspes who is my father; and my country.
>
> (from Henri Frankfort, *The Art and Architecture of the Ancient Orient*, Harmondsworth 1970)

Greek inscriptions, Ros Thomas argues in her book on *Oral Tradition and Written Record in Classical Athens*, were primarily mnemonic. Whether celebrating victories, recording treaties, or allegorizing the contemporary in terms of gods and legends, their function was confirmatory, bringing into the public domain what people knew, through oral tradition, had already happened. Stone inscriptions were a more certain means of preservation than written documents, using paper, and more public than word of mouth. They were regarded as memorials as well as written documents, 'material objects which were a reminder and a symbol of the decision they recorded'. Orators could refer to them freely, because they were so spectacularly visible. Historians, starting with Herodotus, called on them to cast light on events which fell outside the sphere of living memory.

Places of worship, starting with the domestic shrine devoted to ancestor worship, doubled in the character of pantheons, memorializing the illustrious dead. They celebrated worldly rulers as well as the godlike heroes of myth and legend. The Greek temple, the political as well as the spiritual centre of the city, is a famous example. 'Statues were placed in the colonnades, in the front and back porch, and along the sides of the cella . . ., or flanking the chief cult statue . . .' The monumental column of the Romans, celebrating military triumphs, served something of the same function – even Trajan's pillar, dedicated to the greatness of the Emperor Augustus, and giving definition to Rome's best-known ceremonial space, was part of a temple.

Memorials of this kind were one of the fundamental resources of the medieval Church, which relied so largely on visual propaganda to reach the people. The honouring of apostolic and saints' relics is a wellknown example; carved misericords 'with scenes from Scripture or legendary sources, by which a lesson might be taught' another. A still more striking example are those wall paintings which Anglican vicars today are as zealous in preserving as their predecessors in the nineteenth century were in having them scraped away. Medieval churches were filled with brightly coloured images of the Trinity and the saints. Walls and windows were painted with religious scenes and symbols. They served as the poor man's Bible, drawing on folk art to exemplify such lessons as the Seven Acts of Mercy, and illustrating legendary as well as sacred history (local saints, it seems, were the great subject of wall paintings in Anglo-Saxon times, and down to the fifteenth century far more attention was paid to the stories of the martyrs and the saints than to illustrations of Scripture).

Ecclesiastical art was a mine of secular information as well as the ark of the religious convenant. Memories of the Crusades were kept alive by knights' effigies. Family brasses recorded the genealogy and the piety of the great, and from the fifteenth century onwards, according to Duffy, also those in humbler walks of life. Monuments preserved the memory of rich benefactors. Heraldry, from the twelfth century onwards, served as both decoration and information, 'enriching the tomb with precious metal and colour, as well as describing the family history of the deceased'.

Medieval town corporations were not less alert to visual propaganda, buttressing their pretensions with brilliant pageants and processions where legendary histories were displayed. Seals, arms and insignia mimicked those of the nobility. Guildhalls were built as palaces with magnificent tapestries, minstrels' galleries, and portraits of kings, queens and benefactors. The banqueting halls of the livery companies – Unwin tells us that there were twenty-eight by the reign of Richard III – 'were of baronial magnificence and extent'. Like the Church, the medieval town corporations made the most of their foundation myths, laying claim to an impossible antiquity. London, the 'new Troy', was allegedly founded by giants (Gog and Magog, the figures who headed the mayoral processions of Elizabethan times, and who still flank the Guildhall today) or, according to another tradition which has left its mark on the street nomenclature of the metropolis, King Lud. Bath was founded not by the Romans but by one of the ancient British kings, Bladud, the father of King Lear. King Coel – the 'merry old soul' of the nursery rhyme – was allegedly the founder of Colchester.

The architects of the Victorian town hall, who in the 1860s and 1870s established a whole new style of municipal magnificence, were determined resurrectionists, modelling their buildings sometimes on the Renaissance, sometimes on the Gothic, sometimes on classical antiquity. So far as narrative adornment was concerned, they drew on the past indiscriminately. Classical mythology provided allegorical figures for the representation of local industries and trades – a ram's head in the case of the great hall at Leeds, symbolizing the woollen trade; the figure of Vulcan towering above the town hall at Sheffield. Legendary beasts helped to give a masculine charge to municipal heraldry. National history, represented very often by a gallery of English monarchs, was painted into stained-glass windows and sculpted into friezes. (At Bradford, in deference perhaps to the strength of local Nonconformity, the figure of Oliver Cromwell was included among the thirty-four kings and queens.) Great writers and famous men of science were also very much to the fore. An extreme instance is the town hall at Preston where Giles Gilbert Scott, an architect who always went the whole hog when it came to summoning up the ghosts of the past, contrived to have statues of such highly un-Lancastrian figures as Caxton and Linnaeus, and paintings of Clive, Wellington and Raphael, alongside a statue of Sir Robert Peel and an allegory of manufacture and commerce. The Elgin marbles were a possible inspiration here, offering models and poses for sculpted figures, helping to turn the Victorian era into a golden age of civic statutory, and making temple-like friezes into the very essence of town hall art, a feature of Alfred Waterhouse's Gothicist fantasy at Manchester.

Still more historicist, and still more didactic, were the church builders of the nineteenth century. Here the restoration (in fact the installation) of stained-glass windows, to which *The Builder* sometimes devotes a whole column; the popularity of the pseudo-medieval encaustic tiles, patented and manufactured by Messrs Minton, the potters; and the extraordinary proliferation of ecclesiastic ornament, even in some Nonconformist chapels, all testify to the centrality of the idea of 'restoration' in programmes of church reform. For the Cambridge Camden Society, in the 1840s the ideologues of the new movement, church restoration was the great answer to the moral and social evils of the day. It could of itself return England to the certainties of an age of faith – supposedly the hallmark of religion in the Middle Ages. Where others, like the Evangelicals, measured belief by the urgency of prayer, the Cambridge ecclesiologists pinned their faith on the fabric of the church itself.

Quite apart from such self-conscious historicisms and didacticisms as these, there are also more subliminal ways in which the built environment shapes or inflects our island stories. It highlights some moments in the historical past while consigning others to oblivion. It offers its own timelines, in which period styles are the equivalent of historical epochs. It is a palimpsest on which an alternative view of the national or local past is inscribed. Great rebuildings, such as that which followed the Fire of London, take the place of civil wars and interregnums as historical landmarks. The 'Hungry Thirties' become the years of the housing boom and the onward march of the 'semi'; the Great Depression (1873–96) is the time which saw the mushroom growth of grand hotels. At the level of macro-history, or of a Braudelian *longue durée*, it focuses on the grand permanences of national life, as, say, struggles and competition over land use or the difference between scattered and nucleated settlement. More domestically (and more democratically) it gives pride of place to the changing forms of sociability and the history of everyday things.

IV Artifice and Authenticity

Despite, or perhaps because of its apparently solid location, the built environment, as historical evidence, conceals far more than it reveals. For one thing the appearance of continuity is deceptive. Buildings change their uses not once but many times, metamorphosing from one kind of occupancy to another while remaining externally – or even internally – unchanged. Thus, for instance, in the manufacturing districts of the Midlands and the North, the Mechanics Institute, built in the 1840s or 1850s to mark a town's coming of age, may have begun life as an Athenaeum, only to find itself doubling in the character of a town hall and then perhaps serving as a free library before being swallowed up, in the local government expansion of the 1960s, as Council offices. The private dwelling is even more chameleon. The 'period' residence, marketed today as a 'Victorian mansion', may have been, forty years ago, and indeed almost certainly was, in the time of twilight zones and postwar housing shortage, a noisome, multi-occupied tenement, fit only for the bulldozer, according to the conventional wisdom of the planners. Likewise today's 'Georgian town house', such as those elegantly restored in Spitalfields, would have been, in the eighteenth century, given over to live-in apprentices and basement-to-attic workrooms; later perhaps, like the house from which I write, warehouse or wholesale premises.

The parish church, covering as it often does, two entirely different systems of belief, the Catholic and the Anglican, as well as vast changes in the administration of charities, would be a prime example of how the appearance of continuity is deceptive. In local history, it customarily figures as the backbone of village life, and indeed in the older histories the village and the parish are treated as though they were one and the same thing. Every addition to the church fabric is lovingly described and treated as organic, a contribution to progressive growth. The old faith disappears at the Reformation, apparently without leaving a trace; newer ones, represented by the meeting-house, the conventicle or the chapel, do not get a look-in.

As with any other form of historical record, the built environment is apt to give a privileged place to the powerful, and indeed very often to leave them as the only presence in the field. Thus when we think of the 'Georgian' town house we do not think of the one-room weaver's cabin (Tower Hamlets Library, Bancroft Road, London, has an affecting photograph of a group of them), but of the more imposing three-and four-storey residences of business and the professions. The peasant hut in Ulster where the Rev. Patrick Brontë was brought up (there is a fine artist's representation of it in the family museum at Howarth) belongs to any age; it is only the parsonage or the rectory which is dignified as 'period'. Differential survival sets up its own biases. Seats of officialdom are far more likely to survive than the *bidonville* or shanty town, the public square than the back alley.

The whole notion of the 'period' house is misleading. Most Tudor people did not live in Tudor houses any more than in 1920s ones lived in semis. The slums of nineteenth-century London, swept away by town 'improvement', were as often as not – to judge by the photographs which preceded the clearance of Wych Street, and the prints which illustrate *Sketches by Boz* – Elizabethan. Mid-Victorian Gothic, exemplified by St Pancras railway station and the Law courts, was notoriously 'a . . . style . . . which had never existed in England during the Gothic period'. Far more 'Queen Anne' houses were built in the 1870s and 1880s (Kensington and Chelsea are full of them) than in the reign of the queen herself.

The idea of a historic building, one to be restored, so far as possible to its original state, and shored up against the ravages of time, is a comparatively recent one. In Britain the first protective legislation was not passed until 1882; it applied, at first, only to buildings which could be designated as 'ancient monuments'; later it was confined to those which had been built before 1714. Not until the Civic Amenities Act of 1967 was there an attempt to extend it from individual buildings to conservation areas. The idea of a historical walk, mapping the character of a district by means of its 'period' buildings, is still more recent, dating in some cases from the Silver Jubilee of 1977, in others from European Architectural Heritage Year, 1975.

The draft ends abruptly here.

Index

Note: Italicized page numbers refer to illustrations